LEADING
THE LEARNING
ORGANIZATION

Week Loan

SUNY series, Human Communication Processes
Donald P. Cushman and Ted J. Smith III, editors

LEADING
THE LEARNING ORGANIZATION

Communication and Competencies
for
Managing Change

Alan T. Belasen

Foreword by Michael V. Fortunato

State University of New York Press

Published by
State University of New York Press, Albany

For information, address State University of New York Press,
State University Plaza, Albany, N.Y., 12246

Production by Marilyn P. Semerad
Marketing by Patrick Durocher

Library of Congress Cataloging-in-Publication Data

Belasen, Alan T., 1951–
    Leading the learning organization : communication and
competencies for managing change / Alan T. Belasen ; foreword by
Michael V. Fortunato.
        p.   cm. — (SUNY series, human communication processes)
    ISBN 0–7914–4367–1 (hc : alk. paper). — ISBN 0–7914–4368–X (pbk.
: alk. paper)
        1. Organizational learning—Management.   I. Title.   II. Series:
SUNY series in human communication processes.
    HD58.82.B43   2000
    658.4´063—dc21   99–11338
                                                                     CIP

10 9 8 7 6 5 4 3 2 1

This book is dedicated to my father, Robert Julian Belasen,
Zichrono Livracha.

Contents

PART I. STRATEGIC CHANGE

PART II. CONTINUOUS IMPROVEMENT

CONCLUSION

List of Illustrations

List of Tables

Foreword

Sixty years ago, Nobel laureate J. R. Hicks wrote that "the best of all monopoly profits is the quiet life," but few leaders of today's organizations spend their afternoons playing whist at the club. There was once a time when local access to scarce resources or idiosyncratic process knowledge sustained a firm's competitive advantage, but the world is now a changing, global village where technology, raw materi-

Michael V. Fortunato holds the A.B. in economics from Columbia University and the A.M. and Ph.D. degrees in economics from Harvard University. He has served on the economics faculty of Williams College and of the School of Management of Boston University, where he taught a variety of economics courses in the organization of industry and the conduct of multinational firms, as well as courses in the areas of managerial decision making and corporate strategy. Dr. Fortunato has also worked as a strategy and economics consultant to senior executives of more than two dozen firms on the Fortune 1000 as well as for firms in Europe and Oceania. He is informally affiliated with Braxton Associates, the strategy arm of Deloitte Touche Tohmatsu, and has contributed to dozens of Braxton engagements since 1987. His recent research efforts have included writing and publications in the areas of executive education trends, management competencies and education, and the effects of downsizing on managerial behavior and performance, trade and export strategy, and the organizational design of corporations and industries.

als and intermediate products, managerial expertise, and even labor shift rapidly in response to subtle shifts in the competitive environment.

Changes in the way we organize ourselves to do our work have been so profound that at least one critic, ex-Secretary of Labor of the United States, Robert Reich, felt the need to question our identity itself when he posed the query, "who is us?" In *The Work of Nations*, Reich argues passionately that an essentially unregulated wave of corporatism threatens to make even our corporate *nationality* irrelevant, much less basic modes of management. For those whose private calculus does not swing so widely as does Reich's sweeping social agenda, there is still plenty of evidence to suggest that even our best approaches to sustaining competitive advantage may not be up to the challenge of the next competitive wave. Consider Richard D'Aveni's *Hyper-competition*, a counterintuitive indictment of even modern models of strategic management, such as Michael Porter's, in which D'Aveni argues that competition changes so fast that we must actively choose to be our own toughest competitors, *challenging our sources of sustainable advantage even as we create them.*

D'Aveni brings to mind the Italian adage, given permanence a generation ago by Giuseppe di Lampedusa in *The Leopard*. Lampedusa said: *Se vogliamo che tutto rimanga come 'e, bisogna che tutto cambi*. That is, if we want things to stay the way they are, things will have to change. The mathematically inclined, as many analysts are these days, would say that $r=f(i,e(t))$: that is, results, r, are a function of a wide range of inputs, i, and a set of environmental parameters out of our control but changing all the time, $e(t)$. In order to get the same results (i.e., to preserve our way of life), we cannot deliver the same old inputs, but we must change the inputs to compensate for changes in the environment. In this book, Professor Belasen quotes Jack Welch, CEO of GE, who might have put it best when he said that organizations have to change faster than their environments.

The bottom line is that passive or defensive management will not be sufficient, even to sustain the status quo.

Managing at the end of the twentieth century is therefore far from the quiet life, but is an exceedingly demanding challenge requiring constant attention to the best new ideas in management theory and practice. Managers who don't question their operating premises today often find themselves without market share tomorrow.

In *Leading the Learning Organization*, Professor Belasen most emphatically implores us to question those premises.

A fair question you may ask is, with all this attention to meeting the new and increasing demands of competition, what manager has time to absorb even a fraction of the exponentially growing body of ideas generated by academics, consultants, and practitioners that fill the groaning bookshelves in the business section of the bookstore? It is not uncommon for the overworked manager to take the newest tome to bed at night and recall the childhood adage: "Please put fire into the verse or put the verse into the fire!"

I would argue that there is indeed a need for a book like Professor Belasen's, and, while there is a lot of difficult terrain to cover, there is plenty of fire between these covers. The reason Professor Belasen should be allocated a place in your portfolio of scarce, valuable professional reading time is that he has made a noteworthy contribution by integrating an extraordinary volume of recent thinking on the subject of managerial leadership and the learning organization and by organizing that thinking into a coherent, predictive model of managerial behavior and organizational effectiveness. That is, Professor Belasen provides a carefully tested schema for organizing a proliferation of recent thinking that not only makes sense of that thinking for you, but does so in ways especially designed for managers seeking to become better individually—professionally *and* personally—at leading their organizations to greater levels of effectiveness.

That's a tall order, and toward that end Professor Belasen has spent, not surprisingly, the better part of five years. Most of us would nonetheless find the challenge daunting, but a colleague, Professor Robyn Silverman, illuminated this for me when she said: "Professor Belasen is a 180-mile-per-hour train. If you're going to get on, don't dawdle."

Glance at the table of contents and you will see an organizational structure for the book that makes the trip across so much terrain possible. This is no Iron Rooster creaking across the Siberian tundra, but a high-speed monorail on a very straight track. The engine, the organizing device for the book, is the competing-values framework, a thoroughly tested and applied model of the fundamental roles managers play in effective organizations, and how the competing tensions of the organization are satisfied, as well as they can be, by the shifting roleplay of the competent manager. The cars of the train, the wealth of theory and evidence assembled for and explained to us, range from topics such as information technologies, cross-functional teams, quality management and reengineering, downsizing and its impacts on organizations and managers—including those who stay behind and risk hypereffectivity, self-managed teams, communication strategies, competency education for management development, initiating transformational learning, and, of course, *adapting to the changing environment.*

That is, the train has many cars and they are *loaded* with cargo, but they are not presented seriatim, without structure. Each chapter has a place in the organizing framework of the book, showing us not only the importance of the issue but *how to apply it* both to our own individual development as more effective managers and to the development of our organizations. The caboose of this train, I would suggest in the spirit of Professor Belasen's call for continuous improvement, has yet to be built, and if you take on this mission, it will be built by you.

What place does this book have on your bookshelf? Is this a reference work? Assuredly, it can serve that role, and I fully expect that this book will take a favored place on your office bookshelf, because you will return to it often for its extensive review of the thinking on managerial leadership. It is so much more, however. This is not only a dispassionate compendium of recent research and practice, but an advocacy piece as well. Pulling together thinking from a variety of disciplines—communication, managerial leadership, organization behavior and design, even economics—Professor Belasen does not just describe and explain high-performance leadership, but argues forcefully that high-performance leadership is, in his words, "*vital* for the success of horizontal, value-based organizations. Leading the learning organization requires team-based design and flexible structures that cannot run without explicit recognition of the new roles that *must* be played by leadership in the absence of traditional systems of control and authority." [Italics mine.] The advantages of a strong point of view are two: one, an expert who has spent considerable time studying the topic has the conviction to let you know what he thinks, and not only does this conviction add credibility to the work, but the advice of an expert is surely valuable. Two, by marshaling evidence and argument in favor of a position—that organizations *must be strongly led* into the future by managers with special skills and insights—it gives you, the careful reader, a chance to conduct a dialogue with the professor as you go. Disagree if you must, but engage! Ride the Belasen Express!

What place will this book have in the history of thought, in what intellectual stream will it ultimately be placed when we later come to gauge the import of Professor Belasen's ideas? I was trained as an economist, so I will hazard a forecast: Professor Belasen will come to be appreciated as following in the current of Professor Peter Senge, author of *The Fifth Discipline*. As you probably recall, Professor Senge broke new ground with that 1990 publication, in which he argued that without thoughtful preparation, teams performed less well than their *least* able individual members, and organizations were only deluded by their ineffective experiential learning. I think of Professor Belasen as Plato to

Professor Senge's Socrates. Senge threw out ideas that changed the way we see the problem, and Belasen provides the framework and the rationale for how we should fix that problem.

Managers who aspire to be leaders and leaders who aspire to be more (as all leaders do) probably agree with me that Churchill was right when he said, in an address to Harvard in 1943, that "the empires of the future are the empires of the mind." In *Leading the Learning Organization*, Professor Belasen shows us where to begin.

MICHAEL V. FORTUNATO
Director, FORUM/East Management Development Program

Acknowledgments

A large number of individuals have helped bring this book to fruition. First of all is Dr. Donald Cushman from the Department of Communication at the University of Albany whose High Speed Management theory has inspired organizational communication researchers and professors to rethink conventional views of organizational communication and redefine the role communication plays in integrating, controlling, and coordinating high performance organizations. Through conversations with him over the years he inspired me to continue this important work and bring it to a conclusion. Thank you, Don!

I owe special thanks to Dr. Michael Fortunato, Director of FORUM/East Management Education at Empire State College of the State University of New York. Mike has inspired me during the last four years to continue to work on managerial learning and education and has provided much of the intellectual stimulation that helped shaped the ideas and insights of this book. As an economist (Mike has a Ph.D. from Harvard) who is typically interested in rational explications of the external boundaries of the box, Mike's provocative questioning of working assumptions and existing theories of management, leadership, organizational design, and human communication would have amazed any researcher in the field of organization and management. With his enormous aptitude, endless quest for new knowledge, and huge information processing capacity, Mike has constantly reengineered my mind and challenged me to think from a gestalt perspective and develop an integrative view of the intricate world of organizations. I often used the acronym BPR (business process reengineering) as Brain Process Reengineering to describe my professional and intellectual relationships with him. Mike epitomizes the concepts of creative tension and breakthrough thinking, not from a conventional Socratic way of persuasion through logic and reasoning but from a holistic, interdisciplinary approach to staying ahead of the learning curve that has challenged me to think integratively. Dr. Fortunato has an ability to constantly remind people of the importance of meta-learning and the need to develop contradictory forms of knowledge, that is, to create a dialectic within one's mind about the preferred operating assumption and measure it up against competing paradigms. It is through this revolutionary thinking that I was able to rethink the logic of my arguments about the cognitive and behavioral complexity that high-performance leaders must have in leading the organization of the future. Dr. Michael Fortunato has taught me a very important lesson: To write with high quality, one must first fail in order to succeed. To me, it sounds like learning without a finish line! Wouldn't you agree?

I am indebted to Dr. Laurie Newman DiPadova from the University of Utah whose scholarly research has made a significant contribution to the field of leadership and service learning. Laurie's work with me in the area of managerial competency, learning, and education have helped form the intellectual boundaries of this book. Indeed, many pages in this book are dated back to the early summer of 1994 when Laurie and I spent many hours discussing and evaluating different research options using the Competing Values Framework (CVF). At some point when I suggested that it would be interesting to apply the CVF in studying horizontal structures and team-based organizations, Laurie, who was busy polishing her dissertation on managerial leadership and organizational hierarchy, replied with her famous sense of humor and unbinding, compassionate style that I should start working on leadership and communication-based learning in "vertically challenged" organizations and that she will join me later. As you will see throughout the book, our collaborative work in the area of managerial competency has yielded some interesting research and program development outcomes.

I would also like to acknowledge the advice and significant suggestions of Dr. Stuart Sigman, former chair of the Department of Communication at the State University of New York at Albany and currently dean of Emerson's School of Communication, Management and Public Policy, who read an earlier draft of the manuscript and whose invaluable comments helped refocus the direction of this book and improve its logistical plan. A nationally recognized expert in his field and a prolific scholar, Stuart often walked me through the complex maze of writing a book and continuously challenged me to think analytically and critically about the field of management learning and organization communication.

I would like to thank Dr. Sue Faerman, currently with the Graduate School of Public Affairs at the Rockefeller College, State University of New York at Albany, coauthor of *Becoming the Master Manager*, and my partner in our consulting venture, whose multifaceted knowledge of how social systems operate and seminal work and observations about the dialectical nature of the managerial job has helped me to refine my thoughts about organizational and management development.

I must say that the number of people who have helped bring this book to closure directly or indirectly include my graduate students from the Department of Communication at the State University of New York at Albany, as well as my MBA students at Union College, Schenectady, who helped execute some of my field studies in pursuit of stronger evidence to validate working assumptions that I had about managerial leadership. From the Department of Communication, I need to recognize the significant contribution of Brian Engle and Olivia Yang to my research involving communication and leadership processes in self-managed teams. Tina Henderson helped to gather data about the expected behaviors of middle managers while Katherine Germain assisted me in mapping out the literature to identify a pattern in managerial discourse that accepted the assumptions of the movement toward quality. Linda Lawrence is perhaps the individual whose contribution to earlier drafts of the manuscript made the final one more complete and in tune with current organizational histories. Working around the clock to meet the publisher's deadlines for submission, Linda did a magnificent job of collecting updated data about companies' actions and performance outcomes, as well as reading portions of the manuscript and giving me valuable feedback to improve the flow of ideas. From the MBA program at Union College, I'd like to recognize my class of summer 1997 who did a wonderful job in administering and performing a field study involving four different organizations and in such a short period of time: Brian Delf, Bharat Navani, Michael McPartlon, Tracy Whitman, Dominic Arcidiacono, Katie Brazeau, Mayur Patel, Jayne Fake, Bob Wilson, Paul Scampini, Charlotte Yunging Xia, Michelle Gallen, Suzanne Byrne, Rick Gangemi, and Marco DeThomasis.

I would like to mention a few of the individuals at State University of New York–Empire State College who supported me while working long hours and with high speed to complete the manuscript on time. Special thanks to Carolyn Jarmon, Robyn Silverman, and Elaine Handley, who also contributed to the chapter on management education and development. Thanks to Patricia Wheeler who read an early draft of chapter 7 and gave me valuable suggestions and feedback to improve its format presentation. Ginger Knight and Mike Mudd often provided me with the back up and logistical support that has enabled me to continue to write the book while also fulfilling my academic and administrative obligations. Lynda Maciag will always have a special place in my circle of much appreciated people. With a unique combination of wisdom and humor she is always prepared to challenge me with provocative questions.

I would also like to acknowledge the support of the Empire State College Foundation and FORUM, which provided me with grants to update the manuscript and bring it to fruition. Special thanks to VPAA, Marjorie Lavin and Dean Joyce Elliott for making these funds available to me. Special thanks go to Zina Lawrence and James Peltz, State University of New York Press acquisition editors, who were always there when I needed their expertise and good advice. I would also like to thank Marilyn Semerad, Production Manager at State University of New York Press, for her dedication and hard work in bringing the project from manuscript to bound book. I would also like to thank Kelli Williams and Patrick Durocher of SUNY Press, who provided invaluable and cheerful assistance.

This book could not have been accomplished without the intellectual, professional, and moral support of my wife Susan Belasen. With patience and passion, wisdom and intelligence she was the light at the end of the tunnel. For the long hours sitting with my computer and switching back from e-mail to writing, Susan was my source of motivation and my model for high-performance leadership. And it has not been easy for her with five children at home who have friends sleep over often and have turned our home into a small to mid-size organizational apparatus! I will always admire my five children for cheering me on while working on this book. My five A's: Ari, Amy, Anat, Amanda, and Abby.

Introduction: Leading the Learning Organization

Needed in today's business environment is not just a skilled CEO but leadership from hundreds of individuals above and below the plant manager level. The high performing leader of the future will be the individual who acts as a dynamic, but not omnipotent, part of a cohesive, decisive interlocking group of people.

—John P. Kotter, *A Force for Change*, 1990

My most important job is to choose and develop business leaders who are bright enough to grasp the elements of their game, creative enough to develop a simple vision, and self-confident enough to liberate and inspire people.

—Jack Welch, *Industry Week*, vol. 245(21), 1996

This book stresses the cognitive and behavioral shift expected from high-performance leaders transforming their organizations into agile, flexible organizations. This transformation involves a strong commitment to lead the organization through learning to achieve a quantum leap performance. Successful leaders reframe the social architecture of the organization, realign its value chain, and create an organizational climate conducive to learning. At times where the only constant in world markets is exponentially increasing change, high-performance leaders are called upon to reframe traditional management philosophy, reshape leadership vision, and redefine organizational mission. High-performance leaders are confronted with the challenge of remaking their organizations before the environment changes. They develop a vision of success and ensure the availability of resources to support and implement the vision.

Through the initiation of networking and investments in information technology, high-performance leaders link organizational interfaces both internally and externally. Internally, they act to create a value-based, horizontal organization, structured along the lines of empowered, communication intensive, self-contained teams. Externally, they ensure that the organization is linked effectively through strategic alliances and partnerships. They also initiate outsourcing processes and activities that are relatively costly or fall outside organizational core competency. High-performance leaders lead the learning organization by creating conditions that foster teamwork and self-management while deemphasizing traditional structures and hierarchy. High-performance leaders are challenged to increase organizational adaptive efficiency by:

- Temporizing structural arrangements
- Delayering the chain of command
- Creating boundaryless structures
- Forming empowered teams staffed by cross-trained individuals
- Using more flexible and informal forms of coordination
- Enhancing organizational and individual communication capabilities
- Focusing on customer needs
- Implementing quality improvement
- Reengineering work processes
- Investing in information technology
- Establishing partnerships with suppliers

Drawing on innovative approaches to organizational design, leadership, and communication, this book proposes a simple yet powerful idea: High-performance leadership is vital for the success of horizontal, value-based organizations. Leading the learning organization requires team-based design and flexible structures that cannot run without the explicit recognition of the new roles that must be played by leadership in the absence of traditional systems of control and authority. Vertical organizations can run virtually without leaders because centralization and bureaucratic control are effective substitutes for leadership. Tall, hierarchically structured organizations can run through midlevel, transactional managers who rely on the exchange of rewards for performance. The vision of these transactional managers begins and ends with performance and results, not with performance breakthrough and innovation.

It is argued throughout the book that unless these organizations and their managers reshape their strategies, reframe their structures, and renew their management philosophies, they will have difficulty adapting to the increasing change in their marketplace and responding competitively to global challenges. The argument advanced is that horizontal organizations, on the other hand, require leadership by virtue of their decentralized structures, or as in the case of delayered organizations staffed with self-managed teams, due to the absence of supervisory relationships. Successful leaders adopt a value system that is congruent with the new culture and management philosophy. They are expected to develop their employees or team players to become future leaders. Empowered team members think and act like local entrepreneurs who are sensitive to customer demands and can respond quickly and creatively to market changes. In these organizations, leadership roles should be transferred to team members by design (i.e., through delegation, lateral movement, and formal training), or through emergent processes (i.e., inclusive, nurturing, altruistic) supported by vicarious learning and socialization.

As market and technological pressures continue to render traditional methods of management obsolete, organizations compress their structures, become flat, and common management practices are delegated or pushed down to self-directed work teams. Upper management has been faced with a challenge to lead the organization through constant adaptation and renewal, action learning, and continuous improvement. This challenge requires high-performance leaders that are both transactional and transformational. High-performance leaders appeal to employees' self-concepts, values, and personal identities to generate the energy needed to replace the old command structure with a commitment culture.

Multilayered, bureaucratic organizations are being replaced by flatter, less rigidly defined organizational structures. The increased reliance on computers is whittling away at the layer of middle managers. Managers, whose primary responsibility was to process and pass along information, are finding their jobs obsolete. The new information age is toppling hierarchies. Increasingly, employees find their upward mobility buffered, out of reach, or nonexistent and their competitive energy transformed by their creative enterprising spirit (Naisbitt & Aburdene, 1985, p. 30). Middle managers, who spent most of their work lives in traditional command structures, often have trouble trading institutional and quantitative skills for interpersonal and communication skills. Adaptive or strategic middle managers learn to break down old habits and patterned behaviors and embrace the goals of change. Ironically, the price that middle managers pay is too high: Still held accountable for the old management practices and processes, they become obsessed with hypereffectivity, a state of performance that is unsustainable over a long period of time (Belasen, Benke, DiPadova & Fortunato, 1996). Those middle managers who rethink their roles by using inclusive styles of management and who nurture a synergistic work climate that empowers employees are also able to adapt quickly. They rebuild self-confidence and act to gain acceptance of lower and higher managerial levels to their new roles.

The downside of restructuring, networking, and even becoming global is communication problems, at least in the early stage of transformation. Cultural differences, task variety, goal ambiguity, and uncertainty regarding professional development and long-term job retention can lead to low self-esteem, morale problems, and often to a breakdown in managerial and interpersonal communication. However, the long-term payoffs are unmatched as long as organizational leaders confront new ideas and purposes by taking risks without fear of failure. Any restructuring brings with it ambiguity over objectives, frustration, and resistance. But once the new structure is in place, organizational leaders must inspire others, build a common understanding, and mobilize commitment to the new vision. This process requires effective communication skills, mutual trust, and high confidence. GE management values (*Industry Week*, 11/18/96) are quite relevant in this context:

> GE leaders, at all levels, always with unyielding integrity,
>
> - create a clear, simple, reality-based, customer-focused vision and are able to communicate it straightforwardly to all constituencies;
> - reach . . . set aggressive goals . . . recognize and reward progress . . . while understanding accountability and commitment;
> - have a passion for excellence . . . hate bureaucracy and all the nonsense that comes with it;
> - have the self-confidence to empower others and behave in a boundaryless fashion . . . believe in and are committed to Work-Out as a means of empowerment . . . are open to ideas from anywhere;

- have the capacity to develop global sensitivity;
- have enormous energy and the ability to energize and invigorate others . . . stimulate and relish change . . . not be frightened or paralyzed by it . . . see change as an opportunity not a threat;
- possess a mindset that drives quality, cost, and speed for a competitive advantage.

We argue in this book that the core values of high-performance leadership must transcend across all levels and locations to achieve breakthrough performance. Exemplary high-performance leaders develop others by helping them find the right mix between transactional and transformational characteristics of leadership. Leadership can be stretched to its full potential and become more effective through the sharing of technological and informational resources and through the creation of shared meaning and compatible values and beliefs. Levi Strauss & Co.'s CEO Robert Haas has attested to this: "In a command and control organization, people protect knowledge because it's their claim to distinction. But we share as much information as we possibly can through the company. Business literacy is a big issue in developing leadership. You cannot ask people to exercise broader judgment if their world is bounded by a very narrow vision" (Huey, 1994, p. 48). High-performance leaders, and especially executives, must be open minded and listen to sensitive issues and concerns of employees. They must develop credibility through mutual respect and recognition in order to synergize and pull people in the direction of the new vision. High-performance leaders transform uncertainty into creative thinking and excellence, which results in a "special feeling of exuberance" (Quinn, 1988) that helps inspire organizational members to reach peak performance.

STYLE AND APPROACH

This book relies on new perspectives on organizational design, leadership, and communication and on successful applications from a variety of domestic and international organizations. It challenges old truths and paradigms of management, demonstrates the new principles of managerial leadership in a variety of situations, and shows what makes certain leaders successful and their organizations world-class organizations. Attention is given throughout the book to Jack Welch's inspirational leadership and to his role in transforming GE into a world-class organization. In addition, the book draws on the experiences of over one hundred American and international organizations to derive conclusions about successful transformational processes.

Since the book targets organizational leaders, practicing managers, and HR managers, as well as students of management, a balance between theory and practice is maintained throughout the book. This balance is attained without the burden of heavy conceptualization and reliance on theoretical constructs. Instead, analytical frameworks are mentioned in the background or are implied (with the assumption that they are understood or known). When necessary, concepts and models are briefly mentioned and the reader is given a reference for further research and follow-up clarification. Similarly, practical examples that demonstrate the usefulness of concepts or approaches are provided concisely and with pertinent and up-to-date information. Most of the examples draw on cases and experiences primarily from the 1990s.

To satisfy the professional needs of organizational leaders and managers, the book provides numerous examples and illustrations of innovative approaches to management and to organizational design. Process guidelines are often used to suggest prescriptions or checklists against which readers can measure their own practices and draw conclusions for further improvement. Pointers are also used to suggest "how to" or to offer critical success factors (CSFs) to help practitioners enhance as well as apply learning. To satisfy the intellectual curiosity and research needs of professors and students of organization and management, the book contains references to published material on subjects discussed or arguments raised.

INTELLECTUAL NICHE AND PHILOSOPHICAL PREDICAMENT

> Organization is a means to an end rather than an end itself. Sound structure is a prerequisite to organizational health; but it is not health itself. The test of a healthy business is not the beauty, clarity, or perception of its organization structure. It is the performance of people.
>
> —Peter F. Drucker

As figure 1 illustrates *Leading the Learning Organization* is a book that draws on four parallel streams of management literature: *Strategic change, continuous improvement, managerial leadership, and learning and development.*

Intro. Figure 1. The Four Streams of Management Literature

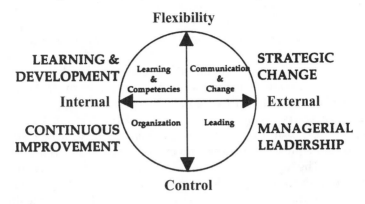

The *strategic change* literature is associated with organizational transformations toward agile, fluid, and adaptive organizational configurations that are supported by outsourcing, global networking, and information technology. Survival in the marketplace is enhanced with speed, flexibility, and creativity, critical success factors that are found in nimbler and highly focused organizations. Breaking down organizational boundaries to form innovative and globally coherent organizational form has become the strategic challenge for managers. The key to organizational success lies with the ability of managers enacting the Broker and Innovator roles to constantly redraw organizational boundaries to facilitate rapid change and adaptation.

The *continuous improvement* literature focuses on streamlining the sociotechnical systems to achieve high consistency in operations and internal processes. Once the organization realigns its structure with the external environment, the systematic integration of structures, processes, people, and technologies must ensure optimal attainment of organizational strategies and goals. This stream of literature stresses the importance of streamlining the value chain and constantly improving organizational value adding as measured by customer satisfaction. Total quality management and business process reengineering combined with empowerment, involvement, and horizontal management ensure that the organization focuses on customer-oriented processes, as well as maintaining a flexible and creative work environments. A culture of high involvement and empowerment is indispensable since front line employees are educated to think and act like local entrepreneurs who quickly and creatively must respond to customer needs and market changes. Managers enacting the Monitor and Coordinator roles develop technical and problem solving expertise and competencies essential for sustaining organizational performance, integrating cross-functional teams, and supporting collective accountability.

The *managerial leadership* literature centers on key behaviors and skills of transformational leaders which result in high performance. Transformational leaders are externally focused and engage in realignment processes between the enterprise and its domain. Within the organization, transformational leaders inspire the creation of a commitment culture with self-led teams and external managers as coaches and motivators. The top manager's role is to ensure the coherence of organizational design and capabilities to effectively compete in the marketplace. The middle manager's role is to productively facilitate the flow of work across organizational units, to maintain organizational viability through the implementation of change, and integrate key parts of the operating core to accomplish organizational strategic goals. The supervisory role is to motivate, counsel, and provide employees with the essentials they need to perform their tasks. In a synergistic culture epitomized by the shift toward organic structures and customer-centered goals, the core values of managers have helped transform the traditional Producer and Director roles into high-performance leaders who are sensitive to external goals and who are skilled in energizing individuals and groups. The new managerial leadership core values are manifested through commitment to the success of others, valuing differences, high standards of ethical behavior, open communication, and actively pushing the responsibility, trust, and recognition to those closest to dealing with products and customers.

The *learning and development* literature emphasizes the importance of double-loop learning and the development of managerial competency to question the underlying assumptions and values of organizational operations. Learning involves systematic evaluation of markets, products, technology, and structures as they relate to personal and organizational performance. Learning is enhanced in horizontal, decentralized organizations in which those who do the work are also responsible for their behaviors and actions. Developing and fostering entrepreneurial drive in horizontal organizations through empowerment and cross-functional teams breed learning that helps support organizational capabilities and business strategies. Once the structural change is accompanied by a cognitive change aimed at unlearning defensive practices and routines, horizontal organizations become the natural incubators for developing and utilizing meta-learning capabilities.

The development of new knowledge becomes the basis for double-loop learning or understanding of causal relationships.

Horizontal organizations also enhance communication-based learning, which in turn supports the capabilities of the organization to maintain decentralized decision making, a greater capacity for tolerance of ambiguity, permeable boundaries, and active networking and connections between subunits. Learning capabilities, which yield fast adaptation, represent internal organizational capabilities that create a sustainable competitive advantage for horizontal organizations. Learning at the organizational level is sustained by the transference of new knowledge and development of new skills and competencies at the personal level. Competency-based management education and development are critical for development of the technical, human, conceptual, and perceptual skills that can match the complexity and sophistication of the environment within which the organization operates. Managers must develop the requisite skills and competencies to see the enterprise as a whole and deal intelligently with changes. As a Facilitator the manager synthesizes and transfers new knowledge to individuals and groups and as a Mentor the manager helps employees break old habits and develop the leadership abilities needed to lead the organization into the future. In enacting these two roles, the manager also supports the viability of the organization to learn and adapt effectively to its environment.

This book, *Leading the Learning Organization*, integrates the four perspectives by examining and demonstrating how change in structures and processes is driven by leaders' cognitive and behavioral responses to that change. Through the initiation of action learning, reflective leaders anticipate the need for change and identify the means by which the social and technical structures of their organizations can be realigned effectively. The book also emphasizes the shift in roles and competencies required by leaders to meet successfully the new organizational challenges.

THEORETICAL BASIS: COMPETING VALUES FRAMEWORK

The management of organization, of society, and of personal life ultimately involves the management of contradiction . . . The choice that individuals and societies ultimately have before them is thus really a choice about the kind of contradiction that is to shape the pattern of daily life.

—Gareth Morgan, *Images of Organizations*, 1986

The theoretical basis and organizing construct for this book is the Competing Values Framework. The Competing Values Framework (CVF) portrays the inherent contradictions facing organizations and managers on two axes or dimensions (The Competing Values Framework is depicted in chapter 1). The horizontal axis is one of focus: internal versus external. This axis reflects the expectation managers have that organizations should be concerned with both what goes on inside the organization and with producing for and servicing an external environment. The vertical axis of the CVF portrays the opposing expectations of flexibility and control. We expect organizations to be controlling systems in order to ensure a predictable and stable work environment. At the same time, we expect organizations to be flexible and adapt to changes in their external environments. The juxtaposition of these two axes forms four quadrants, each of which reflects a different model of organizational effectiveness criteria.

The external horizontal axis and the flexibility vertical axis in the Competing Values Framework define the boundaries of the *open system model* and the domain of organizational *strategic change*. This model reflects the view that organizations are effective when they are able to anticipate changes in their marketplace and even thrive when such changes occur. Fundamental to this model is the need to survive in a turbulent arena. The two managerial leadership roles associated with this quadrant are the Innovator and Broker roles.

The internal horizontal axis and the control vertical axis in the Competing Values Framework define the boundaries of the *internal processes model* and the domain of organizational *continuous improvement*. This model reflects the view that organizations are effective if they are stable and keep track of activities within their operating cores. Fundamental to this model is the need to upgrade the technical systems of the organization to match its structural capacity, coordinate and streamline work flow processes, and monitor progress toward achieving organizational goals. The two managerial leadership roles associated with this quadrant are the Coordinator and Monitor roles.

The external horizontal axis and the control vertical axis appear in the lower right quadrant of the Competing Values Framework and define the boundaries of the *rational goal model* and the domain of organizational *managerial leadership*. This model reflects the view that organizations are effective if they meet their goals. Fundamental to this model is the need for structure and direction. The two managerial leadership roles associated with this quadrant are the Producer and Director roles.

The internal horizontal axis and the flexibility vertical axis appear in the upper left quadrant of the Competing Values Framework and define the boundaries of the *human relations model* and the domain of organizational and management *learning and development*. This model reflects the view that organizations are effective if they are able to tap into the talents and thinking of their employees. Fundamental to this model is the concern for attention to human needs. The two managerial leadership roles associated with this quadrant are the Facilitator and the Mentor.

A key point of the Competing Values Framework (CVF) is that organizations are inherently contradictory entities, and therefore, organizational effectiveness criteria are fundamentally opposing, contradictory, and may be mutually exclusive. While we expect organizations to maintain stability and integration by paying strong attention to their internal workings and procedures, we also expect organizations to be responsive and adaptive by responding to pressures coming from the external environment. This approach, then, highlights the fact that organizations operate under the burden of contradictory, competing, and conflicting expectations. Responding to these expectations is vital for the success (effectiveness) of the organization. Obviously, this burden is not borne by organizations per se, but by the managerial leaders in these organizations. These individuals function within a context of complex and contradictory expectations. In this way, the CVF reflects on the contradictory criteria of effectiveness that describe managerial leadership.

As the discussion in the following chapters reveals, managers at all levels perform the variety of CVF leadership roles to enhance the ability of their organization to adapt effectively to its environment and act in a coherent and consistent way. While a full treatment of these roles appears in *Becoming a Master Manager* (Quinn, Faerman, Thompson & McGrath, 1996), this book sets out to examine the context within which managers perform the roles described by the CVF. Although the eight CVF roles are often mentioned or discussed explicitly throughout, the emphasis of this book is on the contextual factors that shape managerial behaviors or that are affected by the actions taken by managers enacting the CVF roles. Thus, each part of the book begins with a short description of two roles associated with a CVF quadrant and contains two chapters that cover material relevant for the functioning of managers enacting those particular roles. The last chapter brings the discussion back to the role level by describing the roles executives play in leading their organizations through learning and transformations.

PLAN OF THE BOOK

Leading the Learning Organization begins with an introductory chapter that establishes the reasoning and logic for using an integrative approach based on the Competing Values Framework to leadership and concludes with a chapter advancing the concept of high-performance leadership as a medium for achieving transformational learning. The midsection of the book consists of four parts and eight chapters that parallel the quadrants of the Competing Values Framework and the eight leadership roles described by the Framework. A look at the organization of the book appears in Intro. Figure 2.

In chapter 1, "Integrating Management Paradigms: The Competing Values Framework," the Competing Values Framework as a logical scheme that brings together mechanistic and organic concepts of management is presented. The mechanistic or rationalistic school of thought is based on the principles of scientific management and the theory of bureaucratic control. The organic or humanistic school is based on the view of organizations as interactive systems evolving around the need to respond to psycho-social needs of individuals within them. The rationalistic approach has positioned itself as an efficiency-driven, control-oriented ideology with a strong emphasis on centralization and formalization of managerial decision-making processes. This approach relies on the development of clear policies and procedural specifications, unambiguous roles and responsibilities, divisible tasks and high specialization, and standardization of work processes to rationalize resource allocation and achieve stability and control. Drawing on the rationalistic approach as the primary ideology to organize labor, organizations have turned into efficient machine bureaucracies. Flexibility and innovation are accepted as long as they do not dramatically change or interrupt the existing work flow. Organizational strict hierarchy and unchallenged authority were intended to achieve obedience, facilitate administrative innovations, and exchange good performance and compliance with rewards while sanctioning poor performance and undesirable behavior.

The humanistic approach distanced itself from the rationalistic view by catering to individual well-being and by being sensitive to employee work conditions, job satisfaction, training, and communication needs. Evolving into what has been called the human resource perspective, this approach called for giving employees greater opportunities for involvement in decision making over work processes. The philosophy was that freed from the burden of being overcontrolled, and by having more autonomy and greater influence over the outcomes of work, employees would synergize their efforts and perform with excellence. The prognosis was simple, yet powerful—a humanistic approach can lead to high commitment and morale—employees would regain trust and confidence in their managers and ultimately would become accountable for the results of work.

Intro. Figure 2. The Organization of This Book

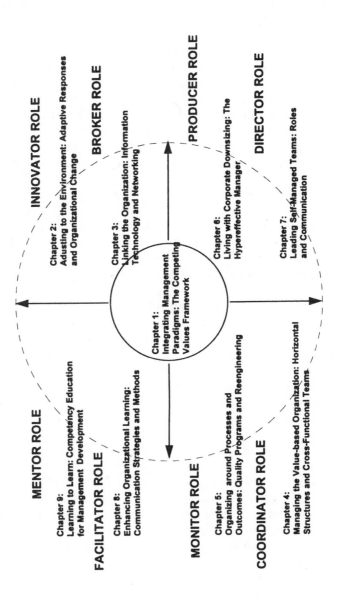

Introduction: **Leading the Learning Organization**

INNOVATOR ROLE

Chapter 2:
Adjusting to the Environment: Adaptive Responses
and Organizational Change

BROKER ROLE

Chapter 3:
Linking the Organization: Information
Technology and Networking

PRODUCER ROLE

Chapter 6:
Living with Corporate Downsizing: The
Hypereffective Manager

DIRECTOR ROLE

Chapter 7:
Leading Self-Managed Teams: Roles
and Communication

MENTOR ROLE

Chapter 9:
Learning to Learn: Competency Education
for Management Development

FACILITATOR ROLE

Chapter 8:
Enhancing Organizational Learning:
Communication Strategies and Methods

MONITOR ROLE

Chapter 5:
Organizing around Processes and
Outcomes: Quality Programs and Reengineering

COORDINATOR ROLE

Chapter 4:
Managing the Value-based Organization: Horizontal
Structures and Cross-Functional Teams

Chapter 1:
Integrating Management
Paradigms: The Competing
Values Framework

High-Performance Leadership: Initiating
Transformational Learning

Other contemporary views of organization and management appeared to avoid the bureaucratic-humanistic dichotomy in favor of an integrative, or holistic approach. Such an approach advanced by the quality movement sought the integration of systems and processes with social and human factors. This approach, often referred to as "gestalt" was aimed at evaluating managerial effectiveness based on universal principles that embrace contextual, informational, and judgmental variables. This integration, however, required a different prism to understand and explain how organizations work and how managers should function. The chapter then reintroduces the Competing Values Framework as a powerful construct allowing the evaluation and analysis of managerial performance from an integrative, multidimensional perspective.

Part I—chapter 2, "Adjusting to the Environment: Adaptive Responses and Organizational Change," and, chapter 3, "Linking the Organization: Information Technology and Networking"—covers the dynamics of change and the need to align the value chain of the organization to optimize organizational performance. The discussion in these two chapters examines the scope of leadership challenges faced by managers enacting the Innovator and Broker roles.

In chapter 2, the isomorphic relationships between organizations and environments and the principles of congruence are discussed. Using examples from a wide variety of organizations, the chapter outlines external and internal adaptive responses used by managers to align their organizations with the environment within which they operate. The common theme emerging in this chapter is the need for managers to act innovatively, creatively, and flexibly. Managers who can change both cognitively and behaviorally can also adjust quickly and learn how to cope with change and deal with stress while helping others do the same. By fostering personal growth and empowering their employees, managers create opportunities for greater organizational adaptability. While most managers appreciate the importance of human capital in the productivity equation, the effective managers utilize their employees' strengths, creativity, and innovativeness to the fullest. The manager's new role in the environment of discontinuity is to cultivate and maintain a nourishing climate for personal growth. Managers do not have to have the answers; just the right questions and the right attitude. Effective managerial leaders transform the entire organization by creating an awareness for the need to change and by enhancing the capability of the organization to adapt.

In chapter 3, the discussion of adaptation and change is continued from a networking and interorganizational relationships point of view.

This form of adaptation involves the creation of a better coalignment of the organization, both internally by rearranging structures and processes, and externally by strategically maneuvering the organization in the direction of greater interdependence with its external environment. This endeavor requires managers to negotiate linking programs with external systems, and therefore, to develop the competencies and skills that are important for boundary management. Brokering, political maneuvering, bargaining, persuading, negotiating, influencing, networking, and managing external linkages become the core competencies of the new leader. Top executives act as brokers to link organizations, to coordinate key players within the network and to monitor the flow of resources across organizations. In a Broker capacity, managers play the role of architect, designing and assembling the network value chain. Once the network has been put in place, managers with coordinating skills assume the role of lead operator to render the network operative. When the network runs smoothly and effectively, other important Broker roles emerge—managers must act as boundary spanners, collecting, screening, and sharing information across the organizations that are part of the network value chain. These maintenance roles are essential for the success of the network.

The chapters included in Part II—chapter 4, "Managing the Value-Based Organization: Horizontal Structures and Cross Functional Teams," and, chapter 5, "Organizing around Processes and Outcomes: Quality Programs and Reengineering"—cover the principles and dynamics of moving toward a team-based design and organizing work around processes and outputs rather than functions. These two chapters highlight the importance of internal consistency in organizational operations through integration and monitoring of interdependencies within and across work units and teams. Thus, the scope of leadership challenges faced by managers enacting the Coordinator and Monitor roles are examined in these chapters.

The principles and characteristics of the value-based, horizontal organization are described in chapter 4. The value-based organization requires managers to develop a unique behavioral flexibility that allows them to balance the need to protect stability and preserve the status quo with the need to manage discontinuity, randomness, and flux. The new style requires managers to be skilled in managing disorder and in coaching, facilitating, and helping employees self-organize and evolve into flexible work groups. Once individuals and groups are organized and their activities coordinated, effective managers must also develop expertise to monitor progress against established performance targets to ensure the smooth and efficient utilization of organizational resources. Enacting the Coordinator role to achieve integration across organizational units and functions complements the efforts of the manager playing the Monitor role. These two roles are essential to support the goals of organizational continuous improvement.

In chapter 5, the concepts and principles of quality improvement programs and reengineering efforts that require managers to enact the Monitor role are discussed. Quality efforts can help organizations increase employee awareness of customers' needs and concerns while focusing on improving existing technologies and processes. When a performance breakthrough is called for, reengineering may be ideal. Organizations already engaged in improvement efforts will find it easier to adapt to the requirements and principles of reengineering. Organizations also need quality improvement techniques to sustain the results of reengineering and to constantly strive to improve the gains achieved through the reengineering effort. The challenge is to know when and where one technique might be more appropriate than the other and to understand how to make rational choices that will maximize economic as well as psychological gains for the organization, its employees, external customers, and suppliers. Where at one time managers acted as aggressors and delegators, the quality movement repositions managers as facilitators and coaches demonstrating understanding and competency in empowering, mentoring, and enabling subordinates. While management literature exalts the significance of the manager's role in the advent of the need for cultural transformation, it also reveals that managers are the most threatened. The requirement to let go and share power rather than use power does not fit the traditional format of managerial roles and responsibilities, especially that of the Monitor. The mental as well as socioeconomic sacrifice is too great to be accepted and the gains are too little to offset the costs. Instead of auditing and evaluating performance retrospectively, the Monitor resorts to a prevention or introspective approach that instills confidence in people and their ability to achieve performance breakthrough. Motivating employees to increase their personal productivity and encouraging them to team up and self-lead, while at the same time adjusting cognitively and behaviorally to the new managerial leadership roles expected from managers are the focus of Part III.

The chapters included in Part III—chapter 6, "Living with Corporate Downsizing: The Hypereffective Manager," and chapter 7, "Leading Self-Managed Teams: Roles and Communication"—cover the dynamics of corporate downsizing, the shifting importance of managerial roles, and the principles of effective self-management and shared-team leadership. While chapter 6 deals with the effects of organizational transformations and particularly with the emergence of managerial hypereffectivity, chapter 7 focuses on the importance of visioning, the initiation of structures, and the transference of leadership roles to self-managed team members. These two chapters examine the scope of leadership challenges faced by managers enacting the Producer and Director roles.

Chapter 6 illuminates the shifting importance of managerial roles during organizational transformations. Restructuring and downsizing require middle managers to adopt different roles and develop different skills and competencies. When positions and jobs are up for grabs at times of restructuring and downsizing, middle managers must enrich their roles and behavioral skills repertoire to increase their chances to survive the change. Through downsizing, the prime strategy for creating a lean organization, top management also hopes to form an organization that is agile and flexible, organic and adaptive. With fewer levels of managers below them, middle managers often perform their roles with a wider span of control. At the risk of becoming hypereffective and stressed out, middle managers experience greater responsibility, less control, and higher task variety in meeting new work expectations. The traditional middle management roles that were effective in hierarchical structures, particularly the Producer and Director roles, can be delegated or transferred and effectively performed by trained members of self-managed teams.

The main characteristics of self-managed teams (SMTs) and the principles that guide their activities and behaviors are discussed in chapter 7. Self-managed teams are unique organizational structures since they exist in a quasi-autonomous state within an organization. SMT members are highly interdependent with other team members as a result of common goals and self-regulation. Rather than being a parallel group or team (e.g., quality circles, task forces), SMTs have the formal power to create and maintain their own systems or working relationships in order to complete a total job. The teams have administrative control and thus contain managerial functions such as those associated with the Director role. SMTs have broad-based and multi-skilled members, integrated responsibilities and duties, training in team functions, and extensive information sharing. As such, SMTs are the result of a major paradigm shift toward cross-functional synergies, joint performance, and teamwork through self-ruled work teams. In addition, the efficacy of the Competing Values Framework of leadership effectiveness as a powerful starting point to facilitate understanding of the leadership roles that have been transferred to SMTs is demonstrated in chapter 7. It is proposed that in the absence of a supervisory structure, the leadership roles suggested by the Competing Values Framework are essential for team effectiveness, and therefore, the emergence of the roles within the teams or building behaviors associated with the roles into the teams must be encouraged.

The chapters included in Part IV—chapter 8, "Enhancing Organizational Learning: Communication Strategies and Methods," and chapter 9, "Learning to Learn: Competency Education for Management Development"—cover the principles, strategies, tools, and methods available to organizational leaders to leverage the professional intellect and knowledge in the organization as the fundamental strategy for successful job, team, or total business performance. These two chapters highlight the importance of building organizational capabilities and supporting human resources through structured learning and competency development. The chapters examine the scope of leadership challenges faced by managers enacting the Facilitator and Mentor roles.

The argument advanced in chapter 8 is that communication-based learning must be embodied in the thoughts and actions of organizational leaders performing the role of Facilitator. Knowledge management and transference require facilitation competencies and understanding of all facets of organizational behavior, processes, and outputs. In the role of Facilitator, organizational leaders must become strategic opportunists— globally aware and capable of managing highly decentralized systems. In addition, they must be interpersonally competent, sensitive to issues of diversity, and be community builders. With a knowledgeable workforce, managers must also shed their traditional responsibilities and become coaches and facilitators of empowered teams. In shifting the emphasis of learning to teams and engaging in experiential, work-based training activities, individuals develop the skills necessary for building cross-functional synergies. The focus of managerial activity is shifted toward reengineering work processes to create high value for customers and achieve innovative breakthroughs, rather than merely eliminating inefficiencies and reducing cost. Skill development and the transference of knowledge require organizational leaders to become effective facilitators and at the same time develop the sensitivity essential for self-improvement and developing others.

The issues discussed above within the context of competency education and development which define the domain of the manager enacting the Mentor role are addressed in chapter 9. Essentially, the discussion in this chapter covers the need for developing the leadership capabilities of managers and future organizational leaders. Particular emphasis is placed on the challenges faced by schools of business and management to meet market and corporate needs in the area of competency education. In addition, the chapter includes an evaluation of the need to redesign management development programs to create the "right fit" talent for management positions to support corporate vision.

In chapter 10, "High-Performance Leadership: Initiating Transformational Learning," I conclude the book with a thorough discussion about the characteristics of high-performance leaders who lead the learning organization. High-performance leaders are self-defining and have strong internalized values and ideals about the future role and direction of their organizations. These leaders have a unique capacity to perceive the world as a constantly evolving system. In creating a cognitive map of their environments, these leaders often combine a highly structured and analytical frame of reference with an intuitive, more flexible pattern of thinking. These leaders thrive on randomness, ambiguity, and contradiction, and are able to transform paradoxes and problems into opportunities for generating innovative responses. High-performance leaders maintain relatively longer periods of peak performance and are better equipped for coping with stress than are average leaders. They have the ability to transcend or reframe perceptual tensions that help them achieve important breakthroughs. Presenting Jack Welch (GE) and Percy Barnevik (former CEO of Asea Brown Boverie—ABB) as models of global warriors and high-performance leaders, the traits, skills, and competencies of high-performance leaders, as well as their visions, actions, and outcomes are traced. I conclude the discussion of this chapter with the roles played by high-performance leaders—Vision Setter, Motivator, Analyzer, and Task Master—and their importance to organizational performance. Taken together these roles frame the four essential traits of high-performance leaders who lead the learning organization: Brightness, self-confidence, creativity, and being inspirational. You are about to begin the journey toward *Leading the Learning Organization*. Good luck!

1

Integrating Management Paradigms: The Competing Values Framework

The best managers and leaders create and sustain a tension-filled balance between two extremes. They combine core values with elastic strategies. They get things done without being done. They know what they stand for and what they want, and they communicate their vision with clarity and power. But they also know that they must understand and respond to the complex array of forces that push and pull organizations in so many different directions.

—Bolman & Deal, *Leading with Soul*, 1995

Control has become a limitation, it slows you down. You've got to balance freedom with some control, but you've got to have more freedom than you ever dreamed of.

—Jack Welch, CEO, General Electric

For much of the past half-century, management philosophy has coalesced around two broad schools of thought: A rationalistic school based on the principles of scientific management and the theory of bureaucratic control, and a humanistic school based on the view of organizations as interactive systems evolving around the need to respond to the psychosocial needs of the individuals within them.

21

THE RATIONALISTIC AND HUMANISTIC APPROACHES
TO MANAGEMENT

The rationalistic approach is positioned as an efficiency-driven, control-oriented ideology with a strong emphasis on the centralization of decision making, development of clear policies and procedural specifications, unambiguous roles and responsibilities, a high degree of formalization, divisible tasks, high specialization, standardization, and functional departmentation to reduce duplication. Running like a machine, this organization is viewed as highly efficient, yet inflexible and anti-innovative. Its strict hierarchy and unchallenged authority is aimed at achieving obedience, facilitating administrative innovations, and exchanging good performance and compliance with rewards, while sanctioning poor performance and undesirable behavior.

The humanistic approach has distanced itself from the rationalistic view by centering on individual well-being, employees' work conditions, job satisfaction, training, and communication. Evolving into what has been called a human resource perspective, this approach calls for giving employees greater opportunities for involvement in decision making over work processes. The philosophy is that free from the burden of being overcontrolled, with more autonomy and greater discretion, and with more influence over the outcomes of work, employees will synergize their efforts and perform with excellence. The prognosis is simple, yet powerful—a humanistic approach can lead to high commitment and morale—employees would regain trust and confidence in their managers and ultimately would become accountable for the results of their work. Proponents of the humanistic approach (e.g., Argyris, Herzberg, Likert, Maslow, McGregor) enthusiastically have called for integration of the needs of individuals with those of the organization.

Particular attention was focused on the idea of making employees feel more useful and important by giving them meaningful jobs, and by giving as much autonomy, responsibility, and recognition as possible as a means of getting them involved in their work. Job enrichment, combined with a more participative, democratic, and employee-centered style of leadership, arose as an alternative to the excessively narrow, authoritarian, and dehumanizing work orientation generated by scientific management and classic management theory (Morgan, 1986, p. 42).

This humanistic approach, then, advocates the need for flexibility, development of employees through delegation and cross-training, open communication, tolerance for ambiguity, the nurturing of creativity, and risk taking. For these reasons, the humanistic approach became quite popular during the 1960s and the 1970s. Many midlevel managers and corporate executives began to participate in T-groups and management development programs designed to enhance self-awareness and interpersonal skills.

POLAR RELATIONSHIPS

> If you are part of the scientific management tradition, you may view competencies as the specifications for the human machinery desired to provide maximum organizational efficiency and effectiveness. If you are part of the humanistic management tradition, you may view competencies as the key that unlocks the door to individuals in realizing their maximum potential, developing ethical organizational systems, and providing maximum growth opportunities for personnel.
>
> —Richard Boyatzis, *The Comptetent Manager,* 1982

The differences between the rationalistic and humanistic approaches have been captured by such popular distinctions as theory "X" and theory "Y," and have been referred to as mechanistic versus organic systems of management (Morgan, 1986). This distinction has also been reinforced in contemporary approaches to management and organization as the contingency and congruence theories, which claim that organizations must develop isomorphic relationships with their external environments to increase their chances to survive. Commonly known as "survival of the fittest," these theories propose that organizations with forms congruent with their environments thrive. Placid, stable environments with little competition and with lower customer expectations enable an organization to predict marginal shifts and respond to them with incremental changes. Changes that are manageable and that do not disrupt the routine flow of work call for a bureaucratic form of organization. In dynamic, changing environments with customers demanding higher product and service quality and with stiff domestic and global competition, organizations are propelled to maintain high flexibility and quick responses of the kind found in organic or interactive systems. Organic systems are nimbler and quicker to respond to market demands. They are decentralized, problem oriented, informal, fluid, and have online information that flows laterally and can reach different parts of the organization at the same time. Organic systems of management provide the flexibility, quickness, and smart response needed to deal with the fluctuations of the environment. NYNEX's chairman and CEO Ivan Seidenberg captured the essence of the differences between the two approaches by suggesting that the technological and market changes in the telecommunication industry forced his company to drift toward an organic configuration. Shaking off one hundred years of traditional, bureaucratic culture to become a market-driven, customer-focused system was necessary to make NYNEX agile and able to respond quickly to external pressures, while competing effectively against the leanest and meanest industry startups. Accordingly, under the pretense of social and economic change, managers found themselves confronting problems for which a bureaucratic system seemed ill-suited to handle. Bluestone and Bluestone (1993) elaborate:

> By the 1980s, bureaucratic firms were too bloated with midlevel managers to be efficient and much too burdened by rules and regulations to keep up with foreign competition. More and more organizations began to realize that top-down bureaucratic control was antithetical to productivity, quality, and innovation. (p. 131)

It was in this context that discourse on organizational culture and employee commitment began to attract the attention of both practitioners and management gurus. Management consultants as well as organizational researchers shared the view that an altered approach was needed to help managers create adaptive, more effective systems that were based on the principles of shared knowledge, accessibility, innovation, empowerment, and high involvement (Bradford & Cohen, 1984; Kanter, 1983; Peters & Waterman 1982; Piore & Sabel, 1984). Quality pioneers such as Juran, Deming, Feigenbaum, Crosby, and Peters have claimed that Japan's industrial success is attributed to the Japanese ideology, which centers on the value of human resources, employee loyalty, free communication, and joint decision making. They suggested that American firms would do well to emulate the Japanese success story by emphasizing and developing strong cultures that foster concern for quality, flexibility, and customer satisfaction (Ouchi, 1981). Deming's appearance on a National Broadcasting Company (NBC) TV program on June 24, 1980, highlighted this necessity: "If Japan can, why can't we?" By the end of the 1980s, the notions of culture and commitment began to gain a stronghold in many organizations. Managers initiated change programs aimed at rethinking the way organizations are structured, work is conducted, and people are managed and rewarded. Organizations began to take on a whole new outlook, as one writer described:

> Ideas provoked action, and business people began experimenting . . . More than anything else, companies began monkeying with their methods of

managing people. New cross-functional teams were designed to break down barriers between departments. New pay-for-performance systems were supposed to get everyone pulling in the same direction. Managers learned new techniques of motivation. Directives were out, coaching was in. Sitting in an office was out, walking around was in. The very word *employee* began disappearing in favor of *associate*. (Case, 1993, p. 83)

More and more companies experiencing severe competition found resolution in the revival of the quality circle movement. Companies wanted to reexamine their operating assumptions about management approaches and experiment with various ways of involving employees in improvement of work processes. Quality circles were the most common vehicles for eliciting suggestions on how to improve operations. However, problems began to arise when little attention was given to how the quality circles fit into the new core values, vision, and mission of organizations utilizing the quality circle concept. Quality circles were quickly subdued by the rigid, autocratic approach to management in which the old style still governed and dominated the infant and not yet proven successful quality circle.

TQM PHILOSOPHY

Other organizational researchers have claimed that TQM brings the two paradigms, rationalistic and humanistic, into agreement by establishing an optimal balance in calling for a sociotechnical approach, where technical and human needs are interdependent with one another (Trist & Murray, 1993) to achieve the goal of adaptation without the need to give up on the premises of either one of the paradigms. These researchers argued that TQM's scientific approach is consistent with the theories of the rationalist school and its emphasis on streamlining and standardizing work processes, while the structural elements of TQM are consistent with the humanistic approach, which centers on individuals and groups (Drucker, 1993; Schmidt & Finnigan, 1992, 1994). Schmidt and Finnigan (1992) succinctly explain how the two major streams of management practices come together in the management ideology of TQM:

Technology-oriented theories have focused on how to do things with greater precision and efficiency and socially oriented theories have focused on how to get people in an organization to work together in ways that are more productive and satisfying. Some managers have been guided more by the first stream, believing that a rigorously controlled approach to running an organization is more realistic than any approach that depends too heavily on the interest, commitment and judgment of people (especially lower level workers). Other managers have followed the preachments of the "humanistic" approach—trusting, developing, and involving people as their strategy for producing organizational health. In Total Quality Management, these two approaches come together in ways that reinforce each other. (p. 12)

Total Quality Management provided frustrated managers with a feasible set of principles to integrate the technical and social systems of the organization into a well-coordinated system unified by external objectives. The message that came from the TQM gurus was astonishingly simple: Take on an outside-in perspective to managing organizations. Effectiveness is not an internal measure but rather an external measure defined by the ultimate consumer of organizational goods and services. Articulating this view into the mission and strategy of the organization has led many organizations to adopt the inverted pyramid structure with customers on top and managers on the bottom. Employees were seen as a resource and were expected to meet customer needs proficiently. Accountability was outward to customers, with managers being responsive to the needs of employees. As organizations increasingly spent million of dollars on training and development programs in support of the quality vision, a puzzling pattern emerged: there were as many ways to implement TQM as there were companies adopting it. Nevertheless, four principles seem to be common to all manifestations of TQM: synergy and empowerment, continuous improvement, process orientation, and customer focus. These principles were supported by the value of:

- Creating a climate of openness and trust
- Harnessing the power of teamwork
- Solving problems systematically by thinking in the long term
- Motivating employees by rewarding both intangible and measurable contributions
- Developing commitment to the goals of continuous improvement and learning in the organization

These principles and values also required ownership that is supported by a shared vision, process champion, and exemplary leadership (i.e., precious commodities in turbulent times in which attention is given primarily to responding to short term pressures, as well as turf and status issues). The implementation of TQM, quite naturally, has turned much attention to the role of the middle manager, the mediator or information transmitter, who is centrally located within the chain of command, between the strategic apex and the operating core of an organization. TQM appeared to be a major threat to the power balance within the organization and a destabilizing, menacing force that should be counteracted, fended off, or extinguished. Paradoxically, those managers who in the past were in favor of change were now opposing it. Change became a self-limiting process. In light of the important position that middle managers occupy, quality practitioners and researchers have offered advice and techniques on how senior managers should handle the middle managers' subversion of the change process (Brigham, 1993; McDermott, 1993). They warned that supervisors and middle managers may not understand or welcome the new roles they must play. McDermott (1993) went on to describe what the senior manager is up against when trying to convince middle managers to embrace and lead a total quality effort. Unless middle managers are convinced that the new world is a better place, they may react negatively. They may engage in battles for turf.

Although other problems with TQM have involved lack of vision and the inability to communicate clearly the goals of achieving greater quality through an organization-wide effort, it seems that the quality movement has never been able to solidify its underlying assumption as a gestalt or an integrative approach to management. Positioning itself on the shaky ground between the humanistic and the rationalist paradigms, TQM quickly became the target for criticism from both sides, with the rationalists leading the way. It was not surprising then to find that seven out of ten TQM efforts were nothing more than enhanced problem-solving efforts aimed primarily at improving processes, with a little lip service given to "changing culture" (Crouch, 1992). Others (Schmidt & Finnigan, 1992) criticized the lack of vision on the part of the TQM sponsors, who neglected to embrace the systemic, integrative notion of TQM and instead focused primarily on design specifications, manufacturing processes, and statistical tools. Still others attributed the failure of TQM to the narrow focus of senior managers, who viewed the quality program as a way of stamping out quality problems, rather than as a transformation in philosophy, values, and ultimately a state of well-being and purpose (Bass & Avolio, 1994). Rationalizing the new reality, Galbraith and Lawler (1993) excused the quality pioneers by claiming that "they are nothing more than engineers, statisticians, and consultants who are naive to the importance of the human behavior dimension" (p. 144).

This shift away from the underlying assumptions of the quality movement must be restored on two levels—cognitive and behavioral. Cognitively, senior and midlevel managers must turn their attention to shifting their thinking and energy toward sustaining the subtle balance between the rationalistic and the humanistic approaches. Behaviorally, they must take the necessary steps to become the architects of change and become accountable for the process and outcomes of the quality effort. Managers must abandon their control stronghold and learn to lead, to unleash the creativity of their staff, and to coach them for continuous improvement (Galbraith & Lawler, 1993). Middle managers are being asked to shift their paradigms by eliminating their entrenched bureaucratic attributes and establishing new ones that are more suitable for an entrepreneurial culture. In other words, instead of being turf conscious and using defensive communication, managers are expected to maintain openness and to see the sociotechnical movement from a broader, more systemic point of view. They see the shift in paradigms from the prism of a cultural transformation that can help the organization transcend to higher levels of performance. Schmidt and Finnigan (1994, p. 11) list the key elements of the newly integrative approach:

- Organizational structure becomes flatter, more flexible, and less hierarchical.
- The focus shifts to continuous improvement in systems and processes (continue to improve it even if it is not broken).
- Workers perceive supervisors as coaches and facilitators.
- Supervisor-subordinate relationships shift to interdependency, trust, and mutual commitment.
- The focus of employee effort shifts to team effort; workers see themselves as teammates.
- Management perceives labor as an asset and training as an investment.
- The organization asks customers to define quality and develops measures to determine if customers' requirements are being met.

Other contemporary views of organization and management appeared to avoid the control-flexibility dichotomy in favor of an integrative, or holistic approach. This approach, often referred to as "gestalt," was aimed at evaluating managerial effectiveness based on universal principles that embrace contextual, informational, and judgmental variables. An example of one such integrative approach came from developers of behavioral models of decision making (Vroom, 1973; Vroom & Jago, 1988):

We were tired of debates over the relative merits of theory X and theory Y and of the truism that leadership depends on the situation. We felt that it was time for the behavioral sciences to move beyond such generalities . . . Our aim was to develop a set of ground rules for matching a manager's leadership behavior to the demands of the situation. It was critical that these ground rules be operational, so that any manager could determine how he should act in any decision-making situation. (Vroom, 1973, p. 66)

This integration, however, requires a different prism to understand and explain how organizations work and how managers should function. One example of this view is the Competing Values Framework of organizational effectiveness developed by Quinn & Rohrbaugh (1983) and expanded by Quinn (1988).

COMPETING VALUES FRAMEWORK (CVF)

Yin and Yang ☯: Two forces through whose essences, according to Taoist cosmology, the universe was produced and cosmic harmony is maintained.

—*Webster's Dictionary*, 1987, vol. 2, p. 1142

The Competing Values Framework (CVF) portrays the inherent contradictions facing organizations and managers on two axes or dimensions. The horizontal axis is one of focus: internal versus external. This axis reflects the expectation managers have that organizations should be concerned with what goes on inside the organization as well as with producing for and servicing an external environment. Specifically, while organizations must be able to manipulate, monitor, and measure internal tasks, technology, and personnel, they must also be responsive to the environment, including demographic changes, global economic events, market forces, government regulations, and competitors' behaviors and actions. The vertical axis of the CVF portrays the opposing expectations of flexibility and control. We expect organizations to be controlling systems. In this way, they provide a predictable and stable work world. At the same time, we expect organizations to be flexible and able to respond to myriad human needs and situations, to adapt to changes in their external environments, and to be a dynamic force in society.

The juxtaposition of these two axes forms four quadrants, each of which reflects a different model of organizational effectiveness criteria (see figure 1.1). The external horizontal axis and the control vertical axis

Figure 1.1. Competing Values Framework Effectiveness Criteria

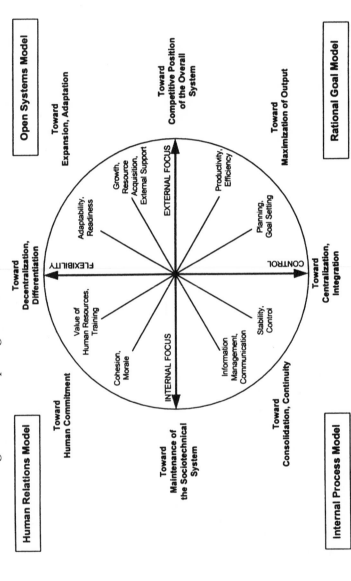

Source: Robert E. Quinn. *Beyond Rational Management: Mastering the Paradoxes and Competing Demands of High Performance* (p. 48). © Copyright 1988 Jossey-Bass Inc., Publishers.

appear in the lower right quadrant and define the *rational goal model*. This model reflects the view that organizations are effective if they meet their goals. Fundamental to this model is the need for structure and direction. The two managerial leadership roles associated with this quadrant are Producer and Director. Briefly, managers in the Producer role are task and work focused with high energy and motivation. They are self-motivated, motivate others, and pursue productivity. Managers in the Director role are decisive, provide direction for others, clarify expectations, and pursue goal clarity.

The internal horizontal axis and the control vertical axis appear in the lower left quadrant and define the *internal processes model*. This model reflects the view that organizations are effective if they are stable and keep track of activities within the organization. Fundamental to this model is the need for stability and control. The two managerial leadership roles associated with this quadrant are Coordinator and Monitor. Briefly, managers in the Coordinator role maintain work flow, analyze task requirements, and organize staff efforts. They pursue stability and control. Managers in the Monitor role are concerned about facts, details, reports, paperwork, rules, and regulations. They pursue documentation and information management.

The internal horizontal axis and the flexibility vertical axis appear in the upper left quadrant and define the *human relations model*. This model reflects the view that organizations are effective if they are able to tap the talents and thinking of their employees. Fundamental to this model is the concern for attention to human needs. The two managerial leadership roles associated with this quadrant are Mentor and Facilitator. Briefly, managers in the Mentor role are sensitive to the needs of employees and help employees plan their career growth and development. They pursue high morale and commitment. Managers in the Facilitator role build cohesion and teamwork among employees, use group problem solving and conflict management. They pursue participation and openness.

The external horizontal axis and the flexibility vertical axis in the upper right quadrant define the *open system model*. This model reflects the view that organizations are effective when they are able to anticipate changes in the economic-sociopolitical environment and even thrive when such changes occur. Fundamental to this model is the need to survive in a turbulent arena. The two managerial leadership roles associated with this quadrant are Innovator and Broker. Briefly, managers in the Innovator role are creative, deal with risk and uncertainty, envision needed changes, and help others to adapt to change. They pursue innovation and adaptation, external support, and resource acquisition.

Figure 1.2. Competing Values Framework

Managerial Competencies

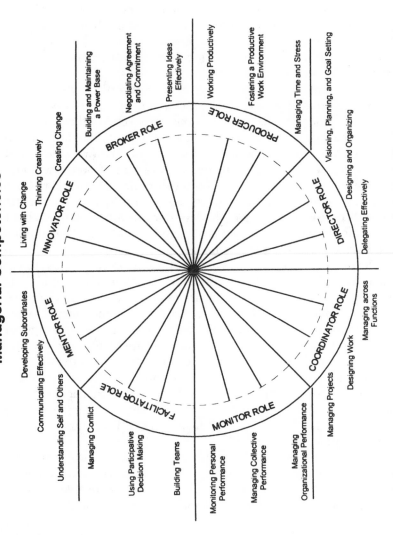

Source: R. E. Quinn, S. R. Faerman, M. P. Thompson & M. R. McGrath. *Becoming a Master Manager: A Competency Framework* (p. 16). New York: John Wiley & Sons. © 1996 John Wiley & Sons, reprinted by permission.

Managers in the Broker role are politically astute and represent the work unit to people inside and outside the organization. Brokers link the organization externally and focus on networking and establishing strategic alliances and partnerships with other organizations.

The CVF represents a universal image of the repertoire of roles manifested in the behaviors of effective managers. For each role, Quinn, Faerman, Thompson, and McGrath (1996) have identified a set of three competencies essential for effective task performance. The CVF leadership roles and their associated competencies are depicted in figure 1.2.

The CVF roles can be viewed as both mutually exclusive (i.e., differentiated) and collectively exhaustive (i.e., integrated). Alone and together, each role subscribes to the need to balance its "time in use" or emphasis against the range of requirements coming from the other roles. For example, despite the fact that in playing the role of the Director, the manager is assumed to have a task orientation, some aspects of facilitation or even mentoring (involving the two roles at the polar opposite in the CVF) must also be manifested in the behavior of the manager to achieve effective managerial leadership. Similarly, while the Mentor is engaged in developing the leadership capabilities of employees to meet new organizational needs and goals, he or she must also balance coaching and counseling skills with the need to achieve synergy across functions, thus entering the domain or "turf" of the Coordinator. The value of this framework is in allowing managers to pursue a systematic journey of self-directed learning and self-development by helping them identify relative weaknesses and strengths and enhance their competence level. More on this is included in chapter 9.

THE SIGNIFICANCE OF THE COMPETING VALUES FRAMEWORK

A key point of the Competing Values Framework (CVF) is that organizations are inherently contradictory entities, and therefore, organizational effectiveness criteria are fundamentally opposing, contradictory, and may be mutually exclusive. While we expect organizations to maintain stability and integration by paying strong attention to their internal workings and procedures, we also expect organizations to be responsive and adaptive by responding to pressures coming from the external environment. This approach, then, highlights the fact that organizations operate under the burden of contradictory, competing, and conflicting expectations. Responding to these expectations is vital for the success (effectiveness) of the organization. Obviously, this burden is not borne by organizations per se, but by the managerial leaders in these organizations. These individuals function within a context of complex and contradictory expectations. In this way, the CVF reflects on the contradictory criteria of effectiveness that describe managerial leadership. The following section is a detailed examination of the Competing Values Framework's utility in facilitating communication across managerial levels within organizations.

USING THE CVF TO COMMUNICATE LEADERSHIP ROLES AND RESPONSIBILITIES

> Life is like a kaleidoscope. We are caught in its ever-changing patterns, but we try to freeze a favorite pattern. We try to control and order life around us and within us.
>
> —Dr. Stuart Atkins, *The Name of Your Game*, 1995

The inherently contradictory nature of organizations is addressed by the Competing Values Framework (CVF) and by the different role behaviors expected from managers. Some of the roles seem to be opposing in that they reflect the conflicting and, at times, mutually exclusive organizational effectiveness criteria. Since managers and leaders presumably are effective within an organizational context, it is particularly important to look at organizational effectiveness criteria (like those mentioned above) when assessing the performance of managerial leadership. But, perhaps, one of the most important benefits of using the CVF lies in enabling managers to increase their self-awareness concerning the strengths and weaknesses associated with playing the eight universal roles. Thus, the utility of the framework as an effective medium of communication to align managers' values and roles within and outside the chain of command is immeasurable.

AVOIDING THE TRAP OF EXCESS: THE KEY TO EFFECTIVE INTERPERSONAL COMMUNICATION

> Weaknesses are nothing more than strengths pushed to excess. Confidence turns into arrogance, flexibility turns into inconsistency, trust turns into gullibility, and analysis turns into paralysis.
>
> —Dr. Stuart Atkins, *The Name of Your Game*, 1995

All too often managers attach values to their own and others' behaviors, form attitudes toward "desired" and "undesired" behaviors,
and develop biases involving what works and what does not work.
These biases are translated into mindsets and patterned behaviors that
guide managers' thinking and actions. Gradually, these values are converted into beliefs, communication styles, and stereotyped behavior
that is expected and predictable. Psychologically, the manager develops
a set of cognitive approaches that is consistent with others' perceptions
of his or her behavior. The drive toward cognitive consonance, although
essential in producing a consistent pattern of expectations, may often
hinge on vertical thinking and tunnel vision or even on insecurity and
lack of confidence. Trapped by his or her style and unable to explore
and use other modes of thinking patterns and behaviors, the manager
very quickly may become the victim of his or her success. The position
of this chapter is that managers must be attentive to their blind spots—
or the behavioral and perceptual areas known to others but unknown to
them—to increase their personal effectiveness. Expanding the "open
window" should help reduce the potential for interpersonal conflict.
Here, however, the *kind* of problem is different since both the perceptual
and behavioral context of the thinking pattern (i.e., as reflected in decision-making or goal-setting processes) and actions taken (e.g., resource
allocations, conflict resolution) are made predictable by the uniformity
of the manager's style. The danger is in overvaluing or overemphasizing a particular type of style and thus creating excess.

Robert Quinn (1988) believes that overemphasizing a style is
pathological and unsustainable. Referring to it as the "negative zone" he
suggested that managers must be alert to the dysfunctionality of
overemphasizing a style and learn how to deal with it. As seen in figure
1.3, in the upper-left quadrant of the CVF, a manager overemphasizing
the human relations criteria encourages extreme permissiveness and a
laissez-faire attitude. The manager lacks decisiveness and totally ignores
the need to articulate the vision for the organization, the charter for the
group, or the objectives for individuals. Individuals and groups take
over by solving problems and making decisions in a noncoherent way,
somewhat reminiscent of the "garbage can" process (Cohen, March &
Olsen, 1972). In the upper-right quadrant there is so much emphasis on
creativity and innovation that discontinuity and disruption occur. Too
much energy is expended on ideas that are not pursued or implemented.
Lack of focus and unclear vision and direction cause the organization to
drift toward an "organized anarchy" (Cohen, March & Olsen, 1972).

The lower-right quadrant contains the "oppressive sweatshop."
Concerns for clear goals and systematic collective efforts are met with

Figure 1.3. The Positive and Negative Zones

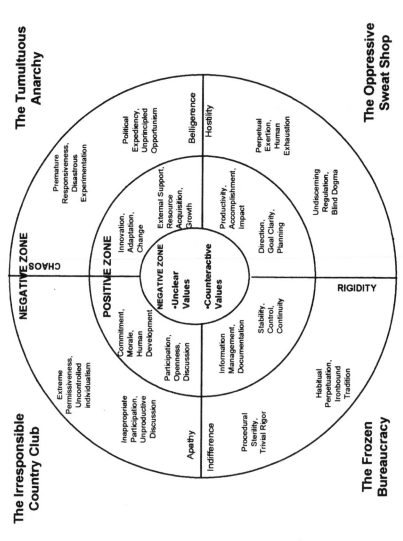

Source: R. E. Quinn. *Beyond Rational Management: Mastering the Paradoxes and Competing Demands of High Performance* (p. 70). © Copyright 1988 Jossey-Bass, Inc. Publishers.

an overemphasis on strict regulation and a build up of a general adaptation pattern that leads to defensiveness in communication and a dogmatic regime that demands to do more with less to meet the bottom-line goals of operating efficiencies and greater profits. The lower-left quadrant conforms to the frozen bureaucracy with an overemphasis on control through documentation and measurement. The organization develops a culture of self-preservation and perpetuation of the status quo. All of these characteristics and outcomes are dysfunctional and result from excess reliance on a particular style, a unidimensional, or simplistic view of the world. When overemphasizing their territory consciously or subconsciously, the Mentor and Facilitator may bring about "uncontrolled individualism" and "unproductive meetings" with their excess pathological behaviors. The Innovator and Broker may create conditions for "premature adaptability" and "unsystematic opportunism." The Producer and Director's excess behavior may lead to human exhaustion and absolute rigidity, while the Coordinator and Monitor's extreme bias toward their domains may breed a "mechanistic system" characterized by excessive formalization, procedural sterility, and inflexibility.

According to Robert Quinn (1988), the effectiveness of managerial leadership is shaped by the ability of the manager to integrate dynamically the demands coming from the full range of the roles expected from a manager. Figure 1.3 illustrates that effective managers are careful to remain within the positive zone and yet have the behavioral complexity needed to move from one set of competing values to another. To become master managers they must frame and reframe or maintain situational flexibility and possess the requisite skills to move comfortably between the various domains represented in the positive zone.

Understanding the concept of the negative zone and the consequences of getting stuck in a predominant orientation is important to improve the ability to manage people and improve interpersonal communication. Stuart Atkins (1995), in his acclaimed Life Orientations* training program, suggested strategies that can be used to avert excess and move back to the positive zone. His typology consists of four orientations or patterns, each with associated values and weaknesses: These orientations are: Supporting/Giving, Controlling/Taking, Conserving/Holding, and Adapting/Dealing. Atkins's typology can help individuals identify their own strengths and weaknesses and can also be used to diagnose the typecasting of key people both intuitively and systematically.

---

*Life Orientations and LIFO are service and trademarks of Dr. Stuart Atkins.

Figure 1.4. Competing Values and Life Orientations

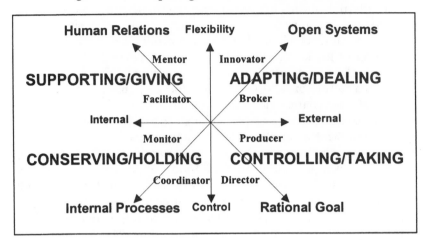

What is striking is the similarity between Atkin's typology and the quadrants (and roles) depicted by the CVF (see figure 1.4). Supporting/Giving seems to correlate with the human relations quadrant and the Mentor and Facilitator roles; The Controlling/Taking orientation appears to include many of the characteristics associated with the rational goal quadrant and its two roles, the Producer and Director; Conserving/Holding tends to reflect the values associated with the internal processes quadrant and the expectations and roles manifested in the behaviors of the Monitor and Coordinator; Finally, the Adapting/Dealing orientation fits the context of the open systems quadrant with its emphasis on the values and criteria associated with change and adaptability and the set of expectations for the Innovator and Broker roles.

Supporting/Giving refers to the principled, cooperative, dedicated, and loyal individual, who is geared toward quality and excellence. Overcommitment to helping others, however, may cause someone to take responsibility for the communication rather than actively listening or empathizing with the communicator. Controlling/Taking describes the competent individual with directing skills, who is task oriented and persistent with a particular bias toward action and urgency. An overemphasis on actions and results may lead to too much aggressiveness, low tolerance for errors, impatience, and coercive use of power to achieve one's goals. Conserving/Holding indicates the practical and reserved individual, who uses reasoning and logic to persuade others. When the strengths of this orientation are pushed to excess, this individual is perceived as stubborn, unimaginative, complicated, and data bound.

Adapting/Dealing is the orientation that is geared toward pleasing others in a tactful, enthusiastic, and flexible way. Adapting/Dealing, however, can slip into placating others, confusion, and ambiguity that may result in the loss of focus and clear direction.

A key element in this typology is the development of self-awareness as well as the understanding of the predominant orientation of individuals, regardless of one's personal biases. This understanding should help individuals overcome their own blind spots, as well as develop a high tolerance toward other, less preferred orientations or styles, and thus improve interpersonal communication. One way to overcome excess and reduce the potential for interpersonal conflicts is to obtain information about other people's thinking patterns and favorite orientations. Giving feedback about one's own orientation should also be used frequently to reduce the risks of high stress and personal tension. But individuals do not need to change their orientations or adopt the successful orientations of others, especially their opposites. What they need is to develop a full understanding of the scope of their associates' orientations and anticipate and organize the form and substance of their communication to capture the positive attention of their associates. According to Atkins (1995, p. 105):

> We don't have to change ourselves to improve our communication with key people in our lives. What is required is that we take a small amount of time to think, to anticipate their questions and to answer them . . . By organizing our communications to answer the uppermost questions of the key person, we provide ourselves with alternatives from our usual way of communicating with the person. It is a change of pace, a different sound and look that can capture attention, get interest and stir action.

COMMUNICATION AUDITS USING THE COMPETING VALUES FRAMEWORK

The Competing Values Framework can be used as a communication audit tool to help management increase the effectiveness of communication on three levels:

Personal or Developmental: to increase one's self-awareness and self-understanding of strengths and weaknesses as perceived by individual performers

Vertical or managerial: to facilitate understanding of leadership roles across hierarchical levels

Lateral or functional: to measure one's communication performance and self-assessment against institutional requirements, organizational core values, and dominant culture, as well as expectations of key individuals across functional lines.

Effective communication audits can alert managers to gaps or overemphasis that might exist between observed and expected communication performance. Such audits can then be used to identify strengths and weaknesses of communication styles as well as to help develop measures to deal with these gaps. As such, a communication audit is an excellent diagnostic and intervention tool to reduce communication anxiety and increase the effectiveness and efficiency of communication flow within and outside the chain of command. Most communication audits touch on many aspects of organizational activities including the boundaries of the organization and its interface with the environment. Environmental scanning and stakeholder analysis, for example, are different means to assess key players in the external environment and their potential impact on the activities of the organization. On the other hand, network analysis or interaction analysis rely on sociometric methods aimed at tracing the communication patterns and processes across formal and informal systems to determine communication interdependencies and key access points to the system. Systematic audits usually cover six important steps: (1) planning to establish the purpose of the audit; (2) conducting assessment of top management's attitudes toward communication, as well as the perceptions of senior managers of specific communication strengths and weaknesses; (3) collecting and analyzing written communication material; (4) conducting focus groups, interviewing, and collecting first-hand data; (5) designing and running a survey instrument to get the broadest possible coverage; and (6) tabulating and communicating the results.

Often content analysis, which looks at messages according to specific criteria and vocabulary usage, is utilized to gain perspective about the fit between the objectives of the message and the form or substance of it. Content analysis, through sensitizing managers to the appropriateness of message composition and message form or substance that is relevant to the context of the communication relationship, is another communication audit tool that can support vertical and lateral communication. The following sections describe communication audit methodologies using the Competing Values Framework.

ASSESSMENTS AT THE PERSONAL LEVEL:
SELF-UNDERSTANDING

To gain insight into one's managerial strengths and weaknesses, it is helpful to gather information from some of the people who have been working together in different capacities and different working relationships. In assessing one's abilities, these individuals will articulate an image of the behaviors manifested in the roles enacted by the focal person (i.e., manager) as they perceive them.

When doing the assessment, five steps must be followed by the user:

1. Distribution of the CVF instrument to build a composite profile of individuals whose opinions you value and trust. These should be distributed to include at least one supervisor, two peers, and a few employees.

2. Completion of the "initial instrument profile" (IIP) to derive a personal competing values leadership profile. Using CVF software and instruments, individuals self-examine their styles, see what role is underempahsized or overvalued, and self-assess their strengths and weaknesses.

3. Compilation of assessments derived from others by using table 1.1 (the average ratings depicted in the last row), and construction of a composite CVF leadership profile as perceived by others. These individuals' assessments are vital to "balance" or "validate" the way in which managers perceive themselves. Once the composite profile has been constructed, it is useful to write a two- to three-page journal comparing and contrasting these results with the profile obtained through administering a self-assessment instrument.

   Reviewing the two profiles—composite versus initial instrument self-leadership profile—should then help managers identify those areas with the greatest gap or perceived discrepancy. In general, the smaller the gap, the greater the strength in particular areas. The larger the gap, the greater the weakness. By rank ordering the discrepancies between the two profiles from the most important to the least important, managers are actually determining the priority they place on each role and skill in terms of job needs or the priority level for future professional development.

4. Using the journal as a frame of reference for future self-directed learning and self-improvement by reflecting on the following questions:

TABLE 1.1.
Compiling Data to Create a Composite Profile

Raters	Director	Producer	Coordinator	Monitor	Mentor	Facilitator	Innovator	Broker
Supervisor								
Supervisor								
Peer								
Peer								
Employee								
Employee								
Employee								
Employee								
Employee								
TOTAL								
AVERAGE								

- Was anything in the assessments surprising?
- What "rang true"?
- How do you account for the discrepancies between your personal profiles and those provided by others?
- What value was gained from these assessments?

5. Evaluating how strengths can be sustained and weaknesses remedied.

The point is that the information coming from the 360-degree radar assessment is valuable in helping managers maintain an overall perspective or "optimal" balance across the variety of the Competing Values Framework leadership roles, rather than focus only on one single dimension of managerial leadership. By comparing the results of self-assessment against the ratings by others, a manager can take steps to deal with higher expectations (e.g., by increasing personal involvement) or lower expectations (e.g., by decreasing an overemphasis on Monitoring behavior) thus reducing tension and the potential for conflict in interpersonal relations. When combined with other techniques (e.g., role analysis transacting technique or responsibility charting method), self-assessment and the information coming from the composite profile can also be applicable to improve interpersonal communication and enable a more effective work climate.

ASSESSMENTS AT THE VERTICAL LEVEL: COMMUNICATION AUDITS IN BANKING, TELECOMMUNICATIONS, POWER LAB, AND DINING SERVICES

The CVF can be used to strengthen the vertical linkage within the chain of command by clarifying the roles and the expectations that managers have vis-à-vis the other levels. DiPadova and Faerman (1993, p. 162) observed that by "examining the transition from one managerial level to the next, managers can better understand how their expected behaviors differ across levels . . . they can see how the roles [are enabled] in different ways in the different [administrative] contexts." An important advantage of using the CVF, then, lies in the creation and maintenance of effective management communication. Problems involving information underload or overload, distortions, and negative filtering can be anticipated and overcome. Clarifying managerial roles and expectations can help minimize role ambiguity and offset the costs associated with dysfunctional role conflicts. Likewise, interpersonal conflicts involving turf issues, status, and power can be avoided in favor of developing a constructive dialogue and having positive learning. As DiPadova and Faerman (1993, p. 168) concluded:

> Often the levels are experienced as so discrete and stratified that members see themselves as separate constituencies in the same organization, rather than as members of the same team. The common language offered by the CVF ameliorates the separateness because it is essentially an organizational language that identifies performance criteria which are common across the hierarchy.

How similar or different is the perceived importance of the eight CVF roles performed by managers across levels? To answer this question, the results of a preliminary study of four different organizations, which was conducted during the summer of 1997, are reported below. To ensure anonymity, company names have been disguised.

The studies used a survey-based methodology, Managerial Leadership and Hierarchy Study, which was developed by Dr. Laurie DiPadova (1995), to explore differences in role expectations at each of the three managerial levels—upper, middle, and first level. The survey, designed around the Competing Values Framework of Managerial Leadership, demonstrates the efficacy of the CVF as a common language for managers across hierarchical levels. The study included samples of managers from organizations in different industries: banking, telecommunications, power lab, and dining services. After acceptance of the study by either the human resource director or vice president of the sampled company was achieved, a packet with a personal cover letter was sent to each participant in the study explaining the request for participation.

The survey was divided into three parts. Part I requested information regarding demographics: gender, highest educational level completed, officer title, and years of service with the organization. Part II, Section A, asked each manager to answer ten questions focusing on how managers view themselves in the context of the organization. Section B contained four questions asking each manager to rate how their peers are different from their direct reports. The areas of focus for these questions were education, income, and commitment to one's job and to the organization. Part III focused on the similarities and differences of managerial tasks and responsibilities in managerial work across the three organizational hierarchy levels. Section A contained measures associated with the eight roles portrayed in the Competing Values Framework: Producer, Director, Coordinator, Monitor, Mentor, Facilitator,

Innovator, and Broker. First, each manager was asked to consider the importance of the various tasks and responsibilities at their level of the hierarchy using a scale of 0 (Not Applicable) to 5 (Absolutely Essential). Then, each participant was asked, using the same scale, to rate the other two managerial levels by responding to the same items. Section B provided definitions of the eight roles of the Competing Values Framework. Each manager was asked to indicate the overall perception of the importance of each role as applied to each of the three levels of management, again using the same scale.

BANKING

In total, thirty surveys were distributed to managers across the hierarchical levels within the bank's sales division in a large metropolitan area. Of the thirty distributed surveys, twenty-one surveys were returned, representing a 70 percent response rate. Average scores and standard deviations for each role at each management level were calculated and t-tests (not reported here) were conducted to verify whether the differences between the samples' means are statistically significant. Tables 1.2 through 1.5 display a summary of top characteristics associated with

TABLE 1.2.
Rational Goal Model: Similarities and Differences in Motivating Others and Goal Setting

Producer	*Director*
All Managerial Levels	
Maintains a high level of energy, motivation, and effort	Makes important work decisions
Motivates Others	Sets goals
	Sets objectives for accomplishing goals
	Defines roles and expectations for employees
First Level	
Focuses on results and accomplishments	Assigns priorities among multiple goals
Gets others to excel in their work	
Uses time- and stress-management strategies to handle delays and interruptions	

(continued)

TABLE 1.2. (*Continued*)

Middle Level

Creates high performance expectations in others	Garners support for goals from managers at lower levels
Focuses on results and accomplishments	
In motivating employees, considers their individual differences	

Upper Level

Creates high performance expectations in others	Establishes context for decision making at lower levels
In motivating employees, considers their individual differences	
Gets others to excel in their work	

TABLE 1.3.

Internal Process Model: Similarities and Differences in Controlling the Work and Tracking Details

Coordinator	*Monitor*
All Managerial Levels	
Ensures that work is going according to schedule	Disseminates information regarding policies and procedures
Reallocates resources to accommodate	Relies on reports from others
Coordinates tasks and people	Assures flow of information among necessary personnel and units
	Sets up and maintains necessary communication channels
First Level	
Anticipates workflow problems	Oversees compliance with procedures
Plans workload adjustments, as needed	
Middle Level	
Anticipates workflow problems	Interprets financial and statistical reports
Schedules workflow of tasks and projects	
Upper Level	
Determines subordinate's assignments based on individual skills and abilities	Carefully reviews the work of others
Coordinates units as well as individual employees	

TABLE 1.4.

Human Relations Model: Similarities and Differences in Dealing with Employee Problems and Enhancing Employee Participation

Mentor	*Facilitator*
All Managerial Levels	
Gives credit to subordinates for their work and ideas	Works to enhance employee participation
Maintains an open, approachable, and understanding attitude toward subordinates	Creates a cohesive work climate in the organization
Takes a personal interest in employees	Creates a sense of belonging to the organization
First Level	
Helps employees work toward and prepare for promotion	Fosters a sense of team work among employees
Does on-the-job training	Facilitates and leads meetings
Middle Level	
Does on-the-job training	Fosters a sense of team work among employees
Creates opportunities for lower-level managers to challenge themselves	Involves subordinates in discussion over work matters
Upper Level	
Advises lower-level managers on how to handle difficult employee situations	Involves subordinates in discussions over work matters
Creates opportunities for lower-level managers to challenge themselves	Facilitates and leads meetings

TABLE 1.5.

Open Systems Model: Similarities and Differences in Managing Change and Negotiation Skills

Innovator	*Broker*
All Managerial Levels	
Supports changes imposed on organization even when disagreeing with the changes	Nurtures contacts with people external to the organization
	Builds coalitions and networks among peers
	Represents the unit to clients and customers

(*continued*)

Table 1.5. (*Continued*)

First Level

Turns problems into opportunities	Interacts with people outside the
Encourages creativity among em-	organization
ployees	Presents ideas to managers at higher
Helps employees deal with ambiguity	levels
and delay	
Helps subordinates see the positive	
aspects of new changes	

Middle Level

Turns problems into opportunities	Represents the unit to others in the
Helps employees deal with ambiguity	organization
and delay	
Assesses the potential impact of	
proposed changes	
Comes up with ideas for improving	
the organization	

Upper Level

Assesses the potential impact of	Represents the unit to others in the
proposed changes	organization
Encourages creativity among em-	Exerts lateral and upward influence
ployees	in the organization
Personally helps individual em-	
ployees adjust to changes in the	
organization	
Helps subordinates see the positive	
aspects of new changes	

---

the enactment of the various roles across hierarchical levels. Top characteristics were determined by ranking least standard deviations with the top five averages for each characteristic for each role. One central finding of these surveys is that there are many striking similarities in the importance of the roles played by managers at different levels. While we have assumed the applicability of the Competing Values Framework across levels of the hierarchy, this study supports the findings coming from the work done by DiPadova (1995) and presents empirical evidence of parallels in perceptual views of leadership roles across levels. Overall, the evidence suggests that at each level managers were able to identify with all eight roles of the Competing Values Framework.

Managers at all levels appear to share similar concerns and have similar understandings of the importance of all managerial leadership roles, with the exception of the Coordinator and Monitor roles, which appeared to be less important for upper-level management. The Rational Goal Model shows a greater alignment with characteristics that make up the Director role, such as making important decisions and setting goals. Within the Internal Processes Model, there appears to be greater consistency among all hierarchical levels regarding the responsibilities manifested in the behaviors of managers performing the Monitor role (i.e., disseminating information and assuring flow of information across the business unit). Consistent views are apparent regarding the characteristics of the Mentor and Facilitator roles in the Human Relations Model (i.e., give credit to subordinates for work and ideas and work to enhance employee participation). Similarly, in the Opens Systems Model the Broker and the Innovator role appeared to be quite important for the performance of managers across all management levels.

TELECOMMUNICATIONS

The surveys were completed by first-, second-, and third-level managers belonging to the General Business Sales regional division. The three levels of management take on much different roles. The first-level managers are responsible for the constant supervision of the craft workers and customer service. The second level has the responsibility to discuss problems and difficulties that have arisen among the subordinates. The third-level managers have more interaction and dealings with the revenue and monetary aspects of the organization, as well as handling large customer complaints. Depending on which department these levels are affiliated with, third-level managers must assume different roles, with the end result being commitment to exceeding customer expectations. Unfortunately, only first-level managers returned usable surveys to us. Despite the low response rate, the data did indicate several interesting observations about managerial behavior of the first-level managers and their perceptions of the other two levels. Figure 1.5 shows the first-level managers' feelings and beliefs relative to their roles in the organization.

These responses indicate that there is a relatively broad spectrum of roles and responsibilities of the managers surveyed. Specifically, conclusions from this data indicate that first-level managers at this telecommunication company:

1. Feel that they have a reasonable "leadership role" within the organization

Figure 1.5. Beliefs of Managers

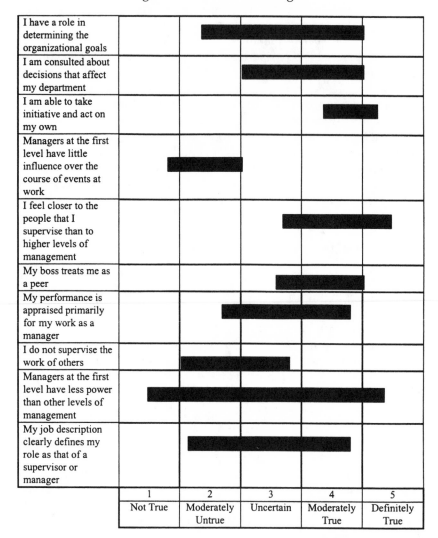

	1	2	3	4	5
	Not True	Moderately Untrue	Uncertain	Moderately True	Definitely True

Row labels:
- I have a role in determining the organizational goals
- I am consulted about decisions that affect my department
- I am able to take initiative and act on my own
- Managers at the first level have little influence over the course of events at work
- I feel closer to the people that I supervise than to higher levels of management
- My boss treats me as a peer
- My performance is appraised primarily for my work as a manager
- I do not supervise the work of others
- Managers at the first level have less power than other levels of management
- My job description clearly defines my role as that of a supervisor or manager

2. Are relatively autonomous and have moderate influence within the organization
3. Are closer to the people they supervise than to their own manager
4. Are appraised for individual contribution as well as that of a manager

5. Have a broad range of power relative to the next level of management
6. Have a relatively unclear job description

The general shape of the leadership roles shown in figure 1.6 seems to indicate that:

1. First-level managers were primarily focused on the Producer, Coordinator, Facilitator, and Mentor roles. They had very little focus on the Broker an Innovator roles.
2. Second-level managers were perceived by first-level managers to have a relatively well-rounded profile, with the exception of a small focus on the Coordinator role.
3. Third-level managers were perceived to be primarily focused on the Innovator, Broker, and Monitor roles. They had very little focus on the Coordinator, Producer, Mentor, and Facilitator roles.

Figure 1.6. First-Level Managers' Perceptions

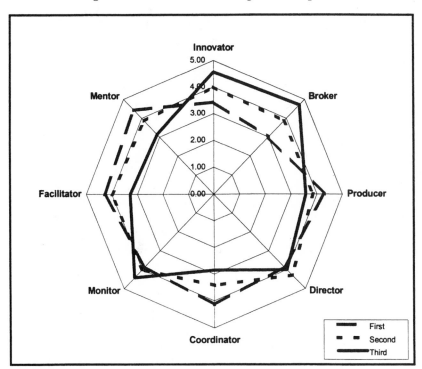

These results indicate that in moving from a first-level manager to a third-level manager within this telecommunication company, there are some expectations for an increase in the importance placed on the Innovator and Broker roles and a decrease in the importance placed on the Monitor, Facilitator, and Coordinator roles.

POWER LAB

The power lab, a functionally organized structure with highly specialized work units staffed with professionals, was expected to have management that was internally focused rather than externally oriented due to institutional and regulatory constraints, which place high premium on control and accountability. This expectation presented managers with an interesting dilemma—Although the Competing Values Framework theorizes that the managers' span of attention must be broad enough to incorporate the different facets of the managerial leadership construct, institutional and structural constraints limit the abilities of managers to perform optimally the full range of the leadership roles. While the focus of managers may be driven by external constraints, they can still develop sensitivity to the subtle nuances of the other roles. As discussed earlier in this chapter, despite the fact that managers, due to job demands, may be expected to (over)emphasize one or more roles, they should also develop the situational flexibility to allow them to incorporate elements from the other roles into the range of their current activities. Developing the capacity to enact the full scope of the leadership roles should also help managers develop the behavioral complexity that is essential to avoid the traps associated with a drift toward the "negative zone" discussed above.

Each manager was asked to consider the importance of the various tasks and responsibilities associated with the competing values leadership roles at their level of the hierarchy using a scale of 0 ("not applicable") to 5 ("absolutely essential"). Then, each was asked, using the same scale, to rate their perceptions of the other two managerial levels by responding to the same items. The results are summarized, by level, in tables 1.6 through 1.8.

First-level managers rated the importance of the eight leadership roles with an overall mean of 3.85 and a standard deviation of .28. They felt that the Coordinator role was the most important (4.0) and that the Mentor and the Broker roles were relatively less important (3.45 and 3.48 respectively). Middle managers felt that first-level managers emphasized the Monitor role (4.55) as manifested most importantly in their be-

Table 1.6.
Assessment of First-Level Supervisors

	Producer	Director	Coord.	Monitor	Mentor	Facilitator	Innovator	Broker	Mean
SELF	3.48	3.70	4.00	3.63	3.45	3.75	3.75	3.48	3.85
MM	4.25	4.40	4.30	4.55	4.10	4.50	4.45	4.05	4.82
TOP	4.3	4.4	4.6	4.3	4.0	4.1	3.8	3.5	3.5

havior, while they indicated the Broker role as the least important (4.05). Overall, they perceived first-level managers as quite effective in performing the range of leadership roles with a mean of 4.82 and standard deviation of .26. Upper-level management perceived the first-level managers strongest in the Coordinator role (4.6) and less active in the Broker role (3.5). These results are interesting for they seem to generate a consistent pattern in which first-level managers' perceptions of the Coordinator role are seen as more important than the Broker role and seem to be congruent with the perceptions of higher-level management.

Middle-level managers rated the overall importance of the eight leadership roles slightly higher than the first-level managers' rating with an overall mean of 4.03 and a standard deviation of .39. They recognized that the Facilitator role was the most important (4.33) and that the Coordinator and Monitor roles (both of which appear in the internal processes quadrant) were relatively less important (3.75). First-level managers discerned that middle managers emphasized the Director role (3.90) as manifested most importantly in their managerial behavior. Moreover, the responses seemed to indicate that the Coordinator role was the least important role (3.20). Again, the rating of the Coordinator role as the least important was consistent with that of the middle managers' assessment. Overall, first-level managers perceived middle managers (mean = 3.54 and standard deviation = .26) as quite effective in performing the range of leadership roles. Upper-level management perceived the middle managers strongest in the Producer role (4.5) and less active in the Coordinator role (3.4). These results are interesting for they generate a consistent pattern across levels, within this sample, in which the ratings of the Coordinator role appear as less important for the performance of middle managers.

Upper-level management rated the importance of the eight leadership roles with an overall mean of 4.0. The Facilitator role was rated as the most important (4.8), while the Coordinator was least important (1.9). First-level managers felt that upper management emphasized the Producer role (3.63) as manifested most importantly in their behavior

Table 1.7.
Assessment of Middle Managers

	Producer	Director	Coord.	Monitor	Mentor	Facilitator	Innovator	Broker	Mean
SELF	4.30	3.85	3.75	3.75	4.20	4.33	4.03	3.80	4.03
FL	3.83	3.90	3.20	3.50	3.67	3.47	3.57	3.50	3.54
TOP	4.50	4.0	3.40	4.20	4.30	4.40	3.90	3.80	3.80

Table 1.8.
Assessment of Top Management

	Producer	Director	Coord.	Monitor	Mentor	Facilitator	Innovator	Broker	Mean
SELF	4.30	3.60	1.90	3.70	4.50	4.80	4.10	4.20	4.0
MM	3.75	3.30	2.70	3.35	3.45	3.83	3.45	3.48	3.00
FL	3.63	3.47	2.03	2.83	3.37	3.23	3.20	3.33	3.17

and indicated the Coordinator role as the least important role (2.03). Overall, they perceived upper management as quite effective in performing the range of leadership roles with a mean of 3.17 and a standard deviation of .26. Middle-level management perceived upper management strongest in the Facilitator role (3.83) and less active in the Coordinator role (2.7). Based on these results, we can stipulate that a "common understanding" involving the relatively low significance of the Coordinator role was evident in this organization. Most of the coordination that was built into the operating core, which was staffed with specialists and run by effective managers, liberated higher-level management to perform other, more important roles such as the Facilitator and Producer roles.

DINING SERVICES

The target organization of this study was the dining services department. The department has a three-layer hierarchical structure. The first layer consists of hourly supervisors who manage line workers. The focus of the first-level managers is on the shift-by-shift operations of the unit. The second layer consists of middle managers who have overall unit responsibility and allocation of resources. The third level, the director, focuses on the programs' overall functional responsibility. At the higher managerial level is the head of the department, who oversees the units' outputs and profitability. Of the twenty managers sampled, thirteen returned their questionnaires, achieving a return rate of 65 percent. Tables 1.9 through 1.11 present the data gathered and compiled for this study.

The findings show that the first-level managers scored highest on the Producer, Coordinator, and Director roles and lowest on the Broker, Mentor, and Facilitator roles. First-level managers felt that the transactional roles are important for the functioning and operations of the dining service. They rated the Coordinator, Director, Producer, and Monitor roles higher than the Facilitator, Innovator, Mentor, and Broker roles for both middle-level and upper-level managers, with the exception of the Broker role that was rated as important for the functioning of upper-level managers. The middle managers recognized that all of the roles, with exception of the Broker role, are important to perform their managerial job. They felt the Facilitator, Coordinator, and Mentor roles

Table 1.9.
Assessment of First-Level Supervisors

	Producer	Director	Coord.	Monitor	Mentor	Facilitator	Innovator	Broker
SELF	4.06	3.74	3.85	3.06	3.15	3.35	3.63	2.93
MM	4.01	4.13	4.21	4.06	3.66	3.88	3.80	3.41
TOP	4.03	4.11	3.14	4.26	3.75	3.91	3.93	4.25

Table 1.10.
Assessment of Middle-Level Managers

	Producer	Director	Coord.	Monitor	Mentor	Facilitator	Innovator	Broker
SELF	4.37	4.00	4.43	4.07	4.33	4.13	4.30	3.83
FL	3.30	3.27	3.33	2.50	3.40	3.47	3.80	2.43
TOP	4.27	4.33	4.00	4.57	3.90	4.23	4.07	4.37

Table 1.11.
Assessment of Top Management

	Producer	Director	Coord.	Monitor	Mentor	Facilitator	Innovator	Broker
SELF	4.45	4.20	4.05	4.60	3.55	4.20	3.30	4.15
MM	4.15	4.20	4.50	4.10	3.70	4.00	3.50	3.45
FL	2.90	3.30	3.55	2.95	2.55	3.80	3.30	3.10

are more important for first-level managers to handle key technical processes and manage line workers. Middle-level managers identified the Monitor, Broker, Director, and Producer roles as more important for the upper-level management, essentially due to the need to monitor performance and handle large accounts and external relations. Upper-level managers rated the Monitor, Producer, Director, Facilitator, and Coordinator roles as the most important for their managerial performance. Again, the "dominance" of the transactional roles over the transformational roles is not surprising in light of the domain of operation or the context of this organization that was geared toward quality in service and the generation of accounts. Upper-level managers felt that the Coordinator, Director, Producer, Monitor, and Facilitator roles are important for the middle managers. The Innovator and Broker roles were rated by upper-level managers as less important for the functioning of middle-level managers.

SUMMARY: MANAGERIAL ROLES AND CONTEXTUAL FACTORS

One common thread that emerged from the CVF audits described above is the importance of the effects of contextual factors on the predominant roles and message orientations used by managers at all levels. While the managers in the sample of the banking organization placed higher weights on the external roles and particularly on the Broker, Innovator, and Producer roles, the managers in the sample of the power lab showed a clear bias toward the Facilitator role. In banking, marketing outreach and relationships with clients led to the emphasis on the external roles, while the makeup of the power lab organization, which was comprised primarily of specialists, naturally demanded more emphasis on the Facilitator role. In both, the Coordinator role was recognized as less important by virtually all levels of management but for different reasons. In the banking organization, due to the higher emphasis on boundary spanning, brokering, and linking activities outside the organization and, in the power lab, due to the nature of specialists whose activities are coordinated primarily via mutual adjustments and lateral relations. The Coordinator role, however, was perceived as important for the managers in the sample of the dining service organization primarily due to quality control and an emphasis on work flow operations.

Another interesting finding was that in the banking organization both the Innovator and the Broker roles were perceived as important by all managers participating in our sample regardless of their hierarchical location. Again, being part of a sales-driven culture may have contributed to this perception and high degree of understanding as to the importance of creative thinking, presenting ideas effectively, and so on—the primary characteristics of effective managers enacting the Innovator and Broker roles. In the telecommunication organization, the profile of the first-level managers in our sample tilted toward the upper-left quadrant (i.e., the human relations) of the CVF, while that of upper-level managers (as perceived by first-level managers) was tilted toward the upper-right quadrant of the CVF (i.e., the open systems). These results pinpoint to the "bias" upper-level managers have toward the external roles (especially in a highly competitive market). First-level managers value more the internal roles, particularly those associated with mentoring employees and facilitating group processes. The profile of the middle managers (as perceived by first-level managers) was right in the middle, between that of the upper-level and first-level managers, illustrating the importance for middle managers to maintain a good balance between the internal and external system requirements.

ASSESSMENTS AT THE LATERAL LEVEL

Most assessments at the vertical level identify energy leaks or communication performance gaps across managerial levels with the goal to improve linkages across managerial lines. Effective upward and downward communication ensure that units and departments are interlocked in a means-ends chain of objectives. Linking the organization vertically must be supplemented with lateral linkages across functional lines to achieve effective integration and optimize organizational performance.

The methodology described here was recently adapted and used by the consulting group of Dr. Sue Faerman (coauthor of *Becoming a Master Manager: A Competency Framework*, New York: Wiley) and Dr. Alan Belasen (author of this book) as a competency-based management intervention program for senior managers at a national systems integration company (NSIC). (To ensure anonymity, the company's name is fictitious.) Belasen and Faerman strongly believed that senior managers would find the program useful in four primary areas: (a) improve interpersonal relations, trust, and understanding among senior managers; (b) enhance knowledge transfer across functional lines; (c) advance double-loop learning, particularly through dialectical thinking and learning about paradoxes; and, (d) strengthen organizational capabilities.

The program was designed to help managers diagnose their performance vis-à-vis key managerial roles and skills, identify strengths and weaknesses, and develop an action plan for improvement breakthroughs. The expectation was that managers would learn to develop ways to communicate more effectively within and across divisions, allowing for increased sharing of best practices. The communication intervention program developed by Alan Belasen and Sue Faerman involved six phases, as described here.

Phase I: Planning Process and Brainstorming Meeting

Consultants conduct brainstorming meetings with senior managers to discuss business plan goals, team goals, and how the team's objectives could contribute to the company. The primary objective is to gather information about the company's core values and guiding principles, as well as to discuss how leadership competency-based tools and applications might help drive organizational performance. The consultants present the competency-based management framework to managers, share expectations, elicit feedback, facilitate discussion, record suggestions, review and fine tune the methodology.

Phase II: Personal and Company Profile Assessment

The consultants administer 360-degree diagnostic instruments and software to derive personal managerial role/skills profiles for each manager. This tool has been designed to provide feedback on managerial strengths and areas needing improvement relative to the competencies needed for success. Accurate, action-oriented feedback is extremely important for personal and professional growth. Consultants also administer a modified cultural assessment instrument to examine how the current organizational culture can support individual and team development efforts.

Phase III: Gap Analysis and Development Plan, Feedback and Coaching

The consultants perform a competency gap analysis comparing the personal profile (a summary of how managers see themselves and how others see them) with the company profile and prepare an action plan for each manager. Working with individual managers, the consultants help managers formulate self-improvement plans for remedying deficiencies and developing core managerial competencies. Managers received ongoing guidelines to help monitor their progress in self-improvement and personal experiences. The consultants also develop an action plan for team building across the management group. This action plan focuses in the short term on how managers can support each other in competency development. It also includes a longer-term focus on developing a team approach to identifying key issues.

Phase IV: Application and Evaluation

Using guidelines developed by the consulting team in Phase III, managers submit self-improvement progress reports that describe applications of the competencies. The consultants review the reports to assess progress against objectives and discuss results, problems, and issues that relate to applications of new or improved competencies with individual managers. At four- to six-week intervals, the consultants bring the management team together for half-day workshops to give the managers a chance to share their successes and get ideas from others about how to manage particular situations. At the completion of the time frame, the consultants evaluate new competencies by readministering diagnostic instruments and by developing feedback reports for each manager, which also address areas for further development.

Phase V: Continuous Improvement Action Plan

The consultants provide senior management with an overall report about the success of the intervention, identify opportunities for improvement, and outline a continuous improvement action plan for future management and team development programs. The action plan also includes recommendations about competency training and development modules to sustain the improvement process.

Phase VI: Competency Review and Final Report

The consultants receive feedback from senior management, adjust and refine the continuous improvement action plan, and submit their final report.

Summary

Assessment at the lateral level within organizations can help improve organizational communication, support corporate vision, and enhance corporate overall performance. The intervention program described above is particularly useful in stimulating organizational learning and self-improvement (see also chapter 8). Communication audits using the CVF help managers develop ways to communicate more effectively within and across divisions, allowing for increased sharing of best practices. Personal and corporate self-evaluation can help managers diagnose their roles and skills, identify strengths and weaknesses, and develop action plans for improvement breakthroughs. At the personal level communication audits enable managers to experience an increase in personal productivity, improvement in interpersonal communication, and decision-making and problem-solving practices. It is expected that managers will have higher confidence in their communication abilities and skills and greater proficiency in dealing with employees, customers, and executives. Managers who use the CVF communication audit tools reportedly develop better understanding across managerial and functional lines and work together as a management team. At the corporate level managers are able to develop a shared understanding of the core leadership competencies required to support organizational capabilities and business growth strategies.

Content analysis, through sensitizing managers to the appropriateness of message composition and message form or substance is another communication audit tool that can improve business and interpersonal communication. The importance of crafting and articulating a message has long been recognized as a skill that can help support communication relationships (Barge, 1994; Conger, 1996). Managers can learn to identify characteristics and orientations that tend to dominate their messages, and more significantly, they can learn about which characteristics are lacking in their messages. The next section describes a CVF tool developed by Rogers and Hildebrandt (1993) to audit and clarify message orientations.

USING THE COMPETING VALUES FRAMEWORK TO AUDIT AND CLARIFY MESSAGE ORIENTATIONS

In the field of business communication, conventional rules tend to stress "power" writing and focused results (i.e., the end product), and build on informative and persuasive messages. A typical management directive is evaluated on seven criteria (the "seven Cs"). The message is expected to be: complete, concise, considerate, clear, concrete, courteous, and correct (Rogers & Hildebrandt, 1993). The effectiveness of written communication, thus, is judged more in terms of its impact (Did the message accomplish its intended objective? Was the stated goal clear enough? Persuasive enough?) and less in terms of the process of writing (Was the argument well presented? Supported with evidence? Documented? Mind stretching? Stimulating?). A good example comes from planning and goal-setting theories such as MBO, or management by objectives (Filley, House & Kerr, 1976; Locke & Latham, 1984). The primary emphasis of these theories is on the development and articulation of clear goals and objectives that are SMART (Doran, 1981). That is, meaningful objectives are Specific, Measurable, Assignable, Realistic, and Timely. In addition, while the literature on developing management skills (e.g., Whetten & Cameron, 1995) tends to emphasize the importance of active listening, interpersonal communication, and public speaking skills, it is clear that writing skills and forming messages are also important. Based on these assumptions, Rogers and Hildebrandt (1993) suggested that each quadrant in the CVF represents a different message orientation with significant parallels and polar opposites: relational, informational, promotional, and transformational. Together, the four quadrants and their characteristics form a framework that illustrates some of the potential conflicts or competing values that managers may experience in face-to-face or written communication. An adaptation of this model appears in figure 1.7.

Figure 1.7. Management Communication: Primary Orientations and Characteristics

	INTERNAL	EXTERNAL
FLEXIBILITY	**RELATIONAL** *Purpose:* establish credibility, rapport, trust *Medium & tone:* conversational familiar words, inclusive pronouns, personal examples, honesty *Focus:* receiver centered *Example:* manager's pep talk, a letter of sympathy	**TRANSFORMATIONAL** *Purpose:* challenge receivers to accept mind-stretching vision *Medium & tone:* visionary, charismatic, vivid, colorful metaphors, symbols, oral delivery, enthusiastic, emphatic, unorthodox written communication *Focus:* future oriented *Example:* CEO speech, written strategic plan
CONTROL	**INFORMATIONAL** *Purpose:* providing clear directions to receivers *Medium & tone:* neutral, precise words, controlled, sequential, standard constructions, factual accuracy, structural rigor, logical progression, realistic presentation, conventional documents, concrete examples, lists, tables, audit reports *Focus:* idea centered *Example:* a plant tour, policy	**PROMOTIONAL** *Purpose:* promoting an idea, selling product or service, persuading receivers *Medium & tone:* decisive, engaging, original, supported by credible evidence, prepositional, assertive, declarative, vivid examples, sense of urgency *Focus:* argument centered *Example:* sales presentations, recommendations to senior managers, press releases

The usefulness of this model is in sensitizing managers to the appropriateness of message composition and message form or substance that is relevant to the context of the communication relationship. Information and feedback are given and received through multiple media and transmission channels and are often complemented by body language, thinking patterns, and communication styles of the people involved. In order to interpret information effectively, managers must consider not only the explicit messages (i.e., substance) but they also need to examine the intrinsic characteristics of the context from which the information comes (i.e., source) and where it goes (i.e., its intention). A successful sales manager, who has been promoted to an administrative position, can use the framework to adjust his or her message orientation based on feedback received from subordinates. For example, by shifting the orientation from one emphasizing "promotional" to one emphasizing "relational" construction of messages, a sales manager can ease his or her transition toward an administrative position which requires a much more balanced approach to communicating the values and multiple objectives of the work unit or department.

CONCLUSIONS: IMPROVING
ORGANIZATIONAL COMMUNICATION

Lower management levels devote more time to direct supervision and monitoring subordinates to meet the operating goals of higher management. Top managers spend more time formulating plans, setting goals, determining priorities, clarifying constraints, and establishing the parameters (i.e., time, objectives, budget, etc.) to guide and control lower-level activities and outputs. While managers at all levels perform the four fundamental functions of planning, organizing, leading, and controlling, their managerial responsibilities, however, tend to vary in important aspects as illustrated in the results of the field studies reported above. This variation typically transpires along the lines of time horizon (e.g., long-term planning versus short-term operational goals), span of attention toward different domains (e.g., market positioning, internal processes, managing professional intellect, organizational productivity, etc.), and range or scope of activities (e.g., micro versus macro issues, external versus internal focus, etc.). Top managers' time horizon and span of attention, for example, are strategic with a focus on the competitive advantages of the firm and its overall strength and positioning within the market. Lower levels, on the other hand, pay more attention to individuals and groups working together to accomplish the unit's goals.

While all managers require a blend of conceptual, technical, and human relations skills to perform their jobs effectively, top managers are expected to have greater conceptual skills than those of middle- or first-level managers. This is because the depth of top managers' responsibilities is much greater and requires mental, analytical, and diagnostic abilities to acquire and interpret information from multiple sources in order to make complex decisions that affect the organization as a whole. Technical skills, including job skills and functional expertise, are more important for first-level managers. Middle managers, who function as communication links between higher and lower management, must have strong human relations skills. Their proximity to the top may also trigger the need to develop strong conceptual skills. These skills, however, must be balanced against the functional skills essential for middle management decision making at the unit or division level. These differences reflect variations in skills that are important to support the distinct responsibilities of the managers. It is important for managers at all levels, however, to ensure that the eight universal leadership roles described above are manifested in their behaviors.

For example, managers at all levels perform the Monitor role. First-level managers use short range scheduling, expense budgets, operations management, and measurement tools to oversee the activities of subordinates and meet performance targets specified by upper-level management. Top managers are engaged more in reading and evaluating financial statements and reports, and are concerned with strategic planning and control systems to meet performance and profit targets at the organization level. Midlevel managers, on the other hand, are involved more in functional deployment and intermediate planning, and frequently use output control systems to monitor the activities of lower levels. Thus, managers at all levels perform the role of a Monitor, but with different nuances and range of objectives. Their scope of activities, again, is also different, with top managers focusing more on broader issues and concerns as well as shaping and controlling business and financial performance and responding to stakeholders' concerns. Midlevel managers pay more attention to internal processes, functional interfaces, and how first-level managers handle the details of subordinates' performance. As managers move up the chain of command, and as they become removed from the points of impact at which the specific information about customers, performance, and the like, exists, they typically rely more on interpretation of the details rather than keeping track of the details themselves (DiPadova & Faerman, 1993). These differences are crucial for the functioning of the organization, since they provide the foundation for effective organizational integration. The three levels appear as part of a means-ends chain of objectives: Accomplishing the goals of lower levels serves as a means to achieve the goals of higher levels.

As the discussion in the following chapters reveals, managers at all levels perform the variety of CVF leadership roles to enhance the ability of the organization to adapt effectively to its environment and act in a coherent and consistent way. While a full treatment of these roles appears in *Becoming a Master Manager* (Quinn, Faerman, Thompson & McGrath, 1996), this book sets out to examine the context within which managers perform the roles described by the CVF. Although the eight CVF roles are often mentioned or discussed explicitly throughout the book, the emphasis of this book is on the contextual factors that shape managerial behaviors or that are affected by the actions taken by managers enacting the CVF roles. Thus, each part of the book begins with a short description of two roles associated with a CVF quadrant and contains two chapters which cover material relevant for the functioning of managers enacting those particular roles. The last chapter brings back the discussion to the role level by describing the roles executives play in leading their organizations through learning and transformations.

Part I

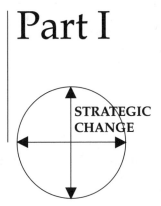

The external horizontal axis and the flexibility vertical axis in the Competing Values Framework define the boundaries of the *open system model* and the domain of organizational *strategic change*. This model reflects the view that organizations are effective when they are able to anticipate changes in their marketplace and even thrive when such changes occur. Fundamental to this model is the need to survive in a turbulent arena. The two managerial leadership roles associated with this quadrant are the Innovator and Broker roles.

INNOVATOR ROLE: THE ENTREPRENEUR

In the capacity of Innovator, the manager is expected to initiate and implement organizational change. The Innovator role involves the use of creativity and the management of organizational transitions. In enacting the Innovator role, the manager has a unique opportunity for affirming the value of individual employees as entrepreneurs. Effective managers acquire, use, and dynamically integrate the competencies associated with the Innovator role in managerial situations. These competencies are: living with change; thinking creatively; and, managing change. The Innovator focuses on adaptability and responsiveness of the organization or the work group as a whole to the external environment. Like its counterpart the Broker, the Innovator, too, acts in the capacity of "knowledge filter," screening and transferring new knowledge to other organizational members. The Innovator initiates ideas and suggestions, stimulates creative and critical thinking, and motivates employees to contribute their talents and skills to deal with change, assume ownership, and support the goals of change and innovation. Thus, both the Innovator and Broker roles subscribe well to the motivation to lead through learning.

BROKER ROLE: THE NETWORKER

In the capacity of Broker, the manager is expected to present and negotiate new ideas, mobilize support for change, acquire essential resources for the organization, and use power and influence strategies to support the mission and objectives of the organization. The Broker also serves as the gatekeeper and boundary spanner for the organization. Effective managers acquire, use, and dynamically integrate the competencies associated with the Broker role in managerial situations. These competencies are: building and maintaining a power base; negotiating agreement and commitment; presenting ideas and effective oral presentations.

The Broker is concerned with maintaining external legitimacy for the organization or the work group and obtaining external resources. Image building, visibility, and reputation are the primary concerns of the Broker (Snow, Miles & Coleman, 1992). The manager in this role is politically astute, persuasive, influential, and powerful (Quinn, Faerman, Thompson & McGrath, 1996). Brokers often act as boundary spanners and liaisons. They meet with people from outside, present ideas and positions, negotiate agreements, and acquire resources. Brokers are the gatekeepers, networkers, and communicators for the organization. They buffer the organization from outside interference by screening the amount of information that flows into the system and they link the organization with the external environment via networking and the establishment of direct lines of communication with external stakeholders (Charan, 1991). As such, managers fulfilling the role of a Broker are also sensitive to transform boundary management into a resilient, permeable, and influential tool of adaptation and change.

Enacting the role of a Broker is often essential for linking organizations and coordinating key players within the network, as well as monitoring the flow of resources across organizations (Snow, Miles & Coleman, 1993). In the broker capacity, managers play the role of architect, by designing and assembling the network value chain. Once the network has been put in place, managers with integration skills assume the role of Coordinator to make the network operative. Brokers and boundary spanners use information technology (IT) and computer-mediated communication (CMC) to quickly collect, screen, and share information across organizational boundaries.

The chapters included in Part I—"Adjusting to the Environment: Adaptive Responses and Organizational Change," and "Linking the Organization: Information Technology and Networking"—cover the dynamics of change and the need to align the value chain of the organization to optimize organizational performance. These two chapters examine the scope of leadership challenges faced by managers enacting the Innovator and Broker roles.

2

Adjusting to the Environment: Adaptive Responses and Organizational Change

The rate of organizational change must exceed the rate of environmental change.

—Jack Welch, CEO, General Electric

CHANGE BEFORE THE ENVIRONMENT CHANGES

In the past, organizations did not have the resources and technological knowledge to create an oversupply in their marketplace. Today, with the accelerating rate of change and the increasing trend toward free trade and globalization, oversupply and market saturation present organizations with the need to move fast and ahead of the competition. Companies today have to maintain flexible structures to respond quickly to new demands. The structure of the past is no longer suited to the new environment. As Heller (1995) rightfully argued, fast change cannot be managed by old methods. Companies, that have survived the stormy transition of the 1980s, such as GE, clearly made significant changes in their bureaucratic structures and revitalized their entire value chain, while once great companies, such as IBM, faltered as they struggled to hold onto their old management systems. Sustaining a

69

competitive edge requires adaptation, learning, vision, speed, boundary management, and above all, taking a hard look at how the organization is structured, what roles managers perform, and how work is conducted.

Often, managers are too late in their adaptive responses—that is, they ignore the need to scan the environment for new trends—resulting in an inconsequential reading of their external environment and poor organizational design. Sometimes managers act in the direction of change, adjusting and rearranging administrative systems and redesigning operating cores. Unfortunately, this is often a reactive rather than proactive strategy. External fluctuations quickly outdate organizational technology and bureaucratic inertia produces internal resistance and turfism, rendering adaptation a self-limiting process and resulting in a loss of focus and vision, missed opportunities, and a loss of market share. The organization becomes subject to natural selection processes and entropy. The outdated and maladaptive is selected out, and unless management takes appropriate steps to revitalize the organization, it dies. Entropy refers to the dissolution of energy, the propensity of a system to run down or disintegrate. Some organizations like Woolworth's paid the price of maladaptation and dissolved, while others like Sears paid a high price for their late response, losing leadership in the marketplace and resorting to dramatic measures to revitalize the company. Others like IBM have gone through a scare, sacrificing their reputation, and compromising their long-term plans in favor of short-term adaptation. Avoiding entropy is important and can be accomplished by recognizing the interdependency between the system and its environment, and by creating more awareness of the environment through boundary spanning, environmental scanning, and internal restructuring.

HOW THE MIGHTY HAVE FALLEN!

The story of how IBM was left behind (McCarroll, 1992) is a classic story of (mal)adaptation. It illustrates the downfall of the company during the late 1980s and the turnaround measures taken by the company to restore its dominance and reputation in the computer industry. By December 10, 1992, IBM stock had sunk to $51, a drop of 63 percent(!) in the value of the company in less than two years. In market capitalization, IBM, the number two in 1981, had slipped to eleventh place by the end of 1993!

IBM had virtually monopolized the industry since computers became commercial commodities during the late 1950s and in the 1960s.

So tight was IBM's market grip that it was practically impossible for any computer company to do business without being tied in some way to IBM. With its absolute dominance of the computer mainframe market, the IBM brand name became synonymous with computers. The comfort of a predictable and stable environment was reflected in IBM's strategy and structure. A huge, functionally integrated machine bureaucracy emerged to support the strategy of dominance and dependence. Structurally, this mechanistic system appeared to be rated high on standardization and specialization. This was an effective strategy because it fit the environment. Although IBM pioneered in the personal computer arena, the company was too devoted to its core business and had too many levels of bureaucracy to adapt to the changing environment.

However, this inertia of bureaucratic dominance was not without its cost. In the late 1980s, IBM found itself overwhelmed by an array of problems in one market after another. Its mainframe business, the core of the company, had been undermined by microchip processors that made low-cost desktop computers and linked workstations as powerful and fast as the big mainframes. IBM's lead in personal computers evaporated. In fact, it is well known that IBM's executives, often quite happily, shared the secrets of PCs with competitors, including Apple. Personal computers never received high priority on their agenda, nor were they part of their vision. *The Washington Post* (3/31/96) reported that by 1993 the problems faced by IBM caught up with them, and the company's decline was "precipitous." IBM lost $8 billion in the second quarter of 1993, compared to the $734 million profit IBM had shown during the same quarter one year earlier.

In software, upstart companies that had not existed before 1980 were running rings around the eighty-year-old behemoth. IBM's hegemony in the computer market started to crack. At a time when companies such as Sun Microsystems and Compaq had been reporting profit increases and rolling out innovative products, IBM was struggling to survive. Recognizing the liability of size, IBM took several drastic steps including shedding unprofitable and ill-fitting assets and slashing its workforce. The first de facto layoffs in the company's history decreased the workforce by about 8 percent. During 1991, it also reorganized its operations into thirteen semiautonomous units called "Baby Blues." IBM also cut 17 percent of its R&D budget for 1993, primarily in mainframe development, in a move that triggered President Clinton's call to corporate America not to cut back on R&D budgets.

IBM's responses, however, have seemed to be dealing with symptoms rather than causes. They are little more than bandaid solutions that cover up deep and very serious structural, technological, and financial problems. Most experts agree that IBM's challenge is not just to shrink in size but to also remake itself completely into a nimbler and more market-oriented player, in much the same way that AT&T reshaped itself after the breakup of the Bell System in the mid-1980s. Not only did AT&T reconfigure itself, but it also regained its spot among the top companies in terms of market value. By the end of 1993, AT&T reached third place with $71 billion worth of market capitalization. Two years later, AT&T announced drastic cutbacks of forty thousand employees and a $4 billion charge against profits. Critics, however, view the latest actions by AT&T in terms of compressed losses. According to the *Wall Street Journal* (1/30/96), AT&T's restructuring may have distorted the company's earnings history by compressing losses into a single quarter in a way that makes future earnings look positive.

Restructuring alone was not enough to restore IBM's competitive edge. Its market share has been decreasing because of its maladaptation. Although the company remained the world leader in the market for mainframes during the 1980s, the demand for large systems has been decreasing rapidly in the 1990s. In 1992, the demand for mainframes was down by about 10 percent. Meanwhile, PCs have been growing in strategic value just as IBM has lost its technological virility. In fact, in 1992, IBM was the only one of the top ten PC manufacturers whose market share declined! This prompted IBM's Chairman, John Akers, to acknowledge the significance of the problem: "The computer industry," he said, "is in a time of fundamental transition; customers more and more prefer smaller computers" (*Time*, Dec. 28, 1992).

But IBM was not alone. During the summer of 1992, Wang Laboratories was forced to file for bankruptcy. Unisys, the by-product of the merger of Burroughs and Sperry, nearly went under after it suffered $2.5 billion in losses in 1989 through 1991. Additionally, huge losses nearly claimed Digital Equipment, whose board ousted its own founder and president in 1992. By contrast, both Apple and Compaq became the leading force in the PC market, while Sun-Microsystems and Hewlett-Packard became the leading manufacturers of workstations. By 1996, the picture for IBM and Apple Computer would change. While IBM took steps and used its size to recapture its dominance in the market, Apple was almost forced out of business. During December of 1996, Apple purchased NeXT Software for $425 million to help support its own R&D and the development of its new operating system in a bid to staunch the exodus of its customers to personal computers that run Microsoft Corporation's software using Intel Corporation's microprocessors. During the spring of 1997, Apple found itself having major problems staying solvent and solicited Microsoft to invest $150 million in Apple to write new programs for the Macintosh. Although quite a risky and surprising move, Microsoft's new stake in Apple has somewhat helped restored Apple's market value and boosted the confidence of many corporate customers in the company's ability to reinvigorate itself.

In the first half of the 1990s IBM made many changes in an effort to adapt to the changing environment. The company has increased the quality of its products by revamping the mainframe series, by paying much attention to customers needs, and improving service quality. IBM has also built strategic alliances with rivals, such as Storage Technology Corporation, in order to make decisions and repair major glitches faster. The *Washington Post* (in an article that appeared in the *Albany Times Union*, November 16, 1997, A5) reported that IBM had formed a new alliance with Netscape Communications, Oracle, Sun Microsystems, and Novell to work on a new technology that could undermine the hegemony of Microsoft in the Internet-browsing software market. The new collaboration had a shared vision of developing a "platform" that would be easily accessible and open to all through the Internet, rather than dependent on Microsoft software and Intel chips. These five companies have been inquiring into three new areas of technology, that is, a computer language known as Java developed by Sun (for writing software that can be transmitted easily on networks and run any computing devices), a low-cost kind of computer known as an "NC" (or network computer), being pushed by Oracle and other companies, and a programming technique known as "Corba" for building Legolike blocks of software. The hope is to develop a technology that will allow a user to access the Internet with any type of operating system or hardware.

Meanwhile, IBM's PC business line has been recovered quite well during 1996, with increased sales and profits. By the end of 1996, IBM ranked number two in worldwide market share, which prompted the *Wall Street Journal* to report during March 1997 that IBM is rebounding from its financial and business woes, and crediting Louis V. Gerstner, Jr., chairman of IBM as leading the reemergence of IBM. By the end of 1996, fast-growing areas, such as personal computers and services, accounted for almost two-thirds of IBM's $76 billion revenue, up from about 40 percent in 1992. However, shareowners were all but dissatisfied with the pace of IBM's restructuring and demanded more aggressive moves that would help IBM to keep up with its competitors. IBM's revenue rose only 5.6 percent in 1996, compared with Hewlett-Packard Corporation's increase of 19 percent and Intel Corporation's increase of

29 percent. Less than one year later, IBM reported a second-quarter profit that rose 7.4 percent above expectations, but the company warned of a "tough external environment." While IBM's computer hardware revenue was essentially flat, software revenue fell 3.4 percent, and maintenance revenue declined 7 percent, revenue from computer services, such as operating computer setups for customers climbed a brisk 24 percent (*Wall Street Journal*, July 22, 1997, A3).

The IBM case example illustrated the importance of organizational strategic responses to the changing conditions of the environment. The next section offers an overview of the theoretical predicament of the open systems and the need to maintain a high degree of congruence between the organization and the environment within which it operates.

ENVIRONMENTAL UNCERTAINTY AND THE CONGRUENCE PRINCIPLE

The effectiveness of organizational structure depends largely on two important variables: First, the extent of the fit between situational factors and the design parameters of the organization, and second, the degree of internal consistency that exists among the design parameters. Together, these variables determine the appropriate configuration of an efficient organization and the level of congruence the organization must maintain vis-à-vis its external environment to be competitive and thrive. The problem is that an increase in environmental uncertainty complicates the interpretation of how the organization should respond to changes. Clark, Varadarajan & Pride (1994), for example, identified three types of uncertainty—that is, state uncertainty, effect uncertainty, and response uncertainty. State uncertainty refers to the overall level of the environment, that is, if the environment is unknown, the state uncertainty is high. Effect uncertainty refers to the difficulty of predicting the effect the environment will have on an organization. Response uncertainty refers to the difficulty an organization has predicting the effects its strategic response will have on an environmental change. The optimum level an organization will try to obtain is low uncertainty about the environment and low uncertainty about the effect of its response to the environment.

When an organization has a good read of the environment but has no way to respond to the changes, the organization can be considered strategically passive. The organization will know what its competitors are doing to advance in the market, but will have no understanding of how to handle the situation. On the other side of the spectrum are companies that have a clear strategy and effective planning but are unable to use them vis-à-vis their competitors because the competitors are unknown and their position within the market is unclear. These companies would try to "sandbag" their strategic position in the market without knowing where the storm is coming from, thus increasing the risk of misinterpreting the behaviors of competitors and of losing market advantages. At best, they will resort to incremental changes that usually follow patterns from the past rather than profound transformations which target the future. K Mart's failure to respond proactively to the emerging challenges in its market cost the company its leadership in the discount store industry in North America.

By 1985, Wal-Mart was closing the revenue gap on K Mart and moving aggressively into bigger cities. K Mart's response was to make its stores more attractive by renovating the stores and by introducing new lines of products, often promoted by celebrities. For example, while Wal-Mart built three new stores in the Albany, New York, area during the early 1990s with sales soaring, K Mart did virtually nothing in response. By 1996, Wal-Mart had established its dominance over the upstate New York area and continued its expansion into Canada. George Stalk, a senior vice president in the Toronto office of Boston Consulting Group, explained K Mart's failure to respond more proactively to Wal-Mart's challenges with organizational inertia, pervasive incrementalism, and management complacency. His analysis, which appeared in the *Globe and Mail*, published in Toronto, Canada (7/11/1997: B8), is a stunning account of K Mart's passive response:

> Through the early and mid-eighties, K Mart continued to grow, but Wal-Mart's sales were also soaring. K Mart took notice, saying "They are good competitors, but they are only in small towns." . . . Wal-Mart took the lead in sales in the early nineties and expanded into Canada. At this point, K Mart replaced its chief executive officer, but at the same time, it retreated even further into denial. To quote one of the company's executive VPs in 1993: "We are where we have to be, and going forward will be minor tinkering." Today, with K Mart frantically selling businesses, entering joint ventures, and trying to stave off bondholders, you can argue about when, exactly, senior management should have responded with more than "minor tinkering." But looking back on K Mart's failure to respond to a competitor that was boldly restructuring its industry reveals a pattern. It starts with blissful ignorance: "There are lots of competitors"; then comes rationalization: "Yes they're out there, but they're only in small towns"; then grudging acknowledgment: "They're gaining on us"; denial follows:

"All we have to do is fix our stores." Finally, panic sets in, which makes headlines weekly at K Mart.

George Stalk went on to propose useful suggestions to avoid the perils of incrementalism and complacency by rethinking the fundamentals of the business during critical points in time:

- When market growth is below the growth of GDP
- When the business has plateaued at a high market penetration.
- If competition is in a stalemate.
- If the concept of the business is not evolving.
- When product improvements are slowing and incremental.
- When performance is good but shareholder returns are poor.

Was it shortsighted or an oversight on the part of K Mart's top managers? Did they underestimate Wal-Mart's strategic goal and capabilities to penetrate the northern part of America? Why use incrementalism or employ inappropriate strategies to attract customers and regain market position in the face of increasing competition? One explanation could involve looking at the management's assessment of environmental uncertainty. For example, Robbins (1990) pointed to three key dimensions which describe organizational environment: Capacity, volatility, and complexity (see figure 2.1). The capacity of the environment largely determines whether the niche can support organizational activities and growth. Abundant environments generate excess resources which can help tolerate mistakes made by the organization and also buffer the organization in times of relative scarcity. In the late 1980s, emerging wireless telephone companies could afford to make mistakes in producing and marketing cellular telephones, since the environment was abundant and had the capacity to absorb these mistakes. The relative success of these companies during the 1990s has saturated the market with new and established telecommunication companies that capitalize on low entry costs to leverage their presence in the marketplace. Today, cellular-telephone companies operate in a dynamic environment that is also scarce.

The degree of instability in the marketplace is captured in the volatility dimension. When the environment presents organizations with the challenge to respond quickly to changing demands, management finds it difficult to predict accurately the consequences of decisions and other organizational actions. Stable environments that are more predictable can typically be handled with routine and programmable decisions. While the computer industry is an example of organi-

Figure 2.1. Structural Responses to Environmental Uncertainty

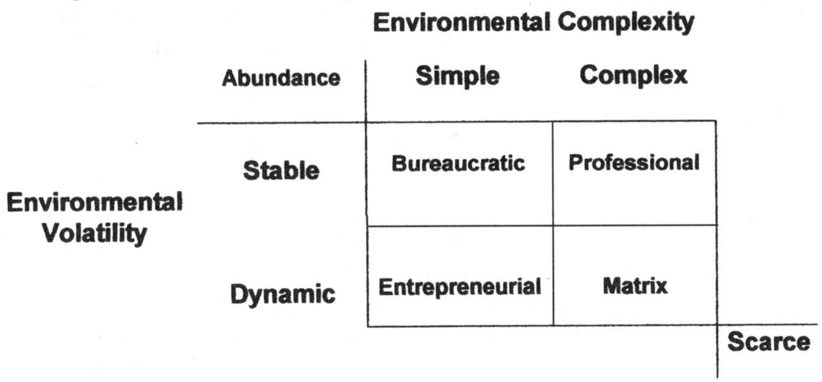

Environmental Complexity

Abundance	Simple	Complex

		Simple	Complex
Environmental Volatility	Stable	Bureaucratic	Professional
	Dynamic	Entrepreneurial	Matrix

Scarce

zations operating in a highly volatile environment, the container industry is an example of a stable and more predictable environment. Finally, the environment needs to be assessed in terms of complexity; that is, the degree of heterogeneity and concentration among environmental factors (Robbins, 1990).

Simple environments are homogeneous and concentrated, while complex environments are heterogeneous and dispersed. The tobacco industry with only a few big players is an example of a highly concentrated industry, while the packaged food industry represents an environment with high heterogeneity and dispersion. According to Robbins (1990), organizations that operate in environments characterized as scarce, dynamic, and complex face the greatest degree of uncertainty, since such an environment has a low tolerance for errors, demands are unpredictable, and a large number of factors must be constantly monitored and handled. This conclusion has led theorists and practitioners to place a high premium on the need to design the organization in such a way that maximizes the fit between the structural arrangements employed by the organization and the conditions prevailing in the external environment (see for example, Mintzberg, 1983; Robey & Sales, 1994).

In a simple environment, organizations can reliably evaluate market conditions and predict the future. Consequently, they can insulate their technical systems, standardize activities and processes, and formalize behaviors. When the environment is also stable, organizations appear as mechanistic, vertically integrated systems which use bureaucratic principles and methods to achieve coordination. Bureaucratic, multilayered organizations that are structured functionally have been successful in simple, unchanged environments. Although often criticized for their insensitivity to psychosociological needs of employees, their advantages are obvious. They were designed to achieve effective control, functional superiority, and internal efficiency through standardization. However, as the IBM example previously discussed demonstrates, bureaucratic organizations have difficulties responding quickly to market pressures for change. Their poor innovation potential and high development costs are often blamed on the lack of cross-functional synergies and on structural complexity. Large bureaucratic organizations, however, can successfully compete with smaller and nimbler startup companies only if they build capabilities that can let the organization act like a small organization, while still relying on the economies of the large system. ABB, for example, has been broken into thirteen hundred small, quasi-independent units with entrepreneurial, innovative leadership. 3M has achieved excellence in product development through the establishment of hundreds of project teams working synergistically. Both companies have virtually revamped their bureaucratic structures and mechanistic systems of management to become successful competitors in their respective markets.

When the environment becomes more complex, organizations often respond by decentralizing their structures. From an information processing standpoint, if the environment contains very few factors, the organization normally will rely on one brain (its strategic apex) to make key decisions. In other words, it will adopt a centralization strategy. To respond quickly to diverse suppliers, different customers' requirements, new regulatory standards, market developments, product innovation, and strategic moves by competitors, managers may choose to relinquish a good deal of their power to others—for example, supervisors, staff specialists, and even operators. The professional organization, for example, is a hybrid design responding simultaneously to the need to differentiate among highly specialized work units and decentralize or simplify decision-making processes. While professionals enjoy autonomy in managing their work, they are also subject to standardization and control. Most hospitals, utilities, and universities adopt configurations resembling the professional organization. Entrepreneurial organizations, on the other hand, are typically small, young, centralized, and organic.

Organizations adopt a strategy of decentralization by empowering functional units with greater autonomy and by giving teams and individuals greater administrative, managerial, and technical discretion over their work. Organizations decentralize decision-making structures via (a) greater vertical loading, by pushing down decision-making authority and by delegating technical and managerial responsibilities to employees; and, (b) greater horizontal responsibilities by giving major units or functions the autonomy needed to perform their jobs.

Organizations operating in dynamic environments, on the other hand, are often faced with uncertain sources of supply, unpredictable customer requirements, short product life cycle and quick market saturation, high labor turnover, and rapidly changing technologies and knowledge. Under these conditions, the organization cannot easily predict its future, and so it cannot achieve effective coordination via standardization of work processes. The organization chooses to employ more flexible, less formal coordinating mechanisms, such as direct involvement, expansion of communication networks, and mutual adjustment to coordinate activities. Evidence suggests that the more dynamic the environment, the more organic the structure of the organization should be (Mintzberg, 1983). In a changing environment management wants an organization flexible enough to adjust quickly to changing market conditions, lean enough to beat any competitor's price, innovative enough to keep its products and services technologically fresh, and dedicated enough to deliver maximum quality and customer service (Hammer & Champy, 1993).

STRATEGIC RESPONSES TO ENVIRONMENTAL UNCERTAINTY

Miles and Snow (1978) devised a typology that can help conceptualize and explain the strategic orientation used by managers in leading their organizations and the subsequent structure employed by the organization in support of that strategy. The four strategic orientations are: defenders, prospectors, analyzers, and reactors. Managers differ along the type and pace of change they adopt in their products or markets, thus leading to different adaptation to the environment and employment of different structures.

Defenders seek stability by using high product differentiation and high market segmentation and by aggressively preventing competitors from entering their domain. They do so by using competitive pricing or producing high quality products. But defenders tend to ignore developments and trends outside their domains and usually expand through market penetration and perhaps some limited product development. Defenders pay less attention to environmental scanning and other external pressures and invest more in streamlining internal processes, cost reduction, and improving operating efficiency. The result is a functionally specialized organizational structure, centralized control, and an elaborate vertical hierarchy for coordination and communication.

All too often vertically integrated organizations, which rely on economies of scale to reduce their dependence on external factors, tend to assess the external environment as less threatening. Top managers in these organizations also tend to perceive the environment as stable and, therefore, requiring less effort on the part of the organization to adapt. General Motors, from its inception through the early 1960s, essentially operated under these assumptions. Management decided on the products it wanted to sell, produced those products, and offered them to customers. Government was generally benign and consumer-advocate groups were nonexistent or had little influence. GM, for the most part, virtually ignored its environment because its executives saw the environment as having almost no impact on the company's performance (Robbins, 1990). In fact, this was the essence of Sloan's management philosophy, which was grounded in the belief that managerial leadership should be reduced to three primary responsibilities: to determine a firm's strategy, to design its structure, and to select its control systems. This model was suited for an environment that was "predictable" and "controlled." It made sense for Sloan to emphasize the values of reliability, efficiency, and machinelike process to achieve coordination and high economies.

At the other extreme are the *Prospectors*, whose strengths lie in scanning the environment, locating opportunities, and aggressively reaching out to new markets and customers with innovative products. Prospectors rely on flexible structures, multiple technologies, decentralization, and low formalization to afford the organization the ability to respond quickly and in a timely manner to market opportunities. Wal-Mart was definitely the Prospector in its industry during the 1990s, while K mart, riding on its relative success in the late 1980s, seems to have become a Defender. The numbers speak for themselves. Wal-Mart had a booming third quarter in 1997 with a 12 percent increase in sales, while earnings were up 16 percent. While K mart's gross profit (net sales minus cost of goods) was $8,444 billion by the end of January 1991 and went down to $7,047 billion by January 1997, Wal-Mart's gross profit for the respective periods were $7,101 billion and a booming $21,196 billion!

Analyzers capitalize on the strengths of the defenders and imitate prospectors with the goal of penetrating existing markets with new products or creating new markets by leveraging their economies of scale. By cloning smaller companies' new products, they use their core technology and mass production to outpace their competitors. Cloning also allows them to cut down on R&D investments and instead focus on the lead of key prospectors to produce high volume at lower costs due to operating efficiencies. Analyzers will tend to have smaller profit margins in the products and services that they sell than will prospectors, but they are more efficient. Typically they pursue both flexibility and stability, and therefore will have hybrid structures with a combination of functional and market-based structures.

Reactors represent a pathology or dysfunctional orientation of managers who respond to change reluctantly. Their responses are inconsistent, nontimely, insufficient, and inappropriate. Reactors are poor performers, whose top managers provide no clear direction or coherent strategies for members to follow and pursue.

A key element in Miles and Snow's typology is that the perceptions of top management concerning how threatening or uncertain the environment is, usually affect the choice of strategy and the predominant method used by the organization in responding to the environment. While Goodyear capitalized on market opportunities by investing in the construction of new tire plants during the 1980s, its rival, Firestone, interpreted the higher gasoline prices as a trigger for less driving and lower demand for replacement tires. Goodyear, the prospector, went on to develop new tires, while Firestone, the defender, closed down a number of its plants and reduced its U.S. tire capacity by over 30 percent.

OPEN SYSTEMS AND BOUNDARY SPANNING

Rummler and Brace (1990) have pointed out that the greatest opportunities for performance improvement often lie in the functional interfaces, those points or "white spaces" at which the baton is being passed from one department to another. This really suggests viewing organizations as open, adaptive systems, in which input factors are imported from outside and are converted by the organization into product and service outputs. The output reflects the premium or value which the organization adds in transforming inputs into outputs. These outputs are provided to receiving systems or markets. The organization adapts by receiving feedback, adjusting its processes, and improving performance. Continuous feedback is essential for aligning the organization with its external environment. Often, this feedback is obtained via activities of boundary spanners or "sensors," such as recruiters, consumer surveyors, and market testers, who monitor change and trends in the external environment. Boundary spanning is vital for the survival of the organization, since it fulfills the important function of information gathering for decision making, implementation, and delivery of organizational outputs. This information is processed so that the organization can make better choices. The activity of collecting information and assessing the environment is called "scanning." Environmental scanning functions are often located in long-range planning, forecasting, or R&D departments.

Boundary spanning units must be relatively permeable or sensitive to significant sectors of the organizational task environment. At the same time, they must buffer or screen less significant sectors—that is, those belonging to the general environment of the organization—and must have a weak, unfelt, or indirect impact on the organization. Boundary spanners must also maintain a high degree of resiliency or adaptability that enables them to adjust quickly to changes and have an effective read of the external environment. To be able to influence business decisions and achieve a higher degree of adaptive efficiency, boundary spanners must also have direct and open communication with decision authority centers. Boundary spanning involves important functions such as:

- *Scanning*: looking for potentially harmful or beneficial external events on an irregular basis and performing SWOT analysis, comparing organizational capabilities (strengths) and gaps (weaknesses) with environmental opportunities and potential threats.
- *Monitoring*: tracking trends and patterns within the domain of organizational operation (task environment) and external events in the larger market (general environment) on a regular basis.
- *Screening and Buffering*: performing a gatekeeping function by selectively communicating information about external trends to key organizational decision makers.
- *Stakeholder Analysis*: managing the boundary of the organization, evaluating the sources of power, and auditing the values of important stakeholders.
- *Linking/Networking*: establishing or maintaining formal and informal relations between internal, interface, and external groups and organizations (e.g., suppliers, distributors, regulators) that are vital for the functioning of the organization.

Internally, organizations consist of subsystems with interrelated functions of management, maintenance, adaptation, production, and those performing boundary spanning activities (e.g., the purchasing

Figure 2.2. An Open System and Its Subsystems

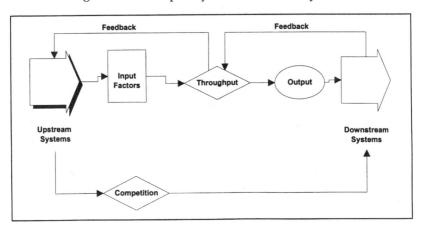

unit on the input side of the system and the marketing unit on the output side). Boundary spanning appears to have reciprocal effects within industries with offsetting results. First, it enhances variation within the system as a response to the need for change. Second, it decreases variation between the systems as a result of industrial imitation and adaptation (Weedman, 1992). Thus, most organizations, within the same industry, if acting in the direction of environmental change, also adopt similar configurations (Mintzberg, 1983). All, however, can be viewed as open systems similar to the one depicted in figure 2.2.

ENVIRONMENTAL SCANNING

The business world is volatile, uncertain, and highly competitive. More than ever before, survival is a key strategy adopted by large-scale organizations. Companies today are competing in a world in which the only predictable constant has become rapid change, requiring management to be both proactive and responsive (Hammer & Champy, 1993). Even the most competitive companies must reinvent and improve their businesses continually to win customers away from competitors. Through external adaptation, organizations can improve internal linkages within their value chain and become better aligned with upstream and downstream systems. Adaptability becomes an organizational competence that must be constantly sustained through environmental scanning activities at the organizational strategic level. This really means: (a) understanding the domain of operation or the market of the organization; (b) choosing appropriate frontiers for development; and, (c) adopting an outside-in (i.e., stakeholder) perspective. All of this requires management competency and the ability to scan the environment. Environmental scanning is "that part of the strategic planning process in which emerging trends, changes and issues are regularly monitored and evaluated as to their likely impact on corporate decision making" (Preble, Rav & Reichel, 1988, p. 8).

Environmental scanning typically involves data gathering, analysis, and strategic choice. Gathering data focuses on products, markets, customers, competitors, and the general environment. Product information includes product innovation and product differentiation. Market information includes the level of market saturation, emerging markets, and actual and potential market share. Customer information includes identifying current and new customers, their needs, changes in preferences, and geographic locations. Competitor information includes potential threats and opportunities, distinctive competencies, R&D capabilities, human, financial, and technological resources. Information about the general environment includes economic trends, governmental policies, regulatory plans, suppliers' availability, and labor markets. Analyzing the data involves making sense of the information by applying qualitative techniques (e.g., trend extrapolation, decision analysis, etc.) or quantitative methods (e.g., expert judgment, Delphi) to generate strategic options that are viable and feasible. An analytical framework for environmental scanning analysis is often used by GE in its strategic planning process. Each business leader is required to present and substantiate answers to five important questions (from Tichy & Charan, 1989, p. 115):

1. What are your business's global market dynamics today and where are they going over the next several years?
2. What actions have your competitors taken in the last three years to upset these global dynamics?
3. What have you done in the last three years to affect these dynamics?
4. What are the most dangerous things your competitors could do in the next three years to upset these dynamics?
5. What are the most effective things you could do to bring about your desired impact on these dynamics?

Strategic choice involves selecting an alignment strategy that should improve the value chain of the organization. Obloj, Cushman &

Kozminski (1994) suggested a range of strategies from which to select an appropriate alignment strategy:

1. Direct confrontation through reenactment of a specialized market (Toyota, for example, introduced the Lexus line to compete directly with Mercedes and BMW in the U.S. luxury car market).
2. Customer focus through technological innovations (VISA, for example, developed a system which shortened the approval time for customers).
3. Circumventing the strategy by which a company avoids or by-passes investments in a key value chain component such as R&D through a linking program such as joint venture to share development or other costs associated with product development (e.g., Chrysler and Mitsubishi).

Withdrawal as a strategy works to preserve reputation, particularly in markets with short product cycle time and rapid technological innovations. IBM, for example, was forced during the 1980s to withdraw its products from the market once its competitors Sun and Compaq introduced more advanced PCs. IBM cannibalized its own product by taking R&D and manufacturing loss to avoid introducing inferior products and to preserve its reputation. The withdrawal was temporary until IBM was able to develop superior PCs (Bryan, 1990).

REORGANIZING

Companies lacking resources to maneuver in their markets cannot escape the adaptation imperative either. They must continually renew their technologies and structural arrangements, plus develop innovative products and services, to keep their businesses afloat. Albany International's Fabric Division in East Greenbush, New York, is an example of a manufacturing organization which was designed from the beginning to achieve higher flexibility in structuring, lower operating costs, and quickly respond to customer needs.

Currently, Albany International's Fabric Division is using a matrix design in which each team is responsible for all three functions performed at the plant, e.g., weaving, needling, and finishing. Team leaders meet on a weekly basis with the process engineer and are informed about changes in procedures or equipment, upcoming new product trials, recent equipment problems, results of field runs, financial or production results, reviews of projects in the area, and processing problems that have been encountered.

Every morning, team members are updated by their leaders and the night-shift leader. This creates a smooth transition from shift to shift and improves decision making. But the highlight of this division is the transformation that has been initiated toward self-management, a change that is expected to result in even greater flexibility and coordination within the system. New self-contained teams will be created along the three core processes performed at the plant. Each team will specialize in one process, have specific performance goals, be supported by a maintenance/ engineering team, and have a process owner. In this way, the process will be given the optimum amount of attention required to achieve greater performance.

A large number of small manufacturing firms are turning away from regimented, standardized, mass-production technologies, and moving toward decentralized forms of organizing labor. Foreign competition is so intense, customers' quality demands so stringent, and product life cycle so short, that a traditional hierarchical organization simply cannot keep track of it all. Structures and processes must become more flexible and responsive. But change can be quite painful for an organization with established routines and regularities. Overly's experience is a clear example.

Overly, a $12 million company, which makes doors for laboratories, nuclear plants, and government vaults, was acquired during 1991 by Reese Brothers, who sought to revitalize the company by making it run like an entrepreneurial, innovative organization. With slow construction, other door makers entering Overly's niche, and falling prices, the new owners were determined to change the tightly controlled culture at Overly to accommodate a more aggressive style of growth and expansion. They broke with the central authority of common structure by giving workers monthly sales figures and quarterly financial reports to help them understand the company's new targets. Next, they put together empowered cross-functional teams to identify problems and suggest innovations. Soon after proposals were offered for implementation, they were met with resistance by frustrated workers who did not like the changes. The turmoil was so menacing that managers saw the company spiraling into "self-directed anarchy." Or as the manager who runs the company's computer systems saw it: "There is some vague idea that Overly wants to become a new democratic organization, empowering people . . . but we've lost the old structure before the new structure is in place, and the chaos scares the s___ out of me." Others complained that the new management was not responsive to proposals that came from the teams. "Every time we came up with what we thought was a good idea, somebody higher up in the company thought it wasn't a good idea" (Levinson, 1993, p. 47). One team even resorted to tactics such as hiding important data from management. The climate was so intense that workers started to question the validity and legality of the cross-training program and reluctantly accepted resolutions offered by management.

Why was Albany International successful while Overly experienced extreme difficulties? Perhaps the transition at Overly was too quick to swallow, too radical to absorb, and too dramatic to accept. The transition at Albany International was gradual and under control. It was supported by a strong psychological commitment on the part of the workers and was accompanied by job-skill training and interpersonal training—that is, the essence of teamwork. Perhaps, the success of the transformation at Albany International can be explained by the "greenfield-effect" phenomenon. The facility was new, people were recruited with prior knowledge about the new culture, and, therefore, acceptance was quite high. Where Albany International's Fabric Division started from scratch and with strong cultural readiness, Overly was an old establishment, deeply entrenched in traditional management practices with managers assuming responsibility for work outcomes, and with workers expected to constantly increase productivity and be responsive to downward commands and instructions. Understandably, a shell, that has hardened under many years of centralized authority and a mechanistic system of management is difficult to crack, let alone penetrate and change.

The lesson from Overly is that a total makeover in a relatively short period of time does not necessarily breed success. Instead, a partial makeover is called for, where incremental adaptation processes are congruent with the current culture and create bottom-up pressures to change rather than top-down imposition. An Overly manager concluded that "most confusing of all is the slowly dawning recognition that the chaos will have no end, that being an innovative, high-quality, low-cost manufacturer is not a one-shot effort" (Levinson, 1993, p. 48).

ADAPTIVE RESPONSES OF QUASI-GOVERNMENTAL AND UTILITY ORGANIZATIONS

In the bureaucratic organization, vertical and horizontal differentiation create a command structure, which is backed-up by clear policies and procedural specifications. This tightly coupled organization creates clear roles and responsibilities, which are governed by direct reporting relationships. Consequently, goals and strategies are unambiguous and accomplishment of tasks at the unit level is intended to achieve goals of higher managerial levels. in the nineteenth century, the dynamics were such that a bureaucratic setup was optimal because there was less competition and lower customer expectations due to lack of choice. Competition has forced companies to look for ways to decrease the time and cost of internal coordination. The forces that prevail today, with customers demanding higher product quality, the increasing role of government in regulating markets, short product life cycle, and overseas competition, make it virtually impossible for organizations to flourish under a bureaucratic structure. A public utility operating in a relatively predictable market can maintain a bureaucratic structure because competition is relatively low and the market is highly regulated. But even in this environment we often find evidence of public utility companies trying to downsize, streamline their operations, and employ more flexible structures.

When Niagara Mohawk Power Corporation of New York (NIMO) was faced with the challenge to undertake a quality effort to improve internal efficiency, it had no choice but to comply with the regulations imposed by the New York State Public Service Commission (PSC). In 1989, PSC issued an order calling for NIMO to restructure its operations if it wanted to achieve rate increases. As Marshall McDonald, president of the FPL group (parent company to Florida Power and Light) said: "Even a utility can be brought to its knees if regulators won't allow you to recover your costs" (*Impoco*, p. 2). Additionally, a NIMO official admitted: "We are moving away from the traditional cost-based regulation and toward incentive regulation . . . Even though we remain in many regards a regulated monopoly, to survive and prosper it's imperative that we conduct ourselves more and more as though we are a competitive business" (Davis, *NM News*, January, 1993, p. 4).

With the Public Service Commission threatening to take actions, NIMO hired McKinsey Consultants late in 1989. The consultants recommended a number of steps the company should take to improve performance, including a process of self-assessment, departmental restructuring, and updating the corporate mission statement. The self-assessment project hoped to accomplish a number of goals. First, the project was designed to make employees feel their input was being acknowledged and used in the decision process. Second, it was used to strengthen the channels of communication among employees, the PSC, and the general public. The ultimate goal was to improve the organization's financial standing. The target was a 40 percent savings for the company. The actual result, however, equaled a 15 percent to 18 percent savings. McKinsey Consultants also proposed dividing NIMO into Strategic Business Units (SBUs) and Corporate Support Units (CSUs). SBUs were separated into groups known as Electric Customer Service (ECS), Electric Supply and Delivery (ES&D), Nuclear (NUC), and Gas Customer (now known as NMGas). Among other objectives, this measure was aimed at providing division managers with more latitude and accountability for their operations. A brief description of the functions of each of these newly structured operations follows.

The Strategic Business Units are largely autonomous. Each unit functions as an independent business with the capabilities to perform individual functions of planning, budgeting, labor relations, and so forth. Each is a separate business, accountable for its own results in support of the overall corporate goals (*Annual Report*, 1991, p. 6). The Corporate Support Units consist of the executive circle, finance and corporate services, human resources, and legal and corporate relations. These units support the semiautonomous divisions and integrate them at a strategic level. Corporate Support Units also handle functions that require overall corporate policy and direction, such as strategic planning, employee benefits, and external affairs. They also handle functions necessary to all units and those that can be handled more economically by corporate headquarters such as data processing.

Niagara Mohawk's quality effort also involved a rightsizing process with a focus on reduction in personnel and plant shutdowns. NIMO announced in late January 1993 that by 1995 it would reduce both management and union staff by approximately fourteen hundred people, or about 12 percent of its total workforce. The reduction in personnel was to be attained via attrition and retirement of about four hundred nuclear employees and one thousand employees from elsewhere in the company, as well as elimination of vacant positions. NIMO maintained that it would review and analyze the functions and necessity of outside contractors, who had ongoing, almost permanent work within the company, and target them for streamlining and elimination as well. The first round of plant closings was announced in April 1994, as the Fossil Generation department of Electric Supply and Delivery led the way by ordering all four of the company's oil and coal-fired stations to scale down operations. These sites were chosen due to the results of the study of each unit's efficiency and projections of the market's future energy needs.

Another bureaucratic organization that is undergoing a massive change is the United States Postal Service (USPS). Despite its high use of automation, bar codes, and high-speed mail flow, which shorten the mail delivery time cycle, the USPS is still faced with the challenge of meeting external competition. The challenges of the external competition are stronger than ever. Technological advances have provided the USPS with competition for every postal product. Fax machines, e-mail, the Internet, and other mass-communication technologies offer alternatives to the public for issuing bills, statements, and personal messages. Third-class mailers, faced with decreasing mail budgets and increasing postage rates, have turned to other mediums, such as telemarketing and cable television to get their messages delivered. Alternate Postal Delivery, the nation's largest private deliverer of second- and third-class mail, for example, has expanded into new markets and is expected to double its sales volume by the end of the 1990s (*Advertising Mail Marketing Association Bulletin*, 1993). In the parcel business (primarily fourth-class mail) UPS, FEDEX, and Air-Born Express continue to dominate the market for urgent overnight mail delivery and packages. UPS alone commands about 80 percent of the market share, while the USPS controls a mere 7 percent of the market (Del Polito, 1993, p. 2).

Market share is dwindling for the USPS due to fierce overnight delivery competition and the rapid influx of electronic forms of communication, such as e-mail, the Internet, and fax. Nevertheless, the USPS is launching aggressive advertising campaigns, introducing new products and services, and installing sophisticated equipment to meet these challenges and improve market share ("Runyon Delivers a Turnaround," *Industry Week, 1997*). For example, to serve its customers efficiently and effectively, the USPS introduced the ZIP+4 (11 digit zip code), which eliminates the need for carriers to case their mail. The mail arrives from the sorting plant to the delivery station in trays, presorted by walk sequence.

In addition, the USPS is also adding a new electronic link that connects the USPS with its airline contractors to improve the reliability of priority and overnight mail ("No More Easy Money," *Traffic World*, 1996). Although the USPS is still a labor-intensive, highly regulated bureaucracy with mounting financial and competitive pressures, it is slowly trying the recover-by-restructuring operations after recording operating losses for three consecutive years. The agency recorded substantial losses in the fiscal years 1990 through 1992. In fact, 1992 ended with a net operating loss of $536 million. This loss is significant considering USPS's unique status as a federal agency, mandated by Congress to operate as a self-sustaining, self-sufficient business, which is required to break even fiscally over the long run.

The Postal Service reorganization of 1992 created a new organizational structure from top to bottom, thus embarking on a three-point plan for change. The plan was intended to reduce postal administrative costs and bureaucracy, to improve service quality, and to stabilize postage rates through at least 1994 (Bounds, Dobbins & Fowler, 1995). By offering early retirements and other incentives, the USPS eliminated four layers of management to speed up decision making and trimmed thousand of overhead positions, without lay-offs or furloughs. This new structure was designed to allow USPS managers to focus their expertise, improve vertical communication, and empower employees to meet the needs of their customers and improve service quality. The restructuring effort at the USPS involved a combination of delayering, consolidation, and reduction in workforce.

Postmaster General Marvin T. Runyon is credited with developing and instituting the plan, turning around the troubled agency, and reporting record profits in 1995 and 1996, only three years after the reorganization began. Runyon's dynamic management skills proved to be the key element in turning around the agency. During the summer of 1992, Runyon started the restructuring by examining the agency inside and out. He sought input from employees to find out exactly what they did, why they did it, and how they did it. He began making changes by forming new VP positions for processing and distribution, marketing and sales, and customer services that reported directly to the newly formed position of chief operating officer (COO). The five regions and their seventy-three divisions were replaced by ten areas headed by managers of customer services and processing and distribution, eighty-five customer service districts, and 235 processing and distribution facilities with direct reporting to the area managers. This new structure created a "matrix" in which plant managers became responsible for processing and transportation functions located within the district territory, and district managers became responsible for delivery and retail operations reporting directly to the same area manager.

As a labor-intensive organization (82 percent of the USPS operating budget goes toward covering personnel costs), only automation and a reduction in workforce could affect the USPS productivity rate positively. Thus, thirty thousand positions (out of about 750,000) were targeted by the GPM, with about 40 percent in the management group, five hundred of which were in Postal Career Executive Service positions, the top level positions at the Postal Service. The early retirement program, however, targeted about 140,000 employees (approximately 20 percent of the USPS workforce) with an incentive of a six-month salary benefit. About five thousand postmasters, fifteen thousand supervisors, twelve thousand city carriers, and fourteen thousand clerks accepted the buy-out, for a total retirement of about forty-six thousand people (*Federal Times*, January 4, 1993). By the end of 1993, the Postal Service lost $1.8 billion. The tough competition, coupled with declining productivity (the improvement goal of 4.8 percent starting mid-1989 through 1995 was only .7 percent by mid-1992, and fell short of the 1.8 percent projected productivity improvement for the same period), led the USPS to initiate its "Quality First!" program, automate the workplace, and develop a participative work environment. In addition, the agency instituted an incentive system, based on the Postal Service financial performance and customer satisfaction, to spur better productivity.

Quality First! program was based on five important principles: customer focus, continuous improvement, employee participation, supplier partnerships, and management systems. However, continuous improvement was the point at which cross-functional teams were formed to target processes for improvement in an effort to achieve performance breakthrough. In 1997, the Postal Service finished the year with a $1.26 billion profit, following profits of $1.77 billion in 1995 and $1.57 billion in 1996. The strong three-year performance trimmed the Postal Service's long-term financial debt from $5.9 billion to $1.36 billion (*The Baltimore Sun*, December 27, 1997, p. 3A).

TRUST THEM! A BOTTOM-UP APPROACH TO CHANGE

According to Beer, Eisenstat, and Spector (1990), revitalization of a company cannot be successfully completed unless the change focuses on the work itself—employees' roles, responsibilities, and relationships—or what they call "task alignment." Effective change can only occur in a nondirective way—top management must specify the parameters for a desired adaptation without insisting on specific solutions. Once a grassroots change in attitudes, behaviors, and habits reaches a critical mass, the CEO must move in by aligning organizational structures and systems, thus leading to a full transformation. The point is that the troops in the periphery must be ready and management practices in the operating core must change before full-scale adaptation can take place. Otherwise, the tension between dynamic units and static management will cause a breakdown in the change process.

Beer, Eisenstat, and Spector advocate a bottom-up, loosely coupled approach to change that steadily moves toward the corporate core and that elicits renewal without imposing it. They note that "the greatest obstacle to revitalization is the idea that it comes through company wide change programs. We call this the fallacy of programmatic change." Change and adaptation are about learning, and CEOs do not necessarily have a complete knowledge of the workings of diverse units. They must learn from ideas and innovative approaches that come from managers and operators who are closer to the points of impact. These authors suggest that adaptation through corporate revitalization should occur along three important dimensions: interfunctional coordination, commitment, and competency. Coordination among product design, manufacturing, and marketing units is essential for product development opportunities. Commitment to cooperation and teamwork and analytical skills, as well as interpersonal skills, is necessary if individuals working together are to identify and solve problems as a team. If any of these dimensions is missing, maladaptation will result. For example, training alone can enhance competency level, but training cannot change the pattern of coordination within the organization. Trained employees may see their new skills go unused and perceive the training as a waste, undermining their commitment to the change process as a whole. Once an intervention program collapses, senior managers often propose an alternative. Pressed by daily business problems, senior managers do not have time for change and adaptation processes and often use "one-size-fits-all" interventions that all too often are isolated, irrelevant, and even inhibit change. Beer, Eisenstat, and Spector (1990) highlighted this problem: "Because they are designed to cover everyone and everything, programs end up covering nobody and nothing particularly well. They are so general and standardized that they don't speak to the day-to-day realities of particular units. Buzzwords like 'quality', 'participation', 'excellence', 'empowerment', and 'leadership' become a substitute for a detailed understanding of the business" (p. 165).

Beer, Eisenstat, and Spector (1990) went on to suggest a six-step change process to help create a self-reinforcing cycle of commitment, coordination, and competence and achieve task-aligned change across diverse units.

1. *Mobilize commitment to change through joint diagnosis of business problems.* Using focus groups, cross-functional teams, or ad-hoc task forces that cover all the stakeholders in the organization, midlevel managers can help people develop a shared diagnosis of what is wrong and what must be done to improve work processes.
2. *Develop a shared vision of how to organize and manage for competitiveness.* Once the problem-solving team proposes workable alternatives, the manager (sponsor), together with involved

employees, can lead the change by redefining task roles and responsibilities. If done in parallel units, this will change patterns of coordination and increase collaboration and information sharing across interdependent functions within the organization.

3. *Foster consensus for the new vision, develop competence to enact it, and mobilize support to move it along.* Not everyone understands the renewal process and not everyone wants to participate in action learning. This is where strong leadership across levels is very crucial. The managers' commitment to change must be displayed up-front through actions: e.g., providing resources, allocating staff, rotating, replacing, and even getting rid of people who aggressively resist the change.

4. *Spread revitalization to all departments without pushing it from the top.* When the roles and responsibilities are reshaped within the departments, teams must decide on the appropriate forms of organizing to accommodate the new concepts of teamwork and coordination.

5. *Institutionalize revitalization through formal policies, systems, and structures.* Once the infrastructure has been built, the need for change is internalized: people are realigned through redefined roles and responsibilities, and teamwork is in place—the changes in structures and systems are complemented with changes in relationships.

6. *Monitor and adjust strategies in response to problems during the revitalization process.* This should be a shared activity by an oversight team that guards the process to ensure that the capacity for continual adaptation and learning is sustained over a long period of time. The purpose of change is to create an asset that did not exist before—a learning organization capable of adapting to a changing competitive environment. The organization has to know how to continually monitor its behavior—in effect, to learn how to learn.

ADAPTATION: LEADERSHIP CHALLENGES

What does this all mean? How will this change affect managerial style, competency, and even professional development goals? The common theme emerging from our discussion is the need to be adaptive, flexible, and resilient. Managers adopting a participative style in leading their employees would find it less difficult to build trust and confidence in employees, establish norms for effective communication, and create adherents that are loyal and supportive of the change effort. Involving others in decision making that might shape the directions of working relationships and affect the outcomes of work will enhance employees' commitment and positively affect productivity. Just as employees are expected to become more involved in shaping work processes and results, so do managers. A manager who knows the secrets of managing by walking around (MBWA) will also be successful in capturing the hearts and minds of employees.

In stressing the importance of MBWA, Wal-Mart includes the principles of this strategy in its training resources. It emphasizes the supporting role of the manager in encouraging employees to become proficient. For Wal-Mart, MBWA means managing by respecting, listening to, and using the ideas generated from employees. It means getting involved and getting others involved. MBWA is not simply tapping into the grapevine or maintaining effective informal communication with employees, but rather it is an active role of frequently encouraging, challenging, and recognizing achievements of employees. MBWA involves listening to demonstrate the value of human resources, teaching to encourage employees to develop high expectations from themselves, and responding by giving feedback, helping, and correcting errors as needed. At Wal-Mart the habit of Sam Walton has been glorified in transforming managers and having them carry the same values Walton had. He was well known for his practices of

- talking to employees (referred to as associates) in their work area
- asking them questions to learn what customers want
- listening to associates' ideas
- showing interest in associates' personal needs and professional goals
- teaching them what he knew

Another version of MBWA is *management by walking away*. The remarkable story of Quad/Graphics, a printing company with its headquarters in Pewaukee, Wisconsin, is a benchmark model of management that has left the company in the hands of its employees for three days (Kehrer, 1989; Kirschen, 1989; Geber, 1988; Gendron & Burlingham, 1986). At Quad, intrapreneurship, creativity, and innovation are the core values if not the ideology of the company. Quad does not depend on formal plans or budgets; each division is set as a profit center measured against its own performance from the previous period. The company is horizontally and vertically decentralized with employees solving problems at the level at which they occur. New employees are expected to internalize the mission and philosophy of the company through socialization and training. The company has no class structure—there are no job titles or punch clocks and very few distinctions between managers and employees.

The underlying philosophy of Quad was defined and shaped by Quadracci, the CEO—a decentralized, unstructured approach that capitalizes on smallness, trust, and high commitment. Ownership in the company is shared with employees, who control over 40 percent of the company's equity. The outcomes are just as remarkable—a growth rate of about 40 percent a year and a reputation as one of the finest printers in the United States. Another example comes from Leyland Trucks, the UK's largest commercial vehicle maker, which found success and improved quality by adjusting quickly to change. Through character assessments and input from employees, management at Leyland Trucks found that employees were not given sufficient responsibility for their work. By adapting quickly to this new-found knowledge, managers placed new emphasis on recognizing contributions of workers leading to the improvement of the company's communication processes and production outcomes. Another company is W. L. Gore and Associates, which fosters personal growth by structuring tasks around commitment rather than managerial authority. Often when new employees join the firm they are told to look around and find something interesting to do (Barge, 1994).

But does all of this change and new expectations diminish the role of management? No, not really—it just changes its focus. Management must transform the way it is evolved, shaped, and sustained. Managers who can change both cognitively and behaviorally can also adjust quickly and learn to cope with change and deal with stress while helping others do the same. By fostering personal growth and empowering their employees, managers create opportunities for greater organizational adaptability. While most managers appreciate the importance of human capital in the productivity equation, the effective managers utilize their employees' strengths, creativity, and ability to innovate to the fullest. The manager's new role in the environment of discontinuity is to cultivate and maintain a nourishing climate for personal growth. Managers do not have to have the answers—just the right questions and the right attitude. Effective managerial leaders transform the entire organization by creating an awareness for the need to change and by enhancing the capability of the organization to adapt. Organizational leaders have four essential responsibilities:

1. Leaders must act as if they are conductors orchestrating the change process but without specifying a particular approach. Top leadership must set new performance standards to realign the organization with its environment and hold unit managers accountable for fundamental changes.
2. Top leadership must identify divisions, plants, etc., that have begun experiencing management innovations. These units become developmental laboratories for further innovation, allocation of adequate resources, and potential targets for internal benchmarking.
3. Top executives must practice what they preach by ultimately applying to themselves the same principles and behaviors that they expect others to apply. In addition they must develop a cadre of young, promising leaders, who are also action-learning oriented, as internal change agents to perpetuate the renewal process. By shifting back and forth between the innovator and mentor roles, effective organizational leaders:

   - Use the criterion of innovative leadership as an important input in promotional decision
   - Rotate prospective leaders between jobs
   - Learn and develop new skills

4. Organizational leaders are encouraged to drift away from a vertical/functional approach to one that recognizes the importance of processes that cut across functional boundaries. They are expected to manage interfaces and boundaries, rather than functions and units. Managers at higher levels should:

   - Think and act strategically
   - Look at dynamics and changes that occur along the value chain of the organization
   - Initiate internal and external networking
   - Create and maintain horizontal linkages that integrate people and units along the value chain

In carrying out these responsibilities, organizational leaders perform the tasks and responsibilities manifested in the behaviors of the Broker. The context for enacting the Broker role is the central focus of the next chapter.

3

Linking the Organization: Information Technology and Networking

> When Wal-Mart sells a light bulb on the register, it goes to my factory instantly—I make the bulb for the one they just sold. The enterprise system is now totally compressed with information.
>
> —Jack Welch, *The Washington Post*, March 23, 1997

The technological information revolution creates more opportunities for redesigning the whole system. Accessibility to diverse databases and expert systems, availability of just-in-time (JIT) training instruments, and shorter channels of communication have all contributed to a shift from task-oriented specialists to result-oriented generalists. Individuals with a generalist orientation possess a broad cross-functional perspective on processes and are free of "turfism." This shift also helps delinearize, redesign, and rebuild sequential processes, an obvious advantage for a reengineering approach to change! (Hammer & Champy, 1993). While management information systems (MIS) tend to have an inward focus, that of linking internal operations within the organization, leading virtually to the creation of a seamless organization, information technology (IT) is more externally oriented. IT provides the organization with the capability to globalize, while simultaneously specializing locally. Information technology has many applications, including networked databases, CD-ROM libraries and vendor-outsourced industry recordkeeping, e-mail, teleconferencing, and facsimile machines. This technology has widely opened up the avenues of communication, making it possible to conduct work in real-time and with quick responses. The competitive advantage of the IT organization in a highly volatile environment is evident. For instance, the electronics industry is using IT to improve efficiency and flexibility to quickly respond to customer demand and a shrinking product life cycle. *Information Week* (9/18/95) reported that many electronics companies employ IT at every stage of product development in order to decrease development time as much as possible. In order to react to ever-changing demands, chief information officers (CIO) are looking at ways in which IT can be used to meet goals. Currently, IT is used in many companies to improve communication by putting people, at synchronous or asynchronous time, in contact with each other at every stage of the development cycle. The ultimate goal is to advance the efficiency and flexibility of the IT capabilities to make organizational resources more available across divisions.

Umanath and Campbell (1994) suggested a number of conditions that facilitate the transition toward an IT organization:

- Market (not command) economy
- Information (not agrarian or industrial) economy
- Relaxed (not imposed) trade policies
- Culture in which uncertainty is tolerated (not avoided)
- Cultures characterized by individualistic (not collectivist) orientations
- Cultures characterized by masculine (not feminine) dispositions
- Abstractive (not associative) cultures
- Low uncertainty (not business risk) in the operating environment
- Ethnocentric (not localized) decision responsibilities
- Value added (not volume maximization) goal orientation
- Composition (not provincial) perspective
- Presence (not absence) of a sophisticated technical core
- Focused (not diverse) corporate goals
- International business strategy (not multinational or global business strategy)

In an information-intensive environment, this transition is almost inevitable. Pen-based computers such as those used by United Parcel Service, Satellite Communications used by United Stationers, and Electronic Data Interchange (EDI) used by Wal-Mart, allow the capturing and dissemination of real-time data through the organization and its network organizations. Sun's Wide Area Network (SWAN) connects more than 120 sites in twenty countries. There are nearly twenty-two thousand active hosts on the network, serving nearly thirty thousand network clients. The network is designed to allow any Sun employee to perform most of his or her normal job functions from any workstation on the network. By design, some job functions requiring authorization cannot be performed from remote workstations for security reasons. However, an employee in Scotland can access files and applications residing on a server in America. With appropriate authorization, Sun employees can obtain current information about customers, orders, or shipments from any system on the network. Sun's telephone system also uses SWAN. Inside the company, five-digit dialing connects Sun offices around the world. SWAN also supports multimedia and video applications. Video conferencing and inter-room connections are provided through a digital network. Other communication-oriented applications involve on-line management information system (MIS) reports which are available to authorized users, and e-mail and fax communications.

Powerful computers help electronically link units and processes, organizations, and their trading partners with greater speed and accuracy. In 1987, Wal-Mart installed a Satellite Network (WSN) that links each Wal-Mart store to the Home Office as well as to a network of large field distribution centers. WSN provides the stores with on-line access to sales inventory and credit information. Forbes (1997) reports that the $100 billion Wal-Mart company spends $500 million per year on information technology and has a storage capacity of twenty-four terabytes; second only to the U.S. government. The investment in information technology provides an avenue for Wal-Mart to share its information with everyone in the stores. This includes information on top-selling items, inventory, yearly comparisons on product sales, competitor prices, products in transit, and consumer purchase patterns. The significance of WSN is by linking the stores directly with vendors and suppliers.

Wal-Mart's electronic data interchange (EDI) links the company with over two thousand suppliers. EDI makes the exchange of purchase orders, invoices, and payment transactions fast and simple by electronically linking the computers of the companies. Scanning at each store provides suppliers with sales and inventory data. When the store's stock falls below a predetermined level, the system activates a quick response (QR) through a replenishment process. The Wal-Mart cash register system is also directly linked from the store to the home office to a credit authorization system, thus minimizing the time it takes to approve a transaction (the entire process takes about six seconds). By using the WSN, the home office is also able to transmit video broadcasts, such as training and updates, to the stores on a daily basis. Since the mid-80s, Wal-Mart has realized that a significant amount of future growth will come from productivity gains achieved via information technology. Although Wal-Mart experienced a flat profit growth in 1995, sales increased 13 percent. Seeing the future in information technology (IT), they boosted the IT budget 10 percent for 1996 and were expected to do the same for 1997 (*Information Week*, 1996).

Texas Instruments (TI) has been undergoing a company-wide reengineering project to redefine the way TI divisions communicate and exchange information. *Information Week* (9/18/95) noted that beginning in 1995, TI planned to invest at least $120 million a year on top of TI's $400 million annual information technology budget. This was TI's response to a slow turnover time to consolidate its calculator and notebook business, which took fifteen months to complete, and to the realization that market changes were happening more quickly than that. The project includes redefining the way the organization is structured by creating teams of IT professionals that can respond quickly to a variety of situations, thus, further decreasing the amount of time to react to business needs and get products to market. Motorola, for example, believed that IT was so important to success that they eliminated the position of a company-wide CIO in 1993 and created equivalent positions at the group and sector levels. This move has given Motorola's individual product divisions more flexibility and, in turn, has contributed to the company's bottom line.

It should not be a surprise to find that more and more organizations increase their investments in computing and communications. Estimates of spending on information technology capabilities range from $1 trillion (Dué, 1994) to 50 percent of total durable equipment corporate budgets (Geisler, 1994). The service industry alone spent over $862 billion in the ten years between 1983 and 1993 to increase organizational communication capabilities and electronic networking (Hildebrand, 1994).

Transitioning the organization strategically toward an IT organization can be patterned along the lines of five modes or levels of development suggested by Venkatraman (1994). The first level is localized exploitation (e.g., the deployment of standard IT applications with minimal changes to the business processes). The second level is internal integration, which involves two types of integration—technical interconnectivity (i.e., different IT systems using a common IT platform) and business process interdependence (e.g., cross-functional teams). Both levels require only minimal changes to existing business processes and are, therefore, classified as "evolutionary." The third level is business process redesign, in which IT functions are used as a lever for designing new organizational and business process (limited to internal functions). The fourth level is business network redesign, which represents the redesign of the nature of exchange among multiple participants in a business network through effective deployment of IT capabilities. The fifth level is business scope redefinition, which implies a shift from the redesign of business networks (level four) to knowledge networks, using IT for "enhanced coordination and control." This framework can help leaders determine the level at which their organization currently operates. Thereafter leaders can position the organization to progress to higher levels; in effect positioning the organization strategically from an "efficient enhancer" to an "enabler of corporate redesign" to achieve competitive advantage.

Can this trend change the ways in which managers perform their roles and motivate employees? One thing is certain: Information technology and telecommuting adds more variety to work conditions and in many ways enriches the conventional way of working. The challenge for managers, however, is to effectively link between organizational interfaces to minimize energy leaks. They also must manage by accomplishments, rather than by line of sight (Nelton, 1993). The dilemma is that telecommuting might lead to an organization that is electronically connected, but socially disconnected. Traditionally, much of the work has been performed by people exchanging written information. Today, however, more than ever before, we are moving rapidly toward the paperless organization that, unfortunately, is also nonverbal. For some, it is a reason to become concerned. People's work becomes divorced from its social and human context. In the absence of human communication and social interaction, employee affiliation with the organization becomes weak. Paradoxically, the technological advances that have increased personal and organizational productivity have also led to the demise of human communication.

As companies are seeing many positive results from IT applications, more employees are encouraged to perform work off-site, saving office space. In addition, computer-mediated communication (CMC) increasingly has become the primary mode of transmitting messages and communicating with individuals and groups. In playing the role of the Broker, the manager is faced with a personal challenge: Linking the organization electronically may require technical skills in addition to communication skills. The next two sections elaborate.

TELECOMMUTING, TELECENTERS, AND
ORGANIZATIONAL PRODUCTIVITY

Information technology increasingly allows for work to be performed off-site, saving office space, and leading to higher personal productivity and worker satisfaction. Employers can save roughly $6,000
to $12,000 or more per person via telecommuting. These dollars saved,
however, are not just from real estate alone. In a 1995 survey of 160 companies conducted by Infonetics Research, only 16 percent said that the
savings from real estate were important. Two-thirds stated that the
most important contributing factors to telecommuting was increased
worker productivity, added sales, and improved responsiveness to customers (*Information Week*, 1/22/96). Additionally, more and more companies are realizing the benefits of telecommuting. For instance,
according to a survey commissioned in 1997 by a research firm known
as IDC/LINK, the number of telecommuters was expected to increase
by a half-million (more than 7 percent), from 7.1 million at the end of
1996 to 7.6 million at the end of 1997 (*Business Week*, 10/7/97).

As companies are seeing many positive results from telecommuting, some employees might be overcome by feelings of loneliness and
isolation and some managers by the fear of losing control. However, for
most telecommuters, it is a confidence booster. Employees feel that they
have more control over their work, and managers can get the job done
even outside of normal working hours. Another effect is what has been
labeled "hoteling"—by having a part-time workplace for full-time
workers, employers save time and money on space and equipment, as
commuters spend less time on the road. Hence, personal productivity
soars (*The Baltimore Sun*, December 28, 1995, 1C). Hoteling entails employees booking the use of a desk or work station in advance with office
or hoteling "coordinators," often at what are called "alternate work
sites" or "telecenters." Otherwise, these employees work out of virtual
centers such as home linking and networking clients with the home office. According to IDC/Link, a New York research company, more than
twenty-nine million Americans telecommute or conduct their business
from home.

One such telecenter is run by the General Services Administration
(GSA) of Southern Maryland telecenter project. Since 1994, the federal
government has opened six telecenters in the Washington area, which
has a high concentration of federal workers. Four of the telecenters, the
first in the United States, are in Northern Virginia. There are plans to
open at least eight more in the Maryland-Virginia region by 1996. Nationwide, the federal government is planning to shift up to sixty thou-

sand employees into hoteling within several years (*The Baltimore Sun*, December 28, 1995, 10C). Two immediate cost savings resulting from telecommuting are that office leasing is being trimmed and overhead costs are reduced. The federal government's projected hoteling would eliminate thirty thousand desks and work stations over the next ten years, with an annual expected savings amounting to $150 million. Ernst & Young, for example, has trimmed its office space leases by about 1.5 million square feet nationwide by setting up hoteling arrangements at 20 percent of its offices. Annual savings for Ernst & Young's rethinking about office space allocation, file cabinets, and telephones amounted to $20 million.

Both Pacific Bell and Bell Atlantic, as well as IBM, use telecommuting to enable employees to perform tasks outside their conventional office. Bell Atlantic saw remarkable results: a 200 percent increase in output, 20 percent time reduction in task completion, and far fewer sick days. By 1996, Bell Atlantic expanded the telecommuting option to include most of its managers. IBM Canada expanded its telecommuting project, during 1994, to include 15 percent of the company's marketing reps, or seven hundred people. During the same year, 20 percent of IBM's workforce nationwide were telecommuters who hoteled at regional offices for office equipment and support. Predictions made during early 1993 estimated the number of telecommuters in the United States to grow to a total of 8.2 million by 1996, or roughly 12.3 percent of the total U.S. workforce (Hotch, 1993). Most of the telecommuting activities seem to be limited to sales and marketing. However, telecommuting and hoteling is expanding to consulting, accounting, and other support systems.

THE HUMAN DIMENSION

One of the most important issues concerning the application of IT, is how it affects complex interpersonal interactions within organizations. The use of Local Area Networks (LANs) and Wide Area Networks (WANs) may have considerable impact on organizational communication since it transforms the way direct communication is transmitted within and outside the chain of command, as well as alters the patterns of the communication. Some have argued that computer-mediated communication (CMC), with its emphasis on speed, outreach, and efficiency, supplements conventional modes of communication or provides immeasurable net benefits for the success of postindustrial organizations. Others have argued that information technology, which provides the basis for complex computer-mediated communication systems, might appear as a buffer rather than an enhancer of communication. For example, sending and receiving messages through e-mail reduces the opportunities for face-to-face communication, and, therefore, could contaminate both communication relationships and communication transactions—the two most important elements of interpersonal communication (see for example, Barnes & Greller, 1994; Jones, 1995; Rice & Love, 1987; Walther, 1996).

Goldhaber (1993) pointed out the interesting issue that, while there is pressure on managers to place a high premium on verbal communication through programs such as involvement and empowerment, the explosion of IT may hinder or inhibit such a purpose. Weick (1985) has suggested that IT, in effect, not only interferes with human interactions, but also interferes with members' ability to make sense of events in organizations. Thus, a major psychosocial need of people—to interact, have exchanges, give and receive feedback, and be able to interpret events through face to face interactions—cannot be fully met. It is evident that CMC does not have the information richness capacity needed for many complex task-related communications. Organizational communication theorists (e.g., Daft & Lengel, 1984; Daft, Lengel & Klebe Trevino, 1987) tell us that more complex decision-making communication must be matched with the greater information richness that accompanies lateral relations, mutual adjustments, direct contacts, and all-channel communication networks based on informal and interactive communication processes. This kind of communication allows ample opportunities for immediacy, reinforcing feedback, and other adjustments, including signals through nonverbal cues that enable communicators to overcome perceptual biases usually instantly or after a short period of free, nonmediated verbal exchange. Rich media are better suited for highly equivocal tasks that require immediate attention and sharing of ideas, whereas lean media are suited more for routine problems or tasks that are unambiguous or unequivocal, and, therefore, can be mediated via written communication or CMC.

The other difficulty with CMC is the amount of time it takes for multiple messages, sent in parallel rather than in sequence, to reach their destination and the opportunity receivers of communication have to use subjective interpretations without the immediate ability to receive clarifications. In addition, typing takes longer than speaking, disruptions in the temporal sequences of messages are frequent, and messages that are perceived as cold, impersonal, and unemotional tend to receive little attention or be ignored all together.

It seems as if IT brings back what the human relations movement has tried to abolish: the mechanized system of standardized work processes and operations governed by rules and prescribed behaviors. Except now, work is automated and self-regulated with people following predetermined codes and procedures, which specify activities without much influence by the people involved. The formal authoritative system of control that has demoralized people and triggered Chester Barnard's famous call to raise interpersonal communication to a high level of priority has reemerged—this time in a transformed fashion— as a high-tech medium that paradoxically increases the information processing capacities of the organization, while simultaneously reducing the amount and rate of verbal communication.

The ability to control the flow of information centrally, by-pass middle managers, and connect directly with front-line employees can lead to another effect of IT—top managers may have an incentive to recover delegated authority. They can avoid vertical loading and decentralization of managerial decision making, depriving middle managers of exercising their legitimate authority over lower levels and eliminating their function as communication transmitters and translators. Top managers can recentralize production control through integrated information processing systems, yet still provide autonomy to front-line employees and teams to manage the work flow with little intervention on the part of the middle manager. Information technology facilitates the shift of managerial responsibilities to teams while stripping midlevel managers of their traditional bases of power. Information technology helps operationalize the need for greater interdependence between employees and develop their awareness for joint accountability, thus rendering the job of the middle manager redundant. As two researchers concluded: "Especially in the areas in which top managers use IT to recentralize authority, middle managers would be eliminated. Those who survive would find that some of their functions are taken over either by a computer or by higher levels of management" (Daniels & Spiker, 1994, p. 186).

Line managers can react directly to communication stimuli generated by top managers, rendering the job of the middle manager unnecessary. This unconventional view of the redundancy generated by the traditional role of middle manager has found some support among consultants of organizational change. Larkin and Larkin (1994), for example, contend that to be successful, any restructuring must be communicated to front-line employees directly by their supervisors, and that supervisors must be the privileged senders and receivers of the information, rather than middle managers. Supervisors are the opinion leaders for front-line employees and have the capacity to change their behaviors. Communication that reaches the front line will be transmitted to employees informally, directly, and verbally, usually in response to employee-initiated questions. Top managers, therefore, should support and enhance this capacity by communicating directly with first-line supervisors and by ensuring that first-line supervisors are prepared for face-to-face communication with their employees. Information technology, much to the dismay of middle managers, provides top managers with the capability to connect directly with first-line supervisors by making them the target of their messages.

Information technology also provides ample opportunities for first-line supervisors to maintain direct links with top managers, thus increasing the possibility that their employees would perceive them as having more power and materializing the Pelz effect (1952)—Increasing the power of supervisors increases both satisfaction and performance among front-line employees. As information technology expands as the primary mode of communication within and outside organizations, it can potentially signal the fate of the middle level. Middle managers, whose popularity in transforming organizations keeps declining (at GM they are referred to as the "frozen middle," while GE connotes them as the "cement layer," and Polaroid coined the phrase "muddle in the middle"), also experience erosion in their real power or actual influence versus their legitimate or formal power. Larkin and Larkin (1994), who advocate direct contacts between top and lower levels, cite research by Harcourt, Richerson, and Wattier (1991) who studied the communication practices of 871 U.S. middle managers. Findings showed 16 percent said their most important source of information was formal channels; 21 percent said the grapevine; and 62 percent, the largest group by far, said their most important information source was their intentionally constructed network. Larkin and Larkin concluded that information is moving in and through middle management. It is not moving out! Therefore, when the change is critical to the survival of the organization, top managers are advised to establish direct communication links with front-line supervisors by calling them directly to see if they have received and understood the message. Information technology and CMC help facilitate the direct contacts between upper and lower levels.

O'Connell's (1988) assessment of the impact of IT on human communication and the system of interactions within the organization is worth mentioning:

- Opportunities for face-to-face contact will be diminished; information from nonverbal cues will be reduced. Consequently, opportunities for random, spontaneous information sharing will be reduced. Managers will need to structure work and relationships to provide more opportunities for face-to-face contact to occur. Meaning will be derived increasingly from text and symbols.

- More informal messages and "short-circuiting" of the hierarchy will occur as new formats are accepted due to the remote nature of an electronic network. Organization structure and formal information flow will be redefined.
- Channel effects will mean that messages of affect and value will decrease. Digitized data, with less context and interpretation, will be the norm. Consequently, decision making may be impaired rather than enhanced. Ambiguity in interpreting information will increase, and the quality of decisions could decrease with the lack of organizational values and context. Organizations will need to work harder at communicating their values and corporate history. Managers will have to seek new ways of communicating the affective component of messages. New and improved decision-making skills will be needed.
- Trust will play a changed role in communication. Trust develops with the shared experience, values, and give-and-take that are the result of human communication. Satellites, electronic mail, and networks could reduce the dimensions of trust to which we are accustomed. New dimensions of trust may spring up in their place.
- The computer imposes the discipline of linear thinking. Data is processed at speeds that increase with each new version of the chip. Consequently, people may become less patient and tolerant for individual styles of communicating. Organizations may find themselves becoming less tolerant of people who do not think or perceive in a strict, linear mode. Organizations will need to find ways to encourage and protect nonlinear thinking and communicating.
- Expectations of work performance may be machine driven. As we become accustomed to the speed and accuracy of the computer, we may expect employees to have the same qualities and produce in a similar manner. Employees in some organizations will perceive this as dehumanizing and cohesive. Unions will take up the human environment as an issue. New ways of defining and using performance standards will be needed. (pp. 480–81)

Whether IT organizations are more centralized or decentralized, one effect is clear: The speed of communication requires that key decisions be made on line in real-time. Real-time decision making will become an essential managerial competency and an important criterion for evaluating the effectiveness of managers in key operational roles. Managers also will have to learn how to deal with information overload and paralysis due to high flood of information. Developing competencies in the design of information systems, data management, and data analysis and interpretation will become increasingly important. In the final analysis, the big question is whether IT threatens the quality of human communication, as well as organizational members' reasoning abilities (i.e., how to make sense of and interpret organizational events).

BUILDING EXTERNAL NETWORKS

Information technology accelerates the use of outsourcing through symbiotic cooperation and networking as a means to reduce environmental uncertainty and manage external interdependencies. According to Alter and Hage (1993) interorganizational networks have four normative characteristics:

1. *Interorganizational networks are cognitive structures*. The organizations share common perceptions of their goals, strategies, values, and needs.
2. *Interorganizational networks are nonhierarchical*. Networks as opposed to hierarchies are linked laterally, influenced by their markets, and have a complex power structure.
3. *Interorganizational networks have a division of labor*. Each organization brings to the alliance a distinct technical competency which enhances the complementary relationships among the members of the network. This division of labor also balances against the development of a dominant player who attempts to control the network.
4. *Interorganizational networks are self-regulating*. Laterally linked autonomous organizations collaborate by relinquishing some of their power and sovereignty to achieve coordination. They do so via a negotiated linking program which evolves through mutual adjustment and self-regulation.

Outsourcing through strategic networking allows a cluster of organizations to keep pace with marketplace changes through pooling their resources collaboratively to produce a product or service. Figure 3.1 illustrates a generic view of such networking. One example of an outsourced function is public relations, particularly crisis management,

Figure 3.1. Outsourcing through Symbiotic Cooperation
and Networking

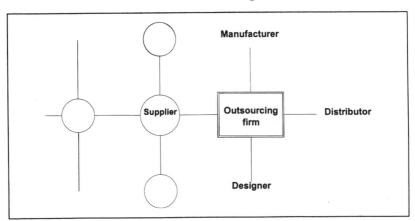

media relations, legislative or regulatory, community relations, and employee communication. Often, functions such as public relations and accounting are outsourced since they exist outside the main core activities within the organization, and hence receive low priority (Patrick, 1994). Another example of outsourced function is customer service. Industry leaders such as AT&T, Microsoft, and Quaker are using a company called MATRIX to improve customer service, reduce costs, and increase sales (*Fortune*, 1995). Some reasons cited in favor of outsourcing are: reduced overhead costs and lower wages and fringe benefits. In addition, companies can outsource functions for which they lack the expertise or the ability to develop or invest in new core capabilities. Other reasons include financial stability of the outsourcing firm, geographic proximity, and quality reputation.

Warren Co., an alliance consulting firm in Providence, RI, proposed the following critical success factors for external networking:

- *Critical driving forces*: There must be essential strategic forces that push the alliance partners together. Without these forces, there is no reason for an alliance.
- *Strategic synergy*: Always look for complementary strengths in a potential partner. For the alliance to succeed, the two partners should have greater strength when combined than they would have independently. Mathematically stated, it must be "1+1=3." If it isn't, walk away.

- *Great chemistry*: Your company must have the managerial ability to cooperate efficiently with another company, which in turn must have an equally cooperative spirit. There must be a high level of trust so executives can resolve difficulties.
- *Win-win*: All members of the alliance must see that the structure, operations, risks, and rewards are fairly apportioned among the members. Fair apportionment prevents corrosive internal dissension.
- *Operational integration*: Beyond a good strategic fit, there must be careful coordination at the operational level where plans and projects are implemented.
- *Growth opportunity*: Is there an excellent opportunity to place your company in a leadership position to sell a new product or service, or to secure access to technology or raw materials? Does one partner have the know-how and reputation to take advantage of that opportunity?
- *Sharp focus*: There is a strong correlation between success of a venture and clear overall purpose that is specific, concrete, timely, and measurable.
- *Commitment and support*: Unless top and middle management are highly committed to the success of the venture, there is a little chance of success. (*Nation's Business*: May 1996, V84, p. 26)

Outsourcing activities that can be performed more efficiently and economically by other organizations and focusing on things in which the leading organization has expert skills have great payoff for organizations. The Outsourcing Institute, a professional association for objective, independent information on strategic use of outside resources, reported that outsourcing is being utilized in every facet of business—from information technology to business support services to human resource staffing to fleet vehicle management. A 1994 survey conducted by the institute, found that, on average companies are seeing a 9 percent cost savings and a 15 percent increase in capacity and quality through outsourcing. Furthermore, the survey showed that the decision to outsource was very much a top-down decision with 61 percent of the outsourcing companies stating that it was the result of a top executive directive.

The motivating principle of external networking is powerful: Interdependence helps boost both speed and quality, two essential ingredients in a world of rapidly increasing product cycles. Close customer-supplier relationships can help trim costs, disseminate quality-enhancing management techniques across boundaries, enlist suppliers' technological expertise where the firm most needs it, and increase speed.

California Steel, for example, no longer produces steel itself, but rather it finishes steel products. It purchases basic steel from a joint venture located in Brazil that is owned by Brazilian, Japanese, and Italian interests. Each firm achieves gains in efficiency with this specialization within the same sector. Another example involves the success story of the synergy that brought together two companies, US Order and Colonial Data Technologies Corp., through symbiotic relationships (*Nation's Business*, 1996: vol. 84, May, p. 20). US Order, a small R&D software company had developed an electronic message transmitter, but had neither the manufacturing core technology nor the capacity to distribute the product. Colonial Data, on the other hand, had no R&D expertise but had the manufacturing and delivery systems needed to achieve economies of scale. The result: US Order is licensing its phone technology to Colonial Data to market to phone companies, and US Order will market to other groups of customers, including banks and paging companies. Each partner will pay the other 10 percent of the profits from products they sell in their respective markets. Both partners projected high returns: While US Order's sales volume reached $25 million by the end of 1996, up from $5 million in 1995 and half of that as a result of the alliance, Colonial Data reported that 25 percent to 33 percent of its 1996 revenue of $110 million were attributable to the alliance.

Firms establish joint ventures, partnerships, or strategic alliances with other firms, including their competitors, to reduce the costs and cycle time of product development and spread the risks associated with the introduction of new products. IBM alone has joined in over four hundred strategic alliances with various companies in the United States and abroad. During 1992, for example, IBM teamed with Siemens and Toshiba to develop a costly new generation of DRAM computer chips. Later it teamed up with Motorola and Apple Computer to develop a microprocessor which can compete effectively with Intel's Pentium chip. Kabi, a Swedish company, joined the U.S. firm Genetech to develop a generically modified bacterium to stimulate human growth. Consequently, once the hormone was approved for sale, the two companies divided the production and marketing of the hormone, with Genetech being responsible for the North American market and Kabi being responsible for Europe. In automobile and aircraft industries, the costs and risks of product development are so high that competitors are actually forced into cooperation. For example, during the 1980s General Motors and Toyota shared the costs of developing the new Nova, costing them $2.5 billion together.

MCI has adopted partnerships as a growth strategy. Partnerships allow MCI to match its competencies in network integration and software development with the strength of other companies making telecommunications equipment. During 1993 and 1994, the company moved toward developing advanced computer technologies that provide wireless communications well beyond traditional cellular phones. The goal was to combine cell phones, answering machines, faxes, computer modems, and print media into one device with one phone number that will work anywhere in the country. Instead of analog technology that uses traditional radio waves, MCI hoped to develop digital mobile networks. In pursuit of this goal, MCI has invested $1.3 billion, buying a 17 percent stake in Nextel Communications, a New Jersey based company specializing in two-way radio systems for businesses. Two other companies have begun partnering with MCI and Nextel. Comcast, a big cable TV and cellular phone company based in Philadelphia, which will help market the products, was the first one. Comcast also owns 17 percent of Nextel. The other company was Motorola, which owns 20 percent of Nextel and will manufacture the phones (*Albany Times Union*, March 1, 1994, B-9). The strategic advantage for MCI was self-evident: MCI did not have to spend its own capital to fund research and development for hardware, which left more resources available for what it does best—network integration and software development. MCI's strategic alliances allowed the company to offer customers a package of hardware and services based on the talents, skills, and resources of as many as one hundred other companies (Byrne, 1993b).

To many organizations, networking appears as a strategic alternative to vertical integration. By decentralizing and linking the organization horizontally with other organizations, interorganizational alliances provide the essential flexibility for capitalizing on market opportunities. When McKesson Corporation, a giant drug distributor, was the subject of takeover rumors, particularly after Merck & Company acquired Medco Containment at the end of 1993 to ensure a high-volume customer channel for its products, its CEO rejected such rumors and reportedly saw no advantage in forging an equity partnership with any pharmaceutical manufacturer. Instead, McKesson expanded its PCS Health Systems division, which specialized in managing pharmaceutical costs for big health plan sponsors, to go beyond pharmaceutical management and become a full-fledged medical-services management company. In January 1994, McKesson bought an interest in Integrated Medical Systems, an electronic network that links doctors with hospitals and medical laboratories. McKesson reportedly uses the system to tie doctors into its pharmaceutical computer network, which is installed in 95 percent of the nation's pharmacies (Mitchell & Weber, 1994).

Partnering often goes beyond a symbiotic relationship to involve full collaborative relationships. Honda Motor Company relies strongly on supplier partnering. According to Honda's Vice President of Purchasing, 80 percent of a car is purchased from its suppliers (*Electronic Buyer's News*, 1995). Honda believes it is important to support the development of its suppliers in order to continue improvement as a company. Honda developed a "mini-reengineering" program for Donnelly, a Michigan-based manufacturer of car mirrors. The purpose of this partnering was to help Donnelly, with its "culture squared perfectly with Honda's," reframe its manufacturing processes to accommodate Honda's specifications (Magnet, 1994). As a result, Donnelly built an entirely new plant to make Honda's exterior mirrors, an unheard-of move that marked the commitment between the two companies. Motorola is another example. Like Honda, Motorola also looks for partners that share its values. Then it hones their skills by training them in its own TQM techniques at Motorola University. In addition, teams from Motorola tour suppliers' plants every other year, evaluating them on how well they stack up against their competitors on cost, quality, and timeliness. Suppliers are then rated, which serves as the basis for allocating Motorola business shares among the suppliers and their competitors. These moves, together with the requirement that suppliers reduce the cost of poor quality are expected to create opportunities for both sides to benefit from the partnership.

Often, partners run into a gridlock because of disagreements, or because of an inability to comanage the joint venture. Two options that the parent companies can use are to give one partner (preferably the one with the superiority in knowledge and skills) operating control over the venture, or to set the alliance up as a completely autonomous operation accountable only to its own board. Mazda markets Ford products under its own nameplate and also engineers some of Ford's small cars such as the Mercury Tracer, while Ford takes care of light trucks such as the Ranger.

Small entrepreneurial firms without the ability to afford staff on a full-time scale and which do not have enough capital are networking with others. They assemble just-in-time groups of organizations to design or manufacture a product. The core organization then coordinates activities within the network. This network is often called a virtual organization (VO), which provides both specialization and flexibility to its members. The VO is a temporary network of independent companies (or specialized individuals) linked through information technology (IT) to share skills, costs, and access in all respective markets. The VO shifts emphasis to electronic files, rather than physical files or even interpersonal verbal or social exchanges. Hence, the VO's computer-mediated communication (CMC) is the dominant pattern of communication, rather than face-to-face communication. VOs, therefore, substitute the need to organize labor into departments and units by areas of specialty with the need to organize information around core organizational competencies. As an organization without a formal structure of authority and without a traditional chain of command, the VO increases opportunities for participation through greater access to information.

The primary goal of the VO is to utilize an apparent competitive advantage. It is a fluid and flexible organization with a group of collaborators who quickly unite to exploit an opportunity. They integrate vertically, pull together their core competencies, and act in a concerted fashion (i.e., as a single company). Once the opportunity has been met, the venture dissolves itself. The rationale behind this temporary network is the optimization of the core capabilities of the systems involved as a whole. The strategy is to gain access to new markets or technologies by capitalizing on each others' distinctive competencies. For example, AT&T, Chemical Bank, and Time Warner have joined together for information technology development. Another example is the formation of the consortium between AT&T, IBM, and MIT to conduct research on superconductors.

The VO and the creation of systemic production networks are common in film, construction, telecommunication, and biotechnology industries. These firms use information technology to achieve functional integration without the liability of size. Firms can operate through highly decentralized units with the economies of scale of a centralized information system, thus becoming more competitive in the marketplace. Byrne (1993b, 98–103) described the virtual organization as the company of the future [and] the ultimate in adaptability with the following features:

- *Ad-hoc partnership*: Temporary network of companies that come together quickly to exploit rapidly changing opportunities. In a virtual organization, companies can share costs, skills, and access to global markets, with each partner contributing what it does best.
- *Information technology*: Informational networks will help link entrepreneurs and partner companies from start to finish. The partnerships are based on electronic contracts to keep the lawyers away and speed the linkages.
- *Excellence*: Since each partner brings its "core competence" to the effort, it may be possible to create a "best-of-everything" organization. Every function and process could be world class, something that no single company could achieve.

- *Opportunism*: Partnerships are less permanent, less formal, and more opportunistic. Companies are banding together to meet a specific market opportunity, and more often than not, fall apart once the need evaporates.
- *Trust*: These relationships make companies far more interdependent, which requires trust and mutual respect.
- *No borders*: This new corporate model redefines the traditional boundaries of the company. More cooperation among competitors, suppliers, and customers makes it harder to determine where one company ends and another begins.

Companies no longer have to own, manage, and control every activity needed to produce a product. They can create partnerships or interorganizational alliances with others to compensate for the missing specialty. Lacking the capacity to produce its entire line of PowerBook, Apple turned in 1991 to Sony to manufacture an inexpensive version of the PowerBook. It was a classic partnership, melding Apple's easy-to-use software with Sony's manufacturing competencies in miniaturization. A year later, after selling more than one hundred thousand Sony-made models, Apple terminated its agreement. AT&T used Japan's Marubeni Trading Co. to link up with Matsushiba Electric Industrial Co. to jump-start the production of its Safari notebook computer, designed by Henry Dreyfuss Associates. IBM and Apple Computer are using an interfirm alliance to develop multimedia systems based on the new chip they are developing together with Motorola to break Intel's dominance of the microchip market. Another example is Corning Glass, which may be a model for creating strategic alliances that work. By early 1993 it had nineteen partnerships which accounted for nearly 13 percent of its earnings in 1992. These alliances have permitted the company to develop and sell new products faster, to penetrate the market more thoroughly, and to generate greater revenues. Alliances are so central to Corning's strategy that the corporation defines itself as a "network of organizations." Through size and power, partnership provides scale but without the mass. The bulky bureaucracy is being bypassed!

NEW CHALLENGES FOR THE BROKER

Perhaps the major challenge for the Broker in initiating and establishing external networks is managing cultural adaptation and orchestrating the integration processes between networked organizations. When conflicts between partners erupt and become intense, these conflicts create pressure to terminate the alliance. TRW's alliance with Fujitsu in 1980—involving the use of the distribution system of the American company to sell the goods of the Japanese company—did not succeed and ended up with the partners blaming each other for the failure. In 1983, the venture was terminated when Fujitsu bought out TRW's interest. The Broker's challenge is to build trust with outsiders, manage interfaces, negotiate, and create win-win situations. Merck's joint ventures with Johnson & Johnson, DuPont, and AB Astra of Sweden took a very long time to craft. As one of Merck's VPs states: "You can hammer out a megamerger deal in sixty days, but these joint ventures can easily take a year to negotiate" (*Fortune,* September, 1992). Bridging between two or more cultures to collaboratively achieve mutual gains is very much a function of friendly relationships, partners behaving as equals, and a lot of trust. Building trust takes time, which requires increasing the time horizon of alliances. Ford and Mazda, at one time stiff competitors, have established a good relationship, which has also linked the two companies on projects where one partner may be less than optimally qualified.

Alliances, particularly with offshore companies, have become an integral part of organizational strategy. It is estimated that since 1985, the rate of joint venture formation between U.S. companies and international partners has been growing by 27 percent annually (*Fortune,* September, 1992, pp. 77–78). These alliances are successful to the extent that their parent companies are involved in long-term contractual relationships. The reason for prolonging the life of an alliance goes beyond making a quick profit. The long-term goal is to penetrate new markets or to exploit or gain access to new expertise. Some organizations are turning away from any linking programs for fear of losing control over the partnership. Moreover, the core organization is at risk of losing control over operations and runs the risk of losing proprietary information or technology. Corning Glass regularly has developed long-term relationships with its partners, as a top executive recalled:

> We are looking only for lifetime associations, because you have to invest an enormous amount of energy to make a partnership work . . . you not only have to deal with the business; you also constantly have to deal with the relationship you have with the partner—nurturing it and maintaining high-level contacts, so that when you deal with items of substance you will be dealing with friends, people you understand and respect . . . a partnership that is going to last only five to seven years simply doesn't warrant that kind of investment. (*Fortune,* Sept., 1992)

In business relationships, mutual economic benefits often help bridge the gap over conflicting interests between partners. Microsoft has maintained and has even strengthened its alliance with Apple Computer, supplying applications software for Apple's Macintosh, even though the two companies compete directly in some areas and Apple is pressing charges against Microsoft for allegedly stealing Apple's intellectual property. Outside of this bitter conflict, Microsoft has helped Apple Computer gain market share in the PC market, while Apple has helped Microsoft increase sales of its applications software. Steve Jobs, founder of Apple, noted that between them, Microsoft and Apple control 100 percent of the desktop market (*Information Week*, 1997). During the spring of 1997, the relationship had become stronger. Apple found itself having major problems staying solvent and solicited Microsoft to invest $150 million in Apple to write new programs for the Macintosh. Microsoft's new stake in Apple had restored Apple's market value and boosted the confidence of many corporate customers.

LINKING THE ORGANIZATION EFFECTIVELY

Senior managers must encourage mutual respect and create a positive work climate, which recognizes the need to transform the organization into a more adaptive and effective configuration. This adaptation involves the creation of a better coalignment of the organization, both internally by rearranging structures and processes and externally by strategically maneuvering the organization in the direction of greater interdependence with its external environment. This endeavor requires managers to negotiate linking programs with external systems, and therefore, to develop the competencies and skills that are important for boundary management. Brokering, political maneuvering, bargaining, persuading, negotiating, influencing, networking, and managing external linkages become the core competencies of the new leader.

The challenge for leadership is to network their organizations with other organizations in concentric circles, which optimizes the skills of the aggregate group. Enacting the role of Broker, organizational leaders identify partners with complementary specialties and develop symbiotic linkages that can help their organizations achieve adaptive efficiency. Multilateral arrangements among diverse organizations require a broader span of attention by organizational leaders—a span of attention with an outward focus that centers on identifying the right partners with expertise and financial resources. Partners are willing to collaborate in the design of new products, share the production costs, and spread the risks associated with the development and marketing of the new products.

Top executives act as brokers to link organizations, to coordinate key players within the network and to monitor the flow of resources across organizations. In a Broker capacity, managers play the role of architect, designing and assembling the network value chain. Once the network has been put in place, managers with coordinating skills assume the role of lead operator to render the network operative. When the network runs smoothly and effectively, other important Broker roles emerge—managers must act as boundary spanners, collecting, screening, and sharing information across the organizations that are part of the network value chain. These maintenance roles are essential for the success of the network (Snow, Miles & Coleman, 1992).

Creating strategic linkages and managing boundaries are not limited just to the territory of the organization's narrow strategic apex. Department and division heads within organizations are increasingly pushed to play a more strategic role in creating cross-departmental collaboration. They are also encouraged, and often are even given a mandate, to take their own journey into the intricate world of their business environment in order to network themselves with others. As one observer notes: organizations are nearly turning themselves inside-out, buying formerly internal services from outside suppliers, forming strategic alliances and partnerships that bring external relationships inside where they can influence company policy and practice (Kanter, 1989).

An important aspect of adaptation is the shift in management paradigms, leadership styles, and communication patterns that reinforces the new organizational forms and the new leadership roles described above. By adopting a loosely coupled structure with fewer hierarchical levels and a wider span of control, leaders must focus their attention on horizontal management. Horizontal management is not an easy task to accomplish. It involves a shift in paradigms, which requires managers to unlock their powerful mindset of vertical doctrine and drift toward a clan culture, which replaces authority lines with communication lines. Middle managers quite naturally become the subject of such change. The significant impact on the roles performed by middle managers is described in chapter 6. Managing and integrating horizontal activities, processes, and structures are important leadership responsibilities that are manifested in the Coordinator and Monitor roles, the subject of the next two chapters.

Part II

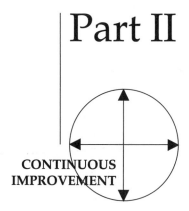

**CONTINUOUS
IMPROVEMENT**

The internal horizontal axis and the control vertical axis in the Competing Values Framework define the boundaries of the *internal processes model* and the domain of organizational *continuous improvement*. This model reflects the view that organizations are effective if they are stable and keep track of activities within the organization. Fundamental to this model is the need to upgrade the technical systems of the organization to match its structural capacity, coordinate and streamline work-flow processes, and monitor progress toward achieving organizational goals. The two managerial leadership roles associated with this quadrant are the Coordinator and Monitor roles.

COORDINATOR ROLE: THE ORGANIZER

In the capacity of Coordinator, the manager is expected to make sure that work flows smoothly and activities are carried out according to their relative importance with a minimum amount of conflict among individuals, work groups, or work units. The Coordinator is responsible for organizing and providing people with needed resources, linking individuals and groups sequentially or reciprocally, and monitoring their performance. Effective managers acquire, use, and dynamically integrate the competencies associated with the Coordinator role in managerial situations. These competencies are: managing projects; designing work; and, managing across functions.

The Coordinator maintains the structure and the efficient flow of work and information and focuses on stability and continuity in the work group. This role involves facilitation in various forms such as organizing the work load, assigning work-group members or professionals and determining job responsibilities, short-range scheduling, reporting and giving feedback, and synchronizing the activities of employees or professionals. Leading and coordinating across functions is an important competency that a team member enacts through knowledge about and understanding of work processes and through having the interpersonal and problem-solving skills essential to achieve joint performance (Rummler & Brache, 1990). In addition, project planning, management, and monitoring require knowledge of PERT, CPM, Gantt charts, and other techniques essential for effective integration. According to Davidson (1994), coordinators must also be skilled in the basics of contracting, business finance, integrating cost/schedule control, measuring work performance, monitoring quality, and conducting risk analyses.

MONITOR ROLE: THE EXPERT

In the capacity of Monitor, the manager is expected to set up an efficient system of information management, which can be used to plan, make decisions, and present information in a meaningful way. The Monitor is responsible for knowing what is actually going on in a work unit. Managers in this role must be able to keep track of the facts, analyze them, and decide which are important. Effective managers acquire, use, and dynamically integrate the competencies associated with the Monitor role in managerial situations. These competencies are: monitoring personal performance; managing collective performance; and, managing organizational performance. As a Monitor, the manager develops means for the work group to achieve compliance with work standards and evaluates whether group members meet their goals. The Monitor functions as an information giver who takes on the leadership role of providing constant feedback to employees about work processes and outcomes. As Senge (1990) points out, feedback allows individuals to draw rational conclusions about their performance and go through self-directed learning and self-improvement.

The chapters included in Part II—"Managing the Value-Based Organization: Horizontal Structures and Cross Functional Teams" and "Organizing around Processes and Outcomes: Quality Programs and Reengineering"—cover the principles and dynamics of moving toward a team-based design and organizing work around processes and outputs rather than functions. These two chapters highlight the importance of internal consistency in organizational operations through integration and monitoring of interdependencies within and across work units and teams. These two chapters examine the scope of leadership challenges faced by managers enacting the Coordinator and Monitor roles.

4

Managing the Value-Based Organization: Horizontal Structures and Cross-Functional Teams

That is the power of teamwork. What we are finding, frankly, is that having fewer people and limited resources does not have to be a liability—not if those resources are properly focused, and not if your people are organized so that they are genuinely turned-on and feel that their contributions really do make a difference.

—Robert Lutz, Research Technology Management 1994

Horizontal management goes beyond flattening organizational hierarchy. It involves changes in management attitudes and orientations, as well as leadership styles and communication patterns. It captures a whole new mindset of interpersonal communication, role relationships, internal motivation, conflict resolution, and reevaluation of work processes. Horizontal management involves creating a high-performance culture through relational management.

W. L. Gore & Associates, a Fortune 500 company, is a horizontal organization that effectively incorporates the principles of relational management in its form of organizing. Gore & Associates, which produces medical, camping, textile, and electronic products expanded from nineteen manufacturing plants with three thousand employees in 1983 to thirty-five plants with over five thousand employees in 1991.

The company's culture is known as a "lattice" organization, in which all employees are considered as equals. The underlying assumption of a lattice organization is that all employees ("Associates") should have direct access to one another in order to get their work done efficiently. Four operating principles are at the core of Gore & Associates' lattice organization (Barge, 1994):

- *Fairness*: associates should strive to be fair to each other, with suppliers and customers, and with anyone else with whom they deal.
- *Freedom*: all associates should facilitate each other's growth in knowledge, skills, and abilities. They should be encouraged to try new approaches and learn about new ways of thinking and working.
- *Commitment*: all associates should honor commitments made to other Gore associates and outside constituencies.
- *Waterline*: if a decision being made could severely injure the financial health of the company, hurt its reputation, or adversely affect its survival, the associates should consult with each other before taking any action.

In horizontal management, transactions and relationships are viewed through a supplier/customer perspective and along the value chain of the organization. From a communication perspective the advantage is self-evident—operators in horizontal organizations have less chance of developing transmission and reception problems because lines of communication are simpler, more direct, and shorter. Horizontal ties between process customers are replacing vertical ties as channels of activities and communications.

For organizational leadership, horizontal management turns its attention to customer needs rather than hierarchical interests. Processes and interfaces replace functions and areas of jurisdiction. Adaptive managers reorient their predominant approach from being auditors and evaluators to being coaches and facilitators by focusing their attention on process management and improvement. These managers take on multiple responsibilities, and therefore, must be cross-trained. An effective manager in a horizontal organization must have both depth and breadth—that is, an optimal mix between being a specialist and a generalist. At Pepsi-Cola Bottlers, located in Springfield, Missouri, all managers are cross-trained and know what is involved in the other managers' jobs. Both the marketing manager and the production manager, if required, can step in and run the other's unit.

Motorola's ten-step process improvement model provides a road map for the new management focus:

1. Identify the requirements of the external customer.
2. Flow chart the process.
3. Determine the major (most important) internal customers in each process step.
4. Determine the major functions/services in each process step.
5. Select the process step with the greatest improvement potential (this is the step with the largest quality problem from the external customer's point of view or with the largest cost or longest cycle time).
6. Determine main customer requirements—these are specifications from the next process customer.
7. Identify measures of effectiveness as negotiated between the customer and the process owner. Typical criteria are timeliness, accuracy, completeness, cooperativeness, etc.
8. Determine the cause of variance or gap in requirements.
9. Improve process steps.
10. Repeat steps 5–9 for the next process step, which is the one with the second greatest potential for quality, cost, or cycle time improvement. (Denton, 1991)

EMPOWERMENT AND INVOLVEMENT

TQM organizations that emphasize the use of cross-functional teams and that allow employees greater access to information, also encourage managers to empower their employees and increase their involvement. Empowerment is getting employees to assume ownership of work and organizational goals. Empowerment involves the delegation of managerial authority to employees and the creation of opportunities for employees to influence the outcomes of their work. Through empowerment, employees are presented with the challenge to take the initiative and control their own destiny. At the same time, employees must be accountable for their decisions, actions, and outcomes.

Employee involvement requires training so workers can participate in a meaningful way. They must know how to contribute. Managers should identify the important areas of job performance and leadership roles that must concern team members. Members also need to have process knowledge and be familiar with techniques such as statistical process control (SPC), just-in-time (JIT), and Pareto Analysis. Management must share information with team leaders and team members on a continuous basis. Initiatives in this direction often boost confidence and morale and lead to more effective communication. Ford's experimental program implementing participative management and employee involvement during the 1980s is a prime example of how such a program can lead to quality improvement and eventually to better performance in the marketplace. The success of the Taurus as the best car in the midsize category, replacing the Honda Accord, which had dominated the market for a long time, is an outgrowth of Ford's cultural shift and implementation of the new management philosophy.

Ford's eight-step process for launching employee involvement programs can also be used by other organizations undergoing cultural transformation. The first step involves gaining the support of management, front-line supervisors, and employees. Second, a joint steering committee must be established to indicate that both employees and management are equal partners in the process. This committee also trains the people who must champion the process. The third and fourth steps involve the diagnosis of potential obstacles and gains from implementing the process, and the selection of a pilot area for testing. The fifth step involves planning and setting up a program in the areas of problem solving, information sharing, and listening to guarantee successful implementation. The sixth step is the actual implementation in which the pilot groups experiment with the new approach to provide the steering committee with important feedback for further consideration and improvement. The final two steps in launching an employee involvement program are fine tuning and expanding the process as an organization-wide initiative.

Ford's experience shows how a highly vertical organization can move toward horizontal management. Ford's management has taken a systems approach and used a variety of employee involvement techniques to improve both employee commitment and global competitiveness. Ford's experience also illustrates that the move toward horizontal management through employee involvement is both evolutionary and revolutionary. Every level within the organization must be involved—it is an organization-wide effort. Empowerment and involvement must be backed up by both management and union leaders to achieve legitimacy of the cultural shift. At Ford, employee involvement received the blessing of the United Auto Workers and the top echelons of the company, including Don Peterson, Ford's president. The shift toward high employee involvement at Ford also involved the "frozen middle" through the initiation of the large-scale Leadership Education and Development (LEAD) program to stimulate transformational behaviors in middle managers.

Ford Motor Company's LEAD was based on cross-functional learning groups and self-assessment using the Competing Values Framework. Spreitzer and Quinn (1996), who conducted field research involving the LEAD program reported several interesting findings: Although all of the managers perceived barriers to change in their work environment, almost half of the middle managers initiated transformational changes. These findings corroborate the statements in chapter 6 supporting the role of the middle manager as a change leader. Second, it was found that middle managers making transformational change were viewed by higher-level managers as more effective than those making transactional or personal changes. On the other hand, those managers receiving the fewest promotions in the organization were the ones most likely to initiate the most profound changes targeted at the organizational level. One explanation is provided by Spreitzer and Quinn (1996, p. 255) who hypothesized that

> given concerns about job security, these plateaued managers may have initiated transformational change targeted at the organization out of fear for their job . . . on the other hand, the LEAD program may have prompted plateaued middle managers to redefine the risk-reward ratio . . . With lessened pressure for political conformity, the person may feel able to listen to his or her inner voice regarding the appropriate path for change.

An important conclusion of these researchers was that middle managers, who normally assume transactional roles, are also capable of making transformational change. Hence, senior managers must be increasingly sensitive to morale and attitude issues, as well as supportive of the middle managers who may initiate, facilitate, and or implement the change. These plateaued middle managers, who are involved in transformational change due to personal change or a value-maximizing behavior to secure their jobs, paradoxically are those who are targeted by the downsizing efforts of senior managers. The downsizing organization may be losing precisely the people who can enhance the organization's responsiveness through transformational change (Spreitzer & Quinn, 1996). A deeper discussion involving this dilemma and other issues relating to behaviors and responsibilities of middle managers is included in chapter 6.

DIMENSIONS OF EFFECTIVE EMPLOYEE INVOLVEMENT

Both employee involvement and empowerment ease the transference of leadership roles to teams and individuals. However, employees are expected to be accountable by accepting ownership to the added managerial responsibilities and leadership roles that have been delegated to them. They must behave responsibly, maintain a positive attitude, and produce the desired expected outcomes. Magjuka (1993) suggested ten dimensions along which the effectiveness of employee involvement can be evaluated. These dimensions are described below:

- *Range of issues*: Most involvement programs are geared primarily toward issues of work load, work conditions, and other HR utilization issues. However, involvement should also concern process improvement issues such as reducing production cycle time.
- *Team staffing*: Involvement has a higher rate of success with heterogeneous, multifunctional group composition. Group diversity involving members of line units and staff units leads to joint performance that is necessary in many continuous improvement efforts.
- *Company policy*: Involvement can range from voluntary to mandatory activity anchored in the company policy. The latter is recommended since it creates a commitment environment in which involvement is a core value of the organization.
- *Supporting teams*: Teams must be given opportunities to meet regularly in order to attain the constancy of purpose for an effective TQM initiative.
- *Training*: Training is essential for both managers and employees and should cover the following: How to use information to improve operations; teamwork; problem solving; administrative/functional (e.g., cost accounting, finance, etc.).
- *Access to information*: Institutional as well as administrative barriers should be removed. Involvement effectiveness can be enhanced greatly when employees' accessibility to institutional and administrative information, including accounting data on profitability and operating costs and information about product and market competitiveness, is relatively accessible.
- *Financial rewards*: Companies which compensate employees on an overtime basis for extra hours spent on employee involvement activities also create highly responsive and highly motivated participants.

- *Performance management systems*: Employee involvement programs should be tied with the company's existing management performance system.
- *Goal-setting structure*: Measurable goal setting helps teams improve task performance. Symbolically, the measurement of performance shows that involvement is highly valued.
- *Leading supervisor*: Groups that are led by supervisors with critical links to networks of communication are likely to have more access to company information essential for their functioning and involvement.

TEAM LEADERS: THE KEY TO QUALITY

Team leaders are to quality efforts what first-line supervisors are to business operations. Team leaders are the critical links between the concept of quality and its implementation through employee involvement. Team leaders tend to come from two groups in an organization: supervisors and technical experts (Isgar, Ranney & Grinnell, 1994). Supervisors, who delegate and encourage participation, and technical experts, who encourage contributions from others, naturally are potential candidates for leading quality teams. Often, supervisors have difficulties in relinquishing control, while specialists are locked in vertical thinking, creating barriers to effective team leadership and communication. Both need to work on their leadership skills and small-group-processes skills. Team leaders are expected to do the following:

- Teach quality concepts and team dynamics
- Get team members involved in problem solving
- Work well with other people across units and levels
- Help the team develop a charter of boundaries and outcomes
- Share information, establish norms and expectations, clarify roles, and build trust among team members
- Resolve conflicts and manage the interpersonal aspects of the team

Team leaders are often assisted and supported by team sponsors, who have direct communication lines with the steering or quality committee within the organization. The sponsor serves as the team's liaison to higher-level managers and helps facilitate internal and external team communications. Sponsoring the teams is critical whether the team is designated by management (top-down team) or by employees (bottom-up). A top-down team is aimed at addressing cross-functional issues. The sponsor mediates the translation of management objectives into operational goals that are carried out by team members. Bottom-up teams are aimed at making improvements within work units and building employee commitment. The sponsor helps the team clarify goals and develop a charter. He or she also serves as the communication link (boundary coordinator) for the team.

ORGANIZATIONAL LEADERSHIP AND EMPOWERMENT

Managers are expected to communicate the goals and tasks clearly and provide resources to employees. These managers specify the extent of authority to be granted, encourage commitment and participation, show trust and confidence in the abilities of employees to perform, stimulate innovative thinking, and give constructive feedback. Implicit in empowerment as an organizational core value is employees' openness to learning and managers' commitment to transfer knowledge to them. To transform organizations into more horizontal structures, the knowledge gap between managers and nonmanagers must be reduced. Effective empowerment can help reduce this gap and facilitate the transition toward the new culture.

Managers in their new capacities as leaders, facilitators, and coaches must encourage employees to take risks and act innovatively. Having a high tolerance for errors (within a range of mutual acceptance) should be a primary trait of the new leader. It should be made clear that horizontal management and empowerment do not breed dependence or independence. The goal is to achieve higher interdependence. No one can empower or be empowered without interactive engagement with others.

Empowerment is transactional in the formation of technical and operational interdependence. It is also transformational in the evolution of a new culture and mindset. Transactional characteristics of leaders and managers must be balanced against transformational characteristics. Bennis (1989) described the difference as "those who master the context and those who surrender to it." Some of his examples are: the manager administers; the leader innovates. The manager maintains; the leader develops. The manager relies on control; the leader relies on trust. The manager does things right; the leader does the right things. Leadership in horizontal organizations does not reside in one location, but rather in all persons. Leadership is fluid: It is distributed, rotated, and shared. Team members are expected to be involved in all phases of problem solving, not only its execution.

Managers and nonmanagers are encouraged to understand the need for continuous improvement through the prism of meeting customer requirements. They must also be provided with a structure that supports and guides the new requirements. Leadership is about constructing a new paradigm, a new ideology, and a new vision through which organizational members can be pulled together. Horizontal management is the framework and empowerment is the means to achieve this transformation. The new management philosophy calls for an empowered organization to continually improve its processes and delight its internal and external customers. All employees and teams must be aligned and motivated to work efficiently and provide defect-free products and services. GE's movement toward horizontal management, which also incorporates the important element of self-confidence, is a case in point. If people do not feel that they are trusted and respected, and do not have a sense of self confidence, both empowerment and employee involvement are doomed to fail. GE also emphasizes simplicity by stripping its organization of redundant work and unnecessary bureaucracy. Coupled with greater delegation of managerial and technical responsibilities to lower levels, simplicity should lead to higher speed and agility. The technique used to create the new culture and motivate employees at GE is called "Work-Out." Later, Work-Out will be discussed in detail. For now, a brief description of its goals and processes should be sufficient.

Work-out was designed initially as a means for implementing organization-wide, cross-functional teamwork. It was intended to identify sources of frustration and bureaucratic inefficiency, eliminate unnecessary and unproductive work, and overhaul how employees are evaluated and rewarded. In New England-style town meetings, which are the essence of Work-Out, participants use brainstorming to identify issues and concerns across the entire spectrum of work activities. The primary goal of these sessions is to "flush out" ideas, agree on recommendations, and identify specific actions for implementation. Some of these ideas can be taken care of immediately or with only short-term, single-person follow-up. Others will require more long-term follow-up procedures by an individual or team before a resolution is achieved, and can evolve into a process quality improvement (PQI). A typical PQI involves a group session where the participants perform an in-depth review of a particular process of concern, with an emphasis on finding ways to improve the process from both employee and customer service standpoints.

Once a process for improvement has been identified, one member is assigned ownership. This member, the champion, is someone who feels strongly that resolution of the issue is important and is willing to take on the leadership role and work with others if necessary to reach the goal of improvement. The champion is supported by a sponsor who helps overcome obstacles, offers advice, secures resources, and so on. Typically, this sponsor is a functional or project manager who is most logically associated with the issue under study. In addition to the champion and sponsor, another member is assigned as a facilitator to help the team through the Work-Out program. This member handles logistics, provides structure, and maintains group focus. The facilitator is not intended to lead or control, but instead serves as a catalyst for the overall Work-Out process.

MOVING TOWARD HORIZONTAL MANAGEMENT

Large, capital-rich organizations, in addition to external networking, must engage proactively and continuously in reengineering efforts geared toward compressing their structures and delinearizing their processes to become more agile and customer focused. They must think and act like small organizations. Thinking and acting small is what Jack Welch preaches and practices. According to Welch:

> Speed is really the driver that everyone is after. Faster products, faster product cycles to market. Better response time to customers. And there is no question that the smaller one is, and the easier the communication, the faster one gets. The customer is a much more real person to you . . . satisfying customers, getting faster communications, moving with more agility, all these things are easier when one is small. And these are all the characteristics one needs in a fast moving global environment. (Smart & Dobrzynski, 1993)

Large organizations with proactive management pursue greater adaptive efficiency by employing elements of horizontal management to realize the benefits of acting like small organizations. GE, DuPont, IBM, and ABB (Asea Brown Boveri) all have shed employees, layers of management, and old ways of doing things. They have reengineered work processes and raised efficiency by implementing quality initiatives, multifunctional work groups, and empowerment. As one observer notes: "Top-heavy organizations are out. Slender, nimble ones are in" (Byrne, 1993a, p. 34). Horizontal management is reinforced by high-speed communications, elimination of useless work and the people who do it, and running what remains with a new set of principles and skills.

Horizontal management is belt-tightening the smart way; it is getting rid of slack resources, because slack, by definition, is the basis for inefficiency. Lawrence Bossidy, the chairman of Allied Signal, captured this idea assertively: "Most struggling companies are over-managed and under-led. Having too many resources is the basis of a lot of failure. I try to make sure my people don't have enough of what they want" (Byrne, 1993a, p. 35). What follows is a description of a cutback process that many organizations use to reduce the number of middle managers and delegate managerial and technical responsibilities further down the lines. By the end of the 1980s, DuPont had cut 25 percent of its workforce and two layers of management were stripped away. Pepsi Cola followed the same path. By 1992 two layers of management were eliminated and the pyramidal structure had been reversed with field representatives put at the top. Ameritech, one of the Baby Bells, uses a wide span of management, as high as thirty to one, in most of its units. Elimination of people often is accompanied by the elimination of nonvalue work or tasks. All of the companies mentioned above have downsized their organizations by doing the following:

- Delayering to 5–6 levels of management
- Widening the span of control to 1/20 ratio as a basis
- Downsizing the workforce and eliminating 25 percent to 50 percent of the work tasks
- Training the surviving managers with new skills and responsibilities
- Compressing major functions into semiautonomous units to gain the economies of entrepreneurship and offset the liability of scale
- Rightsizing corporate headquarters' staff by half or even more

Denton (1991) outlined several prerequisites for moving toward horizontal management and the type of leadership needed in the new culture: Motivation, assessment, knowledge gap, cross-training, partnership, ownership, and lines of communication.

A strong motivation to change: Globalization, tough competition, high-quality products and low-cost production by offshore producers, shrinking market share, and low profits have forced American companies to streamline operations and become more efficient, faster, innovative, and more responsive. Corporations have begun to downsize and delayer their structures to become leaner and decentralized. Ford's eight-step process, discussed above, provides a good roadmap for organizations contemplating change. Ford first built up support and commitment to the change, developed awareness of the new partnership culture, diagnosed what is needed to achieve successful outcomes, planned the change and experimented with the idea, and then assessed, fine tuned, and widely implemented it.

Assessing the outcomes of change: A continuous improvement process requires feedback and self-correction. When Met-Life launched its Quality Improvement Process (QIP), it began with identification meetings intended to verify the type of transaction which existed for each department and its customers. The meetings concentrated on answering the following questions:

1. What are our products/services?
2. Who are our customers?
3. How do we measure our effectiveness? (How do we know whether we meet customers' requirements?)

Next, a product champion was assigned to oversee the quality application of QIP for a particular product or service. Met-Life then built up a quality network consisting of multifunctional work groups from branch to corporate levels. These teams engaged in targeting processes with high complexity for simplification and streamlining. The challenge was threefold:

1. How to improve customer satisfaction.
2. How to measure/increase effectiveness.
3. How to eliminate extra processing (EP) such as rework, scrap, and waste.

- An important element in the improvement process involves the setting up of a system which regulates how well improvement objectives are being met and whether gaps between perceived services and expected services are being reduced or eliminated.

Closing the knowledge gap between managers and nonmanagers: Workers must be exposed to broad factors affecting organizational operations and outcomes. They not only want to contribute, they also want to understand their impact on organizational outcomes, how they fit into the decision-making structures, how they can influence policies and procedures, the direction of organizational strategies and goals, and the vision of the organization.

GE's Work-Out provides an example. In an interview conducted at GE CEO Jack Welch's office in Fairfield, Connecticut by Tichy and Charan (1989), he suggested that Work-Out had practical and intellectual goals. The practical goal was to eliminate the machine bureaucracy that had dominated GE for decades and to move toward a knowledge-based, information-sensitive culture. The second objective, the intellectual one, began with

> putting the leaders of each business in front of . . . their people, 8–10 times a year, to let them hear what their people think about the company, what they like and don't like about their work, about how they are evaluated . . . and spend their time . . . Work-Out exposes the leaders to . . . their business opinions, feelings, emotions . . . we are talking about redefining the relationships between boss and subordinate. I want to get to a point where people challenge their bosses every day: "Why do you require me to do these wasteful things? Why don't you let me do the things you shouldn't be doing so you can move on and create?" That's the job of a leader—to create, not to control. (Tichy & Charan, 1989, p. 118)

- Multidisciplinary workforce and cross-training—"T-shaped skills": Specialists with narrow areas of expertise typically suffer from a vertical-thinking syndrome. They tend to work in series, sequentially linked to one another. Horizontal management demands parallel thinking and processing of information. The creation of flatter organizational structures must be reinforced by people with a wider knowledge and understanding of all aspects of work. Training must support this need by exposing people to a broader range of technical and interpersonal skills. The concept of T-shaped skills captures the essence of this requirement—having a preference for a deep expertise in one discipline combined with enough breadth to see its connections with others. T-shaped skills essential for effective management at the middle level will be discussed later.
- Partnership: Full partnership between managers and non-managers creates an empowered organization. Setting New England town meetings, forming horizontal networks, conducting quality circles, and establishing cross-functional

teams encourages participation and contribution of the people involved. But these methods of involvement must be supported by power sharing and delegation. To avoid having an empowered vertical organization and a partial partnership, employees must have the power to decide and take actions whenever necessary to improve performance. Only by delegating actual decision making, can individuals and teams at all levels become real partners in the transformation toward the new culture.

- Ownership: Having a real stake in the company's equity can influence employees to make the connection between their efforts and the bottom line. As Denton (1991, p. 200) skillfully pointed out: "If they do make the connection, it will empower vertical organizations, but it will supercharge horizontal ones."

- Lines of communication: Lines of communication must replace lines of authority to make the transformation successful. Work flow and lateral communication should take precedence over the chain of command. The customer/supplier relationship should be substituted for the superior/subordinate relationship. Denton (1991, pp. 200–201) succinctly proposed: "Boss/subordinate relationships are unequal; customer/supplier relationships are [even], for they focus not on position in the pyramid, but rather on function . . . whatever the function, organize all work around the function and do not get stuck conceptually on titles, levels, or hierarchies. Ask: what form needs to exist so we best serve our function?"

This function, of course, defines the scope of individual performance within a process. Developing knowledge and having diverse responsibilities within a process is essential both for turning out superior products and services and for effective communication between performers. Top leadership must encourage knowledge acquisition and the development of skills that can support a horizontal form. Salary, rewards, and incentives must be knowledge based rather than position based. Promotions should be through lateral movements rather than vertical ones. Career ladders in flat, horizontal organizations are ladders without administrative steps; they provide performers and specialists with more complex work, greater responsibilities, and more challenging and stretching goals.

Texas Instruments, for example, introduced a lateral approach to career moves called a "technical ladder." Engineers can now move through junior position, associate engineer, engineer, senior engineer, master engineer, member of group technical staff, fellow, and senior fellow. Texas Instruments' technical ladder illustrates that a transformation to a horizontal arrangement eliminates upward positions, but does not necessarily result in the loss of status. People have another direction in which to move and can still earn just as much money. Flat organizations do not necessarily mean that people will plateau or peak earlier in their professional careers. At Price Waterhouse (PW), the "move-up-or-out" philosophy caused them to lose technically oriented consultants to firms that did not have that philosophy. PW either held employees back because they didn't fit a managerial profile or if the firm continued to progress them, they would hit a glass ceiling. PW's response to this problem was to alter its structure and move from an "up-or-out" philosophy to a three-step ladder approach (Management Consultant International, 1995). In this new system, consultants are divided into three steps: consultant, principal consultant/director, and managing director/partner. This approach gives the employees the opportunity to progress or stay at one level and become specialists in a particular area. It is also beneficial for PW because their clients increasingly require more specialized skills and senior personnel than in years past. Thus, other avenues exist to serve as external motivators. The challenge for transformational leaders is to provide enough coaching and training so that professional growth can occur in the right direction.

- Creating efficient work flow: Elimination of artificial functional barriers among performers is one way to move toward a fluid, flexible boundaryless organization—an integrated organization without walls between departments; an organization in which people work in cross-marketing, joint purchasing, and cooperative product and market innovation. Getting rid of functional walls and employing self-directed work teams within the operating core (and perhaps other parts of the organization) can help direct organizational energy toward streamlining and standardizing important processes through an integrated information system. This system can provide timely information about customer specifications, inventory, and the like, to various decision centers within the organization. The system helps speed up communication processes at the shop floor and outside, and also eliminates the need for making decisions. DuPont's successful experience is an example of how decisions can be automated through expert systems.

Mrs. Fields Cookies' information system used by the company in the late 1980s is a good example of how and why decisions sometimes must be eliminated. The company ran a nationwide business of hundreds of stores through a sophisticated computer system. Many of a store manager's daily decisions were routinized and controlled through this information system. The system monitored sales by the hour, offered suggestions to keep actual sales in line with hourly goals, told the manager when to make up additional batches of cookies, scheduled work crews, helped with employee selection, and directed equipment breakdown problems. This automation of decisions allowed the company to maintain a very flat organizational structure, a spatially dispersed operation with low-skilled personnel. This system helped the company maintain highly controlled product uniformity and product quality by bringing Mrs. Field's expertise to every store. At McDonald's a computer program tells the manager what size crew is needed each hour of the next week. On that basis, temporary employees are assigned shorter or longer hours. Since labor is highly substitutable, the high turnover of employees is balanced against quick replacement where a new employee can be trained in twenty minutes and come up to top speed in about half an hour.

LEADERSHIP IN HORIZONTAL STRUCTURES

Once transformational leaders create an infrastructure in which the knowledge gap has been reduced, a full partnership exists, lines of communication substitute for lines of authority, a knowledge-based system of promotion is established, functional barriers are removed, and decision making is automated, the road toward horizontal management is opened up.

Kanter (1989) suggested that horizontal management involves four important transformations:

1. There are a greater number and variety of channels for taking action and exerting influence.
2. Relationships of influence shift from the vertical to the horizontal, from chain of command to peer networks.
3. The distinction between nonmanagers and managers blurs, especially in terms of information, control over assignments, and access to external relationships.
4. External relationships become increasingly more important as sources of internal power, influence, and even career development.

Horizontal organizations are not only leaner and flatter, they also have a variety of different channels for action. Among these channels are:

- Cross-functional projects
- Joint ventures at the division level
- Innovation funds that generate activities outside mainstream budgets and reporting lines
- Strategic partnerships with suppliers or customers
- Comanagement involving union representatives and managers

These channels for action overlay the traditional organization chart, with collateral networks, or power centers substituting for the chain of command. As the need for greater networking within and outside the organization arises, the role of these power centers tends to increase. Meanwhile, the latitude of those with formal authority and position-based power tends to diminish. More and more opportunities for greater flexibility and speed continue to erode the chain of command to the point that it becomes unnecessary or redundant. As a result, the ability of managers to get things done depends more on their horizontal power and less on their vertical power. Network centrality or location within the flow of communication, high visibility, relevance, criticality, and nonsubstitutability become important sources of power. Interpersonal communication, bargaining, dialogues, negotiations, and the use of knowledge and information become the tools for persuasion and influence, instead of unilateral decisions and impersonal commands.

Another source of power and influence comes from the ability of the new manager to manage interfaces, scan the business environment for resources and opportunities, and strategically link business units with external customers, suppliers or partners.

> As managers and professionals spend more time working across boundaries with peers and partners over whom they have no direct control, their negotiating skills become essential assets. Alliances and partnerships transform impersonal, arms length contracts into relationships involving joint planning and joint decision making. Internal competitors and adversaries become allies on whom managers depend for their own success." (Kanter, 1989)

Developing networks of cooperative relationships between key organizational stakeholders helps to link the organization horizontally and better coalign its different components.

According to Denton (1991), the transformation can be accelerated with three factors in place:

1. Fluid leadership that determines goals and objectives based on competency.
2. Cross-functional communication networks that help sustain the new culture.
3. The existence of transparent knowledge and information; communication flows in a nonrestrictive manner and knowledge is readily available to everyone.

When these factors exist, they give rise to the emergence of a decentralized, team-based organization.

DECENTRALIZED, TEAM-BASED ORGANIZATIONS

When it comes to renewal and innovation, size is a barrier to flexibility and adaptation. Large organizations, however, can grow by diversifying themselves in a decentralized way. They can spin off elements of their organizations so that they stand as self-contained, quasi-autonomous units with the ability to self-organize themselves. Organizations can also use multifunctional teams with the essential resources to perform jobs that cut across organizational lines and that are capable of managing themselves. The whole thrust behind decentralization is to create small business units (profit centers) that are staffed with empowered, cross-trained employees who have the ability to adapt quickly to the variations of local environments. Decentralization permits quick response to market changes, allows reconfiguration of organizational structure as needed, and could potentially lead to better coalignment and adaptation processes.

Decentralization stimulates flexibility, and flexibility, in turn, breeds versatility, which is the key to managing shorter production runs and utilizing rapidly advancing technologies. Decentralization creates a fluid network of interactions within the organization as well as between organizations. In team-based organizations that are also decentralized, functional tasks are virtually eliminated and organizational resources are focused on customers. Team objectives are external and span functions and departments. Work is structured primarily around a small number of core processes or work flow performed by multidisciplinary teams linked in a network to outside suppliers and customers. The teams have a trained capacity to deal with all aspects of their processes and are given considerable latitude in managing their work. They are held accountable for measurable performance goals and are evaluated and rewarded through a compensation system which recognizes collective contribution and is based on customer feedback.

The shift toward team-based forms is prevalent in large organizations where both individual and mutual accountability are stressed. Eastman Chemical Company spun off as a stand alone company with its senior executives organized in teams that span several functions and departments. AT&T's Network Systems Division reorganized its entire business around thirteen core processes. Each process has an "owner" and a champion. While the owners focus on the daily routines of a process, the champions ensure that the process is linked with overall business strategies and goals. Budgets are based on processes such as the maintenance of telecommunication networks, rather than on functions or departments. Employee performance is measured and rewarded based on customer feedback and evaluation of how well the teams have met their requirements.

GE's lighting business collapsed its vertical structure to create a senior team composed of managers with multiple competencies, who oversee about one hundred processes worldwide, ranging from product design to improving the performance of production machinery. In virtually all of the cases, multifunctional teams have worked to achieve the goals of the process by looking at the value chain sequentially rather than consequently. The teams are self-managed to perform their daily routines. Team members are rewarded based on their knowledge and skills as they relate to their customers' needs and on the results generated from a 360-degree appraisal system. The senior team allocates resources based on processes, not functions, and ensures coordination across processes.

TEAMS AND TEAMWORK: SHIFT OF EMPHASIS

Quality improvement and its principles of customer focus and process orientation cannot take root in the culture of an organization unless its values are embedded into the underlying design of the organization. Many organizations in the automotive and computer sectors, for example, have already begun to activate the link between human resource initiatives, such as teamwork, and their reward and compensation systems that are based on team performance.

Traditionally, profit-oriented companies rewarded their employees based on individual performance and outputs. But new studies conducted by the American Quality Foundation and Ernst and Young have shown that the profile of practices used to assess the performance of individuals within organizations has shifted. The top four assessment criteria for senior managers in the automotive sector were found to be:

1. Profitability
2. Individual performance
3. Quality performance
4. Team performance

The projection for the 1990s was that profitability would still top the list, closely followed by quality performance and team performance. Individual performance would drop to the bottom in terms of emphasis. This pattern has also been validated in the computer industry, although team performance was found to be ranked ahead of quality performance in both current and projected terms. Similar shifts have been anticipated in both industries for middle management and nonmanagement levels as well (*Industry Week*, April 6, 1992).

Teams and teamwork have become the underlying foundation of many corporate revolutions. Team culture recognizes the need to reconcile individual with collective contributions, whereas the focus of working groups has always been on individual goals and accountabilities. Teams focus on the synergy between individuals and on joint contributions. Work groups hold individuals responsible for their own results, whereas in teams individuals are collectively responsible for team results. Katzenbach and Smith (1993) have provided the following working definition for a team: A team is a small number of people with complementary skills, who are committed to a common purpose, set of performance goals, and approach, for which they hold themselves mutually accountable. Regardless of the initial direction of the teams' objectives, whether they are developed internally or externally, the essence of a team is mutual commitment and collective ownership of the team charter and goals. Building ownership and commitment energizes the team to win, to be first, and to remain innovative and transformational.

Teamwork is the ideological element that holds team members together and is what distinguishes teams from work groups. In a synergized team, performance levels are much greater than the sum of the individual's performances. Teamwork is an integrative process where 2+2=5. Teamwork creates a favorable climate which includes:

- Mutual respect for others
- High trust and confidence in the abilities of members
- Support

- Tolerance for ambiguity
- Acknowledgment of the accomplishments of others

Teams have very specific goals, such as reducing cycle time by 50 percent or developing a new product in less than half the normal time. These specific goals create shared meaning, lead to high cohesiveness, and distinguish the team as a separate entity. According to Katzenbach and Smith, "specific team performance goals help to define a set of work products that are different both from the organization-wide mission and from individual job objectives" (1993, p. 113). This specificity of goal performance holds the team together, facilitates communication, helps resolve conflicts, and maintains their focus on getting results. Specific results make the team's norms and ideology unique and help team members even out the power distance and avoid status or personality differences.

CROSS-FUNCTIONAL TEAM DESIGN

Several characteristics common to all team designs include considerations of function, goal, market, customer, size, composition, cohesiveness, and competencies.

Function: Team members are selected based on their specialized skills and the knowledge they bring to get the work done. Depending on the various objectives for each team, some teams may consist of employees with specialized expertise within the same area, while other teams may be composed of experts with different specialties.

Goal: Teams are also formed cross-functionally or as multifunctional teams. These are the teams in which members are pooled to work together to create cross-functional synergies.

Market: Teams are formed according to the different products that organizations manufacture or the services they render. This approach to designing a team is most commonly used by companies that manufacture products in different ranges or provide various services to their customers. Each team is totally responsible for a specific product line from beginning to end.

Customer: Teams are created to deal with and respond to various types of customers or customer groups. For example, a medical team may consist primarily of physicians in different skill areas, while another team consisting of nurses may handle patients with a specific disease.

Size: Most effective teams have about ten members. Larger teams are more sensitive to process losses, particularly those involving communication and coordination. Larger size may also inhibit interactive relationships among members and create more opportunities for conflicts and cynicism.

Composition: Teams must have the right member composition. Ensuring the right mix of skills (functional diversity) means putting together a team with complementary skills essential for performing the team's job. Diversity can also promote learning from within since the group contains the resources and information needed for performance.

Cohesiveness: No team can work cohesively unless collective accountability is established. Mutual accountability should come from within. It is a cause and effect of mutual trust, understanding, and shared meaning and purpose. "When people work together toward a common objective, trust and commitment follow. Consequently, teams enjoying a strong common purpose and approach inevitably hold themselves responsible, both as individuals and, as a team, for the team's performance" (Katzenbach and Smith, 1993, p. 116). Team cohesiveness can be enhanced when it is built on nondependent trust. Nondependent trust rests on the reformation of a contribution/inducement or psychological contract between individuals and organizations. Employees take responsibility for their own careers and companies give them the necessary tools. To attain this new bond, organizations should:

- Hire employees who think their careers are their own responsibility
- Train workers to be employable people, not employees
- Outline for new employees the skills they need right away and those they will need in the future
- Conduct in-placement (by providing employability opportunities within the organization) before out-placement
- Maximize resources by using contract employees (Sorohan, 1994)

Competencies and skills: Team members individually and collectively can benefit from mastering the following competencies: teamwork, problem-solving and decision-making skills, administrative abilities, cross-functional or implementation skills, and interpersonal skills.

- *Teamwork skills* include learning about the features that make the group a team (e.g., psychological awareness of belonging, high level of cohesiveness, work-flow interdependence), shared team leadership, resolving conflicts, participating in meetings, establishing goals and expectations.

- *Problem-solving and decision-making skills* are important for identifying the problems and opportunities teams face and for evaluating the options and necessary tradeoffs for moving the team forward. In addition, understanding input/output processes, dealing with variances or exceptions, and handling the team's interfaces are crucial for the success of the team.
- *Administrative skills* consists of skills such as record keeping, budgeting, scheduling, and allocating, process control, purchasing, and budget control.
- *Cross-functional or implementation skills* refers to the technical skills essential for task performance, maintenance and operational responsibilities (e.g., work scheduling, safety, planning, ordering supplies).
- *Interpersonal skills* include giving constructive feedback, active listening, and acknowledging achievements of others.

All of these skills must be present in teams at all times. An absence of certain skills (e.g., interpersonal skills) may lead to ineffectiveness in maintaining team harmony and sustaining team commitment. The most essential competence, however, which links all five skills, is giving and receiving useful feedback. The following guidelines for giving and receiving useful feedback are adapted from *Training and Development* (August, 1994, p. 12):

For sending feedback:

- Be specific rather than general.
- Be descriptive rather than judgmental.
- Make sure the feedback is about something the person can control.
- Speak only for yourself, not others or "the group."
- Use "I statements" to accept responsibility for your own perceptions and feelings.
- Make sure you are giving the feedback to be helpful, not punitive.
- Try to give positive feedback three times more often than negative feedback.

For receiving feedback:

- Listen carefully. Try to be open.
- Paraphrase what you hear to make sure you understand what the person giving the feedback means.

- Ask specifically for the kind of feedback you want, and describe the behavior about which you want feedback.

SELF-MANAGED TEAMS

Self-managed teams, like multifunctional teams (see below), are frequently used as a means for continuous improvement, but with varying scope and intensity of activities. Self-managed teams (SMTs) are formed to improve work unit functioning diagnostically by identifying problems and their solutions. Self-managed teams are formal, permanent work units—intact groups of employees that are highly interdependent, multiskilled, and responsible for a whole work process or segment that delivers a product or service to internal/external customers. Self-managed teams seek to create a critical mass of shared leadership. Since they operate as quasi-autonomous groups, leadership does move around fairly easily.

Most observers agree that team members' input skills, process orientation, and quality outputs are the main criteria to judge the effectiveness of self-managed teams (SMTs). Hackman (1990) for example, suggested three dimensions along which group effectiveness can be measured. The first dimension is the degree to which the group's output meets the standards of quantity, quality, and timeliness of the people who receive, review, or use the output. The second dimension is the degree to which the process of teamwork enhances the capability of members to work together interdependently in the future. The third dimension is the degree to which the group experience promotes the growth and personal well-being of the team members. Chapter 7 provides a focused discussion about leadership and communication processes in self-managed teams. In this section, important characteristics of SMTs are described to differentiate SMTs from other kinds of high-performance teams. These characteristics include:

- Work is designed to give the team ownership.
- Multiskilling gives team-based organizations the flexibility needed to handle shifting requirements and cover for absent members. It also provides members with a source of motivation through greater job challenges and a better understanding of the total process.
- The team is empowered to share leadership roles and responsibilities.
- Members perform traditional management functions.

- The team sets its own goals and schedules its own activities.
- Control and coordination are obtained concertively.
- The team trains its own people.
- Members deal directly with suppliers.

Why self-managed teams?

- Higher productivity—technical breakthroughs; cost containment; speed
- Greater quality—continuous improvement
- Greater flexibility—adaptability; problem solving
- Reduced costs—operating; overhead (for the organization)
- Responsiveness—technological changes are challenged and implemented to increase customer satisfaction
- Fewer job classifications—multiskilled
- Higher morale—self-motivated workforce
- Higher retention—committed people

Critical competencies that members of SMTs should have for effective functioning:

- Ability to learn and use a variety of skills
- Problem solving and critical thinking
- Attention to detail/focus on process improvement
- Brokering—being able to persuade/influence others
- Taking initiative
- Job/skills congruence
- Judgment/decision-making skills
- Interpersonal communication—presenting ideas
- Planning, organizing, controlling
- Teamwork and collaboration
- Tolerance for ambiguity
- Mutual training and coaching
- High work standards with a focus on quality

A work group becomes a team when:

- Leadership becomes a shared activity
- Accountability shifts from strictly individual to both individual and collective
- The group develops its own purpose or mission
- Problem solving becomes a way of life, not a part-time activity

- Effectiveness is measured by the group's collective outcomes and products

A team becomes self-managed when:

- Decision making and formal power are transferred to the team.
- No external supervision exists—objectives are adopted internally
- and the team makes/implements its own decisions.
- Interdependence is at its highest level.
- Norms and concertive control replace rules and formal, bureaucratic control.
- Compliance is gained through a shared value system.
- Leadership is distributed or shared reflecting facilitative responsibilities.
- Accountability is collective.
- The team is not a parallel unit, but rather an intact, in-place, multifunctional unit.
- The team has administrative oversight over planning, scheduling, monitoring, and staffing.

Two types of SMTs are common, production or service teams and problem-solving teams. Problem-solving teams, such as GE's Work-Out teams are intended to identify problem areas and derive solutions that are initiated by employees and supported by management. A problem-solving team is often associated with a process improvement team (PIT), which is a functionally heterogeneous group composed of four to six members and a team leader or a technical advisor. At the Press Fabrics Division of Albany International more than ten PITs work concurrently on different problems. These teams typically rely on process-mapping methods, such as flow charts, to target processes for improvement.

Problem-solving teams improve processes by:

- Identifying the customers and their requirements
- Defining the current process to meet their needs
- Determining the problems in the process, analyzing the process using problem-solving techniques, improving the process, and monitoring and planning for continuous improvement

Production teams, such as those employed by Saturn or Hannaford Bros., are intended to function with minimum supervision and with maximum autonomy in goal setting, work scheduling, resource allocation, evaluation, conflict resolution, staffing, training, and compensation. An example of a service team comes from Digital Equipment's Eastern Massachusetts Financial Management Center, which implemented the SMT concept in its accounting unit in 1992. Reportedly, members of the various teams employed high levels of empowerment and resource sharing while experiencing high motivation, high productivity, and improved communication (Cofsky, 1993).

QUALITY CIRCLES

Quality circles (QC) fall between production and problem-solving teams—they involve people from the work unit who are engaged in quality-improvement processes. Ownership and participation of QC are mostly voluntary. There is no obligation for employees to join the circle groups, nor are they penalized for not participating. Quality circles are generally characterized by the following attributes:

- A quality circle consists of a small group of people, usually composed of 4–10 employees.
- QCs are formed outside the chain of command and typically run parallel to organizational structure.
- Circle members are often grouped by their similar job functions, training, and related working background.
- Membership in the quality circle group is voluntary, as is the participation in quality circle activities.
- QC group meetings take place after work hours or after the completion of members' normal work routine.
- Every circle group is assigned a team leader by management to guide, monitor, and/or facilitate group meetings. Team leaders are also responsible for reporting and communicating group progress to management.
- The major emphasis of a QC is on work-related issues and innovative problem solving.
- QC groups only suggest solutions to problems and then present the options to management for review. The final decision about executing the decision is a management prerogative.

Quality circles represent an innovative practice in the workplace that emphasizes group problem solving and working as a team. The concept of QC is to get inputs from members of an organization to identify and propose workable problem-solving suggestions related to their specific jobs. Typically, QC teams formulate a problem statement in quantitative terms, use force-field analysis to map out constraints and opportunities, construct cause-and-effect diagrams, conduct a solution-impact analysis, and agree on an action plan.

MULTIFUNCTIONAL TEAMS

Multifunctional teams (MFTs) are formed to improve inter-unit functioning through integrating activities across organizational value chains. By cutting through functional lines and by cooperating in a process-oriented manner, they enhance the capability of the organization to respond quickly to market changes and to increase productivity. MFTs can be used by both middle-level management, who focus on the redesign of core processes or process innovation, and top levels, who manage the organization's alignment with the external environment. MFTs facilitate the transition to a horizontally structured organization and are usually part of an effort to eliminate layers and make employees think in terms of processes rather than tasks. They have proven especially effective in integrating marketing with production and delivery processes, thus stressing the critical factor of customer focus across the value chain. MFTs foster communication across organizational lines, create a supportive climate within the organization, and help link the organization with important external customers and suppliers. They have also been found to enhance the personal growth and professional development of team members (Hackman, 1990).

The strengths of MFTs lie in their ability to develop a sharper understanding of customers needs and expectations, make better, more balanced product decisions, work in parallel and therefore act quickly and plan and manage complex programs more effectively. MFTs create what Robert Lutz (1994) called "virtual enterprises"—a highly synergized working group that is a seamless value-added chain. Chrysler product development projects that consisted of multifunctional teams have reportedly outperformed their counterparts at Ford. Comparing the 1993 LH project with the original Taurus and Sable models introduced by Ford in 1986, Lutz clearly showed the superiority of MFTs over traditional work groups. Both programs spawned the same number of new vehicles. The Chrysler teams, however, were able to develop their cars in just thirty-nine months compared with the sixty to seventy-two months needed to develop the Taurus and Sable models. Moreover, the total cost for the entire LH program was $1.6 billion, including

$.6 billion for plant modernization. That was $1 billion less than what was reportedly spent on Taurus/Sable.

EFFECTIVE TEAM DEVELOPMENT

Uncovering and eliminating barriers to MFT work and communication processes is critical to the team's success. Prior to designing an MFT, the management team should identify key obstacles in the path of the future team. These barriers to success should be removed before the team is put into place, so as to assure that it has every opportunity to succeed. McKee (1992, p. 38) identified three key obstacles to MFTs: subject-matter barriers that deal with inappropriate team composition (lack of expertise); process barriers that involve institutional constraints, such as the need to receive prior approval by external supervisors before the team can move on with its task; and cultural barriers that may be represented by the old norms and habits of work that must be changed. One way to cope with these barriers is to form a "sacred-cow shooting committee" charged with enabling everyone to understand that no process is unchangeable (Stundza, 1993, p. 17). A more proactive approach is to develop systematically and sustain the capacity of the team to think and act collaboratively. Parker (1990) suggested a ten-step process for effective team development:

- *Get to know the team*: This requires that the team leader get to know about the background and experience of individual members of the team to identify their competencies, strengths, and weaknesses and determine how they will fit in with the team and what roles they might play.
- *Define the team's charter*: The team leader must communicate to the team his/her expectations about timetables, budget, and constraints. All questions must be met with complete openness to address concerns about the team's future. Involvement of team members in the formation of the team's charter and operative goals is essential.
- *Clarify roles*: Having team members understand what will be expected of them from the team will eliminate certain problems that may arise in the future.
- *Establish norms*: The importance of norms lies in the emergence of concertive controls that guide the team's goals and activities.
- *Draw up a game plan*: The game plan serves as a tool to monitor performance, assess progress, and make necessary adjustments.

- *Encourage questions*: The team leader is instrumental in establishing a climate that supports the expression of individual viewpoints and differences. Support and encouragement by the team leader will facilitate the willingness of team members to question the status quo and openly disagree with other team members when appropriate.
- *Share the limelight*: This involves giving recognition to deserving individuals for contributions, as well as acknowledging team results as a whole. It is important for the leader to give all team members an equal chance to be recognized.
- *Be participatory*: This requires the involvement of as many of the team members as possible in work assignments, decisions, and problem solving. When key decisions need to be made, the consensus method can be effective because high involvement usually leads to a better outcome.
- *Celebrate accomplishments*: By encouraging the team to plan celebrations to mark milestones and other significant team achievements, the leader can set the tone for the team to work hard and play hard.
- *Assess team effectiveness*: The team leader is responsible for initiating the process of periodically engaging in a systematic review of the team's competencies as a whole.

Multifunctional team development must be constantly supported via training to ensure that teamwork and the competencies needed to sustain the effort of the team are in place on an ongoing basis. Halpp (1993) suggested a list of fourteen checkpoints to ensure proper training to enhance the capabilities of the team:

- *Team orientation*: Provide a clear definition of the team's goals. Examine the differences between effective and ineffective teams. Show the team development cycle (forming, storming, norming, performing, transforming).
- *Boundaries analysis*: Identify team boundaries, roles, and responsibilities. Have the team identify all of their work inputs and outputs.
- *Communication basics*: Help team members develop their ability to listen, question, provide feedback.
- *Handling problems*: Identify immediate process problems and learn how to respond to them on the spot, as well as how to eliminate them long term.

- *Dealing with conflict*: Help the team understand where and when conflicts might arise and develop tactics for dealing with conflict one on one in a group.
- *Leading/participating in meetings*: Provide a structured agenda for leading meetings. Train members in how to lead and participate in meetings.
- *Coaching*: Have members practice coaching skills with each other. Give each a chance to give and get feedback, as well as to teach interpersonal and technical skills on the job.
- *Identifying quality problems*: Teach the basic continuous-improvement problem-solving methods. Begin with identifying improvement opportunities and analyzing problems using statistical methods.
- *Implementing improvements*: Practice setting improvement goals and planning and implementing projects or changes in work processes.
- *Documenting changes*: Work with the team to help members become adept at documenting improvements in terms of cost/benefit and selling ideas to management and others.
- *Evaluating/standardizing improvements*: Train the team in methods for evaluating and standardizing improvements.
- *Evaluating team performance*: Show the team how to develop work standards and to appraise both group and individual performance.
- *Leadership*: Review the role of the team leader, role rotation issues, situational leadership theory and practice. Help the team identify/select the best leadership styles for themselves.
- *Development planning*: Guide the team in developing skills in administrative areas such as selection, compensation, and discipline.

HIGH-SPEED COMMUNICATIONS

Teamwork effectiveness can be enhanced tremendously through collaborative computing, which allows members to share information without the constraints of time and space (Hsu & Lockwood, 1993). Through network applications, team members can be linked with one another across the room or across the globe. The principle is the same: collaborative or work-group technologies can transmit on-line information simultaneously to multiple users. E-mail, computer teleconferencing, real-time teleconferencing, and video-teleconferencing systems all help to create or to support electronic meetings.

Meeting environments are created through text and graphics on computer terminals or via audio and video messages transmitted from one location to another. Another application is electronic white boards, or live boards as they are often called, which electronically mimic the white board allowing team members to respond quickly to any stimulus.

Collaborative systems, in effect, give support to horizontal organizations by using high-speed communications that link everyone regardless of level, location, status, or personality. ITT in New York, for example, has been able to leverage its diversity to gain competitive advantage by providing its engineers in the electronics division with access to databases in its hotels division. Using the WAN, ITT's engineers seamlessly and electronically can share expertise and, concurrently, design products. Furthermore, using frame relay and asynchronous transfer mode, the company is able to keep employees in Europe, North America, and Asia in contact with one another (*Information Week*, 9/18/95). In essence, collaborative systems add a new on-line culture to the organization by further expanding the communication capabilities of individuals and teams.

MOVING TOWARD TEAM-BASED ORGANIZATIONS: PRINCIPLES AND APPLICATIONS

Ostroff and Smith (1992) proposed a ten-point blueprint for converting vertical structures into team-based horizontal organizations:

1. Organize around core processes and team-based work flow that is linked both upstream and downstream.
2. Flatten the administrative hierarchy by combining related tasks (that have been functionally fragmented) and by streamlining work through the elimination of nonvalue-added tasks.
3. Assign ownership of processes to top managers with multiple competencies.
4. Establish performance control systems based on customer requirements. All team members are expected to be involved in data collection efforts intended to verify whether internal/external customers' expectations with respect to quality, timeliness, cost, communications, and the like, have been met. This data is also used for evaluating and rewarding team performance.

5. Make teams, not individuals, the focus of organizational performance and design. Individuals acting alone do not have the technical skills required to continuously improve work processes.

6. Create self-managed teams by combining managerial and nonmanagerial activities. The teams must be supported by organizational resources and have access to essential points of information. They must be encouraged to take risks and maintain high flexibility in decisions and actions. The teams must be held accountable for measurable objectives.

7. Emphasize that while each employee should develop several competencies, only a few experts are needed with knowledge in a very specific area. Albany International's plant in East Greenbush, New York, is a good example. The company reduced job classifications from fifty-four to only four. Each team member has the technical knowledge of how to operate every machine used in the three important processes of weaving, melding, and finishing. Moreover, team members also have important interpersonal skills that are essential for group problem solving. Having cross-disciplinary competencies helps the team to maintain a high level of flexibility, creativity, and innovation.

8. Inform and train people on a just-in-time (JIT) basis, not on a need-to-know basis. Employees must have direct access to online information needed for task performance. At both Albany International and Hannaford Brothers, team members have access to immediate sources of information with respect to quality, cost, efficiency, and other performance measures. They are also trained in the use of quality tools, such as control charts, Pareto Analysis, and flow charting to track results and improve performance.

9. Maximize supplier/customer contacts to enhance continuous improvement and innovation. These contacts range from obtaining feedback through joint problem-solving meetings, such as those experienced at GE, to Motorola's inclusion of both customers and suppliers as members of in-house teams.

10. Reward individual skill development and team performance, instead of individual performance alone. Team-based organizations use a "pay for knowledge" approach to reward those who gain competence in multiple tasks as well as in interpersonal skills. At Motorola, Supply Management Organization, performance of team members is evaluated by peers based on

ten criteria including customer satisfaction, technical skills, team participation, communication skills, and the efficient use of resources.

AT&T is currently undergoing a transition toward a team-based structure incorporating many of the principles discussed above, in what has been labeled the "future work place." The drive at AT&T has been to change its culture through the following:

- Support of quality of work life/employee involvement
- Supervisors as coaches
- Creation of quality/customer satisfaction teams
- Continuous employee development
- Elimination of dead-end jobs

The goal is to reframe the organization into a team-based organization with the following characteristics:

- Boss becomes facilitator
- Real-time resolution by line teams
- Employees participate in problem solving
- Leaders provide resources and help form strategies
- The system is driven by subunit goals linked to corporate goals
- Understanding business competitors and customers

AT&T's future workplace shares many of the characteristics of horizontal management. The future workplace consists of self-managed teams, which are engaged directly with customers on the one hand, and with the business council on the other. Senior managers and union members form a comanagement group, called a Human Resource Board, which oversees the strategic business unit operations. The vertical hierarchy collapses, giving rise to an inverted pyramid.

Another example of implementation of a team approach is the Albany Veterans Affairs Medical Center (VAMC), a 440–bed facility, which provides comprehensive tertiary medical, surgical, psychiatric, and neurological care. Outpatient services are also provided through primary care, specialty, and emergency room services. The VAMC also operates many clinics, which provide an expansive array of preventive services, as well as a 100-bed Nursing Home Care Unit. The VAMC services a broad geographic area, extending north to south from the Canadian border to the Pennsylvania/New Jersey borders, and east to west from Massachusetts to Central New York. As of 1993, the VAMC employed over 1560 full-time equivalent employees and seventy-six medical residents. More than six hundred volunteers also contributed more than 120,000 service hours during 1993.

The VAMC maximizes resources well beyond its $92 million annual budget by affiliating with other organizations in the Capital District Health Care Community. As a result of this, VAMC has accordingly lowered the costs of services for veteran patients, provided scarce medical expertise, and increased services to the Department of Defense and other federal facilities. Through its many sharing agreements, the VAMC has been able to provide services to three Department of Defense providers and over twenty community health care providers. During 1991 and 1992, the VAMC was chosen as a pilot site from within the VA system to receive consulting support and resources to implement continuous quality improvement (CQI). From its inception, the CQI received momentum through the intellectual stimulation, enthusiastic commitment, and continuing sponsorship of the VAMC director. The following traces this quality effort by briefly describing the strategic objectives, key competitive advantages, core processes, ownership, establishment of multifunctional teams, performance objectives, elimination of nonvalue-added activities, building core capabilities, empowerment and self-management, and training to sustain the effort.

In March 1991, the CQI steering committee was initiated by Frederick L. Malphurs, the hospital director, and included himself, the chief of staff, associate director, associate director for nursing, CQI coordinator, associate chief of staff for education, and president of the medical staff. The committee revised the mission statement to reflect the new quality objectives and also redefined the core values of the hospital to include innovation, excellence, truthfulness, teamwork, trust, quality, empowerment, dignity, and compassion. In 1992, the VAMC developed a four-year plan which addressed three key areas: training, CQI teams, and infrastructure development. The infrastructure development was centered on the mission, vision, and values of the hospital, strategic quality planning, education, communication, and reward and recognition. In addition, an organizational assessment was developed to provide employees with opportunities to participate and be involved in CQI teams.

As part of the national VA system, the Albany VAMC has a competitive advantage in that patients who are veterans receive care at a reduced cost (compared to other health care institutions). A second competitive advantage is the low turnover rate of the nursing staff, which saves on recruitment and training costs commonly incurred by other health care facilities. The "captive clients," coupled with low turnover, also promotes continuity in service delivery and maintenance. Within the larger scope of the American health care delivery system, the Albany VAMC needed to contain health care costs as the trend of rising costs of inpatient hospital care continued to accelerate. Prior to implementing CQI, the VAMC demonstrated its superior performance by being the recipient of prestigious awards within the VA system. One such award was the 1993 Robert W. Carey Quality Award recognizing the VAMC for its benchmarked accomplishments in the area of quality improvement. The medical center also had measurement tools in place to measure outcomes and provide feedback for making competitive changes, as necessary.

Thus, the VAMC was competitive with other hospitals and VA medical centers even prior to implementing its CQI. VAMC wanted to achieve greater organizational capabilities through the CQI process and by organizing around core processes. Seven such processes were initially identified: OR cancellations, Sputum Cytology, ER waiting time, total hip replacement, discharge planning, medical records, and contract hospital. While all employees were encouraged to recommend improvements, only the few vital ideas set the stage for the formation of Quality teams. CQI teams were chartered based on the three levels mentioned below and only when teams had a specific, measurable problem that was promising in terms of the positive outcomes or returns. These three levels were: (1) projects involving large issues that concerned the whole medical center, that is, performance ratings; (2) projects which cut across functional lines or which required multidisciplinary treatments; and (3) projects whose processes were contained within a specific service or group of people, that is, laboratory specimen testing and service quality deployment. The teams varied structurally—Sputum Cytology was interdisciplinary in nature, while the ER was based on self-management principles. By April 1994, there were twenty chartered teams. Virtually all these teams were supported by the CQI education task team, which provided the essentials needed to perform quality control training and analysis.

The steering committee did not eliminate functions or departments but rather revised the way services are provided by making them more sensitive to the needs of veterans and to the institutional goals of the medical center. For example, the contract hospital team identified a need to clarify the procedures for pay reimbursement claims for veterans receiving care in non-VA hospitals. Steps were taken to ensure that veterans understand these procedures and that the outcome was a reduction in unauthorized claims. On another end, the steering committee had placed a high priority on the need for in-house and contract training in the area of quality improvement and self-management. The CQI training plan attempted to meet two objectives: to create and nurture a CQI environment, and to assist the staff with the use of process management tools and techniques. During the first phase of the training plan in 1991, the CQI steering committee held weekly meetings to review and discuss Deming and Quality Process Control (QPC) videotapes and the information gathered by members who had attended off-site seminars. Once this information was accumulated, the committee designed a training plan for all employees.

The first step was to introduce the principles of CQI to all employees. This basic CQI training has become part of new employee orientation at a service or committee level to provide theory and techniques for implementation of the CQI process. The second phase of the plan involved the development of an internal CQI training team consisting of four Master Trainers. These trainers were responsible for conducting Quality Deployment workshops and training other members to lead future training sessions. Once the training staff was developed, members of the CQI training team became facilitators and consultants for individual groups, so that managers and staff could utilize the tools needed for a given situation. This training included:

- CQI awareness
- Team leader/facilitator/member—tools and techniques for process improvement
- Service quality deployment
- When the patient comes first—managing and responding to patient complaints and concerns
- Mentor training
- Cultural diversity in the workplace
- Creative leadership
- Labor/management relations
- Vision through focusing on the customer
- Interpersonal and communication skills
- Employee orientation

In addition, performance appraisal systems have been modified to include elements of quality in areas such as leadership, technical competence, and coaching. Although participation in CQI was said to be voluntary, employees were nonetheless accountable for upholding CQI's principles. Employees, however, were encouraged to participate and be involved in the process improvement teams through team and peer recognition activities. Effective January 1995, the hospital redesigned its performance evaluation reward system. In the previous system the supervisor would meet with the employees, discuss their performance ratings for the past year, and then give a monetary reward. The new system, based on CQI principles, empowers the employees to recognize themselves for various achievements through individual or team efforts. These achievements must be consistent with the mission, vision, values, and critical success factors of the VAMC. All employees are eligible to receive $1,000 during a fiscal year and can submit proposals as often as they wish. Recognition may be noted in the following areas:

- Patient satisfaction
- Quality of work life and staff satisfaction
- All other customer satisfaction
- Cost reduction
- Process improvement
- Teamwork
- Empowerment (shared responsibility)
- Quality of care
- Safety

Three of the success stories at the Albany medical center (VAMC) are the self-directed work teams, Eye Clinic waiting time, and the Sputum Cytology Specimen Process.

Self-directed work teams: The hospital currently has four services that are self-directed or are in the process of establishing an implementation plan to become self-directed. Supply service developed their own plan for self-direction, whereas Human Resources, the Eye Clinic, and Ward 9C were given assistance by an outside consultant. Human resources had been self-directed for approximately one year by the end of 1995 and had projected completing the transformational cycle toward self-direction by 1998. This service was chosen as the pilot because of numerous internal and external problems. The Eye Clinic has been developing an implementation plan since May 1995 with a goal to become self-directed shortly afterward. Ward 9C also began their process in May 1995, but has taken longer to develop it because of the multidisciplinary nature of the group. A fifth team has recently been chosen for self-direction—the newly developed VISN (Veterans Integrated Services Network). The Albany VSN is one of twenty-two newly created VSNs nationwide.

Eye Clinic waiting time: A process improvement team (PIT) was initiated to review the time a patient spent waiting in the clinic. The PIT team used CQI tools and techniques to understand and analyze the process within the clinic. It was determined that a waiting time of eighty minutes total was reasonable. The flow chart and time study then indicated twenty-eight to fifty-six patients waited an average of 1.8 hours with over half of the patients waiting in excess of two hours. The team decided on several improvements, including establishing a receptionist in the clinic and ensuring that the appropriate forms were available in the exam room. The average waiting time was reduced to seventy-eight minutes with only two to twenty-two patients waiting two hours or more in the clinic.

Sputum Cytology Specimens: The laboratory noted that 17 to 28 percent of specimens submitted for sputum cytology were rejected as unsatisfactory. A multidisciplinary PIT team was chartered to study the problem. Flow charts, cause-and-effect diagrams, and Pareto charts were used to identify and verify the data, and based on the analysis of the process, eight improvements were noted. Some of these improvements included establishing a centralized specimen collection center in the laboratory, providing in-service sessions to the medical and nursing staffs to update them on any changes, and developing a computer ward order entry system for the needed laboratory tests.

SOURCES OF MOTIVATION IN HORIZONTAL ORGANIZATIONS

Motivating employees working in a delayered organizational structure is an important concern for HR managers. Limited, or the absence of, upward mobility creates both constraints and opportunities for motivating individuals and groups. While the desire to advance administratively is still strong, it collides with the institutional need to spread responsibilities and shift or transfer managerial tasks downward to teams or front-line employees. Most individuals working in transforming organizations enjoy similar or greater monetary rewards. What they need more is the opportunity to contribute, gain access to information, influence decision-making processes, enjoy high leverage over their tasks and projects, have the freedom to create new things, and be recognized and appreciated. How does management respond to these new needs?

Vision

People are often inspired by the mission of the organization and are motivated by the vision of their leaders. A mission provides the organization with its raison d'être—that is, its social justification for existence.

It shapes the institutional identity of individuals and groups within the organization. A clear and focused mission can eliminate a great deal of unnecessary conflict in an organization and can help productively channel discussions and activities. An inspiring vision can supply individuals with energy and enthusiasm. Vision is the mechanism through which all members of the organization are united in pursuit of the important dream of constantly improving working conditions and organizational performance for the good of all organizational stakeholders: internal, interface, and external.

A clear vision of success provides an effective substitute for leadership. People, particularly in decentralized settings, are able to lead and manage themselves if they are given clear guidance about where they are going, how to get there, the blueprint for success, and how to know if they are on track. More effective decision making and problem solving, then, occurs at a distance from the center of the organization and from the top of the hierarchy, a process that provides an impetus for further erosion of the chain of command and renders it redundant.

Technical Ladder and Agenda Control

When opportunities for upward mobility are limited and lose their potency, members of the organization can move horizontally by advancing into more complex and diversified jobs. Often, the move is to jobs that allow employees to perform with greater discretion and autonomy. Their leaders then emphasize results rather than procedures, and they empower members to choose the means to attain the objectives of their jobs or projects.

Action Learning

Learning is a key element in all continuous improvement initiatives. Companies increasingly try to achieve higher standards of product quality through the integration of continuous improvement programs within organizational processes. Action learning through knowledge acquisition, cross-training, education, and professional development provides organizational members with the skills and tools necessary to perform their jobs. Action learning duplicates work experiences, processes, and cross-functional projects in a structured learning environment. Managers and nonmanagers are taught to deal with changing conditions and respond to them logically and systematically. The learning sessions also provide an opportunity to socialize, blow off steam, and share problems and concerns. Overall, action learning provides an opportunity for continuous improvement.

Communication

The increasing decentralization and entrepreneurship typifying horizontal organizations not only give rise to different kinds of power bases, but also signify the role of interpersonal communication. No longer relying on formal authority to direct and mobilize staff, the new leaders increasingly use their persuasive and inspirational communication skills to attain desired results. A leader's effectiveness will be shaped by his or her ability to motivate through oral media and open communication. Articulate leaders, who can communicate goals and plans clearly while being sensitive to the psychosociological needs of diverse people, will become role models. The leader as role model is no longer a superior whose challenge is to nurture compliance on the part of his/her subordinates, but rather a coach who is versed in interpersonal relationships.

Coaching

Unlike the manager whose role is primarily to manage by results and evaluation, the coach's main interest is to train team members and help them develop new skills, recondition existing behaviors, and acquire new knowledge. The coach provides members with expert input and advice. The coach watches his/her players from outside and gives them an objective viewpoint of performance. World-class players and professional athletes have coaches. Similarly, organizational "stars" and "super stars" can all learn continuously and improve their performance. Coaches are expected to provide direction and set clear goals, train, build relationships, energize, monitor performance, and initiate feedback for continuous improvement.

PRINCIPLES OF EFFECTIVE COACHING

- Goal setting allows both coaches and players to measure progress being made toward achieving goals. Goals act as internal drives to motivate employees to perform with excellence when meeting targets set for them by their coaches.
- An effective coach teaches team players to be technically proficient while also improving interpersonal skills. Supportive skills such as assertion, interpersonal communication, conflict resolution, negotiation, and self-esteem are essential for achieving team goals.

- Coaches are expected to establish continuous growth as a norm, prepare employees to meet challenges, demonstrate confidence and trust in employees' abilities, provide continuous feedback, and reinforce and reward flexibility and cooperation.
- The manager, as a coach, knows that paying more attention to employees and providing them with greater autonomy and responsibility fosters inner motivation to perform with excellence. The "most valuable player" (MVP) is not one of twelve yearly employees of the month. An effective coach provides many opportunities for everyone to receive acknowledgment. The coach also teaches his or her stars to acknowledge the contributions of their teammates.
- Effective coaches watch their players perform directly and provide them with confidence and a sense of security. They keep players energized by constantly measuring stamina and decreasing and increasing workload accordingly. Effective coaches know when their players reach peak performance and look for signs of mental or physical fatigue to reduce or adjust workloads, offer emotional or technical support, and help employees pace their outputs. Successful managers as coaches constantly provide players with feedback about results through regular coaching sessions, a scoreboard that presents actual performance, and post-factum analysis to evaluate progress and suggest improvements.

VALUE-BASED ORGANIZATIONS AND LEADERSHIP ROLES

Managers in hierarchically based organizations tend to rely on formal, vertical sources of power to coordinate activities. They use legitimate authority and positional power to set goals for subordinates, motivate them, and ultimately affect their performance and behavior. Work is usually divided by functional areas of specialty and is defined along departmental lines. In addition, the manager enacting the Coordinator role tends to focus on measuring, evaluating, controlling, and rewarding employee performance. However, in a value-based organization, effective managers adopt new styles by asking the questions that will motivate people to solve problems and make decisions on their own.

Value-based organizational design requires managers to develop unique behavioral flexibility that allows them to balance the need to protect stability and preserve the status quo with the need to manage discontinuity, randomness, and flux. The new style requires managers to be skilled in managing disorder, and in coaching, facilitating, and helping employees self-organize and evolve into flexible work groups. Once individuals and groups are organized and their activities coordinated, effective managers must also develop expertise to monitor progress against established performance targets to ensure the smooth and efficient utilization of organizational resources. Enacting the Coordinator role to achieve integration across organizational units and functions complements the efforts of the manager playing the Monitor role. These two roles are essential to support the goals of organizational continuous improvement. In chapter 5, the concepts and principles of quality improvement programs and reengineering efforts that require managers to enact the Monitor role are discussed.

5

Organizing around Processes and Outcomes: Quality Programs and Reengineering

A primary contribution of a manager (at a second level or above) is to manage interfaces. The boxes already have managers; the senior manager adds value by managing the white space between the boxes.

—Rummler & Brache, 1990

A reengineering effort strives for dramatic levels of improvement. It must break away from conventional wisdom and the constraints of organizational boundaries and should be broad and cross-functional in scope. It should use information technology not to automate an existing process but to enable a new one.

—Michael Hammer, *Harvard Business Review*, 1990

Most organizations focus on functions while processes fall between the cracks. In a complex, highly interdependent system, however, managers are encouraged to shift their orientations from a vertical/functional approach to one that recognizes the importance of processes that cut across functional boundaries. In fact, as Rummler and Brache (1990) noted, everything in the "ecosystem" of the organization (both external and internal) can be viewed as a process connected through supplier/customer relationships (see figure 5.1).

Figure 5.1. Supplier-Customer Relationships

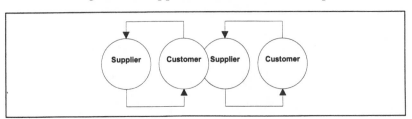

STRATEGIC LEVEL

The organization's anatomy is displayed at the system (strategic) level (figure 5.2). This is the "skeleton" of the major functions that comprise the organization. Variables that affect performance at this level include goals, strategies, structures, and the functional deployment of resources (Rummler & Brache, 1990). According to Rummler and Brache, at this level organizational goals are stated in terms of how well an organization meets the expectations and requirements from outside. These goals must address the values of the organization, the requirements of key customers, financial and nonfinancial expectations, and targets for each major function within the organization. Strategically, the questions to be addressed at this level are:

- What are we going to do? (type of service)
- Who are our customers? (target users)
- What are our competitive advantages? (internal strengths)
- Where should we place our emphasis? (prioritization)

Once a strategy is developed, the infrastructure must be established to support the implementation of that strategy. The two most important questions in this context are:

1. What internal customer/supplier links are required to attain organizational competitive advantage? (the question of structure)
2. How many and what kinds of resources need to be allocated to the various functions? (the question of management)

The two questions above underlie the variable of strategic organizational design involving the following points:

Figure 5.2. Organizational Structure: An Open Systems Perspective

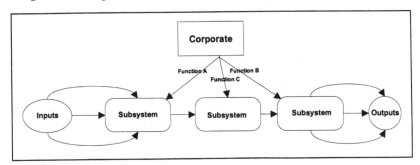

- Are all relevant functions in place?
- Are there any unnecessary redundancies?
- Is the current flow of inputs and outputs between functions both efficient and effective?

MISSION STATEMENT

Often, the strategic-level goals shape or frame the ideological construct of the organizational mission. The mission is intended to rationalize the existence of the organization by legitimizing its outputs. It is the broad definition of the reason for the organization's existence. It is the single statement that differentiates an organization from other organizations. Corporate mission statements can help a company form an identity. Mission statements define what companies do and reflect the operating philosophy and future goals of organizations. A mission can give an organization the focus it needs for survival and growth. It clarifies the values employees must consider when coping with problems and making choices. The mission statement helps refocus attention on shared values and redirects actions toward a shared purpose. Most managers who develop and follow their missions have clear ideas about the future direction of their organizations. This also helps their units and teams relate to the broader goals of the organization rather than to the technical or functional objectives of the units and teams. Experts agree that without a mission there is no long-range future state shared by all the stakeholders to inform and guide day-to-day improvements and to integrate short- with long-term planning (Long & Vickers-Koch, 1994).

OPERATIVE LEVEL

At the process or operative level, looking inside the organization (figure 5.3) we see functions or subsystems that exist to convert the various inputs into products or services. Essentially, we see the work flow that transcends functional boundaries.

A process then involves a sequence of activities that create something of value for internal or external customers. In figure 5.3, functions A, B, and C can represent R&D, manufacturing, and marketing specialists responsible for developing, producing, and delivering a new product line. The Internal Revenue Service (IRS) in 1991, for example, organized its work into five Core Business Systems (CBSs) with "owners" for each CBS as follows: value tracking, informing, educating and assisting, managing accounts, ensuring compliance, and resourcing. The purpose was to adopt a systems perspective for improving organizational performance and customer satisfaction. Thus, the emphasis was shifted from functions to processes and from tasks to service outputs that overlap several functions. Each CBS is composed of many subsystems, processes, subprocesses, and individual products. In addition, each CBS developed quality and productivity measures that indicate how well the subsystem is meeting organizational goals.

Figure 5.4 shows how process goals are linked both to organization goals (vertical) and to customer requirements (horizontal). This level typically involves resource allocation through budgeting the

Figure 5.3. Interdependence among Subsystems

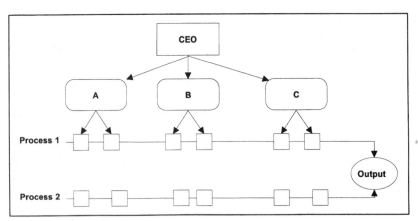

Figure 5.4. Functional and Process Goals

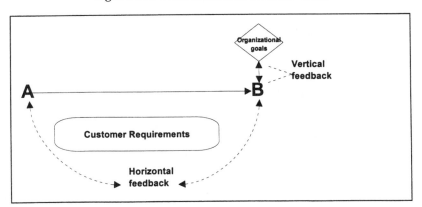

process as a whole and allocating its share of the resources to each function according to its marginal contribution.

From the continuous improvement standpoint, adaptive actions at the process level may include the following strategies:

- Bringing a process under statistical control to make output more predictable
- Eliminating nonvalue-added tasks, rework, and waste
- Reducing cycle time
- Streamlining the process by reducing the number of steps
- Error proofing the process

And if performance breakthrough is needed:

- Redesigning the process
- Standardizing best practices
- Improving process capabilities
- Ensuring that customer requirements are being met

OPERATIONAL LEVEL

Rummler and Brache (1990) noted that at the operational level or the job/performer level we look at goals accomplished by individuals or groups in the organization regardless of their location within the hierarchy (figure 5.5). Presumably, sequential or reciprocal interdependence

Figure 5.5. Interdependence among Performers

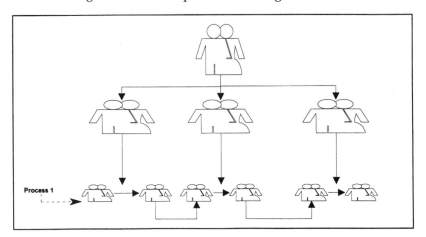

among the performers has greater value than hierarchical relationships since the former connects the different components of work flow rather than separating work by supervisory duties and reporting relationships.

Performers are the individuals or groups who convert inputs to outputs. The four most important variables of goal setting at this level are goal clarity, challenging goals, feedback, and goal acceptance.

Goals must be specific, measurable, assignable, realistic, and time related. Goals should not be too difficult, to avoid rejection, nor should they be too easy, to avoid procrastination and attempts at padding. Goals must be accepted by individual performers for two reasons: they lead to a buy-in climate and they serve as a source of motivation and commitment. Finally, individual performers must also receive feedback about the results of their work performance. Feedback serves as a follow-up and helps individuals maintain high output quality through continuous improvement. Goals at this level must support both functional objectives and process requirements (see figure 5.6).

Rummler and Brache (1990) proposed the following questions in the context of job performance:

- Are process requirements reflected in appropriate jobs?
- Are job steps in a logical sequence?
- Have supportive policies and procedures been developed?
- Are the job requirements ergonomically sound?

Figure 5.6. The Relationship between Functional Goals and
Process Requirements

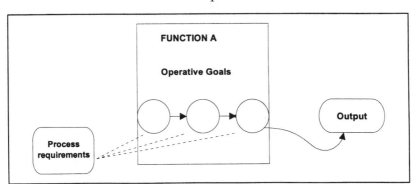

Answering yes to all of the above questions can help the organization achieve horizontal as well as vertical congruence. Accomplishment of objectives and goals at one level (e.g., supervisory) serves as a means to achieve goals at a higher level (e.g., middle), as well as goals of parallel units (e.g., next operation).

CROSS-FUNCTIONAL TEAMS AND MARKET-BASED FORMS OF ORGANIZING

Vertical, hierarchical structures are being replaced by flexible networks, adaptive systems, informal structures, and horizontal structures. At the center of these contemporary organizational structures are cross-functional teams made up of experts with diverse functional skills and abilities who are ready to act quickly and flexibly to adapt to changing organizational needs. But quick response is only one advantage. The other benefit is the ability to contain the competencies needed to perform work within one (sub)structure, thus increasing the likelihood for effective integration and control. Glenn Parker (1994b, pp. 49–50) lists six important benefits of using cross-functional teams:

- *Speed*: Cross-functional teams tend to accomplish tasks quickly, especially in the area of product development, because they utilize parallel development rather than serial development. In other words, cross-functional teams develop different aspects of a project simultaneously instead of sequentially.

- *Complexity*: Cross-functional teams improve the organization's capacity to solve complex problems because such problems transcend traditional disciplines and functions.
- *Creativity*: Cross-functional teams help increase the creative capacity of the organization by bringing together people with different backgrounds, orientations, cultural values, and styles.
- *Customer focus*: Cross-functional teams help focus the organization's resources on satisfying customer needs.
- *Organizational learning*: Members of cross-functional teams learn more about other disciplines and tend to develop new technical and job skills more readily because they work across job functions. They also learn how to work with people with different backgrounds and styles.
- *Single point of contact*: Cross-functional teams create a single point of contact for external customers and foster teamwork among internal customers—that is, their members.

Cross-functional teams achieve greater effectiveness when they are led by internal or external leaders who optimize the balance between technical knowledge of the work process and the interpersonal skills required for joint performance. Once the team has achieved a high degree of maturity (i.e., passed the early stage of its development), the team (external) leader should reduce his/her involvement and empower the team to assume leadership roles in various facets of the team's life. The leader should set clear goals and establish the team charter to optimize its performance. The leader must also ensure that the team's goals are aligned with the larger unit's goals. The team leader should also guide the boundary management activities of the team both internally (with parallel units) and externally (with key stakeholders). Cross-functional teams change the way by which work is conducted and rewards are determined and used within the organization. Parker (1994b, p. 51) stated that

> organizations with cross-functional teams should examine their performance appraisal systems to see whether team participation is taken into account and whether managers are required or encouraged to incorporate feedback from employees' team leaders . . . [In addition] organizations must shift the emphasis of their recognition programs from individual to team rewards.

These issues are very important, for if cross-functional teams are implemented appropriately they change both the structural and cultural makeup of the organization. Shifting from a functional to a market-based form of organizing, containing the work within the team, and making team members accountable for the results while rewarding them based on collective effort, knowledge, or performance, is a major shift from a conventional management and organizational structure. The organization becomes more sensitive to changes in the external environment and can adapt to them faster, while front-line employees become more responsive to customer needs and concerns. In addition, efficiency may increase due to simplification of business processes, reduction in inventory, improving cash flow and improving turnover. A case in point is 3M, which in 1995 and 1996 underwent a major reorganization toward a market-based approach in its businesses. In an interview in *3M Stemwinder* (December 1995, pp. 4–5), L. D. DeSimone, chairman of the board and CEO explained:

> Historically, 3M has been a company driven by technology, innovation and new products. No other company in the world has the track record we have in innovative products, processes and services that change the basis of competition. Our customers like that, but they have been telling us for some time that we are more complicated to do business with than they would like. We need to present one company, with one voice, that's easier to do business with. That's the main reason for a market-centered approach . . . In the past . . . we would often have multiple sales organizations calling on a customer, with each organization having different terms and conditions of sale, different distribution, different customer service representatives, different promotional packages . . . Now that's changing . . . 3M divisions that are going to sell to that company need to be more integrated—in sales, customer service, distribution, everything . . . So, we are fully embracing and accelerating the market-centered effort around the company. Instead of having multiple divisions organized around a technology, we're going to organize around industries, markets and distribution channels. We are going to give our key account customers one primary contact to deal with if they have a problem . . . This also differentiates us from other suppliers, because no other manufacturers in the world can do this across as many product lines as we have.

What this also means is that cross-functional teams must have an "optimal" size that prevents process losses (e.g., coordination and communication) and rather, allows for the development of effective interpersonal relations. From the outside, the success of cross-functional teams requires managerial support that spans over such things as:

- resources (i.e., time, funds, information, training)
- role modeling (particularly in teamwork)
- establishing reward and recognition systems
- communicating the charter of the team
- identifying stakeholders' values and sources of power for the teams
- emphasizing collaborative efforts
- creating policies and procedures that support the team environment

The shift toward a market-based form of organizing and the utilization of cross-functional teams to take advantage of internal expertise and efficient deployment of human resources, also gives rise to the use of broadbanding and organizing around core competencies to achieve strategic advantage. Broadbanding, as an alternative approach to organizing, is discussed in the next section.

BROADBANDING: ORGANIZING AROUND CORE COMPETENCIES

Core competencies involve the value adding of the organization as reflected in its collective knowledge and ability to perform actions upon objects. In a broader context, core competencies include the transference, synergy, and coordination of technology, as well as the human knowledge and skills necessary to create and deliver value. Sony's core competence in miniaturization is the result of bringing together the advanced technology and the collective knowledge of engineers, designers, and marketers who have a good understanding of customer needs and of technological possibilities (Prahalad & Hamel, 1990). Core competence involves using systems thinking, managing across functions, and leveraging the collective intelligence of the organization. Competence is about linking knowledge, networking learning, and integrating and communicating performance targets across organizational boundaries. The skills that encompass core competence coalesce around individuals who recognize the importance of blending their functional expertise with those of others in new and stimulating ways. Core competencies evolve in a cumulative, progressive way—that is, they must be constantly improved to create superior performance.

Broadbanding is a competitive line-management organizational strategy that supports the streamlined, developmental format of organizational structure. By organizing staff specialists according to their contributions to the organization rather than their disciplines, broadbanding supports the creation of networked learning that can enhance the ability of the organization to concentrate its synergistic brainpower on responding quickly and effectively to environmental stimuli. From a human resource systems vantage point, broadbanding throws out the old job classification systems and replaces them with clusters of competencies or broad job bands that allow flexibility and strategic moves that benefit the organization and the workforce. Thus, core competencies, networked learning, and broadbanding are essential components of the architecture of the knowledge-based organization, while at the same time they induce organizational learning and development. Using broadbanding and forming networked learning teams organized around core competencies provides organizational leaders with an integrated approach to organizational transformation. Broadbanding fosters flatter organizational structures and helps deemphasize traditional structures and hierarchy. A number of U.S. companies—for example, Xerox, NCR, MET P&C, GTE Wireless, and Marriott International—have reengineered their internal work processes to achieve greater operating efficiencies and improve customer service using broadbanding. By emphasizing how career planning, performance management, training and development, and staffing are aligned with overall business strategies and goals, these companies use broadbanding architecture to gain a higher degree of proficiency from employees. The critical challenge for organizational leaders is satisfying the corporate need for flexibility and adaptability while at the same time responding to the need for integration and consistency. Marshaling organizational resources through broadbanding and core competencies yields a competitive advantage that competitors may find difficult to imitate. The ability to balance this advantage against the needs of individuals and groups for stability and ownership is a critical success factor that can help sustain banding efforts. The key for successful results is to redesign human resource programs (e.g., competency assessment, job evaluation procedures, and performance management approaches) along the goals of broadbanding and core competencies, as well as linking networked learning teams to compensation decisions.

Broadbanding, organizing around a portfolio of competencies or networked learning, rather than organizing around a portfolio of functions or businesses, is essential to achieve flexibility and high performance. At the same time, the distinctiveness of core competencies must also be nurtured, built, and protected to avoid imitation by competitors. Prahalad and Hamel (1990) recommended three tests to identify core competencies:

- A core competence provides potential access to diverse markets.
- A core competence should make a significant contribution to the perceived customer benefits of the end product.
- A core competence should be difficult for competitors to imitate.

The challenge for organizational leadership is to avoid conceiving the company as a vertically integrated system consisting of a collection of discrete strategic business units (SBUs) that depend on external suppliers for critical components necessary to produce value. The problem is that these are not just components, but rather part of the organization's networked learning. They are core products that contribute to the competitiveness of a wide range of end products. They are the physical embodiments of core competencies (Prahalad & Hamel, 1990, p. 83). Senior managers must think of the organization in terms of a value chain by looking upstream to the operating efficiencies of suppliers and downstream toward distribution and customers. Canon, Fuji, Honda, and a host of other Japanese corporations are successful at least in part because they cultivate their core competencies and have a visionary mindset that spans over their entire value chains. American corporations, however, make post-hoc efforts to rationalize production costs across existing businesses, rather than employ pre-emptive strategies to link business strategy with organizational core competence. While Asian companies like Goldstar, Samsung, and Daewoo have built up advantages in the component markets first and have then leveraged off their superior products to move downstream to build brand share and cater to customers worldwide, American companies use structures and strategies that were devised during the 1970s and that fit domestic rather than global markets. According to Prahalad and Hamel (1990), the need for new principles is most obvious in companies organized exclusively according to the logic of SBUs. When Canon identified an opportunity in digital laser printers, it gave SBU managers the okay to draw on other SBUs to pull together the production skills necessary to achieve its objective. With strategy making that is patterned around the needs of the specific functional unit or division, top managers in American companies lack the vision to blend resources across the units and create core competencies to achieve competitive advantages. When choices are limited and the pressure is on and when implementing an organization-wide change is a matter of survival, the change becomes too costly, as IBM's experience showed (see chapter 2). Often the change is less coherent, done in a reactive, crisis-intervention mode, as Eastman Kodak's experience, described below, illustrates.

By the end of 1989, Kodak had shaved 12 percent of its workforce, reappointed 70 percent of its key managerial positions, reduced the number of top managers by 25 percent, reorganized its structure into five business groups with thirty autonomous business units, and used constant monitoring and measurement of business outputs and value adding. The manufacturing and R&D departments were split up and redistributed into the business units. Kodak required each business to generate a return that exceeded an internally established cost of equity, reflecting its own level of risk and market conditions. Business units unable to meet the required rate of return were given a time limit in which to make it or risk being divested or dismantled. Throughout the organization, managers were involved in creating a sense of urgency and ownership, thus expanding Kodak's dissemination of shared understandings and increasing the effectiveness of Kodak's adaptive response to global changes.

By spring 1994 Kodak announced the divestiture of three large units and its intention to concentrate on the imaging business. The divestiture includes Sterling Drug, which was acquired in 1988, as part of the selling of about $7.9 billion worth of health-related operations (*Wall Street Journal*, 12/22/94, p. B1). Sales of assets have permitted the company to cut dramatically Kodak's debt load by $6 billion between 1993 and 1994. Reportedly, Kodak's strategy has been to extract better profits from the firm's photography and develop digital technologies such as all-electronic cameras and image-storage devices (*Business Week*, 5/16/94, p. 32). To that end, Kodak also acquired Wang Laboratories' document imaging division for $260 million, a strategic move that was intended to reduce Kodak's dependence on wet film analogue technologies and establish Kodak as the "undisputed leader" in document imaging processing, with Filenet and IBM trailing behind.

Kodak also reorganized its sales force into a more integrated scheme of marketing approach to create customized solutions for retailers (*Advertising Age*, 1/30/95, V66, n5). Later that year, Kodak reorganized its digital imaging group to speed the manufacturing and marketing of new products such as digital cameras and imaging software (*Wall Street Journal*, 5/15/95, p. B6). Fisher, the new CEO who came from Motorola, set a goal to shake up the oversized, hierarchical management at Kodak. As recently as fall 1997, Kodak announced the elimination of 20 percent of its one thousand senior and middle managers. With a style more like a coach than an autocrat, Fisher initiated a matrix management system with accountability for outputs. Using his experience at Motorola, he concentrated on quality, customer needs, and shorter product-development time in the hope of paring costs and generating a culture that is more dynamic (*Business Week*, 1/30/95, p. 62). Despite the fact that the diversification into digital technologies risked rendering Kodak's traditional photographic products obsolete, market analysts hailed the move as a "remarkable turnaround" strategy (*Forbes*, 1/13/97, v159, n1, p. 45). Furthermore, the gross profit results of Kodak showed the success of its restructuring and spin-off efforts. From the end of December, 1993, until the end of December, 1996, Kodak's payoffs from its turnaround strategies were $6,016 billion, $6,232 billion, $7,018 billion, and, $7,642 billion, respectively. The year 1997, however, brought bad news: The strong dollar made Kodak's products more expensive abroad, stiffer competition in the emerging markets of electronic photography (Fuji's share of the U.S. market increased by about 3 percent to 20 percent), sluggish sales (Kodak's sales dropped 13 percent during 1997), rising new-product losses (Kodak lost $300 million in its digital imaging business through the third quarter), and declining profits (Kodak reported a loss of $744 million in the fourth quarter of 1997) all contributed to Kodak's poor performance and another wave of job cuts. In addition to the elimination of one thousand managerial positions mentioned above, Kodak announced that it would cut ten thousand jobs and take a $1 billion charge against earnings over the next two years. Kodak is also expected to exit nonprofitable business units, reduce its spending on R&D (much of it in digital photography) by 10 percent to 15 percent, shift more of its manufacturing, and consolidate its plants (*Albany Times Union*, 11/12/97 E5, 1/16/98, E6).

MANAGEMENT RESPONSIBILITY: TAKING CARE OF PROCESSES

The primary contribution of managers at higher levels is not to re-manage functions, but rather to manage interfaces and be responsible for workflow processes. Processes have no natural owners; instead they fall within the gray area that defies ownership. Conventionally speaking, management is responsible for establishing objectives and strategies, monitoring internal and external feedback, evaluating performance, and reallocating resources. But management is also responsible for process improvement. Process Quality Improvement (PQI) involves a number of diagnostic and intervention strategies intended to focus on a process, subprocess, or steps to reduce complexity and achieve higher efficiency of resource utilization. Examples of complexity are interruption (e.g., detection, delay, product testing), scrap (e.g., defects, returns), inefficiency

Figure 5.7. Process Quality Improvement

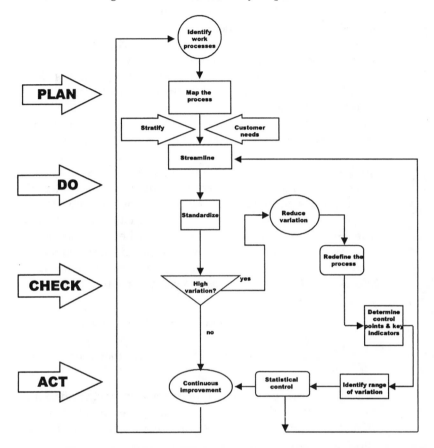

(e.g., unnecessary activities, waste, replacement), and, variation (e.g., idle time, employee turnover, retraining).

A typical PQI involves the following six important steps for dealing with complexity (see figure 5.7 which is based on the commonly used model of process quality improvedment; source unknown).

- *Targeting a process for improvement*: This step often involves the need to stratify a process into sub-processes (components) and subjecting the components to a Pareto Analysis. The basis for Pareto Analysis is the "80/20" rule. That is, 80 percent of the problems (roughly) result from 20 percent of the causes. This analysis can reveal which of the components account for a pro-portionally larger impact on the broader problem. Once the PQI team identifies the component of the problem that produces the greatest impact, this component is then taken forward to the next step in the improvement process.

- *Mapping the process using flow charts*: Flow charts help the PQI team consider what should happen in a process rather than what actually does happen. Thus, charting the process provides a tool that can help the quality improvement team identify sources of complexity.
- *Identifying customer requirements*: Customer requirements must be identified constantly and checked against the process to determine whether they are being met. This step sets the stage for quality evaluation. Quality, in this context, means conforming to valid requirements, or that the outputs produced meet the specifications outlined by the customer. The ultimate criterion to judge product/service quality is via customer satisfaction. The single most important measure is whether customer requirements have been met or even exceeded. Direct communication between partners (customer and supplier) of a process allows the PQI team to answer two important questions and consider some rational actions:

    What problems does the customer have with our current performance?
    What would the customer like to receive that s/he does not receive?

    Evaluating product quality by measuring customer satisfaction is essential for validating whether reasonable expectations can be met. A valid customer requirement should meet three criteria:

    It should fall within the process capabilities.
    It should be possible, objectively, to establish key indicators to measure how well the requirement is being met.
    Employees who are part of the process should accept the requirement and are be committed to conforming to it.

- *Standardizing the process*: The purpose of standardization is to enhance process output uniformity and create a baseline for further evaluation and improvement.
- *Streamlining the process*: The objective of streamlining is to reduce the cycle time it takes to complete a work process from beginning to end. This can be done by determining the ratio of time spent on value-added tasks (V) to total time, including prevention (P), appraisal (A), and rework (R).

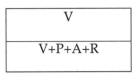

V
V+P+A+R

- *Reducing process variation*: This stage involves the substeps outlined below. The first four substeps make up the diagnostic or clarification phase; the final two cover the fixing or improving segment:
  - Flow chart the process to arrive at a baseline
  - Establish control points (those with a high potential for failure)
  - Identify key indicators or process performance measures (nonconformance)
  - Determine the range of variation (by defining the upper and lower control limits and identifying potential causes of rework, waste, etc.)
  - Bring the process under statistical control (using run-charts and the identification of special causes and any randomness patterns)
  - Eliminate special cause variation (through the implementation of countermeasures and monitoring indicators to ensure success)

BUSINESS PROCESS REENGINEERING

Business process reengineering (BPR) is a redesign not only of the processes within an organization, but also of those processes that link the organization to its customers and suppliers. It is the "fundamental rethinking and radical redesign of business processes to achieve dramatic improvements in critical, contemporary measures of performance, such as cost, quality, service, and speed" (Hammer & Champy, 1993, p. 32). More than just automating the work flow, it focuses on improving effectiveness, speed, and efficiency. Every facet of the operation is up for grabs: jobs, structures, management systems, values, and beliefs. Thus, discontinuous thinking is at the heart of BPR, where managers are expected to identify and abandon outdated practices, rules, and fundamental assumptions underlying current business operations and aim at creating organizational operation breakthroughs. BPR means "starting all over," and from this point of view implementing process reengineering appears to attract senior executives seeking more to adapt their organizations to the environment than to implement quality improvement programs.

During fall 1992, Goll and Cordovano, both of the Business Process Transformation at Price Waterhouse, conducted a survey involving CEOs of 150 mid- to large-scale companies (Goll & Cordovano, 1993). The purpose of the survey was to learn about the reengineering experiences of these companies. About one-third of the companies surveyed responded, with 80 percent of them reporting consideration or application of reengineering; 48 percent reported reengineering as a company-wide effort; 26 percent have been reengineering specific functions such as customer service; and 40 percent have been working on a specific process, such as order management. Most of the companies targeted by the survey reported a range of anticipated improvements. Productivity, quality, profits, and customer satisfaction were expected to improve from 7 percent to 100 percent, depending on the stage of the reengineering effort. Anticipated cost, cycle time, and response time improvements ranged from 10 percent to 400 percent. Other anticipated goals were given as 100 percent on-time deliveries and zero loss of market share.

Ford Motor Company's effort to achieve a dramatic breakthrough in a process illustrates the value adding of using reengineering. Benchmarking Mazda's accounts payable unit staffed by only five people, Ford's executives set to redesign existing subprocesses by installing new computer systems and reducing the size of their accounts payable department by 20 percent, from five hundred to four hundred people. The existing process was too complex and involved too many steps, most of which concerned matching the original purchase order with the receiving document and vendor's invoice. Ultimately, instead of streamlining the process, Ford instituted "invoiceless processing" (vendors are no longer required to send invoices) by which purchase orders and receivable documents are matched by an on-line computerized database, which also prepares checks for accounts payable to send to vendors. Instead of achieving a 20 percent reduction in staffing, Ford was able to reduce the size of its accounts payable department by 75 percent, since the function of comparing mismatches had been totally eliminated. The whole process has been simplified and financial information accuracy has increased.

Ford did not focus only on accounts payable, but rather on the entire goods acquisition process—purchasing, receiving, as well as accounts payable—which was cross-functional by nature. Essentially, Ford could not have achieved these results without looking at the flow of work as a process and the flow of processes as a system. By 1996,

Ford reportedly had begun to restructure its entire information system (IS) operations by testing a client-server Unix software package for core functions such as order taking and manufacturing. These and other changes have created unrest within the ranks. Managers and nonmanagers resist the new program ideas out of fear of losing their jobs. Ford responded by stating that the new reengineering ideas are not about jobs, but about greater efficiency through cutting costs and redundancies and increasing quality.

Reengineering changes everything people take for granted—it realigns organizational structures and authority, and it rethinks the rules of organizing and operations. Rather than looking for opportunities to improve the current process, a cross-functional team must be assembled to determine which steps add value and to search for breakthroughs in achieving results. The team should use information technology not to automate an existing process, but to enable a new one (Hammer, 1990).

PRINCIPLES OF REENGINEERING

Reengineering is a total transformation of the way management systems have existed previously. It changes work fragmentation and narrows task specialization into a more compressed and integrated work flow that negates linear and sequential operations and replaces them with parallel, more decentralized process structures. Hammer (1990) identified seven important principles of reengineering:

- *Organize around outcomes, not tasks*: Instead of sequential processing that defines functions, labor must be organized by the work flow or outputs. The call is to simplify linear processes by compressing them. In late 1990, Aetna Life and Casualty, dissolved its three main business divisions—commercial insurance, personal insurance, and business services—and replaced them with fifteen profit centers, laying off twenty-six hundred people in the process. In 1992, Aetna consolidated twenty auto and homeowner insurance field offices into four business centers, while sixty-five property casualty claim offices were consolidated to twenty-three.
- *Assign those who use the output of the process to perform the process*: By using expert systems and data bases, departments can perform their own purchasing functions. Or, rather than having technicians available on demand to respond to customers calls, have the customer perform the repair. (When the motor on my

Pro-Form treadmill malfunctioned, I called the manufacturer's field service hotline and described the symptoms to the hotline technician, who arranged to send me a new motor with specific replacement instructions.)

- *Subsume information processing work into the real work that produces the information*: The units producing information should also process and use this information. Ford's redesigned accounts payable process, discussed above, exemplifies this principle.
- *Treat geographically dispersed resources as though they were centralized by using information technology and internal networking to link decision-making centers across organizational boundaries*: Decentralization of a resource provides more quality service, but at the cost of redundancy, bureaucracy, and missed economies of scale. However, this tradeoff can be mitigated through the use of EDI, computerized databases, etc., to reap the benefits of scale and coordination, while still maintaining high flexibility and greater service quality. Both Wal-Mart and Hewlett-Packard centralized their purchasing functions and were able to achieve more efficient internal integration. Also, they lowered the costs of goods purchased significantly.
- *Link parallel functions during the process—not after its completion*: Communication networks, shared databases, and teleconferencing can bring the independent functions together so that coordination is built into the system on a perpetual basis.
- *Push decision-making authority to points of impact and build control within the system by using teams and by flattening the hierarchy of authority*: Most organizations follow the scientific management doctrine in which doers are separated from planners. Performers are expected to follow standards and meet quotas and goals. Accountants, auditors, and supervisors monitor, measure, and reward work results. With information technology in place and with on-line databases, doers can now make decisions, check, and take actions to improve their performance. As the doers are organized into self-managed teams, hierarchical management layers can be compressed and organizational structure can be flattened. Albany International's Fabrics Division in East Greenbush, New York, embodies the essence of this principle. The division is currently organized along a matrix design in which teams perform all functions included in the three major processes of the system. As the system moves toward self-management, teams will be reorganized along the processes in parallel activities, with process owners that coordinate the work flow and with

a management team that provides support for the teams. The system, therefore, becomes flatter with empowered teams and with built-in coordination and control. The managerial role is changing from one of monitor and controller to one of supporter and facilitator.

- *Capture information once and at the source*: Avoid redundancy by inputting all data into an on-line database and by making it available to all units.

REENGINEERING, PARADIGMATIC CONSTRAINTS, AND THE ROLE OF LEADERSHIP

Despite its relative success as a tool for change, reengineering appears to be perceived negatively by employees. According to *Business Week* (Nov. 7, 1994, p. 6), 83 percent of the largest Fortune 500 corporations have indicated that they reengineered their workplaces. Of those, 70 percent noted that the outcomes were positive in terms of achieving greater productivity. However, when employees of these corporations were asked for their opinions about the success of reengineering: 69 percent actually believed it was an excuse for layoffs; 75 percent feared job losses due to reengineering; and 55 percent claimed that they were overburdened with work after reengineering was implemented. None of these barriers are quite as fatal to the change effort as those existing within the heads of people. Peter Senge, in his widely acclaimed book, *The Fifth Discipline* (1990), suggested the need for a paradigm shift. A paradigm is a set of rules that establishes boundaries and describes the parameters for solving the problems within these boundaries. It is a construct or a mental map that gives certain people both cognitive and behavioral directions. Paradigms force us to think in certain ways, constrain our reaction to new information, and often disable objective thinking regarding new information.

In and around organizations, paradigms define the set of absolute management assumptions and the philosophy that drives the vision, goals, and plans of the organization. These assumptions are unquestionable. They become ingrained in the thinking patterns and work behaviors of employees and managers, they evolve into norms, and they define the core values of the organization. The paradigm gives meaning to the way people do their work, maintain interpersonal relations, use metaphors, jargon, rituals, stories, and sagas—that is, how they shape the identity of organizational ideology. Senge (1990) discusses how these paradigms filter the way that people process new information and limit their flexibility in considering innovative approaches to work. These paradigms, in and of themselves, are not dangerous as they represent a basic function of human information processing. However, when these paradigms stand rigid and unchallenged they limit organizational agility. Overvaluing a paradigm leads to strong values and ideological views of the world that often are difficult to change. Strong beliefs breed taboos that guide thinking and that may result in inflexible behaviors that inhibit reengineering. The concerns about "getting stuck" in a dogmatic attitude toward change and reengineering prompted Morris and Brandon (1993) to suggest the need for a significant change in the rules, assumptions, and attitudes related to an established way of doing something. Organizations must understand that past success does not guarantee success in the future, and may even be detrimental to the organization if it poses barriers to new opportunities and fosters resistance to change. When significant changes take place in the organization's environment, old paradigms must change to make room for new ones that are consistent with the current situation. If an organization fails to take advantage of these changes, a loss in its competitive position can be expected as the competition will move in to exploit them.

Reengineering can be viewed, not as a new paradigm but rather as a process requiring the willingness to question old paradigms constantly. It is apparent that without the ability to question the old assumptions, reengineering attempts may potentially fail. Hall, Rosenthal, and Wade (1993) believe that even with sufficient depth and breadth, a reengineering effort will fail if it is not championed by senior executives. In their study, five of the companies actually achieved the projected impact of the implemented project. Of those five, four were headed by new CEOs who were familiar with leading an organization through a period of "radical change." Hall, Rosenthal, and Wade (1993) suggested five keys to the successful implementation of BPR:

1. Set aggressive reengineering performance targets.
2. Commit 20–50 percent of the CEO's time to the process.
3. Conduct a comprehensive review of customer needs, economic leverage points, and market trends.
4. Assign an additional senior executive to be responsible for implementation.
5. Conduct a comprehensive pilot of the new design.

Because reengineering involves a total system change, it tends to generate much resistance from people satisfied with the status quo.

Reengineering has no constituency within an organization. It must be sponsored and supported by a committed senior operating manager with a strong transformational leadership style and with a moral obligation to discontinue major systems initiatives that reinforce obsolete processes. This leader must have a natural propensity for entrepreneurial thinking and creativity. The leader must understand the nature and depth of the organization's operations and problems and the potential consequence of reengineering solutions. The leader must act as a catalyst for change to support and integrate the various reengineering efforts that process owners are conducting. It is a charismatic-expertise-based leadership that must be both imaginative, spiritual, and knowledgeable about the need for process breakthrough. But since any process breakthrough can be benchmarked by competitors, its strategic advantage is short term. In a complex, dynamic environment the capacity to reengineer must be institutionalized. Senior managers must have the ability to implement constantly any radical transformation—a core competency of successful leadership (Hammer & Champy, 1992).

QUALITY IMPROVEMENT AND PROCESS REENGINEERING

Quality Improvement (QI) typically centers on enhancing products and services provided to both customers and suppliers. QI involves continuous changes or at least incremental improvement over a long period of time. These changes are generally small and occur within the corporate culture. Reengineering rethinks corporate culture and sets out to redesign processes from scratch rather than through simplifying, optimizing, and/or automating them. Turner (1994) suggested a range along which process improvement and reengineering can be classified:

- *Process improvement*: Incremental innovations at the operational level including minor improvements in process efficiency, eliminating waste and cutting out nonvalue-adding activities. These most likely are local in scope.
- *Process redesign*: An extension of process improvement beyond one department or functional area. This is likely to result in a greater improvement than that of process improvement.
- *Process reengineering*: This would most likely involve a change in a step of the value chain from one side of the business to the other. This type of change is higher risk than the previous two types and usually results in improvements in cost, quality, and

lead time (or possibly all three). This type of change alters the
way that services are delivered to customers and, therefore, can
be thought of as a strategic process.

- *Business reengineering*: A step up from process reengineering,
  this type of change is more environmentally focused than any
  of the previous types, and more often than not, its achievement
  requires transformational change.

Chang (1994) suggested eight areas in which quality improvement
and process reengineering differ:

- *Senior-management involvement:* QI is an organization-wide activity involving everyone. Methodology comes down from the
  top, but the initiative for specific process improvements may
  come up from the front lines or any other part of the organization. At more advanced stages, direct involvement of a senior
  manager is diminished by leaving room for reinforcing and
  supporting roles. In reengineering, senior managers are the
  driving force from beginning to end in order to achieve a significant change in a short period of time.
- *Intensity of team-member involvement:* QI teams are assembled
  on an ad-hoc basis and members take part only as needed to
  work on improving a particular process. With reengineering,
  teams tend to work full-time for shorter periods and are usually
  charged with creating a new process or achieving a process
  breakthrough.
- *Improvement goals*: The goal for both QI and process reengineering is basically the same—that is, improving customer satisfaction. The intensity of improvement is different. QI is
  continuous; it is relatively smooth and gradual and, therefore,
  does not produce dramatic performance results. Reengineering,
  on the other hand, is discontinuous. It focuses on achieving
  massive improvement by radically redesigning the way a
  process operates, without regard to how things were done previously.
- *Implementation approach:* QI focuses on long-term benefits and
  returns, although occasionally a QI effort can result in a breakthrough. Reengineering focuses on outcomes rather than on the
  way things are currently done. Team members review how the
  process should work rather than how it presently works. Thus,
  they are able to fully uncover process complexities such as excess cost and excess cycle time.

- *Magnitude of organizational change:* With QI's emphasis on incrementalism, organizational change is less than comprehensive and typically is based on existing structures and processes with limited disruption to jobs and management systems. Reengineering creates change forcefully and over a short period of time. Radical changes are applied to jobs, management systems, structures, training, and information technology. The rate of organizational change is rapid, not only for internal employees but also for external customers and suppliers.
- *Breadth of focus:* QI tends to focus on narrowly defined processes or subprocesses. Improvement is measured in terms of performance of those processes, rather than on the strategic, broad goals of achieving greater returns (ROI), user satisfaction and retention, or even a larger market share. Reengineering focuses on broader processes with critical significance being placed on the final outcomes and the overall performance of the organization.
- *Benchmarking:* In QI external or internal benchmarking is often used comparatively after the process has been improved. In reengineering it is important to benchmark world-class organizations, functions, and processes before engaging in the improvement process.
- *Dependence on information systems:* QI teams use information systems for data collection and interpretation. Reengineering teams, on the other hand, utilize information systems as enabling mechanisms to access on-line data simultaneously.

Both quality improvement and business reengineering as change strategies have limitations embedded in their change philosophies. While using quality improvement as a change strategy may not be sufficient to achieve a technological breakthrough, applying reengineering to business processes may jeopardize the change or undermine existing interdependencies and relationships. Then how do managers decide whether quality improvement (QI) or process reengineering is more appropriate as a tool for better organizational performance? According to Chang (1994), a complementary approach is desirable. Quality initiatives encourage employees at all levels to produce continuous and incremental improvement of work processes. Targeted reengineering produces breakthrough improvements for a new core business process. Together, these two approaches may help an organization achieve and sustain significant improvement.

RETURN ON QUALITY

Although customer satisfaction is the driving force behind quality improvement initiatives, increasingly companies find it important to tie quality and profit together to remain competitive. There is some evidence showing that managers and organizations are trying to provide customers with meaningful quality products that also pay off in terms of customer loyalty and retention and in terms of market share and profitability (Greising, 1994). Return on quality (ROQ), as it is now called, ensures that quality programs have a payoff. NationBank, for example, measures every improvement in service, from adding letters to offering new mortgage products, in terms of added revenue. Federal Express still stresses speed adjusted to new quality criteria such as accuracy in sorting packages. Quality improvement efforts that are value-adding increasingly receive more attention by management. Many companies believe that applying a bottom-line requirement to quality is vital, especially in volatile markets with short product cycles and fierce competition. AT&T's CEO, for instance, receives a quarterly report from each of the company's fifty-three business units that outlines quality improvement and the subsequent financial impact. Everything from the installation of new technology to methods of improving billing accuracy is held up against an array of financial yardsticks, such as potential sales gains and return on capital. Based on its experience, AT&T found that when customers perceived improved quality, it showed up in better financial results for the next quarter.

Six principles must be followed to create a positive ROQ ratio (Greising, 1994, pp. 54–59):

- *Start with an effective quality program*: Companies that do not have the basics, such as process and inventory controls and other building blocks, will find a healthy return on quality elusive.
- *Calculate the cost of current quality initiatives*: Cost of warranties, problem prevention, and monitoring activities all count: Measure these against the returns for delivering a product or service to the customer.
- *Determine what key factors retain customers* and *what drives them away*: Conduct detailed surveys: Forecast market changes, especially quality and new product initiatives of competitors.
- *Focus on quality efforts* most *likely to improve customer satisfaction at a reasonable cost*: Figure the link between each dollar spent

on quality and its effect on customer retention and market share.

- *Roll out successful programs after pilot testing the most promising efforts and cutting the ones that do not have a big impact*: Closely monitor results: Build word of mouth by publicizing success stories.
- *Improve programs continually*: Measure results against anticipated gains: Beware of the competition's initiative and do not hesitate to revamp programs accordingly: Quality never rests.

TOTAL QUALITY MANAGEMENT: SOME POTENTIAL LIMITATIONS

Total quality management as an adaptive response is intended to link the organization internally and externally for better performance. The principal advantage of using TQM is to improve profitability and competitiveness, increase organizational effectiveness, and improve customer satisfaction. But many TQM efforts have not yielded the expected benefits. Brown, Hitchcock, and Willard (1994) proposed the following reasons for the inherent *limitations* of TQM efforts:

Short-term, bottom-line thinking: While TQM is a long-term organizational improvement strategy, many mistake TQM as a purely cost-cutting, headcount-reducing strategy. When results are not seen immediately, TQM is often dropped for being ineffectual and expensive. Most quality-conscious firms have a hard time sustaining the results of adaptation through TQM over a long period of time. Adaptation is a dynamic process which requires a tremendous amount of energy and which involves constant tradeoffs between competing values and contradictory pressures. TQM as an adaptive tool that places high expectations on people and organizations is no different.

The Wallace Company, a Baldridge Award winner, for example, had difficulty sustaining the results of TQM. Wallace is a $100 million industrial distributor of pipes, valves, fittings, and other specialty products for the refining, chemical, and petrochemical industries. Decentralization was a key element of the Wallace strategy. Organizational units were given considerable latitude to act without first seeking top-level approval. All associates were empowered to make customer-related decisions of up to $1,000 without seeking higher approval. The company also reduced its suppliers from more than three thousand to three hundred and required them to provide Wallace with extensive product-quality information. The company provided its vendors with quality-training programs and required them to pass its vendor certification program. On the other end, Wallace provided on-line computer access to much of its inventory and pricing data for customers to use in making purchases. Through its electronic data interchange (EDI), customers can gain easy access to the Wallace computer system and place orders directly, reducing the chance for errors in order processing and fulfillment. As a result of its quality-improvement program, Wallace reportedly achieved both revenue and profit growth in a still-depressed market. Wallace also became a leader in on-time delivery and defect-free transactions.

Wallace's setback came just a few months after receiving the Baldridge Award in fall 1990. During the first three quarters of 1991, Wallace's revenues were off by about 20 percent and the company lost money. It was claimed that "the Wallace company had focused only on superficial changes to win the Baldridge Award and had made no long-term improvements in its operations" (Hill & Freedman, 1992, p. 79). Although this claim was refuted by Wallace's CEO as "absolute insanity," he admitted that the company paid much more attention to quality processes and less to interfaces and customers. In fact, an anecdote told was that Wallace's Chief Operating Officer was in favor of traveling around the country and giving speeches on the quality movement.

Inappropriate measures: A fundamental tenet of management is that you get what you measure. All too often managers measure the wrong things. For example, the number of calls a service rep took, not the number of customers that were satisfied. Most firms are unable to aim their efforts at the right target, the customer or the end user, which is the one that ultimately determines the chances of a firm to be selected in or out. Allen-Bradley, a large Milwaukee-based manufacturer of industrial automation equipment is a case in point. During the 1980s, the effectiveness of its TQM effort was regularly measured against short-term financial results—"Has quality improved profits this quarter?"—rather than against customer expectations. With less than optimal results, the company finally realigned its strategic focus: "Quality needed to be in the eye of the customer" said the VP for operations (*Economist*, April 18, 1992, p. 67). The company now uses its sales people as a quality task force, continuously surveying customers to pit their expectations against the company's results.

Divergent strategies: Quality is often treated separately from "work." Quality improvement teams are often forced to try to address process-improvement issues at the same time that managers are telling them to just get the product out the door. TQM efforts tend to focus on processes rather than results and products, with the latter receiving only secondary attention. The Baldridge Award allots only about 25 percent of its scores to the actual outcomes of a firm's quality efforts. The remaining 75 percent focuses solely on processes. This can explain the difficulty Florida Power & Light had in sustaining the fruits of the Deming prize it won in 1989. While customers saw some improvements in the quality of its services, these were insignificant when measured against the sheer scale of the firm's quality effort. To a large extent, FP&L was simply going through the motions. It was obsessed with quality within, while ignoring quality outside. The company has taken some steps toward rectifying the situation. Its quality department staff has been reduced to a small number of employees, most of the quality teams have been disbanded, and a higher priority is being given to external customers.

Outdated appraisal criteria and inappropriate rewards: Traditional performance appraisal systems are not suited to teams and teamwork involving synergistic effort and collective accountability. Most compensation systems focus on individual performance as opposed to team accomplishments.

Failure to empower employees: Managers and supervisors often view TQM and the establishment of sociotechnical systems as signaling the abolishment of their jobs and responsibilities. Empowerment is associated with a threat, which is translated into a phobic reaction of nest feathering and overprotection of turf. Empowerment stops at the end of the desk of the insecure manager.

Outdated business systems: Many business planning processes provide no structured methods for front-line employees, who are closest to the customer, to have any input into the business, while information systems still focus on myriad data instead of providing customer satisfaction information.

Failure to communicate learning: In many organizations, innovative approaches to quality issues are seldom shared outside the quality teams that generated them. Learning is not diffused throughout the organization, and knowledge about errors and the lessons gained by correcting them is rarely communicated to others.

Other reasons for the partial success (failure) of TQM include:

- Refusal by organizations and managers to lead the change effort by example and involvement.
- The view that quality improvement is separate from the actual functions and responsibilities of management.
- Using an intuitive (or judgmental) rather than a systematic (or factual) problem-solving process.
- Failure to utilize quality indicators and other measures of process outcomes.
- Failure to change the reward systems as well as transform the culture of the organization.

Arthur Little's survey of five hundred American manufacturing and service companies found that only 36 percent of their executives believe that quality programs improved their competitiveness (read: adaptation). A poll by the Rath and Strong consulting firm found that 38 percent of senior managers from ninety-five corporations gave their quality efforts a failing grade (*Fortune*, May 18, 1992, p. 12). In a cover story on "managing," Labich (*Fortune* 130, 10, Nov. 14, 1994, pp. 52–68) provides an astonishing account of "change fatigue"—a dysfunctional process of adaptation. Between 1989 and 1992, U.S. companies, which had failed to implement quality processes, doubled from 50,000 to 97,000! His analysis suggested that much of this failure could be attributed to the inability on the part of top managers to understand the fundamentals of the competitive business environment, as well as the core competency of their organization. This inability led to an inaccurate reading of the need for change through a strategy of imitation rather than a strategy of change and development. Consequently, managers became reactive, lacked vision, changed only incrementally, and were faced with resistance from within. They, therefore, resorted to the means of authoritative power and top-down communications to impose their objectives.

Effective organizational leaders cannot lose sight of the fact that the pursuit of TQM goes beyond statistical tools and process control. Successful TQM intervention takes individuals' commitment and ownership, trust, confidence, and true belief in the vision of the sponsor. As Peters and Austin (1985, p. 98) said: "Quality, above all, is about care, people, passion, consistency, eyeball contact and gut reaction." Quality comes from people who care and are committed. Doing fishbone diagrams, brainstorming and drawing Pareto charts is relatively simple. Total quality management, however, is a socially binding process: "The heart of quality is not technique. It is a commitment by management to its people and its product—stretching over a period of decades and lived with persistence and passion—that is unknown in most organizations today" (Peters & Austin, 1985, p. 101).

So what separates the winners?

- Although complex information systems are needed for effective quality improvement, the human element is still a key factor in any change or adaptation process.
- Employees must be trained and be empowered to respond quickly to situations and customers with minimum interference from managers.
- A flat hierarchy and reliance on teams ensure faster communication and better coordination.
- The central focus should be on improvement of work processes, but concrete outcomes must not be overlooked.
- Renewal processes should focus on roles and responsibilities of performers and, therefore, must incorporate their views and knowledge in an upside-down approach to change. Meaningful change can originate from within the ranks.

THE GAO REPORT ON THE IMPACT OF TQM ON PERFORMANCE

In 1990, the United States General Accounting Office (GAO) was asked to conduct a study to assess the impact adopting TQM as a strategy of improvement had on select U.S. companies. GAO reviewed twenty companies that were among the highest-scoring applicants for the Baldridge Award during 1988 and 1989. Among these companies were Corning, Digital Equipment, Eastman Kodak, GM, L. L. Bean, IBM, Xerox, and Motorola. Companies that adopted TQM have experienced positive variable improvement in employee relations, productivity, customer satisfaction, market share, and profitability. Most companies used unique approaches to TQM, although many shared common features (critical success factors) that were major contributing factors to improved performance. For example:

- Corporate attention was centered on meeting customer requirements.

- Senior management led the way by creating the vision and mobilizing support for that vision and by building quality values into company operations.
- Training was available and appropriate; employees were encouraged to improve quality and reduce costs through empowerment and involvement.
- Systematic processes were integrated throughout the organization to foster continuous improvement.

None of the companies, however, reaped the benefits of implementing TQM programs in the short term. A common theme was the necessity for sufficient time (these companies improved their performance on average in about thirty months) for results to be achieved. More specifically, the results of the study included the following (GAO, 1991, pp. 3–4):

- *Somewhat better employee relations were realized*: Employees in the companies reviewed by GAO experienced increased job satisfaction and improved attendance; employee turnover also decreased. Eighteen companies reported a total of fifty-two observations (performance measures) in this area. Thirty-nine out of the fifty-two improved, nine declined, and four were unchanged.
- *Improved quality and lower costs were attained*: Companies increased the reliability and on-time delivery of their product or service and reduced errors, product lead time, and the cost of quality. Twenty companies reported a total of sixty-five observations. Fifty-nine out of the sixty-five improved, two became worse, and four were unchanged.
- *Greater customer satisfaction was accomplished*: Seventeen of the twenty companies provided data on customer satisfaction based on the survey results of their consumers' overall perceptions about a product or service, the number of complaints received, and customer retention rates. Twenty-one out of the thirty reported observations improved, three became worse, and six were unchanged.
- *Improved market share and profitability were attained*: A major impact of an organization's quality management practices, as measured by several ratios widely used in financial analysis was improved profitability. Fifteen companies reported a total of forty observations in this area. Thirty-four of the forty increased and six declined.

TQM, BALDRIDGE CRITERIA, AND ISO 9000

Most of the aforementioned critical success factors were primarily based on the Baldridge Award criteria. The Baldridge Awards are granted on the basis of company assessments. The criteria for these assessments cover all facets of TQM pertaining to leadership, information and analysis, strategic planning, human resource development, process management, business results, and customer focus and satisfaction.

The Baldridge criteria were developed in the United States partly to compensate for the lack of management, human resource development, training, and empowerment which have characterized standardized operating procedures such as ISO 9000 to ensure quality. In addition, although the ISO 9000 has contributed to an increase in companies' quality awareness and generally improved the levels of operational quality, the certification procedure failed to incorporate benchmarking and continuous improvement in its evaluation. The Malcom Baldridge Award criteria set out to replace standardization with competition. While ISO 9000 discriminates between ISO 9000 companies and those without the certification, the Baldridge criteria give a measurement of excellence through corporate self-assessment. Companies and their SBUs can receive up to one thousand points when measured against the criteria. The challenge for the companies pursuing quality is to integrate the ISO 9000 requirements and the Baldridge assessment criteria with the strategic quality planning and operational routines. Valmet's Hudson Falls division's self-assessment is a good example. By 1993, the division became ISO certified and by 1996 it began evaluating its leadership, management, and human resource systems to identify and remedy gaps and other deficiencies, as well as to assess its customer relationship management and other aspects of business and process management.

QUALITY IMPROVEMENT: ONE SIZE DOES NOT FIT ALL

In pursuit of greater adaptation, some organizations resort to quality-improvement teams, empowerment, and adoption of best practices to achieve dramatic results. Quality improvement or CQI (continuous quality improvement) is predicated on the assumption that by continually striving to reach higher and higher standards in every facet of business operations, the resulting series of small wins will add up to superior performance. Such improvement efforts typically point in the direction of an organizational ability to learn and adapt to the demands of rapidly changing environments. But is CQI sufficient or are more dramatic changes in structures and systems needed to sustain the improvement effort? The problem is that many firms, in the rush toward a tighter fit with their environments, waste a tremendous amount of resources on quality-improvement strategies that do not improve their performance and, rather, may hamper it.

Organizations must consider a range of possible interventions from which they should carefully select one for greatest optimization. For example, the formation of cross-functional teams can help identify and solve minor problems and, therefore, can be useful for starter companies. However, teams may lose direction and can be distracted from broader strategic issues once corporate performance improves. Benchmarking works best for higher-performing companies with know-how technology and expertise. For lower performers just starting a quality effort, benchmarking may create unreasonable goals, which potentially may jeopardize their entire journey toward better quality. Similarly, the idea of empowerment should not be applied indiscriminately. Empowerment works best in higher-performing organizations; whereas lower-performing organizations, which lack the training to make empowerment work, can benefit more from selective horizontal decentralization. For example, by giving customer service units greater authority to respond to customers' needs.

Fleet Financial Group, a Northeast banking operation with its headquarters in Providence, Rhode Island, is an example of a company using selective horizontal decentralization. During 1994, the company underwent a major restructuring involving the shedding of fifty-five hundred jobs (more than 20 percent of its Northeast banking operation) in an effort to boost profits by $350 million annually and survive in the rapidly changing world of banking (*Crains New York Business*, 2/20/95). The long-term goals are to reduce costs, improve customer service, and reposition the company to grow through acquisitions. But what is more interesting is Fleet's approach to change. To attain these goals, top decision makers at Fleet did not use external benchmarking or drastically change their culture from within. Realizing the risks associated with restructuring, they used internal benchmarking and also increased the amount of discretion given to front-line employees. We "went through our systems and found the best of our practices and adopted them bankwide" (Albany *Times Union*, March 11, 1994, A-8). Many functions in the bank remained centralized and items such as loan applications have been standardized and reduced to a single form. In the branches, tellers have been permitted to cash checks up to $2,500 without seeking a supervisor's approval.

Ernst and Young's study of five hundred organizations in the United States (*Business Week,* Nov. 30, 1992) offers a classification of three levels of organizational performance for implementing variants of quality methods. They used a composite of profitability, productivity, and quality criteria to measure organizational performance. In general, the study suggested that quality efforts work best when companies start with a few, highly focused practices and add more sophisticated ones later. For lower performers, the recommendation was to emphasize teams across and within units with a focus on fundamentals such as reducing cycle time by eliminating bottlenecks in the value chain, while increasing training of all sorts. Low performers do not have the necessary quality infrastructure to support the organization-wide change necessary to emulate the best. They should not use benchmarking or encourage widespread participation in quality-related activities. Low performers, essentially, should reduce their quality journey in pursuit of moderate goals. According to Aggarwal (1993, p. 66), these goals can involve some elements or all of the following sequence:

1. Identify all the quality problems and find their solutions.
2. Establish quality-assurance programs for procurement, production, and service after sales.
3. Expand TQM to all other departments of the company.
4. Train all employees (including managers) in awareness of and commitment to quality.
5. Link product design with process design to achieve the best possible quality. This may require going through several iterations.
6. Try to reduce the overall costs of operations, while simultaneously adding value to products/services.
7. Use a continual improvement program to minimize product and process variability.

The study by Ernst and Young recommended that medium performers simplify such processes as design and focus training efforts on problem solving. They should not select suppliers based on their reputation, but rather make a rational choice based on competitive bidding and by checking out suppliers' quality efforts themselves. High performers (those with returns or assets of 6.9 percent or higher) should use benchmarking to identify new products and services and should encourage organization-wide quality meetings. High performers should not increase the number of departmental teams as this could inhibit cooperation across functions. Florida Power & Light, the 1989

Deming prize winner, for example, disbanded most of its quality teams to ensure an outward focus of its operating units. As such, careful consideration of which strategies and improvement tools to use was essentially determined by the "learning curve" of the firms, as measured by ROI & VAE. The study cited above surprised many "quality" managers as well as consultants with its explosive conclusion: novice organizations can actually harm themselves by trying to imitate the strategies of a world-class benchmark as they simply are not skilled enough to undertake such an advanced initiative.

CONCLUSIONS

Quality efforts can help organizations increase employee awareness of customers' needs and concerns while focusing on improving existing technologies and processes. When a performance breakthrough is called for, reengineering may be ideal. Organizations already engaged in improvement efforts will find it easier to adapt to the requirements and principles of reengineering. Organizations also need quality-improvement techniques to sustain the results of reengineering and to constantly strive to improve the gains achieved through the reengineering effort. The challenge is to know when and where one technique might be more appropriate than the other and to understand how to make rational choices that will maximize economic as well as psychological gains for the organization, its employees, external customers and suppliers.

Chang (1994) suggested five important criteria that can facilitate the decision regarding whether to use quality improvement or reengineering:

- *Marketplace changes*: If the market is highly dynamic with short product life cycles, making gradual improvements to processes that get products to the market is unwise. Instead, redesigning the process for new product development makes more sense economically.
- *Geographic spread*: If a process affects only local work groups, a quality improvement approach may be more cost effective and appropriate than reengineering.
- *Customer and supplier involvement*: Customers and suppliers are often involved in different stages of quality improvement. Reengineering involves only the key customers and suppliers needed to achieve mutual benefits.

- *Resource allocation*: Reengineering is a costly maneuver that requires the commitment of staff, equipment, and other resources on a full-time basis. Part-time reengineering staff efforts, by definition, cannot produce breakthrough results.
- *Level of urgency*: organizations that are new to quality improvement may find that improving a process incrementally is their best choice. Later, if necessary, they can experiment with reengineering to achieve significant results. Reengineering is a good option when a process is misaligned from within, when it does not produce things right, or from outside, when it does not produce the right things. Reengineering is also a good option when improvements are essential for organizational success and when everyone recognizes the urgency for dramatic change.

Despite the fact that recent studies have shown that TQM programs are used by a wide variety of organizations, not all have been successful in achieving their quality targets (Benson, 1993; Brigham, 1993; Cole, 1993; Fuchsberg, 1992; Jacob, 1993; Lawler, Mohrman & Ledford, 1992). While some authors have blamed the failures on many factors, others believe the problem is simply a lack of understanding that cultural change is necessary for complete transformation to occur. From this perspective, moving toward a better cultural fit may result in profound results for the organization (Grant, Shani & Krishnan, 1994). Cultural fit begins with a change in attitudes and style. Where at one time managers acted as aggressors and delegators, the quality format repositions managers as facilitators and coaches demonstrating understanding and competency in empowering, mentoring, and enabling subordinates (Galbraith & Lawler, 1993; Sayles, 1993; Schmidt & Finnigan, 1994). While management literature exalts the significance of the manager's role in the advent of the need for cultural transformation, it also reveals that managers are the most threatened (McDermott, 1993). The requirement to let go and share power rather than use power does not fit the traditional format of managerial roles and responsibilities, especially that of the Monitor. The mental as well as socioeconomic sacrifice is too great to be accepted and the gains are too little to offset the costs.

While TQM calls for systemic changes in management practice, there is a paucity of concrete examples showing how middle managers adjust to their new roles. One study (Belasen, Benke, DiPadova & Fortunato, 1996) suggested that middle managers have become hypereffective in that managers zealously perform a variety of leadership roles, thus increasing their personal and organizational productivity. The study confirmed that restructuring and streamlining affect managerial behavior and that the Competing Values Framework effectively describes those behaviors and how they change. That is, for all roles but Monitor, the managers in the sample of the study perceived the roles to have increased in importance. In the case of the Monitor role, a significant number of managers perceived that the Monitor role became more important, and a significant number also perceived that the Monitor role became less important. This bimodality reflects both increasing ambiguity regarding the importance of monitoring after transformation and the differential impact of specific circumstances on the role itself. For example, when asked specifically about the lack of major increase in the importance of the monitor function, many managers reported that the monitor function had fundamentally changed. Some managers reported that monitoring had become redundant and, therefore, less important due to increasing reliance on computer technology and team-based management. Others worried that with less monitoring, quality standards may be compromised resulting in a decline of customer satisfaction.

The other three transactional roles—Director, Producer, and Coordinator—increased in absolute importance at very high levels of statistical significance. This was not predicted by the traditional managerial leadership models, which focus on shifts within the Competing Values Framework, but was consistent with the study's interdisciplinary model, which predicted—drawing upon the principal-agent literature in economics—that the sign of the effects on the transactional roles is ambiguous and depends upon the relative importance of two forces at work. The first has been the relative shift from transactional to transformational behaviors predicted by most models. The second was the shift in emphasis from discretionary behaviors outside the framework into the set of effective behaviors. That study, however, also concluded that the state of hypereffectiveness is unsustainable and therefore, requires the attention of HR directors and top managers. It may be, however, that managers resort to hypereffectiveness due to a lack of role clarity, ambiguous goals, and an insufficient or unclear understanding of management functions in changing environments. One common cause of this ambiguity is the lack of effective communication across levels and units within an organization. Maintaining open channels of communication and making them accessible is crucial for the success of change.

In contemporary, value-based organizations, a manager performing the Monitor role does not need to resort to authority and command to achieve compliance. As discussed in chapter 4 and elaborated on in chapters 6 and 7, horizontally structured organizations develop a commitment culture in which members of the organization use normative or concertive control to monitor behaviors. Instead of auditing and evaluating performance retrospectively, the Monitor resorts to a prevention or introspective approach that instills confidence in people and their ability to achieve performance breakthrough. Motivating employees to increase their personal productivity and encouraging them to team up and self-lead, while at the same time adjusting cognitively and behaviorally to the new managerial leadership roles expected from managers, are the focus of Part III.

Part III

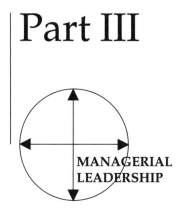

MANAGERIAL
LEADERSHIP

The external horizontal axis and the control vertical axis appear in the lower right quadrant of the Competing Values Framework and define the boundaries of the *rational goal model* and the domain of organizational *managerial leadership*. This model reflects the view that organizations are effective if they meet their goals. Fundamental to this model is the need for structure and direction. The two managerial leadership roles associated with this quadrant are the Producer and Director roles.

PRODUCER ROLE: THE PERFORMER

In the capacity of Producer, the manager is expected to be task oriented, work focused, and highly interested in the technical/operational aspects of the job. The Producer is also expected to exhibit high degrees of motivation, energy, and personal drive. Effective managers acquire, use, and dynamically integrate the competencies associated with the Producer role in managerial situations. These competencies are: working productively, fostering a productive work environment, and managing time and stress. The manager, in the role of a Producer, is a constant learner who must have updated knowledge about organizational and group performance to be able to apply complex solutions to complex problems (Maisel, 1996). Proper and useful analysis of problems can only be accomplished by understanding the full scope of the sociotechnical problems and by possessing the behavioral complexity essential for tagging and handling the number of variables involved in complex situations (Hooijberg & Quinn, 1992). This ability also requires a good number of meta-skills—for example, compassion, consistency, inner drive, and self-discipline—to enable constancy of effort through which problems and solutions are sorted analytically during the search for optimal options to meet performance objectives.

The Producer's high energy and inner motivation are triggered by traits and attributes of "personal peak performance" due to a results-oriented personality and a sense of personal mission. Adams (1984) identified commitment, challenge, purpose, control, transcendence, and balance as essential conditions that stimulate personal peak performance. For example, commitment requires a large investment in time and attention that help employees work together effectively. Valuing internal goals and intrinsic rewards should generate the commitment required for peak performance, while challenges lead employees to be task oriented and purposeful. Managers enacting the Producer role balance the need for control (to achieve efficiency) against the need for flexibility (to achieve effectiveness). They perform a dual role: An administrative role that enforces internal efficiency through operational routines and an entrepreneurial role which executes meta-routines to adapt the operational routines to the changing environment. The use of meta-routines allows employees to transform routine tasks into standard operating procedures and to develop a "grammar of actions" to achieve uniformity (Pentland & Reuter, 1994). The condition identified above as "transcendence" creates a drive toward continuous improvement, or "Kaizen," in which current performance serves as the basis for breakthrough performance (Imai, 1985). Finally, the Producer, who is skilled in time and stress management, also helps employees to manage their stress level in order to achieve a good balance across goals and tasks that often seem to be contradictory. The manager trains employees in the use of strategies and relaxation techniques and the creation of a social support system (Farnham, 1991). Improving time and stress management helps create a sense of overall balance or the perception of a healthy tradeoff between work and social obligations (Quinn, Faerman, Thompson & McGrath, 1996).

DIRECTOR ROLE: THE VISIONER

In the capacity of Director, the manager is expected to clarify expectations through formal planning and goal setting, to initiate actions and problem solving, to establish objectives and strategies, to determine roles and tasks, to generate rules and policies, and to give instructions. Effective managers acquire, use, and dynamically integrate the competencies associated with the Director role in managerial situations. These competencies are: visioning, planning, and goal setting; designing and organizing; and, delegating effectively.

Visioning seems to capture the essence of the Director role by creating the frame of reference for operational planning and setting clear objectives for the work of unit members. Hence, the follow-through process by which the leader communicates powerfully the essence of his or her vision to lower levels is important and highlights the role of the Director (Bassett, 1993; Buhler, 1995; Conger, 1996). This behavior is also congruent with findings that show that whenever a group of employees and even professionals is required to set and pursue specific goals, members of the group invariably increase their productivity substantially over that of groups who do not set goals (Latham & Wexley, 1994). The Director also must have the communication and sensitivity skills required to encourage self-evaluation and self-reinforcement, stimulate employees to acquire knowledge and learn new skills, and administer the reward and recognition systems for the organization or the work unit (Galbraith, 1993).

The chapters included in Part III—"Living with Corporate Downsizing: The Hypereffective Manager" and "Leading Self-Managed Teams: Roles and Communication"—cover the dynamics of corporate downsizing, the shifting importance of managerial roles, and the principles of effective self-management and shared team leadership. These two chapters highlight the importance of meeting external organizational goals productively and effectively while using the strategies of downsizing and self-management. While chapter 6 deals with issues concerning the results of organizational responses to declining markets, and particularly with the emergence of managerial hypereffectivity, chapter 7 focuses on the importance of visioning, as well as the initiation of structures and the transference of leadership roles to augment organizational capabilities. These two chapters examine the scope of leadership challenges faced by managers enacting the Producer and Director roles. Both chapters also contain treatments of managerial leadership roles that are theoretically based and empirically supported by recent research.

Chapter 6 illuminates the shifting importance of managerial roles from an integrative, interdisciplinary perspective. Chapter 7 sets out to demonstrate the efficacy of the Competing Values Framework of leadership as a powerful starting point to facilitate understanding of the leadership roles that have been transferred to SMTs. The CVF is a multidimensional framework, rooted in organizational effectiveness criteria, which allows capturing the complexity and dynamics of leadership adaptation, behaviors, and roles. The CVF can be used to facilitate our understanding of leadership roles in SMTs and help to close the gap between the existing theoretical constructs of leadership, especially those that are heroic-centered, and the reality of SMTs, which operate virtually with no single authority within teams.

6

Living with Corporate Downsizing: The Hypereffective Manager

The toughest problem will probably be to ensure the supply, preparation, and testing of top management people. This is, of course, an old and central dilemma as well as a major reason for the general acceptance of decentralization in large businesses in the last 40 years. But the existing business organization has a great many middle management positions that are supposed to prepare and test a person. As a result, there are usually a good many people to choose from when filling a senior management slot. With the number of middle management positions sharply cut, where will the information-based organization's top executives come from? What will be their preparation? How will they have been tested?

—Peter Drucker, "The Coming of the New Organization," *Harvard Business Review*, January–February 1988, p. 52

In recent years, corporate America has been caught by wave after wave of reorganization and the displacement of managers and professionals. From downsizing to rightsizing to restructuring to reengineering, America's corporations are collectively experiencing a "size reduction" (Gertz & Baptisa, 1995). This trend has been described by these authors as the "great corporate shrinking act." Downsizing, as a natural evolutionary extension of the process of economic development and renewal, has become the tool for reshaping bloated and inefficient organizations. Cameron, Freeman and Mishra (1991) reported that more than 85 percent of Fortune 1000 firms downsized their white-collar workforce between 1987 and 1991. Tough market conditions coupled with globalization and increased competition from offshore companies forced many companies to rethink their TQM and BPR process-focused improvement strategies and shift toward rightsizing and delayering to become flatter, more agile, and market driven. Downsizing is credited with triggering positive results: lower overhead, less bureaucracy, faster decision making, more effective communication, greater entrepreneurship, higher personal productivity, and greater overall organizational effectiveness (Bruton, Keels & Shook, 1996, p. 38).

Byrne reported that by the end of 1993, corporate America had announced 615,186 layoffs (1994, p. 61). Beginning in 1994, the corporate cutback rate was 3,100 people a day and has continued to rise. According to *The Economist* (April 20, 1996), 169,000 workers were laid off during the first three months of 1996. As recent as October 1997, ITT Industries reported that it planned to eliminate 1,900 jobs, or 3 percent of its workforce, and take a charge of over $145 million in the third quarter. A common view has been that, in the short run, companies, especially small to mid-sized with quick turnarounds, generally improve performance after downsizing. Downsizing leads to higher productivity and quality improvement, better customer service and greater willingness to take risks. A panacea? Not so. The cons are as strong as the pros.

THE DOWNSIDE OF DOWNSIZING

Critics have argued that companies obsessed with quarterly results (i.e., that encourage a short-term financial outlook through quick-fix cost reductions) have developed tactical plans to restructure through downsizing to become more "productive." The contrasting approach is strategic downsizing that reflects long-term goals and the overall positioning of the company in its market. One study found, for example, that only 22 percent to 34 percent of the downsized companies increased their productivity in the short run (Trapp, 1996). The American Management Association (AMA) survey (1996) reported that since 1990 morale has slumped instantly in 72 percent of all downsized companies. In addition, employee turnover, absenteeism, and disability claims have all increased as after-effects of downsizing. *Business Week* (April

28, 1997) recently reported that more than 70 percent of American companies undergoing downsizing are grappling with the serious problems of low morale and mistrust of management caused by years of instability and restructuring. Apparently the vast majority of the companies, which have neglected the importance of building and supporting their human resources, also suffered from a loss of productivity (Caudron, 1996; London, 1996; Noer, 1995; Remick, 1991; Tang & Fuller, 1995).

TRAINING AND TECHNICAL SUPPORT

The narrow span of attention and outwardly focused strategy of top managers, which has been aimed primarily at satisfying shareowners' demands for short-run profits, accounts for the loss of productivity. The importance of an inward, people-focused orientation tends to diminish. Consideration of the effects of downsizing on survivors' roles and responsibilities is downplayed or given a low priority. While most organizations undergoing downsizing concentrate on compensating employees who have been terminated, they do very little to improve work conditions for the survivors. For instance, middle managers working at NYNEX have lamented the absence of seminars about resumé writing or job interview preparation. A high percentage of NYNEX employees began their careers immediately after high school and have never worked elsewhere. The thought of job interviews and writing an effective resumé has placed many of these employees outside their comfort zone.

The numbers speak for themselves: AMA's tenth annual survey reported that of those firms that have downsized since 1990, only 24 percent increased their training budgets during the year following the cuts and only 32 percent did so in the long term. This is unforgivable in light of the fact that most job cuts are structural or strategic and, thus, result in different reporting relationships or business processes. AMA's 1996 survey concluded that companies that train their people to work in the new environment are twice as likely to report long-term productivity increases as are companies that cut training budgets when they cut jobs. Employees surviving downsizing are demoralized, confused, and paralyzed. They are subdued by the fear that they are next on the "hit list." Mental fatigue, hostility, and depression are often the inevitable effects of downsizing on surviving employees. There is also evidence that the number of work-related disability claims one life insurance company processed for mental illnesses increased from 7.8 percent of its total volume in 1989 to 10.2 percent in 1993.

SURVIVOR SYNDROME

A number of authors (e.g., Caudron, 1996; Frazee, 1996; Noer, 1995) addressing the need to treat the psycho-behavioral problems associated with the "survivor syndrome," or what has been labeled as "layoff survivor sickness," have described this syndrome in terms of a constant state of anxiety, guilt, fear, anger, sadness, and emotional isolation. Survivors also encounter physical symptoms of sleeplessness, irritability and lethargy. The remaining employees or survivors are left with a feeling of emptiness. Being demoralized and insecure they lose trust and confidence in assurances from organizational leadership that their jobs are safe. Citing a study conducted by the American Society for Training and Development (ASTD), Clark and Koonce (1995) reported that the credibility of senior managers is estimated to drop 35 percent after restructuring. These authors reported the following postdownsizing behavioral symptoms displayed by remaining employees:

- Concerns about future possibilities for promotion and advancement within the organization, particularly if the boss has been laid off or if the career path has been obliterated by the restructuring.
- Anxiety and insecurity about the survivor's own ability to function in or adapt successfully to the new environment, especially when the training budget has been axed.
- Adjusting emotionally, psychologically, and behaviorally to the new culture and overcoming feelings of loss, grief, depression, and inadequacy as a result of changes in the task environment. That is particularly difficult when such losses make the survivors reassess their value to the organization in terms of personal worth and professional competence.

LOSS OF ORGANIZATIONAL ENERGY: CORPORATE ANOREXIA

Downsizing companies are often caught up in a self-destructive syndrome similar to anorexia nervosa. According to Carpenter (1996, p. 37), anorexia, whether it is human or corporate, is a disease, not a cure. Corporate anorexia is a fear-and-denial-driven, dangerous reaction to often real competitive threats. In the final analysis, the status quo may be improved, but temporary gains are, after all, just temporary. Cutting and slashing without adequate restructuring of work must be replaced with common sense. The objective of reorganization is to reprocess the work to provide more customer value and productivity, not simply to eliminate jobs.

Strategically, companies cut costs while seeing no increase in revenue. In addition, by stripping themselves of employees and managers with functional knowledge and familiarity with the system of communication, downsized companies create work conditions that are often both physically and psychologically unsustainable. Carpenter (1996, p. 36) explains that corporate anorexia is the 1990s response to business competitiveness. Anorexia nervosa is a serious disorder characterized by a pathological fear of weight gain leading to faulty eating patterns, malnutrition, and even death. Businesses driven by an obsessive compulsion for short-term efficiency can become caught up in a similar destructive pattern. Whether workers are laid off (via downsizing) or managers are fired (via a shake-up), it means the same thing; removal of a primary cost, in this case, people. And the results are often destructive, as Eastman Kodak's experience has demonstrated. By the end of 1989, Kodak shaved 12 percent of its workforce, reappointed 70 percent of its key managerial positions, reduced the number of top managers by 25 percent, reorganized its structure into five business groups with thirty autonomous business units, and used constant monitoring and measurement of business outputs and value adding. As recently as fall 1997, Kodak announced the elimination of 20 percent of its one thousand senior and middle managers. From the end of December 1993 until the end of December 1996, Kodak's payoff from its turnaround strategies were $6.016 billion, $6.232, $7.018, and, $7.642 respectively. The year 1997, however, brought bad news: A strong dollar made Kodak's products more expensive abroad and stiffer competition in the emerging markets of electronic photography (Fuji's share of the U.S. market increased by about 3 percent to 20 percent). In addition, sluggish sales, rising new-product losses (Kodak lost $300 million in its digital imaging business through the third quarter), and declining profits (Kodak anticipated a 25 percent slide in profits for 1997) rendered the company less competitive. Kodak, presumably, did not have the technological and managerial capabilities—that is, its core competence—to handle the pressures. By November 11, 1997, Kodak announced that it would cut ten thousand jobs and take a $1 billion charge against earnings over the next two years.

Rubach (1995) noted that remaining employees feel less loyal to an organization that has deceived their friends and also feel guilty about retaining their jobs while others lost theirs. *Training and Development Journal* (January, 1996: 16) reported on studies conducted by the Hay Group of Philadelphia that, from 1991 to 1994, 50 percent of employees in downsized organizations claimed to have neutral feelings about staffing issues, while the other 50 percent reported negative feelings. Pointing to the psychological trauma survivors face in dealing with their emotions, Remick (1991) noted that survivors discuss feelings of anger, sadness, and guilt, and refer to physical symptoms of sleeplessness, irritability, and lethargy. Low morale, a sense of helplessness, and a lack of self-confidence tend to lead to a downward spiral.

LOSS OF ORGANIZATIONAL MEMORY: CORPORATE AMNESIA

Employees who were laid off through a generous buyout program, such as those used by telecommunication companies, have been surprised by subsequent offers to serve as consultants and resell their expertise to the company. Both AT&T and Lucent Technologies, for example, increased their hiring in the New York region despite the voluntary buyouts and layoffs worldwide (*New York Times*, 6/8/96, B1). The *Wall Street Journal* (3/11/97, B10) reported that AT&T cut about fifty-seven hundred jobs (out of about forty thousand individuals targeted for elimination by 1999) during 1996. However, the company ended the year with a slightly larger head count than it did at the end of 1995 because of increased hiring in other AT&T businesses including wireless communications, local phone services, and AT&T Solutions, a network consulting and outsourcing service. Other companies have taken steps to hire employees on a part-time status, thus avoiding large overhead costs such as fringe benefit payments. Paradoxically, relying on "temps" or LOs (low overhead), as these employees are called at Procter & Gamble, increases efficiency and flexibility, but it also could lead to a loss of institutional memory, an organizational capability or asset that is extremely essential in developing well-orchestrated and sustainable responses to pressures coming from turbulent environments. Hence, the short-term gains from downsizing appear to be offset by a long-term loss of organizational capabilities. How does the financial market measure up to these important findings? Not with great enthusiasm. AMA's 1996 survey reported that during the years 1994 to 1996, the share of the companies offering outplacement to their departing employees decreased from 58 percent (1994) to 44 percent (1995) to 38 percent (1996).

John Challenger, executive VP of Challenger, Gray, and Christmas, a consultancy and outplacement firm that monitors downsizing plans, used the "corporate Alzheimer's" metaphor to explain the risks companies take when losing investments in their intellectual capital, particularly intuitive skills and knowledge that employees take with them upon being laid off. Relating to this syndrome in terms of the loss of important organizational memory, he claimed that companies risk losing intangibles such as their collective business experiences, successes and failures, culture, and shared vision (*The Economist*, April 20, 1996). The main critique is that although companies such as Delta and NYNEX are leaner and more efficient, they are not necessarily more competitive. Corporate amnesia is particularly evident in service companies that rely heavily on networking and informal structures of relationships and common understandings to do their job. Once employees are laid off, the formal arrangements still in place are left without their collateral structures; that is, the informal networks of communication that transmit and disseminate important business and customer information.

The 1996 AMA study found that downsizing tends to hit middle managers in a much higher proportion than their numbers belie. While comprising only 8 percent of the U.S. workforce, middle management accounted for 20 percent of the jobs eliminated between July 1995 and June 1996. During the same period, there was only a 7 percent increase in middle management jobs. Unfortunately, middle managers also possess much of the organizational memory essential for effective business functioning. Although empowerment and self-managed teams (Belasen, 1997), as well as computer networks and information technology (Belasen, 1996), have rendered middle managers relatively less valuable in the decision-making and communication processes within the formal structures of the organization, their knowledge about and contribution to the informal networks of communication that tend to make up corporate memory is indispensable. Memory serves the organization and its members by preserving learned identities, causal maps, and daily routines, thus reducing uncertainty as to how to act (Robey & Sales, 1994). Companies, worrying about the consequences of memory loss or corporate amnesia have used communication audits to trace the flow of information and retain organizational knowledge before losing key middle managers. Others, such as IBM and NYNEX, have rehired their laid-off managers as subcontractors or consultants.

CHANGING STRATEGIES RATHER THAN
CUTTING PERSONNEL

In the long run, organizational downsizing, with a strategic emphasis on cutting costs, has been promoted as a means of ridding organizations of everything that fails to make them competitive or add value. Some observers note that in a downsizing program that is implemented by upper management to cut costs, insufficient attention is usually paid to both the intended and unintended effects of downsizing on the productivity of individuals and work units (Rubach, 1995). The question of whether aggregate cost savings should be combined into subunit productivity gains (and if so, how) is seldom considered by downsizing strategists. This lack of attention to cross-level effects helps explain why the goals of improving overall organizational productivity are not met. When a cut-back strategy is used without making long-term technological, structural, functional, and behavioral considerations, the organization's capability to efficiently transform inputs into outputs is effectively curtailed (Rubach, 1995). Four conditions are essential for successful downsizing:

- Long-term effects in terms of market share and penetration, new product development, and so on must be considered before making any cutback.
- Employee morale, motivation, and the sustained commitment to the organizational goal to increase productivity should be a top priority for management.
- The downsized organization should streamline its operations and reengineer the way it conducts business.
- Targeting processes for improvement should also evolve into cultural reengineering and the creation of sociotechnical systems. A process orientation along the value chain of the organization can be reinforced by cross-functional teams with teamwork and joint performance leading the way toward a full transformation.

Cameron, Freeman, and Mishra (1991) examined downsizing practices in the automotive industry with a special focus on white-collar employees in thirty organizations by inquiring about perceptions of strategies, corporate culture, leadership, and outcomes of downsizing. Measures of effectiveness were obtained by asking respondents to compare their organization's current performance against its (1) stated objectives; (2) previous performance; (3) domestic and global competitors' performance; and, (4) perceived customer expectations. These researchers concluded that a downsizing strategy that is integrated within the strategic planning of the organization tends to yield better results and higher organizational effectiveness.

Cameron, Freeman, and Mishra (1991) suggested three downsizing strategies that were associated with the most effective organizational outcomes: (1) strategies implemented by decree from top down, but also initiated from the bottom up; (2) short-term and across-the-board strategies, but also strategies that are long-term and selective in emphasis; and (3) strategies that focused on paying attention to those employees who lost their jobs as well as the survivors. They found that the best downsizing strategies were recommended and designed by employees, not top managers. Downsizing from the top down provided consistency, vision, and clear direction as well as visible commitment and hands-on involvement. Downsizing from the bottom-up helped foster innovation and improvement that would not have been possible had top management simply mandated headcount reductions (Cameron, Freeman & Mishra, 1991, 61). These researchers found that effective organizations provided outplacement services, personal and family counseling, relocation expenses, and active sponsoring of employees whose positions were eliminated. Special attention was paid to survivors through access to and sharing of information about the organization's plans and performance results versus those of its major competitors. These findings were corroborated by Covin's (1993) study, which found support for the notion that personalized means of communication are generally more effective means for communicating the need for and impact of downsizing.

Larger companies like GTE, Chrysler, Hewlett-Packard, IBM, and Motorola, which have also transformed parts of their operating core into multifunctional teams, have seen an increase in net income and profit margins. However, no one has even come close to GE, which reduced its personnel by almost one half (over 220,000 people!) over a decade, tripled its net profits, and more than doubled its revenues. In 1989, GE was ranked third in terms of its market value added (MVA) and by 1994 it had reached number one with over $55.5 billion and a 13.1 percent return on capital (*Fortune*, Nov. 28, 1994, p. 144). GE's emphasis on downsizing via limiting its core businesses and focusing on the most successful ones, and IBM's experience with elimination of large segments of its business portfolio, also suggest that large corporations seek to improve effectiveness by altering the range of their activities. As Bruton, Keels, and Shook (1996) reported in their study: firms successfully downsizing actively manage their portfolios to build new competitive strengths or reinforce preexisting ones. As Catherine

Arnst, an analyst with *Business Week* (1/22/96, p. 41) concluded: corporate America's downsizing continues to be driven by changing strategies rather than lower profits.

PREEMPTIVE STRATEGY

Through the reinvention and utilization of TQM and BPR techniques, downsizing as a turnaround strategy, has also become a preemptive strategy (Bruton, Keels & Shook, 1996). AMA's 1996 survey reported that 82 percent of companies reporting job elimination cited rationales such as organizational restructuring, reengineering of business practices, and improved staff utilization. The same survey, however, found that product or service quality and operating profits proved elusive in the wake of job cuts. Fewer than 33 percent of those companies that have downsized since 1990 have seen improved productivity and higher operating profits. Approximately 50 percent made rapid gains in productivity and increased their operating profits. And just 26 percent of the firms surveyed reported short-term improvement in the quality of customer relations, products, and services. Other surveys reported similar results: only 30 percent of the downsized companies experienced the expected profit increases and only 21 percent achieved satisfactory ROI increases. However, 46 percent reported that the workforce reduction did not reduce expenses as much as expected (Cascio, 1993). Reporting on the outcomes of corporate downsizing, *Business Week* (April 28, 1997, p. 26) concluded that "On average, organizational structuring, mainly downsizing, had little if any positive impact on earnings or stock market performance." Evidence shows that the stock value of most downsized companies tends to depreciate two years after the reduction in force has been initiated (Dorfman, 1991).

To remain competitive, NYNEX, for example, initiated a downsizing program with the goal of eliminating 20 percent of its employees. This reduction was projected to slash the operating budget by 40 percent while improving customer service. The story of NYNEX (Byrne, 1994, pp. 62–63) illustrates the drama of achieving the four criteria mentioned above and the human dynamics associated with the attempt to remake the company. Since 1990, about six downsizing efforts have been introduced by NYNEX Finance and Administration. Since then, the company has rid itself of 19,200 employees, mostly managers. In January 1994, NYNEX took a $1.6 billion charge to earnings and during March 1994, NYNEX acknowledged that the cutbacks would cost an additional $1.3 billion in charges for severance terms more acceptable to union leaders.

Delta Air Lines, like NYNEX, reportedly slashed its workforce by almost 17 percent to become more productive. Both companies, however, suffered from a major setback in service quality and customer satisfaction. NYNEX, for example, was forced to pay its customers a rebate. Although NYNEX's management linked the reduction in force (RIF) plan with a relatively attractive buyout offer, many of its lower and middle managers resented the uncertainty surrounding the offer and their career stability. The outcomes of the RIF have been measured against the strategic goals of the company, but implementation has been inconsequential and unsystematic. One middle manager recounted that "the 1994 Employee Opinion Survey showed that morale is at an all-time low. Additionally, there appears to be no rhyme or reason as to how workers are rated to determine who stays and who goes." Moreover, "while NYNEX made an attractive retirement offer to those who are pension eligible, the majority of employees were forced to sweat out their job security . . . Ideas such as leaves of absence or part-time work were never introduced." Another problem is when a company makes an early retirement offer, HR managers cannot easily determine who will accept the buyout offer. The same middle manager recounted: "In my department, the most experienced, knowledgeable workers left. Our department was left with an inexperienced, depressed workforce." Micklethwait and Wooldridge (1996, p. 206) wrote about the tension involving the need to obtain high productivity through overworked employees:

> One of the developing world's biggest problems is that modern economies seem to combine rising unemployment with longer working hours for those in jobs. On balance, Handy's rule (about half the number of people being paid twice as much to do three times as much work) looks like an exaggeration, but even if they are working only one-and-a-half times as hard as they used to, most workers feel shattered.

Even among middle managers the sense of foreboding is strong. The very same managers that seemed to be impervious to changes now feel that their world is falling apart.

MIDDLE MANAGERS: THE "IN-GROUP"

> It is interesting that although many organizations seek to empower people and encourage greater leadership from middle managers, their downsizing efforts are targeted at exactly the people who were found . . . to make the most transformational change . . . plateaued managers were

most likely to take the greatest risks . . . The assumption that plateaued managers should be the initial targets of downsizing efforts through such things as early retirement buyouts may be terribly destructive to organizational responsiveness. The organization may be losing precisely the people who can enhance the organization's responsiveness through transformational change. (Spreitzer & Quinn, 1996, pp. 256–57)

This section summarizes the tenets of social identity theory (SIT) to help explain self- and cross-perceptions between human resource managers and middle managers, the "in-group." According to Ashforth and Mael (1995), SIT is the tendency of individuals to classify themselves and others into various social categories (e.g., religious affiliation, gender, sports fan, etc.) defined by characteristics shared by all members. The organizationally situated identity of an individual may be comprised of multiple disparate and loosely coupled identities derived from a developing sense of who one is as complementary to where one is and what is expected of him or her in relation to the group or organization. Identification is the vehicle whereby an individual attempts to manage his or her life in order to establish continuity in their identity with relationship to the group. From a social identity theory (SIT) perspective, every personal experience may potentially affect behavioral patterns within any social affiliation. When social identity is salient, the individual tries to assimilate his self-concept to that of the typical group member, thereby satisfying a need for group inclusion (Ashforth & Mael, 1995). Studies have shown that at either extreme of inclusiveness, a person's sense of self-worth may be threatened. Total individualization leaves one vulnerable to isolation and stigmatization while complete deindividualization leaves no room for comparative self-definition (Tajfel, 1978; Hogg & Turner, 1985; Brewer, 1993). Previous studies by Turner (1981), Tajfel (1982), and Brown (1986), found that when identifying with a group, people may actually feel that they personify the group or organization, and interestingly, these studies also found that identification persists tenaciously in the face of group failures, personality conflicts, and absence of strong leadership. Consequently, social identification with a group formed via an individual's personal experiences has been found to directly impact employee satisfaction and overall organizational functioning (Mael & Tetrick, 1992).

While most people tend to slide between social identities with relative ease, occasional conflicts arise with respect to those loosely coupled organizational identities in which integration proves cognitively taxing to the individual due to the need to juggle across a number of important identities. This cognitive conflict may be resolved in several ways. The individual may attempt to define him/herself in terms of the dominant identity to which he or she relates most closely; or the individual may apply sequential action between conflicting identities so that inconsistencies need not be resolved for any specific identity; or the individual may buffer identities via a developed hierarchy that prioritizes his or her perceptually most valued identity. Adler and Adler (1987), as cited by Ashforth and Mael (1989), described an example of how this occurs when college sports players tend to resolve conflict between athletic and academic roles by defining themselves as athletes first and students second. Apparent hypocrisy may occur when an individual attempting to compartmentalize identities fails to integrate values, norms, and attitudes inherent in these identities into his or her outward persona (Ashforth & Mael, 1989).

Social identity theory assigns referent memberships to in-group and out-group categories due to the relational and comparative nature of social identifications. Awareness of out-groups reinforces awareness of one's in-group. For example, Kanter (1977) found that the presence of females in a male-dominated sales force induced male exaggeration of perceived differences between the sexes. Given the desire of group members to seek differences between themselves (in-group) and other reference groups (out-groups), much intergroup conflict exists, thus allowing groups to segregate from one another and fall into competition for existing organizational resources. This is especially true with respect to relations between high- and low-status groups. The phenomenon of in-group bias, which justifies distancing and subordination of the out-group occurring as a result of competition, is in fact greater in the absence of strong organizational identity and with respect to increasingly comparable out-groups (Ashforth & Mael, 1989).

The hypocrisy that occurs when the individual fails to integrate a variety of conflicting identities extends to groups where individuals become sublimated within the dominant organizational culture. Although a strong identification with an organization by subgroups is likely to enhance support and commitment toward organizational goals, in-group and out-group subcultures may take on norms, traditions, and values that may have negative effects on the organization. One instance is that while subgroups may internalize an organization's culture, they may not necessarily identify with the organization itself (Ashforth & Mael, 1989). Charles Heckscher (1996), for example, reported that in downsized firms that "successfully built a shared commitment to the accomplishment of a mission" (p. 121), middle managers developed identities as professionals rather than loyalties to the firm as a way to avoid psychological denial of change. Middle managers in such firms had high morale and initiative even without job security. Another example may be seen in middle-manager hypereffectiveness (Belasen, Benke, DiPadova & Fortunato, 1996). This tends to occur when manager subgroups under the threat of downsizing are increasingly unwilling to relinquish roles and responsibilities in the belief that everything is of top priority under the old middle-management paradigm where groups were expected to respond to contradictory demands from other upper-level management subgroups. These examples demonstrate ways in which in-group and out-group subcultures may take on roles and behaviors counter to optimal organizational efficiency. The resulting conflicts existing between subgroups and organizational identity give way to increasingly low employee morale and below-optimum organizational functioning. This may also help to explain the frustration of middle managers who are the prime target for elimination during corporate downsizing.

MIDDLE MANAGEMENT TRADITIONAL ROLES

> The question is not whether to have middle managers, but how to use them without letting them indulge their weaknesses for hierarchy building and paperwork.
>
> —Micklethwait & Wooldridge, 1996, p. 203

Since traditional, bureaucratic organizations are geared toward maximizing efficiency, they also adopt a strategy of centralized control through vertical hierarchies and functional departments (Perrow, 1986). Using horizontal differentiation, standardization of work processes, and formalization (through rules and procedural specifications, training, and coordination), management reduces uncertainty and achieves effective integration (Robbins, 1990). In these organizations, middle managers exercise positional power to achieve greater compliance and conformity to organizational goals and strategies in lower levels (Kanter, 1979). Purposive middle managers provide clear direction and common patterns of behavior that reduce randomness and ambiguity. Acting primarily as gatekeepers, middle managers translate the objectives and strategic plans of higher-level managers into operational goals and plans that are clear and understood by lower levels (Daughtrey & Ricks, 1989). They respond to reports, inquiries, and quests for clarifications that come from lower levels and are sensitive to demands for accountability and responsiveness flowing from higher levels. Thus, middle managers focus on the coordination of activities performed by others and the integration of their efforts. Middle-level managers help link the means-ends chain of management; they ensure the smooth flow of information and work between upper and lower levels (Barge, 1994).

Midlevel managers also intervene in the flow of decisions (Mintzberg, 1983). Exceptions, emergencies, proposals for change, decisions requiring authorization, and so on, flow upward. Some of these decisions are made at the midlevel, while others are passed up for action at a higher level in the hierarchy. Resources that middle managers must allocate in their units, rules and plans that must be communicated and clarified, responsibilities that must be divided or shared, and projects that must be implemented flow down. Middle managers in bureaucratic settings are communication transmitters, goal translators, and organizational custodians. They use their legitimate power to create and manage dependencies, as well as measure, evaluate, control, reward, or sanction performance (Kanter, 1979). Midlevel managers also engage in boundary management, maintaining liaison contacts with other managers or creating internal and external interdependencies between units (Daft, 1989).

Building on Parsons (1960), Thompson's (1967) taxonomy of three levels of management also identified strategies used by managers in dealing with their task environments. Thompson suggested that top managers assume open systems strategies and roles, while lower levels use closed systems strategies and assume internal process roles, and midlevel managers utilize situational management. Upper-level managers deal with elements in the institutional environment of the organization including markets, goals, strategies, and overall structure, and therefore appear to use an open systems strategy (i.e., strategic planning, SWOT analysis, environmental scanning) and must have conceptual skills. Lower-level managers deal with elements in the work flow and the technical system including production processes, supervision, and motivation of employees, and therefore, appear to be using a closed system approach (i.e., organizing and controlling the work unit) and require technical skills. In dealing with organizational stakeholders, upper-level managers must master skills that are associated with the broker role (i.e., how to negotiate better terms for the organization), while lower-level managers and first-line supervisors use the skills associated with the producer as well as the monitor roles that are essential for motivating people and coordinating activities to increase work productivity. Thus, both upper and lower levels share similar concerns for human relations and both must also have effective interpersonal communication skills.

Middle managers, on the other hand, by virtue of their position within the chain of command, must use a situational strategy by blending conceptual, human, and technical skills and applying them in a variety of situations. These situations include linking internal systems both vertically and horizontally, managing information and control systems, resolving intergroup conflict, allocating departmental resources, and using power to resolve turf issues and protect functional territories.

Middle managers rely heavily on rules and quantitative skills to generate compliance and achieve desired results. Constrained by middle managers' hegemony, lower levels perceive middle managers' roles as auditors and evaluators and their managerial style as directive and autocratic (Kanter, 1979). Middle managers, in turn, influence these perceptions with their own behaviors by creating and enacting an image of an authoritative and powerful position protected by their centrality, criticality, visibility, relevance, and nonsubstitutability (Whetten & Cameron, 1995). Participation and delegation are relatively less important in this work environment. Instead, monitoring, coordinating, directing, and producing skills are needed to ensure stability and predictability. Defending the status quo and maintaining the equilibrium become critical and receive high priority (Pfeffer, 1978). Change is marginal; it is accepted only as long as it does not disrupt the daily routine and stable work flow. When administrative change occurs, middle managers tend to resist it by sealing off their functional turf and by creating alliances with their loyal followers and peers to ward off any attempt to shake up the power balance within the organization. Often, it is not difficult for middle managers to demonstrate that the socioeconomic costs of change outweigh the benefits. As McDermott (1993, p. 38) succinctly stated:

> In effect, middle managers are being asked to alter their world, a world they know and in which they're comfortable. Unless they're convinced that the new world is a better place, they may react negatively. They may engage in battles for turf. They may let themselves become sidetracked by everyday work activities. They may spend their work days worrying about whether they will eventually lose their jobs if they relinquish their power to peers and subordinates. (McDermott, 1993, 38)

Bureaucratic organizations have limited capacity to change due to inertia and preservation of the status quo, and also due to systemic barriers such as limited resources, high specialization, and such formal constraints as rules and standardized work processes. Kaufman (1985) postulated a range of reasons as to why managers, in general, would tend to resist change: sociopsychological, economic, and functional. The sociopsychological reasons are reflected in the need for collective stability. Working together in social systems requires a great deal of regularized behavior. Middle managers are reluctant to replace known imperfections with unknown ones and prefer, instead, to preserve the status quo. They create rules and standard operating procedures (SOPs) to sustain authoritative relationships and stabilize the system. Economically, middle managers are reluctant to risk the rewards, status, influence, fame, security, reputation, and network that they have built up over the years and which benefit them (Perrow, 1986). In addition, they encourage routine, patterned behaviors, and intensive specialization, essentially forming functional walls and mental blinders between units and individuals, which buffer against any innovation. Change, even an incremental one, becomes self-limiting (Belasen, 1996).

Bureaucratic organizations, however, are not immortal. They do and must change to survive the changing conditions of their environments. The existence of multiple layers of unnecessary managers creates a series of filters and obstacles that slow down organizational responses to change and innovation (Berry, 1991). The typical hierarchical structure is the result of the need to oversee mass production and render the system's outcomes uniform and predictable through high specialization and the use of command and control structures. Traditionally, as organizations grew larger and production and delivery processes have become too complex, hierarchical structures have evolved to ensure uniformity. The growing number of midlevel managers was one of the prices organizations paid for the benefits of fragmenting their work into simple, repetitive steps and organizing themselves hierarchically (Hammer & Champy, 1993, 16).

There is evidence to suggest that the more dynamic the environment, the more organic the structure of the organization should be (Lawrence & Lorsch, 1967; Mintzberg, 1983). Organizations operating in dynamic environments are often faced with uncertain sources of supply, unpredictable customer requirements, short product life cycles, high labor turnover, and rapidly changing technologies and knowledge. Under these conditions, management cannot easily predict the future, and so it cannot achieve effective coordination via standardization of work processes. Management must employ more flexible, less formal coordinating mechanisms such as direct involvement, expansion of communication networks, and lateral relations (Drucker, 1990; Ledford & Mohrman, 1993; Manz, Keating & Donnellion, 1990; Morgan, 1993). In other words, the organization must have a flexible, organic structure (Galbraith & Lawler, 1993; Robey & Sales, 1994).

When the environment also becomes more complex, organizations tend to become nimble and must adopt decentralized structures of decision making. To respond quickly to diverse suppliers, different customers' requirements, new regulatory standards, market developments, product innovation, and competitors' strategic moves, managers must relinquish a good deal of their power to supervisors, staff specialists, and even operators. Midlevel managers are expected to decentralize decision-making processes vertically by pushing down decision-making authority and by delegating technical and managerial responsibilities to supervisors and employees, and also horizontally by providing specialists with the autonomy (i.e., managerial, technical discretion) needed to perform their jobs.

MIDDLE MANAGEMENT TRANSITIONAL ROLES

> The strategic [role] of middle management has . . . become increasingly multifaceted. In essence, it has shifted from merely promoting stability to coping with ever increasing complexity . . . Middle management's strategic roles therefore have to do with change: understanding the need for change (synthesizing), preparing for it (facilitating), stimulating it (championing), and ultimately, managing the process (implementing).
>
> —Floyd & Wooldridge, 1996, pp. 50–52

As organizations are restructured and adopt more flexible, decentralized forms of operations, old styles of management must be reshaped or transformed into new styles that recognize the changing needs of the organization. The traditional (old-style) middle manager told people what to do, how to do it, and when to do it. A new-style middle manager asks the questions that will get people to solve problems and make decisions on their own. This transformation involves a shift in mindset from one which adheres to the traditional, bureaucratic style that favors stability and preserves the status quo, toward one suitable for managing discontinuity, randomness, and flux. The new style requires middle managers to be skilled at managing disorder and helping employees self-organize and evolve into a flexible, more relevant mode of grouping such as self-managed work teams (Belasen, 1994). However, Traditional middle managers whose jobs have consisted primarily of interpreting and carrying out plans and directives from top management, must accept change or face losing their jobs (Kanter, 1986). When adaptive responses to environmental change require cultural, structural, and technical change within the organization (Tichy, 1983), middle managers have two choices: to collaborate and contribute or to resist and risk their reputation, image, and often, their jobs. The most difficult yet challenging task for them is to unlearn old habits and styles and to learn new ones. This creates a very confusing situation both cognitively and behaviorally (McDermott, 1993).

The transition toward a more flexible, organic system of management creates ambiguity that is not easily facilitated or resolved. While the surviving middle managers are expected to collaborate by sharing power and transforming the culture of the organization (Dobbs, 1993), they are still held accountable for the old management practices and processes. To remain viable, middle managers must change their traditional roles (Sherman, 1995). During this transition they find themselves responding to a simultaneous and often contradictory set of pressures from the top, from external stakeholders to mobilize resources around new ideas (Fulop, 1991), and from lower levels to maintain constancy of purpose, stability, and continuity. Trying to link organizational activities across technical and institutional levels (Van Cauwenbergh & Cool, 1982) is both challenging and frustrating.

The shift in management paradigms, leadership styles, and communication patterns is an important aspect of adaptation that reinforces the new organizational forms and the new leadership roles. Adopting a loosely coupled structure with fewer hierarchical levels and a wider span of control also requires midlevel managers to reorient their cognitive map and focus on horizontal management, often beyond merely adjusting their behaviors. Horizontal management reflects a change in management attitudes and orientations, as well as leadership styles and communication patterns (Denton, 1991). It requires a whole new mind-set of interpersonal communication, role relationships, internal motivation, conflict resolution, and reevaluation of work processes. Horizontal management involves creating a high-performance culture through relational management where coaching and facilitating skills are essential. Horizontal management turns the attention of organizational leaders, and particularly middle managers, to customer needs rather than hierarchical interests. Processes and interfaces replace functions and areas of jurisdiction. Midlevel managers must take on multiple responsibilities, and therefore, must be cross-trained. An effective middle manager in a horizontal organization must have both depth and breadth, a T-shaped set of skills that is an optimal mix between being a specialist and a generalist. In other words, s/he must have the leadership, administrative, interpersonal, and cross-functional skills essential for task performance. However, middle managers reluctantly agree to transform their roles.

Middle managers, who have spent most of their work lives in traditional command structures, often have trouble trading institutional and quantitative skills for interpersonal and networking skills. Those who rethink their roles learn to let go by empowering and by sharing information with employees. They develop and articulate exactly what the organization is trying to accomplish, and then recreate an environment within which employees can perform with high quality to meet the needs of their customers (Kotter, 1990). Effective middle managers reorient their predominant approach from being auditors and evaluators to being "employee coaches," "facilitators," and "process managers." They focus their attention on process management and continuous improvement efforts (Micklethwait & Wooldridge, 1996). Mid-level managers who take on multiple responsibilities can benefit by having both depth in their related discipline and breadth of administrative and problem-solving skills. This involves mastering brokering and interpersonal skills, as well as the cross-functional skills essential for task performance. Being a broker is often essential for linking organizations and coordinating key players within the network, as well as monitoring the flow of resources across organizations (Snow, Miles & Coleman, 1992). In the broker capacity, managers play the role of architect, by designing and assembling the network value chain. Once the network has been put in place, midlevel managers with coordinating skills assume the role of lead operator to make the network operative. Acting primarily as boundary spanners, middle managers collect, screen, and share information across the organization that is part of the network value chain.

Department and division heads within organizations, or middle managers, are increasingly pushed to play a more strategic role in creating cross-departmental collaboration and conceptualizing solutions from the perspective of organizational stakeholders. Middle managers are centrally located within the structure of decision making and their participation in strategy making is important (Nonaka, 1988; Westley, 1990). Middle managers are also encouraged and are often given a mandate to make their own journey into the intricate world of their business environment in order to network themselves with others. As one observer noted: Organizations are nearly turning themselves inside-out, buying formerly internal services from outside suppliers, forming strategic alliances and partnerships that bring external relationships inside where they can influence company policy and practice (Kanter, 1986, 1989). In this highly interdependent network of organizations and clients, middle managers' role as change architects is extremely important: They carry much of the responsibility to transform the organization into an agile and adaptive system (Delavigne & Robertson, 1994; McDermott, 1993; Schmidt & Finnigan, 1994). Katzenbach (1995), for example, supports the notion that middle managers should transform themselves into real change leaders who provide a rock-solid linkage between the realities of the marketplace, the aspirations of top management, and the actions of the workforce. Real change leaders influence and make a 360-degree performance impact on people all around them. To do so, however, they need to unlearn their heroic or great man model (i.e., analyze, leverage, optimize, delegate, organize, and control, in essence the manager who knows best) and learn to become emergents or real change leaders (i.e., do it, fix it, try it, change it, and then do it all over again; no one person knows best).

Middle management roles must also evolve into facilitator and mentor roles, where coaching and counseling and interpersonal communication are important skills that must be acquired and used. They are expected to use lateral rather than vertical communication to coordinate work schedules and activities. First-line supervisors are delegated the authority that traditionally has been kept away from them. They are expected to make decisions without being second-guessed and make themselves more valuable to their employers. The value adding of middle managers in the downsized organization is not monitoring results, but rather linking processes; not managing functions, but managing interfaces. They are expected to lead people, facilitate conflicts, coach teams, initiate action learning, anticipate crises, reengineer processes, scan the environment, link interfaces, and communicate the mission of the organization to teams and individuals.

Perhaps the best description of middle-management roles in transforming organizations comes from Floyd and Wooldridge's (1996) conception of the strategic middle manager. Being centrally located at the interplay between strategic purpose and organizational action, middle managers influence strategy in upward and downward directions. These authors bring evidence to support the argument that when middle managers are involved in the substance of strategic decisions (not just implementation), organizational financial performance improved significantly. They describe four important strategic roles (see figure 6.1): vis-à-vis top management, middle managers champion strategic alternatives and synthesize information, while toward lower levels they facilitate adaptability and implement deliberate strategy. Although each role is distinguished by its vertical orientation, the need for effective lateral communication and influence across the organization is common among the roles (Floyd & Wooldridge, 1996). Becoming a strategic middle manager is a challenge that involves the need to learn strategies from three different perspectives: being sensitive to and understanding values and needs of external constituents; becoming intimate with

Figure 6.1. Strategic Roles and Communication for
Middle Managers

STRATEGY

	Divergent	Integrative
COMMUNICATION		
Upward	Championing	Synthesizing
Downward	Facilitating	Implementing

Adapted from: S. W. Floyd and B. Wooldridge (1992) Middle Management Involvement in Strategy and Its Association with Strategic Type: A Research Note,
Strategic Management Journal, 13, 153–167. Copyright © John Wiley & Sons Limited. Reproduced with permission.

internal operations and understanding how the technical skills and
competencies of employees and units are integrated across the organizational value chain; and, knowing, understanding, and influencing top
management's view of strategic priorities (Floyd & Wooldridge, 1996).
However, as Spreitzer and Quinn (1996) pointed out, becoming a strategic manager presents senior management with the special challenge of
stimulating middle managers to redefine their roles and to experiment
with more transformational behaviors.

ADOPTING TRANSFORMATIONAL ROLES

> From our perspective, it is surprising when middle managers fail to take
> an interest in broadening their strategic involvement. In these times of re-
> structuring and downsizing, it seems obvious that organizations are likely
> to place a greater value on middle managers who understand the strategy
> and who are actively engaged in it . . . Apart from the organization's inter-
> ests, therefore, we see strategic role performance as in the middle man-
> ager's self-interest. Why then are so many managers reluctant?
>
> —Floyd & Wooldridge, 1996, p. 128

Evidence shows that since they have more to lose, high-potential
middle managers tend to place more emphasis on transactional roles
and take small, incremental steps to change what is within their domain
of control (i.e., within their work units). In contrast, managers reaching

a plateau experience less role conflict, and having less to lose, they are able to assume transformational roles and initiate change outside their domain of control (Spreitzer & Quinn, 1996). These researchers also observed that

> although many organizations seek to empower people and encourage greater leadership from middle managers, their downsizing efforts are targeted at exactly the people who were found . . . to make the most transformational change . . . Plateaued managers were most likely to take the greatest risks on behalf of the company . . . The organization may be losing precisely the people who can enhance the organization's responsiveness through transformational change. (pp. 256–57)

Surviving corporate downsizing can have negative bearings on managers, both at emotional and cognitive levels. The managers still employed will be expected to assume more work responsibilities with fewer employees, cope with stress and low morale, defuse anxiety and mistrust, streamline processes, and plan, organize, lead, and control activities under tight schedules. They need to deal with employees who feel insecure about their jobs and psychological contracts (i.e., in a traditional sense of transacting or trading loyalty and performance for rewards and employability) with the organization. They are advised by management consultants to become "doers" by accomplishing more with less (Morris, 1996). Managers concerned about their inability to measure up against the added demands from the job and the additional responsibilities often ask for workload reductions, reduced hours, voluntary simplicity, or downscaling only to find that they are expected to give the company no less than total commitment.

According to Moats Kennedy (1996, 53), a career planning strategist, "those managers who raised the idea of playing a lesser role were ruthlessly dealt with: some were eventually fired even though they did not reduce effort. Candidates who tried to negotiate a lesser role going in were simply not hired." Most survivors of downsizing, including middle managers, share the following symptoms described by Nadler, Gerstein, Shaw, and Associates (1992):

- *Priority stress*: Everything is important. There is no clear view of critical issues nor clear tradeoffs among tasks and responsibilities. The outcome is a level of productivity unsustainable over the long run.
- *Unclear strategies*: Conflicts arise over future direction. Lack of clear vision creates ambiguity that makes it difficult for lower

levels to operationalize goals. The result is constant subopti-
mization.

- *Perceived powerlessness*: Self-fulfilling prophecy that managers
  perceive themselves as having no control over the situation. Yet,
  they are held accountable for work results. Since the effects are
  detrimental and contrary to the call to empower, managers
  tighten control over their direct reports rather than relinquish
  power. Yet, they still feel vulnerable and helpless.

- *Role overload*: Managers are doing more of everything to satisfy
  expectations coming from senior managers. Consequently, they
  reduce the autonomy of lower levels and restrict access to channels of communication. Employee morale goes down the tube;
  e.g., once a manager feels that his or her immediate superior
  lacks the support of upper management, trust and confidence
  in the ability of the manager to influence tends to diminish. The
  manager then places restrictions on the quantity and quality of
  upward communication.

BECOMING HYPEREFFECTIVE

The study by Belasen, Benke, DiPadova, and Fortunato (1996),
which examined the reactions of middle managers to downsizing,
found that managers have become hypereffective in performing their
roles. The significant increase in seven of the eight roles, including the
critical Producer and Director roles of the Competing Values Framework, suggested that the sample of managers studied may have become not only more effective but what the researchers labeled
"hypereffective." Movement toward the efficiency frontier was not sin-
gularly conclusive, but the pattern of change in the tasks and responsibilities underlying the roles suggested a severe loss of discretionary
time and an increase in the sense of powerlessness among the managers surveyed. Further, the indepth interviews supported these preliminary findings. The reason transactional roles (e.g., Director,
Producer, Coordinator) increased was that the managers had been
working much longer and harder. Increased organizational efficiencies
have come about only in part due to changes in work processes (reflected in part by shifting roles within the Competing Values Framework). The larger source of productivity gain was most likely the result
of the vastly increased allocation of managerial activity from personal
(nonvalue-maximizing) activities to activities enhancing organizational effectiveness. The researchers were treated to many stories re-

peating this theme: managers understand how important these roles have become ("as we downsized and became more competitive, the roles became much more explicit"); managers do not emphasize merely some but rather all of the roles more heavily ("since there are fewer managers, each . . . must take on more functions"); and managers do so at the expense of the other activities in their personal and professional lives.

These managers need training and support for the performance of a significantly enhanced set of roles and competencies. In this light, human resource professionals in transforming organizations need to assess their organization's current inventory of capabilities and managerial competencies, compare them to the changed needs of the organization, and develop requisite training programs. Middle managers need assistance in redefining the scope, intensity, and range of behaviors and competencies associated with managerial leadership.

Roles such as Innovator and Broker, previously considered the domain of upper management, are important for the functioning of middle managers in the transforming organization (see table 6.1). In addition, support and incentive systems must be linked to the new organizational structures. A second major finding was somewhat counterintuitive: Unlike common agreements among researchers (e.g., Spreitzer & Quinn, 1996) that middle management roles must shift from transactional managers charged with maintaining the status quo to transformational leaders (Bass, 1985; Bennis & Nanus, 1985) who stimulate change (Johnson & Frohman, 1989), Belasen, Benke, DiPadova, and Fortunato (1996) found that the importance of transactional roles has increased as well. Human resource professionals must, therefore, exercise care to ensure that their own increased emphasis on the importance of developing the competencies associated with the transformational roles does not come at the expense of the traditional skills of management; that is, those residing within the transactional roles. Coordinating, directing, and producing (the latter in particular) remain absolutely critical to managers in organizations undergoing severe transitions. (See tables 6.1 and 6.2 for a full explication of the most important roles versus the least important roles as rated by the managers in the sample of Belasen, Benke, DiPadova & Fortunato's study cited above). The findings suggest that these roles are particularly important for managers of organizations faced with real threats to their survival.

Managers who perceive an increase in the importance of most roles clearly find few opportunities to diminish the performance of some in order to increase their attention to others. For example, managers who perceive that the producer role has increased in importance may choose

Table 6.1.
The Most Important Tasks and Responsibilities, by Roles

PRODUCER	Maintains a high level of energy in motivating others Creates high performance expectations in others, focusing on results
DIRECTOR	Sets objectives for accomplishing goals Assigns clear priorities among multiple goals Sets goals in a participative context
COORDINATOR	Reallocates resources to accommodate necessary changes in workflow
MONITOR	Sets up and maintains necessary communication channels Disseminates information regarding changes in policies and procedures
MENTOR	Gives credit to subordinates for their work and ideas Maintains an open, approachable, and understanding attitude toward subordinates Encourages participation in professional development activities
FACILITATOR	Fosters a sense of teamwork among employees; helps subordinates resolve conflict Works to enhance employee participation and cohesive work climate Involves subordinates in discussions over work matters; encourages participation in group decisions Facilitates and leads meeting
INNOVATOR	Comes up with ideas for improving the organization Suggests changes in work processes and procedures to superiors Turns problems into opportunities Personally helps individual employees adjust to changes in the organization Encourages creativity among employees; helps employees deal with ambiguity and delay Assesses the potential impact of proposed changes Helps subordinates see the positive aspects of new changes
BROKER	Builds coalitions and networks among peers Nurtures contacts with people external to the organization Presents ideas to managers at higher levels; represents the unit to others in the organization; exerts lateral and upward influence in the organization Represents the unit to clients and customers

Source: A. T. Belasen, M. Benke, L. N. DiPadova, and V. M. Fortunato (1996). "Downsizing and the hypereffective manager: The shifting importance of managerial roles during organizational transformation." *Human Resource Management Journal*, 35(1), p, 107. © Copyright by John Wiley & Sons, Inc.

Table 6.2.
Tasks That Are Less Important Than Those in Table 6.1

Items in *italics* are those tasks reported to be less important now than before the organization began downsizing efforts.

PRODUCER	In motivating employees, considers their individual differences
	Develops policies and procedures that foster the motivation of all employees
	Uses time- and stress-management strategies to handle delays and interruptions
	Helps lower-level managers deal with the difficulties of their role
DIRECTOR	Defines role and expectations for employees
	Presents goals to higher levels for consideration
	Delegates tasks to employees
COORDINATOR	*Coordinates units as well as individual employees*
	Determines subordinates' assignments based on individual skills and abilities
	Makes sure that space, supplies, and other needed materials are available
MONITOR	Relies on reports from others
	Analyzes detailed written and verbal reports
	Oversees compliance with procedures
	Interprets financial and statistical reports
	Writes technical reports on unit performance
MENTOR	*Helps create policies and procedures to help employees experiencing personal problems; deals with the personal problems of employees*
	Advises lower-level managers on how to handle difficult employee situations
FACILITATOR	Works to obtain consensus across functional areas
	Helps create policies and procedures to encourage employee participation
INNOVATOR	*Has a fair degree of input into organizational change decisions*
BROKER	Seeks to expand the resources of the division or work unit
	Speaks at public gatherings and hearings
	Emphasizes important organizational values through ceremonies, celebrations, and other events

Source: A. T. Belasen, M. Benke, L. N. DiPadova, and V. M. Fortunato (1996). "Downsizing and the hypereffective manager: The shifting importance of managerial roles during organizational transformation." *Human Resource Management Journal*, 35(1), p. 108. © Copyright John Wiley & Sons, Inc.

to do less monitoring, as some of the managers studied implied they had done. But what of the manager who perceives that all roles have increased? What is to be sacrificed? Managers, who are unwilling to let go of any of their roles, are vulnerable to hypereffectiveness.

As bad as it sounds, hypereffectivity has also transformed middle managers into conservative and overworked managers, who are pushed to the limits by the expectations of those above them who demand nothing short of better results. Indeed, AMA's 1996 survey showed that 38 percent of the companies that reported job cuts also have extended working hours for remaining employees in lieu of new hiring. Paradoxically, the very same idea of horizontal management through empowerment and flexibility has also bred a paranoid manager obsessed with getting the job done.

NEW CHALLENGES FOR HR PROFESSIONALS

Human resource managers should attempt to understand the conditions that lead to hypereffectiveness, as well as the costs of ignoring their effects. While middle managers worried about plateauing in traditional organizations, they now worry about termination or survival. According to David Wigglesworth (1996), a human resource development consultant, HR professionals are faced with the task of revitalizing surviving employees and realigning the corporate culture. They play a critical role in creating new strategies that empower, retain, and develop new incentives for the survivors, as well as facilitating the transition through effective communication, training, work redesign, and reinvestment in human capital to sustain the organization's own survival. Myers (1993), for example, listed five important tools to help employees cope with morale and other transitioning issues:

- *Teambuilding*: Including the full range of team-oriented production methods for employee involvement programs aimed at involving employees in decision making, participatory management, and productivity improvement.
- *Empowerment of middle managers*: Especially in giving and receiving feedback about present restructuring strategies and future goals to help middle managers maintain their morale, productivity, and drive.
- *Mentoring/training programs*: Dedicating time and resources to cross-train employees and counsel them about mobility and other career options.

- *Recognition programs:* Adopting special recognition ceremonies, bonus plans, and promotional opportunities.
- *Restructuring benefits:* Implementing benefits to fill the special needs of the surviving employees such as attendance and production bonuses and even longevity awards.

Human resource professionals must face the challenges created by the two perspectives. First, they must treat the issues from the viewpoint of changes in the psychological contract; and second, they must help senior management understand that business plans linked to unsustainable human resource systems are unlikely to succeed. The challenge for human resource managers is how to build a new commitment among survivors in a newly restructured organization.

Managers who perceive themselves as powerless and without much influence over work processes and outcomes may be unable to sustain current levels of productivity growth without purposeful interventions from human resource managers. Increased stress, emotional fatigue, lack of responsiveness, apathy, and overall dissatisfaction with work have been found to emerge in such environments as detriments to productivity. Counseling and coaching are important but insufficient tools for coping with the causes of hypereffectiveness, which is rooted in an unsustainable work plan. Rebuilding trust and confidence of the survivors in the system and recreating the vision of success should become a top priority for human resource managers. But productivity must also be addressed at a fundamental level with attention being paid to training and development and matching managerial competencies and job requirements.

3M's Vice President for Human Resource highlighted the following resources that his company makes available to employees whose jobs are eliminated due to the company's reorganization (*3M Stemwinder,* December 1995, p. 3):

- *Job information system:* for making job openings visible
- *Unassigned list:* being placed on the list gives salaried employees up to six months to look around the company for another job
- *Part-time jobs and job share:* reassigning or dividing employees across segments of the same jobs
- *Leaves of absence:* allowing employees to exhaust different opportunities outside the company
- *Job search assistance:* outplacement services
- *Career counseling:* internal support

- *Employee assistance counseling*: offered to any employee having difficulty dealing with change and the uncertainty it causes (not limited to those directly affected by the reorganization)
- *Transition workshops*: enabling employees to acquire technical and administrative skills in different areas and preparing them for new jobs within or outside of the company
- *Support groups*: helping employees facilitate small-group discussions, share concerns, experiences, successes, and support each other
- *Voluntary separation plans*: in areas where there is a need to reduce the workforce
- *Communications services*: through newsletters, management responsiveness, and feedback
- *3M feedback line*: twenty-four-hour 800 number established to record employees' comments, questions, and suggestions about the change

AT&T, for example, created an expansive network of "resource centers" to help people find new jobs. These centers provide office space, telephones, computers, and career counseling, as well as a database of job openings at other companies. The computer automatically tries to match a person's goals and qualifications with job listings and mails out a list of possible matches to each person in the program every week (*New York Times*, 2/13/96, D1).

Another example of a successful intervention to reduce the negative effects of downsizing was achieved by the state of Maine and described by Robinson and Drucker (1991). The administration and the state employees' union developed a joint strategy aimed at encouraging employees to take advantage of the various alternatives offered under the Voluntary Cost Savings Program. All employees received letters signed by the governor and their respective commissioners. A toll-free number with on-line help was also provided to answer questions, clarify the different options, and provide general guidance. Administrators and union representatives felt that midlevel managers might resent the goals of downsizing for fear of having to do more work with a smaller staff. The governor and top administrators showed leadership and commitment to support the affected staff by meeting with groups of managers and supporting their claims that there would be a reduction in services with fewer resources. As the program developed, both management and the union emerged as winners (Robinson & Drucker, 1991). For employees and the union, the program:

- Provided new flexible employment options while maintaining benefits
- Developed a language in the agreement that acknowledged the need to reorganize and prioritize work so that remaining employees would not be overburdened
- Initiated an agreement not to use temporary or contractual employees to replace employee work hours.

For management, the program:

- Represented two-thirds of the targeted savings ($10 million) (the rest would be achieved via attrition and vacancy freezes)
- Fostered a spirit of voluntarism that lead to more creativity in the area of performing tasks and utilizing time efficiently
- Sustained employee morale and loyalty

Once they survived the major cut, both employees and managers could increase their chances to adjust to the new conditions successfully by following a few simple suggestions:

- Cope with the uncertainty of the situation by focusing on short-term objectives and targeting the present rather than the future
- Think innovatively about ways to either recreate your niche or consolidate different facets of your work into a meaningful job (in other words, redesign your own job, but remember to do it creatively)
- Unlike others who focus on the need to stabilize, move ahead in the direction of change by seeking out ways to improve your work conditions, by increasing the complexity of your work in terms of its depth and breadth to make your job difficult to evaluate and by becoming highly proficient
- Become visible, by interconnecting with others and by locating yourself centrally within informal and formal networks of communication
- Look for jobs that are linked directly with the bottom line— those jobs that generate revenues for the organization and that would make you critical and therefore nonsubstitutable
- Manage your stress and anxiety level by sharing your concerns and problems with peers and by seeking professional counseling and help

Top management, however, should also concern itself with supporting the surviving employees both emotionally and materially by:

- Sharing ownership of the organization
- Providing opportunities for greater participation and self-management
- Renewing the vision of the organization and mobilizing support for that vision
- Stabilizing career systems and supporting job security
- Establishing reward programs, such as gain sharing, above a predetermined baseline performance
- Sponsoring innovative programs to enhance efficiency
- Tolerating errors, rewarding creativity, and encouraging risk taking

THE ROLE OF SENIOR MANAGERS

Senior managers planning to use the downsizing axe must also pay attention to the human dimensions of their plans including dealing with anticipated low morale, role ambiguity, and mistrust. To help boost morale, senior managers with visionary skills know how to mobilize the support of middle managers for the newly created vision. Senior managers must encourage mutual respect and create a positive work climate that recognizes the need to transform the organization into a more adaptive and effective configuration. This adaptation involves the creation of a better alignment of the organization—both internally by rearranging structures and processes and externally by strategically maneuvering the organization in the direction of greater interdependencies with its external environment. Top managers are expected to negotiate linking programs with external systems, and therefore, develop competencies and skills that are important for boundary management. Brokering, political maneuvering, bargaining, persuading, negotiating, influencing, networking, and managing external linkages become the core competencies of the new leaders.

The challenge for senior managers is to network their organizations with other organizations in concentric circles that optimize the skills of the aggregate group. The new role-set for leadership is to identify partners with complementary specialties and develop symbiotic linkages that can help their organizations achieve adaptive efficiency. Multilateral arrangements among diverse organizations require a broader span of attention by organizational leaders—that is, a span of attention with an outward focus that centers on identifying the partners with the right expertise and financial resources. These partners should be willing to collaborate in the design of new products, share the production costs, and spread the risks associated with the development and marketing of new products. Internally, senior managers are challenged to develop the next managerial leadership cadre that will lead the organization into the future. As Drucker (1988) stipulated: top managers must concern themselves with succession planning and building the leadership capability to sustain the continuity and effective functioning and operation of the information-based organization.

CONCLUSION: WORKING SMARTER BY DEVELOPING NEW COMPETENCIES

Downsizing must and should be integrated within the strategic planning of the organization. Long-term effects in terms of market share and penetration, new product development, and so on, must be considered before making any cutbacks. Employee morale, motivation, and the sustained commitment to the organization's goals to increase productivity should be a top priority for management. The downsized organization should streamline its operations and reengineer the way in which it conducts business. Targeting processes for improvement should also evolve into cultural reengineering and the creation of sociotechnical systems. A process orientation along the value chain of the organization can be reinforced by cross-functional teams with teamwork and joint performance leading the way toward a full transformation.

Restructuring and downsizing require middle managers to adopt different roles and develop different skills and competencies. When positions and jobs are up for grabs at times of restructuring and downsizing, middle managers must enrich their roles and behavioral skills repertoire to increase their chances to survive the change. Above all, they should become leaders (Lawler, Mohram & Ledford, 1992). Through downsizing, the prime strategy for creating a lean organization, top management also hopes to form an organization that is agile and flexible, organic and adaptive. With fewer levels of managers below them, middle managers often perform their roles with a wider span of control. Subsequently, they experience greater responsibility, less control, and a greater variety of expectations. They still must focus on results and the relationships required to achieve these results. They need, however, to think and act strategically by virtue of their proximity to the top, and they must understand the technical requirements of the operating core by virtue of their proximity to the points of impact.

In short, effective midlevel managers maintain an optimal balance between enacting the roles of Innovator and Broker vis-à-vis senior managers, and enacting the roles of Director and Producer vis-à-vis lower-level managers. They also adjust their styles to suit the transformation. Middle managers must learn to let go, empower, involve others, communicate openly, encourage innovative thinking and risk taking, maintain a high tolerance for errors, and synergize the efforts of employees. They attend to the value of the human resource by increasing their sensitivity to the psychosociological needs of employees. They train them, listen to their problems, resolve conflicts, and provide employees with opportunities for professional development. The middle managers' role is critical for the success of the organization, for they carry much of the transformational burden by becoming change architects (Delavigne & Robertson, 1994; McDermott, 1993, Schmidt & Finnigan, 1994).

With change comes ambiguity and added frustration. In the old paradigm, middle managers were fully expected to respond to contradictory demands from both lower- and upper-level management. First-line supervisors called for clarity in goal setting and planning, for direction in resource allocation, scheduling, and task prioritization. Senior managers, however, put pressures on middle managers to become more responsive to the values and expectations of key stakeholders.

Flexible middle managers sense intuitively when they need to relinquish their formal power to lower levels and push decision-making authority downward, while simultaneously providing supervisors with greater access to information and other resources. Middle managers are also expected to have a high tolerance for ambiguity toward first-line supervisors, to enhance their self-confidence, and to boost innovative thinking and action learning. These expectations are consistent with theories of horizontal management and self-direction (see chapters 7 and 4, respectively), which position the middle manager outside his/her traditional turf, since multifunctional teams are also self-contained and self-led (Belasen, 1997; Wellins, Byham & Wilson, 1991). Often, these teams are directly accountable to senior managers, thus rendering the role of the middle manager redundant or at best supportive. In addition, as discussed in chapter 4, computers have transformed information handling from a difficult, time-consuming job to a far easier and quicker one. Zap! In an instant, historically speaking, the middle manager's traditional functions have been vaporized (Dumaine,

1993). While self-managed teams rendered the job of the middle manager and traditional supervisory responsibilities obsolete, information technology has made it easier for higher managerial levels to monitor and control activities directly without the need to rely on middle managers (Dopson & Stewart, 1990).

Middle managers, whose main source of power came from withholding or modifying messages within the chain of command in ways that enhance that power, can no longer claim ownership over the communication channels. Their location centrality and visibility within the interlocking networks of communication has deteriorated and almost vanished with the emergence of high-speed communications and the realization of powerful electronic means of communication and information technology. What remains for them is the burden of proof that their positions are still critical and that their pay is justified. To communicate their value-adding, middle managers operate beyond any sustained level of performance, overworking and subjecting themselves to high stress and vulnerability (Belasen et al., 1996). The surviving middle managers must assume leadership roles that have never before existed. These roles may include the following variants:

- *Socratic manager*: a manager who asks questions to stimulate further thinking and who teaches management techniques such as statistical analysis and pay-for-skills methods to line employees.
- *Open manager*: a manager who provides timely and relevant information to employees. NeXT, Steve Jobs's computer company, is using this approach. Jobs believes that every employee must contain the company's DNA, and therefore, must be privy to crucial information like profits, sales, and strategic plans. But NeXT takes openness a step further: everyone knows everyone else's salary and stockholdings or at least can find out by asking.
- *Renaissance manager*: a manager with a breadth of knowledge across many functions. A versatile manager who can manage almost any function on demand, and with a wide range of overlapping responsibilities. Experience shows that when a manager has a thorough understanding of jobs, skills, and needs, people respect the manager and accept his or her influence.
- *Radical manager*: a manager who is an innovator and constantly seeks to change and improve processes and outcomes. Sony Medical is a manufacturer of color printers and other peripherals for use with medical imaging equipment like ultrasound

machines. As an entrepreneurial laboratory, the company has at least a half dozen new seed ventures going at all times. The general manager and his people spend a lot of time with doctors and HMOs, their key customers, and constantly scan the rest of Sony Medical for technology that might serve those customers. Once they hit on one, they start a small cell of about ten people from different disciplines and let them run with it. The idea is to experiment constantly, move quickly, see if the idea works, and if it does not, move on to the next idea. The key is to constantly create, juggle, shift, and finally destroy organizations as the market demands!

- *Scavenger manager*: with resources becoming scarce, budgets tightening, and costly technologies, the new manager must beg, borrow, and steal anything he can. The scavenger manager fights for survival by exerting opportunistic behavior. The purpose is to exploit and take advantage of opportunities as they arise. The scavenger must be creative and proactive, but also diplomatic and tactful.

- *Humane manager*: in an environment of change, new managers must balance the tremendous demands of work with the other demands in their lives and help others do the same. Managers must be concerned about causes of stress and help reduce their negative effects by talking to employees and taking actions in the direction of relieving their stress through counseling, providing flex work time, and conducting sports events. (Dumaine, 1993, pp. 81–84)

Under the old paradigm, middle managers focused on internal processes and monitored the work flow and integration processes within the organization. In the new paradigm, they are expected to shift their focus. Adaptation and market positioning become important parts of their management responsibilities. Thus, the traditional roles of middle managers vis-à-vis senior managers must be modified in scope and variety. Middle managers are now expected to support and sustain the vision of senior managers, to scan the external environment for opportunities and threats, to align the organization value chain, and to constantly create interdependencies that can help the organization to adapt effectively to its environment. Middle managers can support the new organizational vision and increase their own personal effectiveness by:

- Adding strategic value to the range of their responsibilities and activities (to remain viable, the traditional role of middle managers must change "more like the phoenix bird than the dinosaur, a new breed of middle managers—whose roles are more strategic than operational—should be rising from the ashes of the delayered corporation" [Floyd & Wooldridge, 1994])

- Improving downward communication, giving feedback, and interacting more often with and listening to first-line supervisors
- Becoming more accountable for performance results
- Balancing their legal power with greater freedom granted to first-line supervisors to interact and communicate laterally and diagonally
- Providing first-line supervisors with more opportunities to interact directly with top managers and participate in frequent decision-making meetings
- Increasing the value-adding and indispensability of middle managers by generating and mobilizing resources around new ideas; linking activities and ideas between technical and institutional levels; selling critical issues to top managers; and, shifting from being transactional managers charged with maintaining the status quo to being transformational leaders who stimulate change
- Reorienting the tasks of middle management from developing coordination within functional boundaries to achieving relationships across organizational boundaries; from controlling growth to finding innovation and championing initiatives; from executing plans to encouraging an evolving mindset and synthesizing information; and, from applying new technologies to production to transferring technology within the organization and facilitating learning
- Using strategy from the middle out by combining strategic awareness with operating experience and by employing lateral communication at the middle level; overcoming communication and functional barriers by recognizing external goals; and getting rid of the "turf conscious" syndrome by changing their cognitive road map and behaviors
- Combining situational flexibility with sensitivity to the needs of upper- and lower-level managers (upward by championing ideas and mobilizing support for these ideas and/or synthesizing different approaches to achieving the goals of the organization; downward by facilitating assimilation of ideas or transitioning the organization toward a new state of affairs, and/or using their problem-solving expertise to implement the change)

Once downsizing has been completed structurally, managers must develop the behaviors and skills essential for the new task environment. Predictably, they should place less emphasis on the Director and Producer roles. The greatest emphasis should be on the roles of Facilitator, Mentor, Coordinator, and Innovator. These roles and their associated competencies, particularly creativity and change, interpersonal communication, and developing others are extremely important for a full revitalization of the organization. Downsizing creates a more agile and lean organization. Moreover, when downsizing is combined with the right dose of managerial skills, it can breed an effective, adaptive, and efficient organization with core capabilities that are innovative and constantly improving. The hypereffective manager who zealously performed the role of the Producer can become a major force that leads organizational transformations through multifunctional, self-led teams. Middle managers, who used to direct and motivate employees to work productively, are expected to provide the teams with the administrative and technical support needed to link the teams' tasks with the mission and objectives of the organization. The traditional middle-management roles that were effective in hierarchical structures, particularly the Producer and Director roles, can be delegated or transferred and effectively performed by trained members of self-managed teams (SMTs). Chapter 7 discusses the main characteristics of SMTs and the principles that guide their activities and behaviors. Leadership roles and communication processes central to SMTs are also examined.

7

Leading Self-Managed Teams: Roles and Communication

The most distinctive (and unsettling) feature of the transition to self-directed teams is a gradual transfer of operational decision-making authority from managers to work teams . . . Self-directed teams are not unmanaged teams; they are differently managed teams. Over time, teams earn the right to exercise increasing authority over their own activities, but even fully empowered teams operate within firm boundaries.

—Orsburn, Moran, Musselwhite & Zenger, 1990

THE ORGANIZATIONAL CONTEXT FOR
SELF-MANAGED TEAMS

Increasingly, hierarchically based organizations turn to self-direction as a means of transforming their organizations into more flexible, team-based organizations with normatively controlled self-managing

The theoretical discussion in this chapter is adapted from: Belasen, A. (1997). "An application of the competing values framework to self-managed teams." In Rahim, A. M., Golembieski, R. T., & Pate, L. E. (Eds.), *Current topics in management*, vol. 2 (79–111). Greenwich, CT: JAI Press Inc.

teams. Large-scale organizations, as Eastman Chemical, Xerox, GM's Saturn, GE's Lighting, and AT&T's Network Systems Division, have all initiated a shift toward self-management. Federal Express (Fedex), for example, has been particularly successful at using SMTs in its back-office operations in Memphis. As part of its reorganization plan, Fedex formed over 150 teams and provided them with the training and authority to manage themselves. In 1989, these teams had helped cut incorrect bills and lost packages by 13 percent (Dumaine, 1990). Organizational theorists (e.g., Cummings, 1978; Manz, 1992), researchers (e.g., Barker, 1993; Barry, 1991; Manz & Sims, 1987; Tompkins & Cheney, 1985), and consultants (e.g., (Orsburn, Moran, Musselwhite & Zenger, 1990; Ostroff & Smith, 1992) have all described this phenomenon as a paradigmatic shift in management orientation, resulting in a transformation of the vertical authority structure into a horizontal, team-based system. They have argued that with flat structures and empowered teams and individuals focusing on horizontal processes, organizations become agile and flexible, more efficient and adaptive, thus increasing the likelihood of surviving environmental turbulence. They have claimed that self-managed teams (often called high-performance teams) are likely to emerge in organizations undergoing a shift in paradigms, and that SMTs help organizations become more productive, and therefore, more competitive and profitable. SMTs are prone to technical breakthroughs, cost containment, and quick response. They offer higher quality through continuous improvement and have greater flexibility through adaptability and problem solving as a way of life. Team members enjoy relatively high morale and greater satisfaction. They display a high commitment to the team mission and objectives, and their retention rate is reportedly high (Wellins, Byham & Wilson, 1991).

Bureaucratic, vertically controlled organizations experience an insufficient capacity to foster learning (Nadler, Gerstein, Shaw & Associates, 1992). In contrast, decentralized, empowered organizations are often led by transformational leaders who use conceptual, nonautocratic power to inspire employees. The leaders create a new vision, reshape the organizational mission, and articulate values in support of that vision. The leaders sponsor the transformation and sustain its momentum through the constant mobilization of commitment to the new vision and the internalization (ownership) of the new values (Bass & Avolio, 1994; Byrd, 1987). These leaders are also highly instrumental in institutionalizing action learning as an overarching goal. By framing and redefining the vision and core values of individuals and teams, attributes of learning systems are adopted and anchored in a continuous process of adaptation and performance breakthrough. Learning is also augmented in these organizations through town meetings, cross-functional improvement teams, adoption of best practices, and identification of technical and behavioral problems that were not allowed to surface previously. The organization is fluid and loosely coupled, permitting the emergence of internal networking as the landscape for innovation and creativity. Information flows faster and in a nonbureaucratic way within the system through communication bridges, direct contacts, and other electronic devices, that connect individuals and teams.

Organizations that employ self-managed teams tend to evolve into what Mintzberg (1989) termed "missionary organizations" and what Barker (1993) refers to as "concertive organizations." Through the creation of a rich system of values and beliefs, a thick culture is developed that distinguishes the organization from other organizations. What holds SMTs together is not bureaucratic rules and regulations, planning and formal control—that is, utilitarian forms of control—but rather the standardization of norms of behavior and the sharing of values and beliefs among members of units and teams. This is what Etzioni (1961) labeled "normative control" and Ouchi (1979, 1980) termed "clan control"—organizations place a high premium on shared values and trust. This type of control is invisible, yet powerful. Controls are conceptual not procedural! Normative control elicits and directs the required efforts of members by controlling the underlying experiences, thoughts, and feelings that guide their actions. Organizational members comply, not because of incentive motivation, but because they are driven by internal commitment, strong identification with the mission of the organization, and intrinsic satisfaction from work (Kunda, 1992). Paradoxically, team members set boundaries that define and enable action, but also simultaneously constrain the kinds of action members can take (Barge, 1994).

THE NATURE OF SELF-MANAGED TEAMS

Self-managed teams are small, multifunctional work teams, responsible for an entire work process or segment. The teams have built-in coordinating mechanisms and external managers typically act as coaches and facilitators, rather than planners and auditors. The reward system tends to be team based and is tied to skills and knowledge, rather than seniority. Information, such as productivity data, quality data, sales figures, and profit margins, is shared readily with all team members, not just among the few top managers. Team members are cross-trained and their job skills usually cover all facets of the work process. The transformation from a bureaucratic, supervisory-oriented organization to a worker-run, team-based organization presents team members with challenges different from those existing in traditional forms of organizations. Instead of being told what to do by the common supervisor, members of SMTs are given considerable freedom to design their jobs, set objectives, discipline and reward team players, and often recruit and select their own members.

Self-managed teams are unique organizational structures; they exist in a quasi-autonomous state with common goals and self-regulation. SMTs are also highly connected from within, but are loosely coupled from outside. Rather than being parallel groups or teams (e.g., quality circles, task forces), SMTs have the formal power to create and maintain their own systems or working relationships in order to complete a total job. The teams have administrative control over managerial functions such as planning, scheduling, monitoring, and staffing. SMTs are characterized by a broad base of multiskilled members with integrated responsibilities and duties, training in team functions, and extensive information sharing. As such, SMTs are the result of a major paradigm shift from cross-functional synergies and joint performance through teamwork to self-direction and self-ruled work teams. Self-managed teams change the impact of individualized rewards, management and leadership roles, and segmentalism by adopting the attributes of a learning system that is creative, adaptive, and responsive to change. This learning system has a built-in bias toward an outside-in perspective; that is, the team's emphasis is on the supplier-customer relationship, rather than on a single function. SMTs have what Nadler, Gerstein, and Shaw (1992) have called the capacity to act. SMTs focus on core priorities, are biased toward performance results, and are empowered to pursue internal goals—the three dimensions that also enhance learning and experimentation.

SMTs AS HIGH-PERFORMANCE TEAMS

According to Orsburn, Moran, Musselwhite, and Zenger (1990), SMTs improve productivity because deep employee involvement builds intense commitment to the corporate vision of success. There is growing evidence that SMTs help their organizations reap the benefits beyond the capacity of traditional, functional work groups. SMTs are more productive than their counterparts. The SMTs at the GE plant in Salisbury, North Carolina, reportedly achieved a staggering 250 percent increase in productivity as compared with plants using conventional work units. SMTs helped their organizations streamline functions and processes. Anything that does not support the team is a target for potential elimination or termination. Organizations also become more flexible in adjusting to changes in their environments. The teams help drive a quality improvement effort into every level within the organization and their high involvement breeds increased commitment to organizational goals. Self-managed teams also promote customer satisfaction through quick response and improved quality. One example of a SMT success story comes from a Postal Service station in the northeast (Engel, 1995).

The formal structure of one Postal Service station in the northeast is fairly simple. There are three groups of city carriers who are labeled by zone and correspond to the local zip code of delivery. All three zones are similar in size (approximately twenty-five employees). Each has a front-line supervisor who takes responsibility for the zone, issues daily instructions, and monitors performance as a means to achieve coordination among the routes. Typical duties include determining vehicle assignments, scheduling, overtime assessment, completing required reports, and so on. However, in the SMT, for the most part the supervisor takes a "hands off" approach to the daily operations and plays more of an administrative role. Members of the SMT carry out some of the duties performed or directed by the traditional supervisor. These include, measuring and reporting on the daily volume of mail, handling customer complaints, determining individual workloads via pivoting and auxiliary assistance, and flexible scheduling/incidental leave. Direct supervision while "on the street" was also eliminated. Internally, disciplinary problems are reportedly handled by informal norms, peer pressure, and mutual adjustment. Contractual limitations relating to labor agreements prohibit the carriers from taking on further responsibilities that are often associated with SMT's. These prohibited responsibilities include scheduling, hiring, firing, budgeting, goal setting, and designing reward systems (Jacob, 1992). Participation in the self-management process is voluntary. At the outset of the agreement, fifteen of the zone's twenty routes were involved, and this number has remained constant over time. The SMT is officially overseen by the Self-Management Committee (SMC), which consists of the Station Manager, the Zone Supervisor, two shop stewards (NALC) and two carriers. The agreement for self-management has no termination date, and according to the team's EI charter, can only be ended by a consensus of the SMC.

The permanence of self-management was put to test in 1992 when a change in front-line supervisors led to major outbursts of conflict. The new supervisor came from another post office and was unfamiliar with the principles and agreement for self-management. He, in turn, did not honor the agreement and tried to "revoke" the self-management pact. The struggle that ensued brought a drop in all measures of performance outcome. This traditional, authoritarian supervisor was subsequently transferred, at which time performance levels increased. Zone supervisors report to the Station Manager, who besides being responsible for the city carriers also oversees the window/customer service operations. The Station Manager in turn reports to the county Postmaster. An exponential increase in the span of control accompanies the next level of management. The three largest offices are managed by Post Office Operations Managers (POOM's) who additionally oversee the operation of the 683 smaller facilities within the region that are managed by Postmasters. The district's three largest post offices, in addition to fourteen functional managers, report directly to the District Manager, who was instrumental in the implementation of the SMT. There are four layers of management between the SMT and the District Manager.

PERFORMANCE MEASURES

The USPS is a very number-driven organization, and frequently sets goals based on the statistical analysis that is generated from finance departments. Although productivity goals have been specifically set for the SMT's zone, they have been based solely on the preceding year's performance adjusted for predicted trends with no input from the teams. Differences in the geographic/physical parameters (weather, traffic conditions, population density, etc.) prevent a comparison between different Postal facilities. For this reason a systems model approach to effectiveness will be used to compare the three zones at the observed station. However, in terms of deliveries per hour (DPH), a direct comparison remains misleading. All other measures are comparable, as are general trends for the past five years. Figures were not available for 1988, the year prior to self-management. Table 7.1 depicts the standard performance measures used to determine the effectiveness/productivity of operations as it relates to City Carriers:

- *Office foot/hour* (OFPH): measure of productivity/efficiency of carriers in sorting/preparing for delivery all pieces of mail to be taken on a route. Mail arrives in standardized flats or tubs, and is measured by length in feet. On average, there are 250 pieces of mail to a foot. The number of feet taken for delivery is divided by the number of hours spent in the office. For example, if twelve

Table 7.1.
Performance Measures for 1989 through 1994 Year to Date

Office Foot/Hour	'89	'90	'91	'92	'93	'94	5-Year D
Zone A	3.70	3.64	3.58	3.47	3.56	3.55	−.15
Zone B	3.61	3.44	3.54	3.75	4.16	4.12	+.51
SMT	**3.28**	**3.34**	**3.59**	**3.44**	**3.88**	**4.08**	**+.70**
Office Average	3.56	3.49	3.57	3.54	3.81	3.85	+.29
			Delivery/Hour				
Zone A	81.7	82.3	78.4	78.4	78.1	77.0	−4.7
Zone B	68.2	68.3	71.9	73.6	73.9	74.5	+6.3
SMT	**81.5**	**82.4**	**82.7**	**80.7**	**81.6**	**82.5**	**+1.0**
Office Average	77.2	77.8	77.5	77.6	77.8	77.8	+0.6
			Sick Leave %				
Zone A	1.7	2.5	3.3	2.8	3.9	2.4	+0.7
Zone B	4.4	4.1	2.8	3.0	1.9	2.2	−2.2
SMT	**3.1**	**3.0**	**2.3**	**2.7**	**3.1**	**3.1**	**0.0**
Office Average	2.9	3.1	2.9	2.8	3.1	2.5	−0.4
			DCEA				
Zone A	17.49	17.45	16.89	16.74	16.94	17.24	−0.25
Zone B	15.64	15.25	15.78	16.22	16.95	17.39	+1.75
SMT	**16.72**	**17.05**	**17.46**	**16.93**	**17.99**	**18.49**	**+1.77**
Office Average	16.70	16.65	16.71	16.65	17.25	17.64	+0.94

feet of mail (approximately three thousand pieces) were taken for delivery, and three hours were spent in the office on preparation, the OFPH would be 4.0. The minimum performance level, as delegated by the national labor agreement, is 3.44 OFPH.

- *Deliveries/hour* (DPH): the number of deliveries to a mail receptacle per hour. The number of addresses delivered to on a given day, divided by the number of hours spent "on the street." Comparison is difficult in that an apartment complex with a lobby and eight centrally located mail boxes is "equal" to eight separate street residences. If a carrier has four hundred receptacles on his/her route, and spends five hours to complete the route, the DPH would be 80.
- *Delivery and collection efficiency analysis* (DCEA): a complex and comprehensive measure of all letter-carrier functions derived from a formula only applicable to USPS operations. The rating includes DPH, OFPH, Relay Times, and Measurements of Bulk Mailings and Parcel Post.

- *Sick leave* (SL): a generalized measure of absenteeism, which has been shown to be correlated to morale and job satisfaction and is expressed as a percent of total hours used. For example, if ten full-time carriers were scheduled to work four hundred hours in a week, and one of them called in sick one day because of the flu, the SL for that week would be 2 percent The "lost" eight hours are assumed to be made up through the use of overtime.

In each of the measures shown in table 7.1, the SMT performed as well or better than the other carriers. Using DCEA, the most accurate and comprehensive measure of performance, the SMT clearly outperformed its counterparts with a rating of 18.49 and an overall increase of 11 percent. In addition, improvement was shown in OFPH, where the SMT increased productivity by 21 percent. Sick Leave for the five-year period was unchanged. However, the range of variation (.8) in SL was half of the other zones. Although a direct comparison of DPH is misleading, changes in DPH are not. While the SMT leads the station in DPH and has shown a slight improvement, Zone A's performance has steadily declined. Surely there are postal facilities and groups of carriers that outperform those at this station. However, using a systems approach that isolates self-management as a variable, it becomes clear that this structure is a viable alternative to the mechanistic one that relies on direct supervision and standardization.

NOT LEADERLESS TEAMS

Leadership is vital for the success of nonbureaucratic, team-based organizations. Vertical organizations can run virtually without leaders, because centralization and high formalization are effective substitutes for leadership. Tall, hierarchically structured organizations can run through midlevel managers, whose primary role is to manage functions, integrate units' efforts, and monitor their performance. Flatter organizations, that are also decentralized and use SMTs, require leadership due to the absence of an institutionalized reporting relationship.

Self-managed teams are often referred to as bossless teams. It is true that external leaders of SMTs are former managers whose roles and responsibilities have been transformed into facilitators and coaches. Self-managed teams, however, are not leaderless teams (Jessup, 1990; Wellins, Byham & Wilson, 1991). The shift to SMTs is not an elimination of supervisory tasks, but instead is a structured transfer of many of those tasks to the team (Dumaine, 1990; Fisher, 1993; Orsburn, Moran,

Musselwhite & Zenger, 1990). It has been suggested in the literature that the transition from a command structure (i.e., with emphasis on extensive rules and procedural specifications, hierarchical control, etc.) to a commitment structure based on shared values and the creation of meaning involves giving employees greater responsibility, ownership, and accessibility through employee involvement programs (Lawler, 1992; Manz, 1992; Walton, 1985). These programs (e.g., quality circles, QWL, etc.), coupled with a gradual movement toward self-direction and empowerment, provide employees "with greater freedom and responsibility than under the control-oriented approach, but significantly less than under the commitment condition" (Manz, 1992, p. 1128).

Delayered organizations provide former supervisors and managers with new managerial opportunities to become coaches, consultants, and sponsors. This process, however, also creates a vacuum requiring SMTs to co-opt traditional leadership roles. Since team members are empowered to undertake traditional managerial roles and responsibilities, they are also encouraged to initiate directions and assume leadership roles in areas where their distinctive competencies are evident. Over time, multiple leaders emerge and a dynamic pattern of shared team leadership evolves. Leadership is rotated and often fulfilled simultaneously and complementarily by multiple members who assume different functions and job responsibilities (Belasen, 1997).

MISFIT OF CURRENT LEADERSHIP THEORIES

> Theories of leadership and management, irrespective of what label is used or how participatory they claim to be, contain core assumptions that actually prevent excellence from being obtained in contemporary organizations.
>
> —Bradford & Cohen, 1984, p. 10

Normative (traditional and participative) theories of leadership position the manager at the center of the action. The manager is assumed to have inherent personal qualities that significantly affect the process and outcomes of work, and therefore, his/her centrality, criticality, and responsibility are crucial for the effectiveness of the work unit. As Bradford and Cohen (1984) described: the manager is attributed a heroic image with the ability to identify unique solutions to problems. These authors claimed that the perception of heroism breeds a self-defeating cycle. Employees, constrained by their managers and without much discretion over work processes and outcomes, shift responsibility upward and outward to their managers for answers and for accountability. Hence, the vertical hierarchy quickly becomes overloaded by the rate, amount, and complexity of communication moving upward in an attempt to obtain answers to unambiguous or routine questions. By developing perceptions compatible with conformity and intolerance for errors, employees are less likely to take risks, or use innovative thinking and initiate change. They feel committed only to particular subgoals and strive only for adequate performance. The heroic, dependable stereotype of the manager as a central figurehead portrayed by traditional theories of leadership is reinforced and sustained by a self-fulfilling prophecy that hinders the attainment of excellence. In contemporary, team-based organizations, however, this conventional view of the leadership role is fragmented, constrained, and at best irrelevant for it prevents excellence from being obtained (Bradford & Cohen, 1984).

Observations of SMT members in action reveal that they can take on multiple leadership roles. Team members enact the team's environment, manage channels of influence, network horizontally, and handle external relations (Belasen, 1997; Fisher, 1993). To this end team members take on the role of gatekeeper by shielding the team from inappropriate distractions or unnecessary confusion. They also play the role of translator by helping team members interpret and comprehend the often ambiguous and unclear external environment. These roles require excellent interpersonal abilities and strong negotiation and presentation skills. Thus, the challenge facing organizational researchers and theorists is to develop a theory which captures the complexity and dynamics of SMT leadership roles and communication processes.

While the study of leadership in SMTs requires a group-centered approach, most existing theories of leadership are person centered, heroic, static, and permeated with bipolar differentiation. Take, for example, the vertical-dyad linkage model of leadership (Dansereau, Graen & Haga, 1975), which may be applicable to organizations exemplifying command structures but is less useful to team-based organizations, particularly those characterized by horizontal management. Horizontal management depends less on vertical supervision and more on lateral relations and mutual adjustment for coordinating members' activities and communicating change and goals to team members (Denton, 1991). Even discussions regarding ambiguous situations and leadership styles (Blake & McCanse, 1990; Hersey & Blanchard, 1993) have not been able to capture the essence of leadership in SMTs, perhaps because SMTs are goal oriented and performance driven, but not externally governed. The task is not accomplished to please the boss, but rather to complete the SMT's internally adopted goal.

Manz and Sims (1987) compared traditional leadership behavior dimensions (e.g., goal orientation, coordination, information giving, being solutions driven) with self-management dimensions (e.g., self-reinforcement, self-observation, self-expectation, self-goal setting, rehearsal) of leadership and concluded that there is a high degree of incongruence between the two sets of dimensions. More specifically, they suggested that while traditional leadership theory implicitly assumed that the power and initiation of actions lie virtually entirely with the leader, SMT leadership requires a group-centered approach. Their conclusion is quite central to the argument being advanced in this chapter:

> The implicit assumption underlying the set of self-management dimensions is quite different from those of the earlier, more traditional behaviors. Instead of a top-down philosophy of control, these dimensions imply a bottom-up perspective. [S]ubordinates can perform leadership functions for themselves and the leader's job is to teach and encourage subordinates to lead themselves effectively. In the self-management system, organizing, directing, and monitoring functions, all part of traditional notions of leadership, are largely centered within the group. (Manz & Sims, 1987, p. 121)

One of the reasons the role of SMT multiple leaders is difficult to explain is because it involves more than just actions, styles, and behaviors. The SMT leadership role also includes the leader's cognitive map: The way leaders think, their core values and beliefs, and their vision of success. Leadership in SMTs requires that both behavior and thinking be shifted concomitantly. A team leader must embrace a new way of thinking about work and relationships in his or her actions and have varying mental images of how to motivate in empowered environments.

Another set of theories, commonly known as participative leadership (Meadows, 1980; Vroom & Jago, 1988), although useful in explaining the impact of using participatory programs on organizational performance (see for example, Denison, 1984; Guzzo, Jette & Katzell, 1985; Miller & Monge, 1986; O'Dell & McAdams, 1987), falls short of offering guidance as to how such participation or involvement can be carried out through the behaviors of team members. In addition, these theories seem to be less useful in providing members of SMTs with the tools for successfully coping with significant autonomy or work contexts in which a formal, legitimate leader is absent. Arguably, even Kerr and Jermier's (1978) "substitutes for leadership" theory fails to recognize the need for other types of roles outside the traditional task-process dichotomy.

Self-managed teams also handle the interface between the team and its immediate environment and must manage the team's boundaries. Boundary management is a nontraditional role (Cummings, 1978; Kanter, 1989). Boundary management typically involves creating a positive image and mobilizing support, assuming liaison positions, building communication bridges with other groups, and establishing important alliances. Boundary management expands the focus of team members beyond internal processes to include external affairs, thus requiring team members to perform multiple, often contrasting roles in an integrated and complementary way (Parker, 1990).

LEADERSHIP IN SMTs AS AN EMERGENT NETWORK

Attempting to fill the gap in the study of leadership roles in SMTs, Barry (1991) suggested viewing leadership as a collection of roles and behaviors that can be split apart, shared, rotated, and used sequentially or concomitantly. His model, labeled "distributed leadership," emphasizes the active development and enactment of leadership abilities by all members of a team. The pattern of distributed leadership is emergent, evolving, and appears to correspond to the needs of the team at different points in time and in different situations. Distributed leadership helps define the social construction of the team's reality and create a social process by which individuals playing various leadership and communication roles are interlinked. By mutually adjusting to each other's behaviors and responsibilities, members of SMTs assume leadership roles collaboratively. This collaborative action is informal, emergent, and dynamic; that is, it evolves socially rather than being formed authoritatively. Collaboration brings a relatively uncoordinated, underorganized group of people into more tightly coupled relationships characterized by concerted decision making (Gray, 1991). With the absence of rules and direct supervision in SMTs, collaboration substitutes for the institutional requirements of coordination and cooperation with reciprocity and tradeoffs. Paradoxically, it also generates the emergence of formal, institutionalized relationships among team players. Understanding how this process unfolds over time is an important intellectual contribution to the study of leadership in SMTs. Barry's notion of distributed leadership may very well be positioned within this developmental frame of reference.

While similar to the life-cycle models emphasizing the shift in predominant behaviors used by team members during the transformational cycle (Hersey & Blanchard, 1993; Lawler & Mohrman, 1987),

Barry's model also set out to identify critical leadership roles that are compatible with different stages of team development. These roles are envisioning, organizing, spanning, and social leadership roles. Envisioning centers on initiating a vision of success for the team. Leading this process requires innovation and creativity, frame-breaking thinking, setting clear goals for team members, and identifying conceptual links with other subsystems in the team environment. Organizing involves integrating the various components of the team's task environment. It includes a focus on details, scheduling, performance, and structure. Spanning leadership concerns facilitating the activities essential to link the efforts of SMTs with outside groups and individuals. This process normally involves networking, image management, intelligence gathering, securing resources, bargaining, and negotiation. Finally, social leadership focuses on developing and maintaining the sociopsychological aspects of a SMT's members. This process involves providing reinforcement and encouragement, bridging differences and fostering a collaborative team environment, resolving interpersonal conflicts, and developing a high commitment. According to Barry (1991), these roles are mutually exclusive and must be differentially emphasized during the various phases of a team's life to achieve the highest rates of success.

Although suitable for the study of leadership roles in SMTs, Barry's model is not without its weaknesses. First, the validity of the argument that the predominant roles are mutually exclusive is questionable. For example, envisioning and spanning are not distinctively different from one another: perceptually they are very similar since both stress the important function of networking and both empirically require the enactment of similar behaviors. These behaviors and functions include linking the team with its institutional environment, maintaining and developing managerial critical thinking and creative problem solving, adapting and accommodating externally induced changes, and gathering and evaluating information that is important for the team's task performance.

Second, the claim that the predominant roles must be used differentially is at odds with the very nature of teamwork, which requires a holistic approach to leadership and the management of paradoxes (Quinn & Cameron, 1988). Postmodern organizations are replete with dilemma and paradoxes that cannot be managed without inspirational leadership. The use of symbolic activities provides organizational members with superordinate goals that allow them to navigate paradoxes. Superordinate goals appear to alter the nature of the leader-follower relationship for the demand is for commitment to the goal rather than to a person, which in turn implies less coercion and a greater likelihood that joint problem solving will occur (Bradford & Cohen, 1984). In the absence of managers, team members draw on the superordinate goals for the common vision, inspiration, excellence, and external objectives to create meaning and achieve cross-functional synergy. SMTs free the group, department, or organizational leader from the burden of providing, or at least reinforcing, the vision and goals. The team becomes the source of meaning for its members and this allows the paradoxes to be accepted.* Thus, team members must enact a cognitively complex strategy by responding simultaneously to the competing demands of the transformational cycle. They must maintain a dynamic fit with their environment and use creative tension to deal simultaneously with opposing demands in their task environment. Team members, individually and as a whole, must continually change and balance the competing values that are an integral part of their work environment.

NEED FOR AN ALTERED APPROACH

These criticisms suggest that a more thorough model of shared team leadership is needed to understand and explain the dynamics and complexity of self-managed teams and the leadership roles that are required for SMT success. This model should also address the communication skills and abilities essential to fulfillment of the various leadership roles in nontraditional organizations. Since we are not looking for a "team coach," "single authority," or "assigned responsibility," understanding SMT requires a renewed or altered notion of leadership. As discussed above, when implemented appropriately, SMTs assume collaboration that includes shared responsibility, interchangeable roles and activities, and a simultaneous loose-tight internal structure. Since roles within the team tend to vary circumstantially, the team resembles a loosely coupled subsystem with dynamic patterns of interaction in a network of relationships. These loosely coupled SMTs and the individuals within them are different from the traditional loosely coupled systems that are relatively uncoordinated (Weick, 1976). Individuals within SMTs are highly interdependent. The emergence of concertive control through the standardization of norms helps integrate the team quite tightly (Barker, 1993).

---

*Bradford and Cohen (1984: pp. 283–89) suggested that many of these paradoxes should not be eliminated or cannot be clearly identified beyond the superficial level.

The study of team leadership in SMTs requires a different leadership format and responsibilities as a positive attribute differentiating SMTs from traditional work groups and teams with limited authority (Katzenbach & Smith, 1993). Wellins, Byham & Wilson's (1991) "empowered team" comes close to recognizing distinctively the uniqueness of leadership in SMTs. Nevertheless, and similar to the traditional approaches to leadership, their notion of empowered teams does not capture the multiplicity in values, goals, roles, and behaviors required simultaneously of team members filling the vacuum created by the absence of formal, institutional authority. Described correctly as open systems (Fisher, 1993), SMTs appear to enact multiple environments and their members seem to engage in a wide variety of task and maintenance roles with contradictory expectations. These expectations should be addressed by a theoretical framework that is both exclusive and conclusive and that has both descriptive and explanatory power. Of course, were it easy to develop a theoretical model for the SMT context, it would have already been developed! The Competing Values Framework of leadership (Quinn, 1988) seems to provide what has been missing.

COMPETING VALUES FRAMEWORK OF LEADERSHIP EFFECTIVENESS

The eight roles suggested by Quinn (1988) offer a unique opportunity to explore how leaders in traditional settings perceive their work environment (cognitive complexity) and the behaviors they display in response (behavioral complexity). The Competing Values Framework of leadership roles provides a framework for conceptualizing and measuring behavioral complexity in managers (Hooijberg & Quinn, 1992). What differentiates effective from ineffective managers is the extent and intensity or the scope of behavioral complexity managers display in playing the various leadership roles (Quinn, Spreitzer & Hart, 1992). The Competing Values Framework has been used primarily in research and applications involving traditional forms of organizations (i.e., vertical hierarchies supported by a cadre of managers organized in a pyramid) and therefore, its relevance and applicability to SMTs might be naturally limited. It has been widely recognized that understanding the major shift in the way contemporary organizations are being designed and operated, as well as understanding the complexity and variety of SMTs, requires a new format of leadership responsibilities and roles. It is also believed, however, that the Competing Values Framework might be useful in offering significant insights that could enhance our understanding of the leadership roles and communication in SMTs and therefore could be a powerful starting point for investigating SMTs. The eight roles are discussed extensively by Quinn and associates (Quinn, 1984, 1988; Quinn, Faerman, Thompson & McGrath 1990). What follows is an adaptation of these roles to the unique context of SMTs. Communication media used in performing these roles are also discussed.

MANIFESTATION OF QUINN'S LEADERSHIP ROLES IN THE BEHAVIORS OF MEMBERS IN SMTs

> Diversity and fluidity of leadership are hallmarks of boundary crossing "teamnets." These groups sport a variety of leaders—like owners, brokers, experts, strategists, managers, networkers, and facilitators. Within any particular teamnet, multiple leadership arises from the multiple roles, skills, and knowledge required to address the complex problems taken on by the group.
>
> —Lipnack & Stamps, 1993

Since SMTs are relatively small, the task roles requiring job skills and technical knowledge can remain relatively constant (although there is extensive cross-training). However, the generic roles, such as those described by the Competing Values Framework, interchange depending on the requirements and the availability of specific members. The following is an adaptation of these roles to the unique context of SMTs.

The first role, the "mentor," is engaged in coaching, teaching, and counseling team members. Mentor or peer relationships are vital and significant for all team members since they depend on each other for support and development, particularly in the absence of hierarchical relationships within the team. Kram and Isabella (1985) found that mentoring in more symmetrical work situations transcends into peer relationships. Peer relationships can "provide a forum for mutual exchange in which an individual can achieve a sense of expertise, equality, and empathy that is frequently absent from traditional mentoring relationships" (Kram & Isabella, 1985, p. 129). Moving through the team transformational cycle (see below), team members develop information peer relationships, which help get the job done; collegial peer relationships, which involve job-related feedback and conversations about evolving professional roles and job performance; and special peer relationships, which center on providing confirmation, emotional support, personal feedback, and friendship.

By playing the role of "facilitator," team members help sustain the collective effort, build cohesion and teamwork, and manage interpersonal conflict (Tjosvold, 1993). The facilitator is the quality advisor or process consultant who supports the team by acting as a resource person. The facilitator trains team members in the use of quality tools and coaches team members in all stages of the problem-solving process, including problem diagnosis and identification of alternative solutions. The facilitator also suggests ways to improve processes and recommends the use of experts/staff specialists as needs arise. Moreover, the facilitator observes the process and monitors the team's progress, gives feedback and provides guidance, facilitates team meetings, and intervenes to resolve intragroup conflicts whenever necessary (Belasen, 1997).

Perhaps, the most important role of the facilitator is to strengthen group cohesion through team building and development (Dyer, 1995; Harrington-Mackin, 1994; Liebowitz & DeMeuse, 1982; Sundstrom, De-Meuse & Futrell, 1990; Tannenbaum, Beard & Salas, 1992). Team building can be approached using quality-improvement techniques such as cause-and-effect analysis, Pareto charting, and interrelationship digraph; communication approaches such as responsibility charting (Beckhard & Harris, 1977), role analysis technique (Dayal & Thomas, 1968), role negotiation (Harrison, 1972), reflective listening (Whetten & Cameron, 1994), and life-cycle models (Hersey & Blanchard, 1993). Understanding and using the appropriate behaviors during the transformational cycle of the team is essential for the team's success. Both the external leader and the team member, who assumes the role of the facilitator, have important responsibilities throughout the different stages of team development (Dyer, 1995; Orsburn, Moran, Musselwhite & Zenger, 1990). These stages are testing, organizing, establishing interdependence, and producing and evaluating (Quinn, Faerman, Thompson & McGrath, 1996).

During the initial stage, the facilitator spells out expectations, clarifies the team's charter and responsibilities, explores the boundaries of acceptable team behavior, and begins team-building exercises. Acting primarily as the group process consultant, the facilitator assists the external leader in setting the agenda and specifying guidelines for future activities. The second stage, "organizing," is the most crucial—that is, both the external leader and the team facilitator are involved heavily in retaining the team's focus and in keeping the team from backtracking. The member acting in the role of the facilitator is active in identifying blocking roles and in creating a balance between task and relations roles. By asking effective questions, placing group discussions in context, encouraging responsibility, helping in problem-solving processes, and communicating time constraints, the team facilitator can help team members regain focus and perform effectively. The third stage, "establishing interdependence," is typified by acceptance, constructive feedback, and positive attitudes toward the team's area of responsibility. While the external leader may encourage team members to continue to contribute, the member acting out the role of the facilitator shifts focus from relations to the task at hand. Finally, during the fourth stage of team development, "producing and evaluating," team members exhibit high levels of maturity through constructive behavior and willingness to synergize their efforts to achieve effective results. While the external leader's involvement diminishes, the facilitator continues to provide support through counseling and coaching.

The "director" is a team player who provides team members with a clear sense of their goals and objectives and who clarifies expectations through processes such as operational planning and goal setting, time management, resource allocation, and prioritization. Team members in this capacity use reports, documents, files, records, charts, and diagrams as the primary vehicle of communication for collecting information and giving performance feedback to the team. Interactive mechanisms of communication, such as meetings and group brainstorming, are also used by the director to discuss performance targets, identify root causes of problems, and generate ideas for solving problems (D'Andrea-O'Brien & Buono, 1996). Typically, this member has a vision of success that encourages self-goalsetting and self-expectation among team members (Manz & Sims, 1987) and also the choice of strategies to achieve group goals. This behavior is congruent with findings showing that whenever a group of employees, and even professionals, is required to set and pursue specific goals, members of the group invariably increase their productivity substantially over that of groups who do not set goals (Latham & Wexley, 1994). The director also has the communication and sensitivity skills required to encourage self-evaluation and self-reinforcement, stimulate team members to acquire knowledge and learn new skills, and administer the reward and recognition systems for the team. Team members would be rewarded, not only for personal contributions but also for their contributions to the team and their development of new skills to support the new form of the organization (Galbraith, 1993).

The "producer" is a task-oriented, work-focused player, who is highly motivated to complete assignments, maintain high productivity, and manage time and stress. Effective enactment of the producer role implies that the team member is personally productive, motivated, empowered, and committed. This role involves energizing team members, usually through oral communication, to increase production and accomplish the stated goals. Under the producer's leadership, the team becomes a high-performance work unit in which the sociotechnical system is optimized (Mink, Owen & Mink, 1993). The producer's high energy and inner motivation are triggered by traits and attributes of "personal peak performance" due to a results-oriented personality and a sense of personal mission, the ability to display the dual capacities of self-management and team mastery, and the capability to make appropriate adjustments and manage change (Garfield, 1986). Adams (1984) identified commitment, challenge, purpose, control, transcendence, and balance as essential conditions that stimulate personal peak performance. These conditions are particularly important in the context of SMTs. For example, commitment requires a large investment in time and attention that can pull team members together. Valuing internal goals and intrinsic rewards should generate the commitment required for peak performance (Garfield, 1986). While challenges require team members to be outcome or results oriented, the member playing the producer role is also the one who helps set clear performance objectives for team members who do not always rise to the challenge. Team members need to know the reasons for making important decisions about tasks and targets and need to agree with the decisions and overall direction of the team.

The producer also needs to balance the need for control to achieve efficiency against the need for flexibility to achieve effectiveness. While SMT members act with relative autonomy, they are also highly interdependent, requiring structure and standards of performance. As such, members enacting the producer role, in effect, perform a dual role: an administrative role that enforces internal efficiency through operational routines and an entrepreneurial role which executes metaroutines to adapt the operational routines to the changing environment. The use of metaroutines allows team members to transform routine tasks into standard operating procedures and to develop a "grammar of actions" to achieve uniformity (Pentland & Reuter, 1994). The fifth condition, that is of transcendence, is triggered by the SMT's drive for continuous improvement or "Kaizen" in which current performance serves as the basis for breakthrough performance (Imai, 1985). Breakthrough performance is the condition that elevates the value adding of the organization to new highs and signifies the transformation toward horizontal organization and self-management.

The "broker" is concerned with maintaining external legitimacy for the team and obtaining external resources. Image building, visibility, and reputation are the primary concerns of the broker (Snow, Miles & Coleman, 1992). Team leaders in this role are politically astute, persuasive, influential, and powerful (Quinn, Faerman, Thompson & McGrath, 1996). Brokers often act as boundary spanners and liaisons. They meet with people from outside, present the team's ideas and positions, negotiate agreements, and acquire resources. Brokers are the gatekeepers, networkers, and communicators for the team (Baker, 1994). They buffer the team from outside interference by screening the amount of information that flows into the system and they link the team with the external environment via networking and the establishment of direct lines of communication with external stakeholders (Charan, 1991). As a broker, a team member may use negotiation and networking skills, as well as influence strategies, to shape team-related boundaries and boundary-spanning roles, to optimize members' integration, and to achieve externally driven goals or performance targets (Baker, 1994).

The "innovator" focuses on adaptability and responsiveness of the team as a whole to the external environment. "The innovator role involves the use of creativity and the management of . . . changes and transitions, and provides a unique opportunity for [team members] to affirm the value of individual employees within the organizational setting" (Quinn, Faerman, Thompson & McGrath, 1996, p. 336). Managing change in SMTs is facilitated by the unique structure of the group, its diversity, cross-functional synergy, and the mutual support that exists among team members sharing leadership roles. The innovator initiates ideas and suggestions, stimulates creative and critical thinking, and often plays the role of the group energizer to bring about positive change. This role resembles the developer style suggested by Bradford and Cohen (1984)—the member in this capacity centers on the SMT's processes and outputs as a joint venture, a team effort. Members are encouraged to contribute their talents and skills to deal with change, assume ownership, and support the goals of change and innovation.

The "coordinator" maintains the structure and the efficient flow of work and information and focuses on stability and continuity in the group. This role involves facilitation in various forms such as organizing the work load, assigning team members and determining job responsibilities, short-range scheduling, reporting and giving feedback, and synchronizing the activities of team members. Assuming this role, the team leader is concerned with the resources and the necessary tools of project planning, resource allocation, and project monitoring to do the work (Badiru, 1993; Kerzner, 1989). According to Quinn, Faerman, Thompson, and McGrath (1996), effective coordination requires skills and competencies such as managing across functions, managing projects, and designing work. Leading and coordinating across functions is an important competency that the team member enacts through knowledge and understanding of work processes and through having the interpersonal and problem-solving skills essential to achieve joint performance (Parker, 1994; Rummler & Brache, 1990). On the other hand, project management and obtaining measurement of the most efficient use of resources requires knowledge of PERT, CPM, Gantt charts, and other techniques essential for effective integration of members' efforts.

Designing work in SMTs usually centers around the sociotechnical approach or the requirement to balance the technical with the social elements of members' interactions (Cummings, 1978). Under the guidance of the team coordinator, the SMT is fully responsible for managing the process and has the authority to make decisions on work methods, quality standards, purchasing and inventory, and production goals (Quinn, Faerman, Thompson & McGrath, 1996). This set of responsibilities and behaviors is consistent with the argument made by Lawler (1992), that "a team must be given responsibility for enough of the creation of a product or service so that it controls and is responsible for a clear input and a clear output. All the factors that influence how successfully a particular transformation is done should be included within its scope of responsibility" (Lawler, 1992, p. 90). Following Hackman and Oldham (1975), this view is also consistent with the job enrichment model, which assumes that rather than using pay and close supervision as incentives to motivate team members to do their work, the work itself could become the incentive.

As a customer-driven work group, the SMT's internal operation is integrated in a value chain that may include processes such as product development, inventory management, order-to-payment, and customer service (Kotler & Armstrong, 1994). Monitoring in a group context involves making sure that systems work efficiently, tracking and analyzing process variation, and leading team members to self-correct errors and deficiencies. As a "monitor," a team member develops means for the SMT to achieve compliance with work standards and evaluates whether team members meet their goals. The monitor uses quality tools such as Pareto diagrams and control charts to evaluate performance, identify nonvalue-added tasks, and improve work processes (Harrington, 1987). Thus, the monitor functions as an information giver or the member who takes on the leadership role of providing constant feedback to team members about work processes and outcomes. As Senge (1990) points out, feedback allows individuals to draw rational conclusions about their performance and go through self-directed learning and self-improvement.

PLAYING THE ROLES EFFECTIVELY IN SMTs

Team members are expected to act out the eight leadership roles and to simultaneously consider and balance the competing demands that are represented by each set of expectations. These expectations are also in line with the agreement among experts that a balance in playing the roles is essential for effective leadership (Bradford & Cohen, 1984; Hooijberg & Quinn, 1992; Yukl, 1989). Team players are encouraged to shift their styles and roles as needed and to broaden their knowledge and skills in the various areas of the team's operations. Team players cannot achieve effectiveness by emphasizing two or three roles while ignoring others. As Quinn (1988) persuasively noted: "Effectiveness is the result of maintaining a creative tension between contrasting demands in a social system. When the tension is lost, the perception of effectiveness is altered. The roles that are emphasized are seen negatively. A perceptual inversion occurs" (p. 106). Like master managers (Quinn, Faerman, Thompson & McGrath, 1996), team members are encouraged to have the ability to see their work context as a complex, dynamic system that is constantly evolving.

To interact effectively with the system's requirements, team players must be familiar with the sociotechnical aspects associated with all of the roles. They must go beyond their predominant behavioral style and technical expertise to recognize the need for greater cognitive and behavioral complexity. Effective SMTs abandon the "its not my job" syndrome of leadership format and responsibility—a member can be a director, monitor, or coordinator in sequence, simultaneously, or intermittently—essentially a dynamic application of Quinn's concept of creative tension to shared team leadership. Shared followership is also important for team success (King, 1988). A team member might take a leadership role synchronizing team activities and work schedule (coordinator role), and yet play a follower role in a conflict resolution session mediated by the leadership role of someone else (facilitator). The roles shift between leader and follower depending on different situations. Since effective team members need to lead and follow, a team requires both shared leadership and followership to be successful.

LEADERSHIP ROLES AND COMMUNICATION
MEDIA IN SMTs

Observations of SMTs in action have confirmed that ongoing performance feedback and the reinforcement of communication within the team are perhaps the most important mechanisms to leverage collective accountability and high commitment to the team's goals (Orsburn, Moran, Musselwhite & Zenger, 1990; Parker, 1990; Ray & Bronstein, 1995). Playing the leadership roles effectively also requires access to and sharing of information that traditionally has been limited to managerial turf or considered to be an integral part of the supervisory domain. In team-based organizations, the value of removing the manager comes from shifting the information from a power source for the manager to an empowering source for the team. SMTs remove communication barriers through ongoing interactions and learning that require the constant sharing of information. The predominant pattern of communication is not institutional nor does it follow a reporting relationship within the chain of command. The pattern is interpersonal and involves direct communication and lateral relations.

Self-managed teams are communication-intensive, learning-oriented systems with a great need for ongoing, highly accessible, and usable information. Team leaders depend on information directly from the source (e.g., supplier, customer) and dispense it through face-to-face, question-and-answer types of communication media. One particular mode of communication that is quite common in many SMTs is the team scheduled meeting. Meetings, one of the few "formalized" mechanisms of communication within teams, are forums for exchanging information and giving many types of feedback—operational, evaluative, reinforcing, or corrective. Typical topics of team meetings are external customer requirements, budget review, vendor information, problem-solving activities, process simplification, role clarification, organizational values, assessment of team performance, resolution of conflicts, and quality review. Meetings and ongoing information sharing between members are important for team success. Without meetings the team would have no institutionalized forum for information sharing, timely feedback, problem solving, rule formulation, or decision making.

Meetings provide linkage mechanisms in flat, team-based organizations in the form of a forum for coordinating activities that typically would have been coordinated by a traditional supervisor (Manz & Sims, 1987). Meetings facilitate decision-making processes by providing a platform for discussions and constructive feedback aimed at ensuring that members have a mental reference map for actions and follow-ups compatible with the overarching goals and organizational needs and strategies. Meetings also appear as a form of unobtrusive control used collectively to socialize individual members through adherence to and belief in a rule system. When SMT members orient their activities around a particular set of normative rules, these rules both constrain and legitimize certain acceptable behaviors. Thus, SMTs manifest the essential element of concertive control, and their value-based interactions become a social force controlling their actions (Barker, 1993). Indeed, team meetings serve the important function of linking and integrating the various roles played by team members and controlling them concertively. Meetings become a medium that serves as a substitute for hierarchy (Fisher, 1993).

ENACTMENT OF THE LEADERSHIP ROLES

Thus far, the a-priori assumption throughout the discussion has been that the Competing Values Framework offers an alternate approach for facilitating the understanding of leadership roles and communication processes in self-managed teams. But how do we know whether the eight roles described above, which have been found to surface in the behaviors performed by managers across hierarchical levels (DiPadova & Faerman, 1993), are also those manifested in the behaviors of members in self-managed teams? How can we determine whether team members stress certain indispensable roles and downplay other "less" important roles? How do we measure the relative importance placed on each role by team members? What is the inherent association between the various roles and communication media and the abilities used by team members? Answering these questions empirically can help confirm the relevance of the Competing Values Framework for facilitating understanding of leadership roles in SMTs and can also provide guidance to organizations and managers who choose to use SMTs and perhaps other variations of high-performance teams.

SMTs OPERATING IN A DISTRIBUTION CENTER

A small-scale preliminary study was conducted at a distribution center located in upstate New York which employs SMTs in its operating core. The distribution center was a newly established operation with a flat, decentralized organizational structure and with very little managerial control. The distribution center also utilized a sociotechnical system (STS) in which an optimal balance has been continually sought between the technical complexity of the tasks and work flow and the personality types and behaviors of participating team players. By any industrial measure, the distribution center's performance in 1992 was very high. For example, while the injury rate per two hundred thousand hours worked for the industry was forty-five, that of the distribution center stood at sixteen. The turnover rate for the industry averaged 35 percent, while that of the distribution center was 7 percent. Errors per one thousand items selected at the distribution center were 2.93, while the comparable industrial figure was around 20. Finally, product damage due to shipping cost the distribution center $.08/ton, while the industry average was $.35 per ton shipped.

The distribution center was also recognized by others to be an exemplary organizational setting. It served as a learning site visit for many firms and academic institutions. Several organizations, as large as IBM and Kodak and as small as Ben & Jerry's and Scott Paper, have benchmarked the distribution center. For comparison purposes they have targeted in particular the key processes, practices, and critical success factors of the seven teams operating at the distribution center. Finally, the distribution center was rated as one of the top employers in the region in which it is located, a major metropolitan area. This rating was conducted by the Regional Human Resource Association, a group of personnel managers representing 250 area companies, who looked at such items as pay, benefits, employee relations, and community involvement. Of the 900 companies invited to participate, 120 began the selection process and 35 completed it. From that 35, the top 10 were chosen. In the large business category the distribution center was rated as the second best employer.

The goal of the investigation was quite modest and limited to finding a preliminary answer to the question of how frequently the eight leadership roles described by the Competing Values Framework are manifested in the behaviors of SMT members. The research procedure included interviews of key people in a managerial capacity (referred to as "resource"), team leaders (called "team coordinators"), and team members ("associates"), as well as a self-administered questionnaire similar to the one recommended by Quinn (1988) that appears in *the Instructional Guide to Becoming a Master Manager* (DiPadova, 1996, pp. 79–92). The objective was to collect data on the Competing Values Framework leadership roles performed explicitly by members of SMTs. The interviews demonstrated the efficacy of the Competing Values Framework in creating a shared meaning across team members. The interviews (with the "resource") also helped identify two parallel teams with similar functions and work flows (processes), but with different sizes. Team 1 was made up of twenty-two members who were responsible for handling grocery items, and Team 2 consisted of twenty-seven members who were responsible for the supply of meat and dairy products.

A total of twelve individual interviews were conducted involving two resource team members, two team leaders, and eight SMT members belonging to the two teams mentioned above. Interviewees were first asked to describe generic roles that are important for the success of the team as a whole and that are performed frequently by team members. Other questions involved the skills and competencies essential for effective leadership role performance. None of the answers provided information about distinct leadership roles and behavioral skills outside those proposed by the Competing Values Framework. A common response was that team members must adapt to change (brokering and innovating), follow accepted guidelines (monitoring and coordinating), be personally motivated and productive (directing and producing), and yet, collaborate with others and work as a cohesive team (mentoring and facilitating).

The interviews then were structured around the Competing Values Framework, in essence to provide the participants with primary information about each of the eight leadership roles and how performing them could involve, at a perceptual level, the need to deal simultaneously with opposite demands or paradoxes. Participants were then asked to provide descriptions in their own words of how the different roles appear in the behaviors performed by SMT members. An important finding of these interviews was the common agreement that the roles are important and relevant and that, on balance, team members are perceived to be playing all of the roles. However, most interviewees suggested that some roles are less important than others due to the unique structure of the teams, strong ownership of team goals, internalization of certain functions and responsibilities, trust and confidence in members' mutual support, and the teams' "built-in" coordination mechanisms. For example, the simultaneous loose/tight structure of SMTs tends to breed intensive communication among team members, as well as mutual adjustment as the primary mode of coordination, making the facilitator and coordinator roles somewhat redundant, and subsequently perceived as being less important. A remark such as: "All of us are involved in coordination anyway" was characteristic of this phenomenon. Cognitively, facilitation and coordination are shared activities and all team members are expected to contribute to team integration.

Another finding was that the age of the organization and its transformational cycle was also identified as a factor in effecting members' perceptions of the importance of certain leadership roles as compared with others. Moving from concept to implementation of self-management, this thirty-month-old organization has also shifted from the entrepreneurial stage to the collectivity stage of organizational evolution. During this stage, team members seem to emphasize the values of human resources, interpersonal communication, teamwork, cooperation, and involvement and are much less concerned with planning, direction, and initiation of structure (Kimberly & Quinn, 1984; Quinn & Cameron, 1983). Members' spans of attention seemed to encompass social processes and mutual adaptation as well as quality outcomes, even more so than internal monitoring and external affairs. The relative importance of performing the monitor and broker roles appeared to become diminished in relation to other predominant roles such as the mentor role. Armed with these initial findings, self-administered questionnaires were sent to the forty-nine members of the targeted teams in this preliminary study in an effort to collect sufficient data to "profile" the leadership roles played by team members collectively. Thirty usable responses were returned, a response rate of 61.2 percent. The questionnaires contained sixty-four statements, eight for each leadership role. The respondents were asked to agree/disagree with each statement on a seven-point Likert scale.

ANALYSIS AND RESULTS

The analytical procedure consisted of measuring the extent to which the eight roles were perceived as important (manifested in the behaviors of team members). Each individual's responses to the survey were arranged by key item into the eight leadership roles. Next, each of these individual's role scores were averaged with those of the other members of the same team to produce a mean value and standard deviation for each role per team. Table 7.2 provides the means

Table 7.2.
Means and Standard Deviations for the Two SMTs

Roles	Team 1 (N=12) Mean[a]	σ	Team 2 (N=18) Mean	σ	combined (weighted) Mean	σ
Facilitator	4.927	0.827	4.812	0.418	4.858	0.604
Mentor	5.156	0.919	5.208	0.596	5.188	0.727
Innovator	5.423	0.636	5.264	0.511	5.327	0.559
Broker	4.649	0.893	4.653	0.412	4.651	0.634
Producer	5.385	0.654	5.257	0.526	5.308	0.573
Director	5.396	0.593	5.181	0.646	5.267	0.624
Coordinator	4.781	0.512	4.597	0.615	4.671	0.574
Monitor	4.604	1.133	4.840	0.660	4.746	0.869

[a]Based on a seven-point Likert scale.

and standard deviations for each of the eight leadership roles of both teams, as well as for the teams combined.

Through an examination of the mean of each of the roles and from discussions with respondents about the practical meaning of the behaviors associated with the roles, team members' perceptions of the existence of the eight roles in their managerial behaviors appear to be very similar across the two teams. The overall mean in the combined sample was 5.002 with a standard deviation of 0.702 indicating that these specific role behaviors were reported as being performed frequently. The small sample size tends to magnify the differences between respondents. In our preliminary study, the low variability seemed to imply uniformity in performing the leadership roles.

The profile of the teams combined seemed to be uniform in shape and size for two reasons: (a) the highest role scores and the lowest role scores for each team were within one standard deviation of their means; (b) both teams produced relatively higher scores on the roles of mentor, innovator, producer, and director, and slightly lower scores on the roles of facilitator, broker, coordinator, and monitor. Although there was some variation, as a natural consequence of human behavior in such contexts, collectively, however, all of the roles described by the Competing Values Framework appeared to be shared. The relatively low variability in role distribution correlated with uniformity in performing these specific role behaviors. No one role was overemphasized to the extent that other roles were ignored. The significant positive correlation that was found between the polar as well as parallel roles (e.g., facilitator vs. its polar opposite, the producer; and the facilitator vs. its parallel, the mentor) indicated support for the specified relationships between roles (Belasen, 1994).

SELF-MANAGED TEAMS IN ACTION

In a study involving the SMT operating in the Northeast USPS station described earlier, Engel (1995) found that on balance all eight roles were perceived as important and appeared in the behaviors of team members, both individually and collectively. Table 7.3 lists each of the leadership roles in terms of means and standard deviations. It is not surprising that the roles of the Monitor (mean 4.875) and Broker (mean 4.938) were perceived as less important and reportedly have been fulfilled less often than the others. The role of Monitor is in part carried out by an elected Coordinator, who acts as a liaison with the zone supervisor and reports the daily activities. While the Monitor "knows what's

Table 7.3.
Leadership Roles in USPS Self-Managed Teams

Roles	Mean	Standard Deviations	
		Individuals	Group
Coordinator	5.146	0.790	0.844
Monitor	4.875	1.057	0.313
Facilitator	5.073	1.079	0.144
Mentor	5.146	0.882	0.634
Innovator	5.521	0.844	0.356
Broker	4.938	1.090	0.549
Producer	5.323	0.805	0.535
Director	5.344	0.891	0.532
Overall	5.171	0.930	0.488

going on within the team," the nature of the task also influenced responses. The core responsibilities of city carriers remain individualistic and a majority of the day is spent on sorting and delivering the mail for one's own route. If a carrier requires assistance, he or she either informally or formally gets help by approaching other team members. If necessary, the group makes a decision regarding assistance. Additionally, due to the national labor agreement, the zone supervisor and station manager must ultimately take responsibility for the SMT's performance. Therefore, they are more apt to fulfill the role of Monitor.

Similarly, the role of Broker, while extremely critical for the formation of the team, and since the 1992 change of supervisors, has also become less crucial recently. The relatively low score in Broker fulfillment is offset and balanced by the high scores on the Innovator role (mean 5.521). As a whole, the SMT can be viewed as very innovative. According to the team charter, prior to self-management the zone "had a low level of morale . . . was the butt of disparaging remarks . . . and had 67 grievances filed." For fiscal year 1994, there were only three grievances filed by the shop steward. Given the conditions in 1988 and the freedom to make changes, the carriers involved in the EI process responded creatively by coming up with, at least as far as the culture of the USPS is concerned, a "radical" idea. Contributing to the success of the group is the frequent enactment of the Facilitator (mean 5.073) and Mentor (mean 5.146) roles. Together these roles maintain the group's collective efforts and are associated with the human relations movement. Without fulfillment of these roles, personal conflicts could spiral out of control and negatively effect the whole group's performance. Reportedly, interpersonal conflicts are handled informally at the lowest possible level and everyone "gets along well together." If these roles were not fulfilled, the traditional zone supervisor would have to step in and resolve problems on a regular basis. Officially the SMT coordinator is the final authority for resolving disputes within the team.

Means for the roles of Producer (5.323) and Director (5.344) were relatively higher than those of other means, illustrating the behaviors that in a sense are used to measure performance (OFPH, DPH, DCEA—see the section on performance measures). Producers are work-focused and task-oriented individuals. This description fits well with the daily routine of city carriers. Elimination of direct supervision necessitates that all of the carriers in the SMT become Producers. Also, the relatively low level of task uncertainty and minimization of interdependence once the carriers are out on their routes make it necessary for team members to actively engage in this role. These behaviors are similar to those associated with the role of Director. Both roles are in the rational goal quadrant of the Competing Values Framework. Directors take initiative and set and clarify goals. This is applicable to the team as well as individuals. The standard deviations for the roles were relatively small, indicating a high degree of role sharing and dependability. All but one of the group standard deviations were lower than those for individuals. Low scores by individuals in certain roles were generally counterbalanced by higher scores of other team members.

The members of the SMT described above create a dynamic tension in the social system between roles, thus creating synergy and balance. Individuals at one time or another engage in all eight roles, depending on situational factors. Leadership is the process of influencing people to direct their efforts toward the attainment of a particular goal. This process by its nature requires effective communication. It is the effectiveness of this communication and thus shared team leadership that has enabled the Postal Service SMT to sustain and increase the performance levels of the unit (Engel, 1995).

IMPLICATIONS FOR MANAGEMENT AND TEAM LEADERSHIP

Although preliminary, these results may hinge on the fact that some roles may be internalized, while other more "vital" roles may emerge pending contextual factors and the team's transformational cycle. Most interviewees suggested that some roles are less important than others due to the unique structure of the teams, strong ownership of team goals, internalization of certain functions and responsibilities, trust and confidence in members' mutual support, and the teams' containment of coordination. This finding is corroborated by Manz and Sims's (1987) study of leadership behaviors in self-managed teams. Manz and Sims concluded that the underlying theme of leadership practice was to influence the team and team members to be able to perform tasks and responsibilities through self–goal setting rather than for the leaders (coordinators) to exercise direct control or perform the tasks themselves. They also found "an abundance of deliberate and calculated efforts to foster independence rather than allow the dependence of more traditional work groups" (Manz & Sims, 1987, p. 114).

Does this mean that the requirement (coming from the leadership literature) to balance the different leadership roles is congruent with the reality in which some of the roles are internalized? Another variant of this question is whether we should expect to find the full range of leadership roles, internalized or enacted, once a team transcends its early stages of development and achieves maturity. If confirmed, however, this may lead to yet another interesting avenue of research. It would actually prove that leadership is not part of SMTs and that role versatility, adaptability, and flexibility are more critical to the success of the teams than merely leadership roles. This conclusion is important since it underscores the learning nature of SMTs.

Learning is an important attribute of team development, ownership, and functioning. The team's learning and knowledge is developed through a system of shared leadership, training, and continuing experimentation. The focus of this learning is on collective skill development or a skill set that places emphasis on team training and learning. Once team members are cross-trained and master the technical, interpersonal, and administrative skills essential for high performance, sharing information and transferring knowledge across team members becomes a way of life (Orsburn, Moran, Musselwhite & Zenger, 1990). In implementing the concept of self-management, it is expected that organizational decision makers have made a conscious effort to give members of SMTs opportunities to develop the skills and responsibilities that supervisors possessed in the past. Status and power are now devalued, while a greater premium is placed on collaboration and broad skill acquisition (Ray & Bronstein, 1995). This is particularly true during the later stage of team development, where relationships, expectations, roles, and processes become clear and effective. When implemented appropriately, team members move toward collaboration, which includes shared responsibility, interchangeable roles and activities, and a simultaneous loose-tight internal (normative) control structure. This also means that self-leadership, self-efficacy, self-direction, and self-improvement characterize the way members behave. High satisfaction with the collective performance and the group accomplishments is what makes the outcome of shared team leadership and the enactment of the leadership roles successful as is "illustrated by spontaneous celebrations and individuals accepting identification with, and loyalty to, their team" (Ray & Bronstein, 1995, pp. 171–72).

If good teamwork promotes productivity and quality improvement, then why are productivity and quality levels sometimes lower in a team environment? Drawing on the work of others (Nahavandi & Aranda, 1994; Allender, 1993), Tudor, Trumble, and Diaz (1996) suggested that many employees believe working in a team environment is a waste of productive time since too much time is routinely spent on building trust and agreement. They cite the example of Florida Power and Light, which reduced the number of the teams established in the company after employees expressed dissatisfaction with the constant need to meet and reach collective agreement over decision situations. Reductions occurred just prior to FP&L winning the coveted Deming Prize.

One reason for the failure of teams is that they do not provide opportunities for personal gratification. For the most part, people are individualistic and they value the independent spirit and competitive relationships. Team members often choose to opt out of teams that require high levels of interdependence, mutual reliance, and shared team leadership. USA Today (2/25/97, section B) cited a study by the Hay Group, which reported that 45 percent of team failures occur due to the lack of effective leadership. In spite of these problems and others, evidence shows that many companies embrace the notion of SMTs (Nahavandi & Aranda, 1994). In fact, one in five companies reportedly has or will implement SMTs (Hitchcock & Willard, 1995). Sounds quite paradoxical, doesn't it?

Self-managed teams are important, for they help reduce operational costs (Orsburn, Moran, Musselwhite & Zenger, 1990). The use of SMTs can eliminate the need for an entire level of middle management and the results at Kodak, Texas Instruments, Ritz-Carlton Hotels, and other companies prove that SMTs are indeed cost efficient (USA Today, 2/25/97, section B).

So how can SMTs be made more effective? One answer could be through the creative use of information technology, such as computer-mediated communication (CMC), voice mail (V-M), e-mail and so on, thus reducing the need for actual meetings in favor of virtual ones, or by increasing the sharing of information before meetings. Second, as learning teams SMTs require extensive training in cross-functional skills, interpersonal relations, and problem-solving, administrative, and leadership skills.

With adequate support and resources coming from human resource managers, leaders of SMTs could satisfy essential training needs for themselves and for their teams (Dyer, 1995). Saturn, for example, provided its 150 SMTs (each with about fifteen associates) with eight hundred thousand training hours in 1990 alone. This training included areas such as quality control, purchasing, budgeting, participative decision making, and staffing (Tudor, Trumble & Diaz, 1996). Each team has the additional responsibility of creating specific training schedules based on current needs for each of its members (Solomon, 1991). All employees at Saturn spend 5 percent of their time in training every year (Geber, 1994). Today Saturn is well known for its quality and customer service (Bluestone & Bluestone, 1992).

Training programs could also focus on eliminating "blind spots" or gaps which might exist as a result of differing role expectations across team members (Sendelbach, 1993). Since team members spend much of their time in meetings and other communication relationships, strengthening communication and listening skills and learning to give feedback must also be among the primary goals of SMT training programs (Wellins, 1992). These communication skills are essential in all four domains of the Competing Values Framework: for the mentor and facilitator roles, problem solving (behavioral), participative decision making, conflict resolution, and interpersonal communication are vital; for the broker and innovator roles, bargaining and negotiation, selling ideas, persuasion, influence and power, and consensus building are crucial; for the coordinator and monitor roles, responsibility charting, role clarification, business communication, assertiveness, monitoring, and evaluation are important; for the director and producer roles, goal setting, giving instructions, presentations, and problem solving (analytical) are critical. Although many skills can be developed through training, certain skills may be difficult to build as a natural course of human behavior. Thus, a team must carefully select members with the required competencies to play the eight roles as well as providing members with training to develop and strengthen leadership skills. Any deficiency in the performance of these roles should inspire further educational and developmental activities aimed at building the roles and the set of competencies associated with them into the teams.

Team members are often trained in the use of personality-typing methods such as the Myers-Briggs Type Indicator (MBTI), allowing them to self-assess their personality type and to recognize the weaknesses and strengths associated with their own types as well as others. MBTI displays sixteen combinations of personality typing based on four functions (Sensing, iNtuition, Thinking, Feeling) and four attitudes (Extraversion, Introversion, Judgment, Perception). During my visits to sites with SMTs operating in the field, I observed how team members interact and refer to each other by their personality typing. It was a fascinating experience to observe. It was not uncommon to hear a discussion where a few members would turn to their associates and suggest that the member take care of the problem directly and uninterruptedly "since you are an ISTJ" (which implies decisiveness and dependability). Team members also teased each other and often referred to the relative weakness of a particular member by suggesting that the "cause" correlates with the personality type of that member. The use of techniques such as MBTI, however, can help reduce conflicts, increase communication and understanding, and above all help in the recruitment and selection process. For example, the teams observed used the criterion of complementary leadership skills to avoid hiring a person with incompatible skills in favor of someone with skills that could support or supplement the needs of the team as a whole. This observation is important, for it underscores the learning attributes of SMTs—understanding personality differences and similarities can help moderate the way by which team members behave or perform their technical and leadership roles effectively.

CONCLUSIONS: THE SIGNIFICANCE OF SELF-MANAGEMENT

Value-based organizations organize work around self-managed teams in which nonmanagers operate with delegative responsibilities and a high degree of latitude. The structure of these organizations has no one in the middle. Middle managers have always handled two main jobs: supervising people and gathering, processing, and transmitting information. Self managed teams are empowered to take over such standard supervisory duties as scheduling work, maintaining quality, and even administering pay and vacations. The transformation from a bureaucratic, supervisory-oriented organization to a value-based organization with worker-run teams presents team members with challenges different from those existing in traditional forms of organizations. Instead of being told what to do by the common supervisor, members of SMTs are given considerable freedom to design their jobs, set objectives, discipline and reward team players, and often to recruit and select their own members.

Self-managed teams use communication lines as an effective replacement for authority lines. They conduct meetings and use participatory decision making as a substitute for hierarchy. Meetings are the forum for exchanging information and giving feedback of many forms—that is, operational, evaluative, reinforcing, or corrective. Without meetings, quality improvement teams (QIT), for example, have no institutionalized forum for information sharing, timely feedback, problem solving, and policy or decision making. These meetings are an important linkage mechanism in team-based organizations employing horizontal management. Meetings are used to coordinate activities that typically would have been coordinated by a traditional supervisor. Effective meetings, however, are also a reflection of a healthy organizational culture that supports the value of teamwork, interpersonal relations, and constructive feedback. Both strong culture and effective communication contribute to the emergence of norms of behaviors that are positive, the maintenance of cohesive work groups, and the formation of committed personnel.

Self-managed teams are unique organizational structures since they exist in a quasi-autonomous state (loosely coupled) within an organization. SMT members are highly interdependent (tightly coupled) with other team members as a result of common goals and self-regulation. Rather than being a parallel group or team (e.g., quality circles, task forces), SMTs have the formal power to create and maintain their own systems or working relationships in order to complete a total job. The teams have administrative control over such managerial functions as planning, scheduling, monitoring, and staffing. SMTs have broad-based and multiskilled members, integrated responsibilities and duties, training in team functions, and extensive information sharing. As such, SMTs are the result of a major paradigm shift toward cross-functional synergies, joint performance, and teamwork through self-ruled work teams.

Horizontal management and self-managed teams require leaders to have the competencies essential to facilitate boundary management. These competencies are particularly essential for performance in a discontinuous environment. They include:

- Thinking of oneself as a sponsor, team leader, or internal consultant
- Communicating laterally and diagonally with anyone necessary for getting the job done
- Changing organizational structures in response to market change

- Engaging others in decision making
- Sharing information
- Mastering a broad array of managerial disciplines
- Demanding accountability and requiring improved results

These new competencies and roles enhance organizational action learning or the process by which organizational members increase knowledge, develop new skills, and maintain the creative tension needed to successfully survive environmental discontinuity. Learning and acquisition of new knowledge, as well as transference of knowledge within the organization, are important facets of the Facilitator role and are used by the manager performing the Mentor role to develop employees' leadership capabilities. In Part IV, chapter 8 examines other important attributes of learning that enhance the capacity of organizations to take action and then adapt to the changing condition of their environments. Chapter 9 provides a thorough review of management education and learning with a particular emphasis on competency assessment and development.

Part IV

**LEARNING AND
DEVELOPMENT**

The internal horizontal axis and the flexibility vertical axis appear in the upper left quadrant of the Competing Values Framework and define the boundaries of the *human relations model* and the domain of organizational and management *learning and development*. This model reflects the view that organizations are effective if they are able to tap the talents and thinking of their employees. Fundamental to this model is the concern for attention to human needs. The two managerial leadership roles associated with this quadrant are the Facilitator and the Mentor.

FACILITATOR ROLE: THE COACH

In the capacity of Facilitator, the manager is expected to foster collective effort, build cohesion and morale, and manage interpersonal conflict. The Facilitator uses some of the same competencies as the Mentor, such as listening and being empathetic and sensitive to the needs of others. The role of Facilitator, however, centers around the manager's work with groups. As a Facilitator, the manager's primary activities focus on generating ownership and commitment to the group or work-unit goals in support of the overarching goals of the organization. Effective managers acquire, use, and dynamically integrate the competencies associated with the Facilitator role in managerial situations: building teams, using participative decision making, and managing conflict.

The Facilitator clarifies the roles expected of individual members, the procedures and processes through which team members interact, and the "sharing of information and building on each other's knowledge to create generative rather than simply adaptive learning patterns" (D'Andrea-O'Brien & Buono, 1996, p. 6). Facilitators specialize in group processes—they intervene in interpersonal disputes, use conflict reduction techniques, maintain cohesion and high morale, develop communication links with the outside, and facilitate problem solving (Bucholz & Roth, 1987; Katzenbach & Smith, 1993; Ray & Bronstein, 1995). Perhaps, the most important role of the Facilitator is to strengthen group cohesion through team building and development (Dyer, 1995; Harrington-Mackin, 1994; Liebowitz & DeMeuse, 1982; Sundstrom, DeMeuse & Futrell, 1990; Tannenbaum, Beard & Salas, 1992). Team building can be approached using quality improvement techniques such as cause-and-effect analysis, Pareto charting, and interrelationship di-graphing. Other approaches to teambuilding include communication methods such as responsibility charting (Beckhard & Harris, 1977), role analysis technique (Dayal & Thomas, 1968), role negotiation (Harrison, 1972), reflective listening (Whetten & Cameron, 1994), and lifecycle models (Hersey & Blanchard, 1993) .

As a Facilitator, an effective manager is able to anticipate dynamics associated with the different stages of the transformational cycle of the work group: testing, organizing, establishing interdependence, and producing and evaluating (Quinn, Faerman, Thompson & McGrath, 1996). During the initial stage, the Facilitator spells out expectations, clarifies the team's charter and responsibilities, explores the boundaries of acceptable behavior, and begins team-building exercises. The second stage, "organizing," is the most crucial. As a Facilitator, the manager is heavily involved in retaining the work group's focus and keeping the group from backtracking. The third stage, "establishing interdependence," is typified by acceptance, constructive feedback, and positive attitudes toward the team's area of responsibility. Finally, during the fourth stage of team development, "producing and evaluating," active facilitation tends to diminish and although the Facilitator continues to provide support through counseling and coaching, the Monitor role "kicks in" to monitor the group's collective performance.

MENTOR ROLE: THE COUNSELOR

In the capacity of Mentor, the manager is expected to be helpful, considerate, sensitive, approachable, open, and fair. The Mentor listens, supports, conveys appreciation, and gives recognition. Employees are seen as essential resources to be understood, valued, and developed. The manager sees that employees have opportunities for training and skill building. Effective managers acquire, use, and dynamically integrate the competencies associated with the Mentor role in managerial situations: understanding self and others, communicating effectively, and, developing subordinates.

The key to successful mentoring is to recognize that mentoring involves developing and maintaining a relationship between the Mentor and other team members (Bolman & Deal, 1995; Covey, 1989; DePree, 1990). Kram (1983), for example, studied the cycle of developmental relationships between pairs of mentors and mentees and found that a mentor relationship moves through the phases of initiation, cultivation, separation, and redefinition with each phase characterized by particular affective experiences, developmental functions, and interaction patterns that are shaped by both individual needs and organizational circumstances. A mentoring relationship has the potential to enhance the career and professional development of team members. Through career functions, including sponsorship, coaching, protection, exposure and visibility, and challenging work assignments, team members can learn the ropes of organizational life. Through psychosocial functions including role modeling, acceptance and confirmation, counseling, and friendship, team members can develop a sense of competence, confidence, and effectiveness in the leadership roles (Kram, 1983, pp. 614–15).

Although the majority of mentorships are informal, mentoring is so important that in large organizations such as Chrysler Corporation, Dow Corning, Kraft Foods, and McDonnell Douglas Aircraft, a structured program teaching skills and competencies for effective mentoring has become an integral part of the organizational culture. In this role, managers develop a new mindset that supports and fits organizational transformations: they are helpful, considerate, sensitive, approachable, and open. The Mentor listens actively, supports legitimate requests, conveys appreciation, provides compliments, and gives credit. In addition, the Mentor provides advice and training in the areas of interpersonal communication, group dynamics, conflict management, and professional planning.

The chapters included in Part IV—"Enhancing Organizational Learning: Communication Strategies and Methods" and "Learning to

Learn: Competency Education for Management Development"—cover the principles, strategies, tools, and methods available to organizational leaders to leverage the professional intellect and knowledge in the organization as the fundamental strategy for successful job, team, or total business performance. These two chapters highlight the importance of building organizational capabilities and supporting human resources through structured learning and competency development. The chapters examine the scope of leadership challenges faced by managers enacting the Facilitator and Mentor roles.

8

Enhancing Organizational Learning: Communication Strategies and Methods

> We find it ironic that top management devotes so much attention to the capital budgeting process yet typically has no comparable mechanism for allocating the human skills that embody core competencies.
>
> —Prahalad & Hamel, 1990

To be successful, organizations adjust structural arrangements, adapt to the dynamics of the external environment, and anticipate future trends and new interdependencies. Decentralized, organic organizations that are linked in a network of strategic alliances enhance their capacity to learn by way of the experimental nature of their structures and the futuristic orientation of their strategic approach. Flexibility and an outward perspective provide the context and the momentum for learning and renewal more so than formalized structures, which reinforce past patterns of behavior. By scanning the environment and by looking to capitalize on networking opportunities, even at the profit-center level, an interpreted reality is constructed and learning starts to take shape. Meaning is created, symbols and metaphors are shared, mutual understanding becomes commonplace, and often a new culture emerges that is sympathetic to the renewal process. When an organization operates in a dynamic environment with shifting interdependencies, learning becomes the context for realigning the organization with its environment through reinvention of the organizational setting. New missions are formulated, new plans and goals are set, structures are re-designed, processes are reengineered and improved, strategic beliefs are modified, and the operational causal map is altered. A true cultural transformation is taking shape.

INCREMENTAL VERSUS BREAKTHROUGH LEARNING

Incremental learning recognizes the difficulty involved in the constant need to change and revise organizational memory. Instead, it views learning as evolving gradually, over time, throughout the organization and with only minimal disruption to the organizational functioning. Thus, minor modifications and small adjustments are made to existing formal arrangements or norms of behaviors until new forms of interactions or new modes of behaviors are adopted. Learning becomes an ongoing part of the members' commitment to the value of continuous improvement to support organizational capabilities and upgrade organizational information systems. While any particular change may be relatively unimportant, the piled-up stacks of revisions can accumulate over time to cause significantly new understandings. Incremental learning is evolutionary and occurs through socialization, training, communication, and networking within and between work groups and cliques. As Robey and Sales (1994, p. 434) explain: Incremental learning confirms the emergent process approach to management. Rather than issuing edicts for instant and dramatic change, managers should allow time for organizational frames of meaning to be revised.

Breakthrough learning calls for quantum revisions to organizational memory in a short period of time. Quantum learning is thought to be more effective than incremental learning because it offers a direct challenge to established routines, identities, and causal maps. Learning occurs rapidly and the change process is revolutionary rather than evolutionary. While incremental learning supports the TQM perspective of continuous improvement, breakthrough learning aligns more with the reengineering school of thought. Change is from the root rather than the branch; by using revisions less frequently, the organization also avoids the cost of continuous self-assessment. Breakthrough learning, on the other hand, affects relatively larger parts of the organization and seeks to establish new formats of working relationships and common understandings. Neither incremental or breakthrough learning is categorically better. As discussed previously in chapter 5, neither TQM nor reengineering is superior, and organizations adopting one approach or another should probably consider the complementary relationships between the two methods.

While small, organically structured R&D organizations are less likely to change incrementally, large organizations with mechanistic structures of management and control seem to avoid the costs associated with breakthrough learning and dramatic revisions to organizational memory. As discussed above, shifting toward the mental map of horizontal management and cross-functional synergies, however, may help large organizations increase their capacity to learn, in addition to their ability to accept quantum change and respond effectively to the faster-paced global market.

Eastman Kodak's fundamental revisions during the 1980s and the 1990s moved from a structure relying on a functional approach to one that uses a market-based approach to doing business. This is a prime example of adopting breakthrough learning. Breakthrough learning is facilitated by the ability to unlearn and champion changes outside the existing organizational memory. There are possibilities that adoption of breakthrough learning as a change strategy may be inhibited by institutionalization processes gravitating in favor of incremental learning that is ingrained in memory. However, the experience of Kodak also demonstrates how large, bureaucratic organizations attempt to unlearn and create new causal maps that link breakthrough learning with organizational outcomes.

ACQUIRING, ACCESSING, AND REVISING KNOWLEDGE

> A learning organization is an organization skilled at creating, acquiring, and transferring knowledge, and at modifying its behavior to reflect new knowledge and insights.
>
> —David Garvin, 1993

According to Robey and Sales (1994), for an organization to learn, it must be able to acquire new knowledge and update its memory with that knowledge. Organizational design researchers (e.g., Galbraith, 1978; Galbraith & Lawler, 1993; Miller & Friesen, 1982; Nadler, Gerstein & Shaw, 1992) have argued that fluid organizational structures increase the capacity of organizations to process more information, acquire greater knowledge, and enhance organizational memory and learning. Thus, what an organization has already stored in its memory affects its ability to absorb and process new information and knowledge. New knowledge must be codified and disseminated among organizational members to enable learning. Codifying can be done formally through recording knowledge in formal documents and developing standard operating procedures, rules, and policies. In addition, it can be done informally through sharing core values, common beliefs, and stories. Incorporating the new knowledge into routines, regularities, and causal maps should facilitate accessibility to and institutionalization of organizational memory. Causal maps are shared beliefs about the relationships between particular actions taken by individuals, groups, or an organization along with the effects of these actions. With direct access to memory and with an implicit understanding of the tangible and intangible costs and benefits associated with using the memory, members can act without analysis. Enacting organizational memory helps sustain the common beliefs and culture of the organization through the construction of shared reality and the development of organizational culture. Learning is institutionalized by becoming part of the core values and normative control used by individuals and groups within the organization.

Robey and Sales (1994) see memory as both constraining and expanding. Memory is constraining when it is (1) based primarily on tacit knowledge embedded in routines; (2) is unobservable; and consequently (3) is difficult to change. However, while the existing knowledge and memory make it difficult to access recently acquired knowledge, new knowledge is often compared to old knowledge to upgrade and expand organizational memory. By retaining the old and the new together, meaningful contrasts can be made and the organization can become more aware of the process of learning (Robey & Sales, 1994, p. 431). Four sources of organizational learning are common, all of which depend critically on communication (Levitt & March, 1988; West and Meyer, 1997):

- *Learning by direct experience*: This type of learning results from the creation of causal maps and knowledge-response learning loops. Characteristics of communication systems include the choice of media used to facilitate the communication-based learning and channel transmissions which affect message routing, summarizing, revision, or delay. As communication-intensive institutions, value-based organizations are capable of transferring knowledge across organizational lines rapidly and effectively. As discussed in chapter 4, multifunctional teams facilitate direct contacts and mutual adjustments between individuals and provide opportunities to enhance learning by direct experience.

- *Interpretations of history*: Learning occurs by drawing on the construction, management, and sharing of meaning and common understandings. The ability of organizational members to develop shared language, symbols, and rituals that glorify and rationalize the history and existence of the organization facilitates the institutionalization of core values. Additionally, it also aids in the development of integrative and consensual organizational response to external and internal challenges.

- *Retrieval of knowledge from organizational memory*: Knowledge is stored and retrieved by conforming to established patterns of communication and regularized behaviors. Organizational members, predictably and uniformly use symbols, sagas, and rituals that differentiate them from members of other organizations. But they also make decisions and do work in a way that is consistent with the core values and the pattern of expectations established over time.

- *Learning from the experience of others*: While personal learning can occur through reflections and experimentation, organizational learning is enriched through the sharing of experiences and cross-fertilization between people. GE exposed many of its managers, who were targeted for global management, to the cultures and customs of its partners in the Pacific Rim to increase the managers' sensitivity to the values and behaviors of these partners. Horizontal organizations that use multifunctional teams to do work also benefit from an increase in the capacity of the organization to learn more than do organizations which use command structures and centralized networks of communication.

Hamel (1991, p. 98), cited by West and Meyer (1997, p. 41), proposed that "firms with a history of cross-functional teamwork and inter-business coordination were more likely to turn personal learning into corporate learning than were firms where the emphasis was on individual contributors and independent business units." As Henry Beam (1997, p. 73), in his review of Tobin's *Transformational Learning* (1996), suggested: Companies can be changed, or transformed, only when employees have acquired the knowledge and skills they need to take command of their careers and to see how their own work contributes to the larger work of their companies.

ENHANCING ORGANIZATIONAL LEARNING: COMMUNICATION, STRATEGIES, AND DEVELOPMENTAL APPROACHES

In an article addressing the issue of how to achieve strategic advantage via organizational learning, Carlvert, Mobley, and Marshall (1994, p. 41) generated a list of principles and guidelines involving the following: What are the steps to becoming a learning organization? What signifies a learning organization? What do learning organizations learn that other organizations do not? A learning organization can evolve by:

- Questioning current assumptions about learning
- Getting an outside perspective
- Tying the goal of becoming a learning organization to its organizational vision
- Finding or creating a champion in top management
- Looking for the "pain" in the organization, i.e., the place where more effective learning could help
- Articulating learning-organization ideas plainly
- Rewarding group as well as individual learning, success, and failure
- Finding an external enemy to spur greater cooperative learning
- Finding ways to collaborate internally in and unhampered by boundaries

A learning organization is characterized by:

- Learning collaboratively, openly, and across boundaries
- Valuing how it learns as well as what it learns
- Investing in staying ahead of the learning curve in its industry
- Gaining a competitive edge by learning faster and smarter than competitors
- Turning data into useful knowledge quickly and at the right time and place
- Enabling every employee to feel that every experience provides him or her with a chance to learn something potentially useful, even if only for leveraging future learning
- Exhibiting little fear and defensiveness; rewarding and learning from what goes wrong ("failure" learning) and right ("success learning")

- Taking risks while simultaneously avoiding jeopardizing the basic security of the organization
- Investing in experimental and seemingly tangential learning
- Supporting people and teams who want to pursue action-learning projects
- Depoliticizing learning by not penalizing individuals or groups for sharing information and conclusions

A learning organization learns to:

- Use learning to reach its goals
- Help people value the effects of their learning on their organization
- Avoid repeating the same mistakes
- Share information in ways that prompt appropriate action
- Link individual performance with organizational performance
- Tie rewards to key measures of performance
- Take in a lot of environmental information at all times
- Create structures and procedures that support the learning process
- Foster ongoing and orderly dialogues
- Make it safer for people to share openly and take risks

For learning to become institutionalized as an organization-wide activity, knowledge must be transferred quickly and efficiently throughout the organization. Two means of communication processes to facilitate the transference of knowledge are internal networks and horizontal arrangements. Two strategic means to improve the ability of the organization to learn are linking programs and benchmarking. Finally, two developmental means that enable organizational members to innovate and learn systematically are problem solving and training and education using 360-degree assessment tools.

FACILITATING LEARNING: INTERNAL NETWORKS AND COMMUNICATION PROCESSES

In a high-tech environment, organizational boundaries are redrawn and reconfigured, giving impetus to the need to continually realign structures and authority, redefine goals and strategies, and redesign systems and processes. These dynamics give rise to a new paradigm in which an organization does not stop at its boundaries and, hence, having no boundaries, is part of a network.

Internal networks, whether formal or informal, enhance organizational learning and adaptation by moving information around the organization with greater speed and accuracy. Organizational members are often formed informally into cliques that facilitate the flow, dissemination, and interpretation of information that reaches units and individuals through the formal channels of communication. Within the informal network, status and power are personal rather than positional and are formed by members' perceptions of participants' personal credibility and location centrality within the flow of communication in the organization.

Formal or prescribed structures of communication and informal or emergent networks of communication coexist and both are indispensable for the success of organizations. In order to fully understand informal networks of relationships, there has to be an understanding of the formal structure of the organization. The emergent and prescribed networks are in constant interplay with one another. Informal networks can be understood as a response to formal structural arrangements within the organization. Formal structures limit the actions of organizational members, giving rise to emergent processes of communication to get the job done. A formal communication network is typically made up of interlinked individuals occupying different roles and extends beyond the authority networks within the organization. The network usually involves a relatively small number of managers who are drawn from across the organization's functions, strategic business units, geographic locations, and different hierarchical levels. Managers are selected for participation by virtue of their skills, personality, motivation, control of resources, and location within the flow of communication in the organization. Core networks operate through subnetworks, teleconferencing, e-mail, and other computerized information systems.

In many organizations, formal networks emerge as a top management initiative for three reasons. First, senior managers clearly and specifically define the business outputs they expect of the network and the time frame in which they expect the network to deliver. Specificity in goal setting and tight scheduling force network members to show real results and make changes that are linked directly to the improved work and financial performance of the organization. Second, senior managers can guarantee the visibility and free flow of information to all members of the network and promote communication among them. At Cornell Glass, for example, all forty-six members of the managerial network are connected through a management information system called

Commander. They receive daily reports on critical business indicators and share information and expert judgment across boundaries using e-mail. This way, people are always informed about and focused on the company's performance. Managers can communicate freely across organizational units, offer their unique perspectives on problems and developments, and receive immediate feedback. Third, senior managers develop new criteria and processes for performance evaluation and promotion that emphasize horizontal collaboration through networks. The focus is on getting answers to questions such as: "Does a manager share information willingly and openly? Does the manager ask for and offer help? Is he or she emotionally committed to the business? Does the manager exercise informal leadership to energize the work of subnetworks?" (Charan, 1991, pp. 112–14).

The informal network is a much more flexible and effective mechanism of coordination than is the vertical hierarchy for performing tasks and responding to the social needs of employees. Organization members optimize their self-interests through the initiation of informal networks (Ibarra, 1992). Informal channels of communication allow for direct contacts among individuals who would not normally interact. The informal network helps reduce the uncertainty and anxiety associated with new tasks or the introduction of change. Informal networks also help to include members of formal networks (e.g., ad-hoc committees, task forces) in communication in which they would not otherwise be included.

Networks are quite different from cross-functional teams or task forces. Networks function as horizontal linkage mechanisms within the organization, but are often charged with problem solving, policy recommendation, or with proposing change. Charan (1991) observed the workings of one particular internal network at the Royal Bank of Canada, which had undergone management reforms intended to accelerate its retail strategy. The reforms, which grew out of an intensive effort by a network of twelve field officers, were adopted by senior management and implemented with the help of the network. An offshoot of this success story includes a plan by top management to affiliate all area managers with networks that share the most successful practices and learn from each other's experiences. Networks generate loyalty from their members due to the long-term nature of the networks. Frequent meetings and dialogues build friendship among the members and create a shared understanding of strategic issues facing the organization. Unlike most task forces, networks are dynamic and take initiatives. They become the vehicle for redirecting the flow of information, decisions, and the use of power to attain specific goals. They also put demands on top managers through requests for resources.

HORIZONTAL STRUCTURES, LEARNING, AND COMMUNICATION PROCESSES

The creation of horizontal organizational forms enhances the capacity of organizations to respond more swiftly and effectively to changes in the external environment and manage internal interdependencies more effectively. Horizontal organizations also enhance communication-based learning, which in turn supports the capabilities of the organization to maintain decentralized decision making, greater capacity for tolerance of ambiguity, permeable boundaries, and active networking and connections between subunits. Learning capabilities which yield fast adaptation represent internal organizational capabilities that create a sustainable competitive advantage for horizontal organizations. According to West and Meyer (1997, p. 27), "organizational learning capabilities are embedded in organizational communication processes designed to create knowledge and deploy intellectual resources." Horizontal organizations leverage these communication processes through the creation of lateral relations that increase the capacity of the organization to process information. Cross-functional teams and self-directed work units enhance organizational responsiveness to customer needs and link the organization internally. The organization operates as a value chain with reciprocal relationships and built-in coordination mechanisms that facilitate the dissemination of information and transference of knowledge.

Organizations are made up of interlocking networks of relationships with members communicating vertically, laterally, and diagonally within a complex web of relationships that make sense and provide meaning to their work and goals. Managers who communicate regularly with others within and outside the organization recognize the importance of communication as a means to establish trust and enhance confidence. Networks of communication are systematic means of disseminating or retrieving information for effective functioning. Without formal communication networks, managers would find it difficult to coordinate activities and achieve organizational goals. Networks help managers avoid chaos and prevent actions from being random. Networks often evolve as an outcome of a social need or task interdependence or as an initiation of individuals participating in a meeting. Cushman and King (1994) pointed out that traditional competitive strategies such as cost leadership or product differentiation are supported by organizational communication processes that center on manufacturing and R&D. However, when a quick response to market changes is pursued by horizontal organizations, then organizational communication becomes the primary organizational focus. This view sharply contrasts earlier assumptions of classical management theorists (e.g., Thompson, 1967; Lawrence & Lorsch, 1967) that predicted the creation of differentiated work units and specialized boundary roles and gatekeepers as an organizational strategic response to shield its core technology from disruptions and fluctuations coming from outside. Instead, horizontal organizations are expected to increase interdependencies and external networking and make their boundary-spanning activities more sensitive to the environment by becoming both resilient and permeable.

Horizontal organizations increase their learning by obtaining information externally through formal scanning processes and boundary spanning activities, as well as through the dissemination of information through nondirectional communication relationships between organizational members. The conversion of environmental data into meaningful information enhances organizational knowledge, and more conclusively, guides decision making through the organization's idiosyncratic communication processes (West & Meyer, 1997). The new knowledge becomes part of an organization's distinctive competence, which competitors can only partially clone. As West and Meyer (1997, p. 35) pointed out: "The unique direction, focus, and transformation of information within a firm's boundaries as a result of its communication processes lead to the creation of unique knowledge which cannot easily be imitated or developed by other firms." A rival might acquire some of the technologies and production skills that comprise the core competence of the organization but, ultimately, will find it difficult or too costly to duplicate the intricate learning and complex coordination required to produce the product.

Organizational capabilities that are embedded in routines and decision-making structures determine the kind of information acquired and how it will be accessed by organizational members. Routines, rules, procedural specifications, and regularized behaviors act as unobtrusive or normative controls that guide members' communication relationships and practices. Routines and established communication patterns constrain the interpretation, storage, acquisition, and revision of new knowledge (Huber, 1991). In a double-loop format in which routines affect capabilities to develop updated knowledge, learning to enhance capabilities also depends on routines (Cohen & Levinthal, 1990). The development of new knowledge becomes the basis for double-loop learning or understanding of causal relationships. When third-order learning (i.e., learning how to learn) occurs, learning becomes an important strategic capability that creates competitive advantages for the organization. Operating under the working assumptions of reengineering, third-order learning questions the predicament of a particular operating strategy and its utility for the organization. The Work-Out program initiated by GE and described below is one example of an organization pursuing third-order learning.

Once the structural change toward horizontal organization is accompanied by a cognitive change aimed at unlearning defensive practices and routines, horizontal organizations become natural incubations for developing and utilizing meta-learning capabilities. "Exhibiting many points of contact with the competitive environment, these organizations are perfectly positioned to generate contradictory forms of knowledge, to create a dialectic within management about the preferred operating logic through effective transfer of competing perspectives throughout the organization, and to implement changes resulting from revolutionary thinking back through the organization" (West & Meyer, 1997, p. 42).

IMPROVING LEARNING: LINKING PROGRAMS

To achieve an effective organization/environment alignment, learning and cultural transformation must evolve and be enacted in a proactive, adaptive mode by the management of small as well as large organizations. As Jack Welch has often put it: "Change before you have to." This is the essence of Senge's (1990) advice to managers to develop anticipation skills and make rational choices based on such anticipation. Small companies that lack resources (e.g., capital) often create greater interdependencies outside their boundaries through linking programs such as strategic alliances and joint ventures. Partnership and strategic alliances benefit small companies that lack the necessary scale. Caterpillar has relied on Morton Metalcraft for the supply of construction equipment. Gradually, Caterpillar has entrusted more responsibility for product design to Morton, which could do the design better and more economically. Merck and Co. has increasingly relied on partnerships with small companies for product innovation to enhance their own research and development efforts. Large companies, unable to achieve the same rate of learning, entrepreneurship, and adaptation as small companies can, benefit from such partnerships as well. Partnership is a competitive strategy helping companies leverage their technological and informational advantages. Manpower International, the $3 billion plus temporary employment service, established a partnership in 1993 with a $50 million minority-owned company. This move allowed Manpower to better tap the U.S. minority labor pool and to respond to calls for diversity in manpower supply.

As discussed in chapter 4, companies increasingly use information technology (IT) to form partnerships with each other or with larger companies. In addition, computer controls on machine tools and electronic exchange of data help small organizations produce high-quality products and services equal to or better than those of larger companies. Larger, resource-rich companies, constrained by their ability to spin back the wheels of entrepreneurship and innovation, forge partnerships with small companies. Drug companies such as Eli Lilly, Merck, and SmithKline have synergistic relationships with pharmaceutical startups to gain access to their path-breaking technologies. Manufacturers like Motorola and DuPont regularly cut costs by tapping their product design and manufacturing expertise into that of small companies.

BENCHMARKING

Benchmarking is a process by which managers target key improvement areas within their organizations, identify and study best practices by others in these areas, and implement new processes and systems to enhance productivity and quality (Kendrick, 1992). Organizations use benchmarking to:

- Avoid reinventing a common or known solution to a problem (i.e., how to remedy process deficiency)
- Achieve performance breakthrough
- Accelerate the pace of change in support of continuous quality improvement
- Move forward or redirect reengineering efforts
- Become competitive in the marketplace using the same or better technologies than those of competitors
- Provide managers with measures to assess organizational performance and outcomes
- Motivate employees to become cohesive and support the mission of the organization vis-à-vis aggressive competitors

Benchmarking requires companies to focus on what customers value, to determine the key factors contributing to success, and to identify the resources needed for top performance. Benchmarking is an important diagnostic and planning device that enhances the learning capabilities of the organization. Chung (1993) suggested the following steps for effective benchmarking:

- Identify the key success variables
- Identify top performing organizations
- Measure performance of best-in-class versus the performance of your own organization
- Identify performance gaps
- Establish performance targets
- Specify programs to achieve performance targets
- Implement the programs

Strategically, benchmarking is intended to create long-term value for shareholders as measured by return on assets (ROA) and value added per employee (VAE). Process benchmarking looks at important processes within the organization (e.g., product development, customer service), identifies a world-class organization that excels in that same business process, and develops a plan to adopt the process. Customer benchmarking is often used to (1) survey which product attributes customers consider in making purchasing decisions and then (2) adopt these attributes as key quality indicators. In general, however, benchmarking methods can be classified as internal, competitive, industrial, and generic.

Internal benchmarking is often used diagnostically prior to external benchmarking. Fleet Financial Group, mentioned earlier, is an example of a company pursuing internal benchmarking. Although information is readily available, internal benchmarking suffers from limited applicability. For example, basic processes such as R&D are not relevant benchmarking targets for billing units. Internal benchmarking, however, can help a company take a hard look at the way work processes are conducted by asking What are we doing (key steps)? Why are we doing it (purpose)? Who is doing it (individuals and groups)? and Why are those people involved (their value added)? Competitive benchmarking, on the other hand, is a study of internal functions and processes of competitors. The crucial element in competitive benchmarking is understanding the organizational structure of the competitor, particularly when certain functions and processes of the organization are located outside its value chain or are outsourced. The third type of benchmarking, industrial benchmarking, is noncompetitive in the sense that both partners in the process imitate each other by adopting the best practices used within the industry.

Finally, generic benchmarking allows an organization to look outward to world-class organizations and imitate their best practices regardless of their type and domain of operation. The idea is to look at management, control, and information systems, as well as vital processes, and adopt them partially or fully. Many companies, especially in the chemical industry like BASF are finding value in generic benchmarking. Benchmarking within the industry can only improve company performance to the level of its competitors. By the time the benchmarking company implements new practices, its competitors will have developed new ones. Generic benchmarking, on the other hand, allows companies to go outside the industry to achieve maximum benefits. Whatever type of benchmarking a company uses, however, a key success factor involves implementing the benchmarking strategy.

PROBLEM-SOLVING COMMUNICATION

Most quality tools are simple diagnostic or problem-solving techniques that allow a quality-improvement team to look at a process in a remedial or interventionist fashion. The idea is to identify problem areas and solve them before serious damage or unnecessary costs are incurred. Since most problems are expected to occur along the "white spaces" or the points in the process with the greatest potential for energy leaks, it is also important that the quality team takes an overall look at the process rather than a segmentalist view. This way, the team can be assured that the causes of the problem will not be overlooked or restricted by the narrow focus of a particular discipline or function. These tools include flow charts, fishbone diagrams, Pareto charts, interrelationship digraphs, and storyboards.

THE FLOW CHART

In many organizational processes, internal units linked in a customer/supplier chain must have a good understanding of what the other units are doing. From an organizational standpoint, goals and objectives can be met with greater success if work activities and tasks that cut across units and/or functions are also coordinated effectively. A flow chart can help clarify the interunit relationship and establish the communication and common understanding required for performing an interdependent task. A process flow chart, on the other hand, shows the activities (steps, tasks, operations, and decisions) and the sequences in which they take place. A well-constructed flow diagram can help individuals and teams avoid unnecessary or wasteful steps such as rework. Preventing rework loops can reduce both costs and time cycle for performing a task. The purpose of the flow chart is to highlight the inefficiencies by identifying excessive or unessential movements of resources (e.g., people, material). A common flow chart contains circles denoting the beginning and ending steps, boxes denoting steps and activities (or functions) within the process, diamonds denoting points where decisions are required, and arrows indicating the direction of flow from one activity to the next in sequence.

Usually a macro flow chart is sufficient to achieve a common understanding of problem areas. If the quality team, however, needs a greater focus, it should construct a detailed flow chart. Detailed flow charts are used to describe process activities at the task level. Tasks are described in boxes, while decisions (yes/no type) are depicted by diamond-shaped symbols. Arrows indicate the sequence of events. The two most important rules to follow in mapping out a process are to break down activities if they are too complex and to combine activities if the flow chart becomes too detailed. The following is a step-by-step procedure for constructing a flow chart:

- *Define the boundaries of the process*: Get a clear idea of the end result. This will help to define the whole project. It is often useful to work backward from the end point, as well as forward from the starting point, to generate a flow chart. This can be done by answering the following questions:

  Who supplies the input?
  Who receives the input?
  What is the first thing that is performed with the input? Subsequently, this should be followed by listing the process output activities: Who receives the output? Who provides the output?

- *Identify the major actors or objects involved in carrying out the tasks*: Which individuals, organizational units, or other entities are involved? What documents, reference materials, or resources are used to do the work?
- *List the activities and decisions necessary to complete the project in chronological order*: Break down the project into discrete activities or tasks. These should be listed in rough chronological order. Note where decisions have to be made to direct the flow of activities down one branch or another depending on the status of the work at the decision point.

- *Diagram the activities necessary to complete the project in order of precedence*: Activities should be diagrammed in order of precedence to show when one activity requires that another activity be completed first. For example, binding a report cannot begin until all pages of the report have been printed.
- *Reiterate to ensure that all activities are listed and are in the proper order*: The first time around it is not so easy to tease out all the activities and get them in the right order. Some activities might be laid out in great detail while others are glossed over. Look for circular flows or feedback loops that might have been overlooked. Make sure that critical steps, on which other activities depend, are included.

Flow charts help employees better understand the importance of individual parts of the process and how each part fits into the whole. The chart provides employees with a sense of the interdependence of the process parts, allowing visualization of the process requirements, measurements, and control. Ideally, two flow charts should be constructed—one describing the actual process, the other portraying how the process should flow. By comparing the two charts and analyzing the gap between the two processes, a powerful roadmap emerges to guide the effort for self-improvement and streamline the process to achieve the best results.

FISHBONE DIAGRAM, PARETO ANALYSIS, HISTOGRAM, INTERRELATIONSHIP DIGRAPH

The fishbone diagram (often called a cause/effect diagram) is used to breakdown a complex issue into components and subcomponents to further understand, analyze, and improve it. When properly drawn, it clearly illustrates the various causes effecting a process by sorting out and relating the causes. It should be noted that for every effect, there are probably several causes. The effect or problem is stated on the right side of the chart and the major influences or causes are listed on the left side of the chart. Most cause/effect diagrams include the generic elements of a system (i.e., the five Ms—material, manpower, machine, method, measurement). Teams, however, may customize these categories to fit their processes. In customizing the fishbone, the team may consider looking for a common thread in each category that captures the central idea and ties all of the subcomponents of the cause together. When examining each cause, it is important to look for things that have changed, deviations from the norms, and patterns. Reduction of the number of subcomponents or consolidation into larger categories is possible through techniques such as multivoting, Pareto analysis, and interrelationship digraph.

If the number of subcategories is too large to handle, the team can rank order the items and vote to eliminate up to one-half of the list. Next, the team can use a Pareto charting to display the results to identify the vital few causes and separate them from the trivial many. Pareto analysis reveals which of the components account for a proportionally larger impact on the broader problem. The basis for Pareto analysis is the 80/20 rule. That is, about 80 percent of the problems result from 20 percent of the causes. Pareto analysis aids in determining a starting point for problem analysis and it highlights the results of improving projects when multiple diagrams are compared in a before/after context. Often, a simple bar graph called a histogram is used to display the distribution of the data or shows the variation in the system. Frequencies are always presented on the vertical axis while categories are always presented on the horizontal axis. Histograms are useful for showing the shape of the distribution and the pattern of variation in a process-output measurement. They are also helpful for summarizing and communicating data and variables with relative ease.

If team members agree on the importance of the item that receives the highest score, the team can end the discussion at this point and concentrate on identifying possible treatments to reduce the effects of the problem and eventually eliminate it. If disagreements exist, the team can proceed with interrelationship digraph following these steps:

- Write down all of the subcategories (subcomponents of the causes) on index cards with each subcategory on a separate card.
- Lay out the subcategories randomly on the work surface.
- Choose one card from the total and place it in the center of the sheet. Then answer the following question: Does any other card either cause or result from this chosen card?
- Draw arrows that connect the different cards in terms of influence and direction. When asking the question, Which other cards are caused or influenced by this card? avoid two-way arrows by making a decision as to which item is the major influence and build bridges. When one arrow crosses another, it becomes easier to read the interrelationship digraph.
- Identify the cards with the most outgoing/incoming arrows, the next highest number, and so on (rank them in descending order).

- Outgoing arrows dominant: indicates a basic cause that, if solved, will have a slipover effect on a large number of items.
- Incoming arrows dominant: this may represent a secondary issue or bottleneck that may actually be as important to address as the original item.
- Confirm by consensus which items with the greatest number of arrows are really the key factors to be tackled. Decide whether there are any other items that do not pass the "arrow test" but should be included.
- Single out the ideas/causes selected in a double-outlined box.

There are several benefits to the cause-and-effect diagram. First, it helps sort and segregate possible causes of a problem into logical categories. It also identifies areas for data-gathering activity. Third, it educates participants in problem-solving processes through their involvement in structured brainstorming and interpretation tasks. The cause-and-effect diagram also serves as a guide for discussions and helps to keep meetings on target. Finally, it can be developed into a complete project management tool that displays actions taken and results achieved.

THE STORYBOARD

The storyboard summarizes the continuous quality improvement process in a few well-chosen words and graphics, such as those listed above (e.g., flow charts and histograms). The team prepares a storyboard which is then displayed publicly for guidelines and directions and also for comments and revisions. The steps in constructing a storyboard are simple:

- Define the boundaries of the problem, issue, or opportunity for improvement.
- Identify the process improvement team leader and the members that most likely have an interest in solving the common problem.
- Map out the process by targeting or singling out areas with the highest potential for improvement.
- Determine the tools to be used.
- Systematically display your analysis and findings by identifying the problems encountered in one column, the actions taken or interventions in a second column, and the current status of the problem in a third column.

- Holding the gains stage—address the point of whether improvement has occurred over time by evaluating the effectiveness of the intervention through measuring the outcomes. Use diagrams to display the results and identify what future considerations could evolvĕ from this process or whether other opportunities for improvement can be identified.

DEMING'S FOURTEEN PRINCIPLES AND THE LEARNING CYCLE

Deming, the most prominent theorist and proponent of TQM, proposed fourteen prerequisites for successful implementation of a TQM strategy (Deming, 1982; Walton, 1986):

- Create constancy of purpose for the improvement of product and service in order to stay in business and be competitive.
- A new economic age demands a new philosophy. Quality must become a way of life because customers do not stand for the past level of mistakes and defects.
- Quality must be built into the process and product as quality cannot be achieved through mass inspection and control.
- Minimize total costs and end the practice of awarding business on the basis of price tag. Strive for good relations with single suppliers based on trust and loyalty.
- Strive for constant improvement of quality and productivity.
- Institute ongoing training on the job that enhances process improvements.
- Institute leadership that facilitates workers and managers to do a better job by understanding tasks, placing employees in the right position, and identifying and eliminating barriers that hinder performance.
- Empower the workforce: allow the expression of new ideas and concerns, and drive out fear so that everyone can work effectively.
- Break down barriers between functional departments and use cross-functional teams to ensure proper coordination and open communication.
- Eliminate slogans and targets (that only promote frustration and resentment).
- Eliminate standards and management by objectives that do not assist employees in improving the work process.

- Remove barriers that rob people of pride in their workmanship.
- Institute a vigorous program of education, training, and re-training.
- Take actions to accomplish the transformation.

According to Deming, once implemented, these fourteen principles establish the climate and conditions for successful improvement of business processes. Only when these principles are fully implemented and become an integral part of organizational core values and ideology should the improvement be pursued. Deming offers the Shewhart cycle as the proper model for "learning and improvement." This simple four-step model simply directs the organization to: Plan, Do, Check (or Study), and Act. It is consistent with the process improvement definition discussed above. The Shewhart Cycle for learning and improvement has multiple applications: it can be used as a problem-solving technique, planning and control, or checkpoints to monitor progress toward predetermined goals. The cycle starts with "Plan"—a proposition of a change or a test aimed at improvement; "Do"—carrying out the change, experimenting with or validating the test on a pilot; "Study"—taking a hard look at the findings to determine potential and actual performance gaps, What have we learned? What went wrong?; "Act"—adopting the change or best practice, abandoning it or running through the cycle all over again.

This simple model was expanded on by Redding and Catalanello (1994) who strongly believed that successful change is dependent upon three variables of learning: speed, depth, and breadth. The speed at which the organization can work through the "cycle" is crucial to an organization undergoing the change process. Each cycle represents an innovation that, at the very least, will result in an increase in the organization's competitive position in its environment simply by virtue of increasing its knowledge. The greater the speed of the cycle, the greater the opportunities for more cycles. This represents the higher organizational flexibility necessary in complex organizational environments. The second variable, depth, represents how deep the level of questioning is that the organization undertakes throughout the "cycle." Speed alone does not guarantee that learning is taking place. However, there are three levels of depth noted by Redding and Catalanello (1994):

- *Symptomatic learning*: This is surface-level questioning that tries to resolve the obvious symptoms through simple solutions and is limited to fine-tuning or quick fixes.

- *Systemic learning*: This is a deeper level of analysis that attempts to develop systemic solutions for the root causes. This usually results in a change in fundamental norms and management practices.
- *Learning to learn*: This level serves to evaluate the organization's ability to learn and attempts to improve that ability. This level provides the greatest possibility for the deepest form of organizational learning.

The third variable, breadth, represents the degree to which learning is integrated throughout the organization. The breadth of learning tends to increase, as does the depth of learning, as the number of learning cycles increases. Complex organizations (with high structural differentiation) disseminate knowledge that comes from learning through experimentation and collaboration. When new knowledge gained in one part of the organization is transferred to another part, learning becomes a strategic advantage for the organization. That is, when insights generated from the cycles are applied to or integrated into other parts of the organization, learning is broadened and benefits the whole organization.

Other researchers have tried to measure the success of companies' quality interventions along the three interrelated dimensions. Hall, Rosenthal, and Wade (1993), for example, studied twenty companies along the depth and breadth dimensions. They found that companies engaging in a surface "unidimensional" depth change faced a 19 percent cost reduction in process costs, while the "multidimensional" depth changes yielded a 35 percent reduction in process costs. In examining breadth, they discovered that narrow-process improvements served to produce less than 1 percent reduction in business-unit costs, while the broad-based process improvements yielded an average of 17 percent reduction in business-unit costs. This data is consistent with Redding and Catalanello's (1994) study; however, it failed to acknowledge speed as an important factor influencing the cycle's breadth and depth.

RADAR FEEDBACK TO ENHANCE LEARNING

Learning can be enhanced by making peer evaluation and critiquing both implicit and explicit dimensions of the learning process. Called radar feedback or full-circle feedback, it is a reliable and consistent source of job-related information that is also easy to implement and rooted in self-improvement goals. Bracken (1994, p. 49) listed the benefits derived from using full-circle feedback. Referred to as multirater systems, these systems:

1. Complement other popular organizational initiatives, such as empowerment, employee participation, downsizing, and teamwork.
2. Respond to the need for a richer source of information in situations involving a wider span of management.
3. Create incentives for implementing organizational change through greater commitment and accountability.
4. Give managers the opportunity to operationalize a vision for success, through descriptions of behaviors that support organizational values.
5. Provide a variety of perspectives since people generally assume that these viewpoints add up to an accurate and reliable assessment of an employee's performance.

Many U.S. companies increasingly follow GE's lead in the utilization of 360-degree assessment instruments to develop leadership competencies. Some of these companies are Sprint, Xerox, AT&T, Chase Manhattan Bank, Shell Oil, and Allied-Signal. At GE, the 360-degree leadership assessment has been designed as a flexible development tool to respond to the diverse needs of managers working in unique work environments. The assessment normally contains feedback on performance and work behavior given by the manager, peers, and subordinates, along with a self-rating. The assessment involves the following criteria and measurements:

- *Vision*: Has developed and communicated a clear, simple, customer-focused vision for the organization; forward thinking, challenges imagination; inspires and energizes others to commit to vision; captures minds, leads by example.
- *Customer/quality focus*: Listens and responds to customer needs and satisfaction, including internal customers; inspires and demonstrates a passion for excellence in every aspect of work.
- *Integrity*: Maintains unequivocal commitment to honesty/truth in every facet of behavior; assumes responsibility for his/her own mistakes; practices absolute conformance with company policies; actions and behaviors are consistent with words.
- *Accountability/commitment*: Sets and meets aggressive commitments to achieve business objectives; demonstrates self-confi-

dence to stand up for ideas; fair and compassionate yet willing to make difficult decisions.

- *Communication/influence*: Communicates in an open, candid, clear, complete, and consistent manner; listens effectively and probes for new ideas; breaks down barriers and develops influential relationships across teams, functions, and layers; uses facts and rational arguments to influence and persuade.

- *Shared ownership/boundarylessness*: Has self-confidence to share information across traditional boundaries and be open to new ideas; encourages/promotes shared ownership for team vision and goals; trusts others, encourages risk taking and boundaryless behavior.

- *Team-building empowerment*: Selects talented people, provides coaching and feedback to develop team members to fullest potential; delegates whole tasks, empowers team to maximize effectiveness; is a team player; recognizes and rewards achievement; fully utilizes diversity of team members to achieve business success.

- *Knowledge/expertise/intellect*: Possesses and readily shares functional/technical knowledge and expertise; constant interest in learning; demonstrates broad business knowledge/perspective with cross-functional/multicultural awareness; makes good decisions with limited data, applies intellect to the fullest; quickly sorts relevant from irrelevant information, grasps essentials of complex issues and initiates actions.

- *Initiative/speed*: Creates real and positive change, sees change as an opportunity; anticipates problems and initiates new and better ways of doing things; eliminates bureaucracy and strives for simplicity and clarity; understands and uses speed as a competitive advantage.

- *Global mindset*: Demonstrates global awareness and sensitivity in building global teams; values and promotes full utilization of global and workforce diversity; considers the global consequences of every decision; treats everyone with dignity, trust, and respect.

LEARNING TO DEAL WITH PARADOXES

Paradoxes are conflicting choices or conditions that demand equal attention. For example, managers want their organizations to be flexible and adaptive, yet integrated and stable. They want higher internal efficiency and profitability and also higher employee commitment and morale. The art of managing and leading organizations today lies in embracing incompatible forces, rather than choosing between them. Organizational leaders must learn to deal with paradoxes through a new mindset—one that combines and optimizes rather than splits apart and differentiates. The problem is that despite the prevalence of paradox in organizational life, the part of our mind that seeks certainty and precision rebels against the very notion of contradiction. In addition, corporate cultures traditionally value such abilities as "hard choices," "setting priorities," and "biting the bullet," behaviors that eliminate certain alternatives in favor of others (Stroh & Miller, 1994, p. 30).

There is a tendency to think in a dichotomous way, develop discriminatory attitudes and behaviors, and maintain a linear, either-or orientation. Meeting the challenge of managing paradoxes requires a dialectical approach that synthesizes and balances between opposite forces. Effective managers often consciously create opposition and subsequent opportunities for new alternatives: from thesis and antithesis, a more powerful synthesis could emerge. This is where a learning organization can reap the benefits of inquisitive managers who challenge existing myths and truths and who are both factual and idealistic—that is, asking questions about what is known and asking questions about what should be done, respectively. These managers are not driven by the need to preserve the status quo or their personal legacy, but by the opportunities created via a multidimensional, simultaneous orientation that encompasses the whole rather than the part. Effective managers face the challenge of a paradox rather than avoid it, and they know how to harness the synergistic tension contained in seemingly incompatible options to optimize problem solving.

Stroh & Miller (1994) outlined four ways of facing paradoxes:

- *Both-and thinking*: Managers must continuously brainstorm the question, How can two incompatible values be true? For example, increasing quality in the long run requires a short-term investment, therefore, improving quality costs money while it saves money.
- *Best of both thinking*: Managers must strive to create conditions that allow simultaneously for the emergence of contradictions through creative tension. Examples are loosely coupled structures, controlled entrepreneurship, and conservative innovators. The idea is to make personal values explicit by inquiring into both the positive and negative qualities of two seemingly

contradictory paradigms and develop a synergistic solution or
a synthesis.

- *Expanding the construct space and time of a paradox*: When profits
  are down, managers tighten controls, and when sales are up and
  profits are soaring, managers increase responsiveness to customers. Thus, current market conditions require that managers
  simultaneously use belt-tightening and creative responses. Similarly, expanding the time frame should help managers optimize
  the management of paradoxes by concentrating on aligning
  short-term with long-term goals. Spatial and temporal constraints often lead to creative solutions (synthesis) using a systems approach. Stroh and Miller (1994) provide an example in
  which a company has a strategic dilemma involving redeployment of the manufacturing or marketing function. While manufacturing claims that only through development of high quality
  products can market share be increased, it can also provide competitors with an incentive to increase the quality of their products. Thus, it can potentially lead to lower industry margins and
  an increase in the company's overall profitability. Marketing has
  polarized its position by claiming that it is through customization the company can maintain its leadership and, therefore, its
  dominance in the market. These seemingly paradoxical claims
  can be reconciled to reflect adjustments in manufacturing
  processes and quality standards in the short run while increasing the company's competitiveness and overall profitability in
  the long run.
- *Neither/nor thinking; or, choosing a third option*: Paradoxically,
  this way of thinking replaces "both-and" by focusing on the
  outcome instead of the choice. Should management base its
  product development decisions on existing organizational technologies or on customer needs? Sometimes companies understand what will best serve customers before the customers
  know it themselves. In these cases, technology pushes the company. At other times, companies recognize that the customers
  know what they need most clearly. It is during these times that
  they let the customers lead the way. The road taken is the one
  that leads to making the world a better place. The paradoxical
  forces of "technology push" and "market pull" both help drive
  the company along the road (Stroh & Miller, 1994, p. 37).

Successful managers, who recognize the tradeoffs between opposite requirements and who are prepared to manage paradoxes, need

supporting structural arrangements that can help them confront and synthesize these paradoxes. One such arrangement is the matrix structure, which simultaneously optimizes the need of the organization for functional expertise and the requirement to maintain a market focus through flexibility and innovation. Other examples are the information technology and the network organizations discussed earlier. These organizations are fluid, team-based systems that continually redefine themselves within their contexts to capture emerging opportunities. Most successful transforming companies use multiple strategies to respond simultaneously to function, business, and geographical challenges. They use a global approach that takes advantage of centralized resources and standardization to achieve economies of scale. This is a multinational strategy that decentralizes resources to adapt uniquely to local needs through specialization and customization. It is also an international approach that centers on taking advantage of the parent company's organizational capabilities through worldwide diffusion and adaptation.

THE COMPETING VALUES FRAMEWORK AS A TRAINING INTERVENTION

Sendelbach (1993) described a variety of management training and development activities based on the Competing Values Framework used by Ford Motor Company. First, the framework has been used to map out an aggregate profile of Ford's culture at significant points in time. For example, in the early days of Ford Motor Company, there was much focus on the rational goal quadrant with its emphasis on maximizing operating efficiency and outputs through mass production. The open systems quadrant was equally important due to the need to innovate and increase market share. Since the financial controls and measures were less important, the documentation and MIS were minimal. Likewise, the premium placed on the values of the human relations quadrant was relatively low. Ford was geared in its early stage of development toward production, and management primarily used scientific principles and economic incentives to increase productivity. Later, and especially during the 1950s, the company's profile shifted to reflect a predominant emphasis on control, monitoring, information systems, and measurement associated with the internal processes quadrant. This analysis provided participants in the training program with an opportunity to explore leadership styles and decision-making processes within the historical context of evolution and change.

Since the 1970s Ford has experienced tremendous change and competition both domestically and internationally. The old bureaucratic structure with its emphasis on stability and control was no longer suited to deal with the volatility of the environment. The need was for a more responsive and involved workforce and greater innovation and creativity. The learning aspects of profiling the emergence of different cultures within the company, with different weights given to different values, involved developing a full understanding of organizational needs and the strategies required for improvement. An analysis of the overall profile, for example, concluded that while improvements in the internal processes quadrant may be possible, the necessary shift is a reduction in emphasis placed on elements within that quadrant and a relative increase in emphasis on the open systems quadrant. Thus, managers can use the model to map out their current needs and match them against the existing organizational capabilities to determine the direction of change.

Another area for applying the Competing Values Framework at Ford involved the impact of cross-functional relations on the overall operation of the company. The profile of the perceived functional stereotype completed by managers of that function provided them with opportunity to test their assumptions as to how others perceive them. Managers of functional units were also asked to use the framework to depict the gap between how they currently view themselves versus how they should be operating. Sendelbach (1993, pp. 86–87) summarized the significance of that learning: "Functional groups do not always have a good understanding as to how they are perceived by the organization. Their 'now' profile may be seen as too optimistic by other functions. They may be told that they have not made as much progress as they think they have. They may also hear that they do not have as good a conception of what the rest of the company needs from their function as they report in their 'should' profile."

Moving from the organizational and unit level, the third level of training and learning activities at Ford was applied to the managerial leadership level. The method permitted managers to conduct assessments of their own managerial profiles against the managerial practices and personal values embedded in the CVF. Participants were asked to respond to behavioral statements ranging on a scale of one to seven from totally uncharacteristic to totally characteristic in relation to how they perceive their actual behaviors and in relation to how they think they should behave. The underlying assumption of this intervention was that via the process of self-assessment, managers will be able to identify essential managerial skills and competencies required for effective job performance. Still, another objective was to help them discover values and attitudes, determine professional goals and needs, and guide themselves through a process of self-directed learning. Ultimately, the objective of this program was to help managers build confidence in their ability to learn a method for assessing management-related knowledge and abilities, diagnose their own strengths and weaknesses, and formulate plans for skills development.

As Sendelbach (1993) pointed out, the real key to this learning process was to have the participants examine the difference between the score they gave themselves in the "is now" section and their score in the "should be" section. Participants then calculated the "gap scores"— the difference between the now and be scores. Two types of gaps are common: One describes an increase from the current level of behavior, while in the other the desired behavior is seen as a reduction of the current behavior. The point is that the information coming from the self-assessment has been valuable in helping participants maintain an overall perspective or "optimal" balance, rather than focusing only on one single dimension to improve their managerial competence.

The assessment tool described above is typically used to diagnose the alignment between a person's skills level and his or her perceptions of the roles and responsibilities that are manifested in his or her managerial leadership behavior. At Ford, participants were also asked to compare the ratings of their self-assessment against the aggregate profile of the work unit to have a sense of the "degree of fit" or compatibility between the individual profile and the aggregate. Although useful in "measuring the gap" between the personal and work-unit profiles, this measurement is not without limitations. First, the ratings are based on perceptions that could be influenced by self-serving biases, therefore skewing the results. A radar assessment such as the one described above, as well as measurements conducted at multiple points in time, which also include concurrent ratings of "now" versus "then" as a postassessment, can respond quite effectively to this challenge. Second, any assessment should take into account work and job (specialization) characteristics. As Sendelbach (1993, p. 88) pointed out: "The results from a participant engaged in advanced scientific research should probably look different in profile than the results from a participant in manufacturing."

One can also expect to find differences in ratings between people with different work experiences as measured by the length of time spent in managing people. Naturally, a person who begins to work in a managerial capacity for the first time may have different values and a different level of intensity than a person who has been managing the same work unit for over two decades. Finally, people may have different understandings about the future direction of the organization and the work unit. Such understandings may lead to different perceptions about the current and future needs and goals of the organization, and consequently, to the adoption of different leadership styles and managerial practices. Nevertheless, according to Sendelbach (1993), the idea was to provide participants with important clues about how they see themselves as "measured" against the profile of the work unit as seen by the compiled assessment of everyone participating in the program. This also provided participants with a fuller scope of the evolution of their work unit and an understanding of emergent structural and social dynamics processes at different points in time.

By understanding the process of organization life cycles and the shifting criteria of organizational effectiveness (Quinn & Cameron, 1984) as well as the need for differing managerial profiles for different situations, participants were able to compare their assessment of what they believe their work-unit profile should be and make subsequent adjustments to their managerial styles and behaviors. Often managers may find that a misfit exists between what they think they should become and the needs of the work unit. This gap may trigger a chain of events aimed at modifying the work-unit needs or readjusting the existing managerial practices in order to reduce the gap. Creating the dual profiles of both a personal behavior set and the work unit that is the context for the behaviors provides a rich database from which to consider action planning (Sendelbach, 1993).

As mentioned above, a more "balanced" view of how one functions can be provided through the prism of how others perceive the competency and effectiveness of that person. At Ford, another wave of instruments was used to generate data feedback about the assessment of how others perceive the effectiveness of the managers involved in the training program. The value of this activity was in highlighting blind spots—areas of managerial leadership behaviors that seem less important or unnecessary by the focal person while others see them as important behaviors. The discovery of a blind spot can help inform managers about future personal training and professional development.

The CVF, much like existing communication techniques (e.g., role analysis technique, responsibility charting), when used properly can help inform users about discrepancies that exist between their perceptions and perceptions of others and take steps to remedy the problem. For example, others may inform the focal person that despite his or her self-perception of high competence in playing the mentor role, they do not see that intent manifested in actual behaviors. Having feedback data represented in the CVF helps the participant to understand the issue and how it relates to his or her overall managerial leadership process. By covering a range of organizational and managerial work facets, the CVF provides users with meta-learning experience and the ability to make important adjustments to their managerial behavior to match the causal map and values of the work unit.

MEASURING LEARNING

One of the laws of industrial economics calls for companies to leverage their experience by rapidly increasing production, cutting down costs, and lowering prices in a very predictable way. The end result is an expected increase in market share ahead of competition. Experience curves that help companies leverage learning and predict costs and prices are common in industries such as aerospace, defense, consumer electronics, and semiconductors. Experience curves, however, are limited to output measurement and generally ignore process variables such as quality, delivery, or new product development. Although they are quite effective in helping upstart companies or established companies with new product lines, experience curves are less effective in mature industries with a flat growth. Experience curves do not provide information about the learning that occurs nor do they say something about the levers of change. David Garvin (1993, p. 89) described the "half-life" curve as a response to these concerns. A half-life curve measures the time it takes to achieve a 50 percent improvement in a specified performance measure. When represented diagramatically, the performance measure (e.g., defect rates, on-time delivery) is plotted on the vertical axis using a logarithmic scale and the time scale (days, weeks, months, etc.) is plotted horizontally. Steeper slopes represent faster learning. Likewise, moderate slopes represent lower rates of improvement, and therefore signal the need to "shift gears" and apply learning at a faster rate.

The logic of using half-life learning is that constant measuring and monitoring is expected to yield short learning cycles that will be converted into superior performance. Half-life curves are feasible, convenient, flexible, and can be used in almost any industry. "Unlike learning and experience curves, they work on any output measure and they are not confined to costs or prices. In addition, they are easy to operationalize, they provide a simple measuring stick, and they allow for ready comparison among groups" (Garvin: 89). Nevertheless, half-life curves are geared toward results and are less likely to capture learning that requires heavy investments in knowledge acquisition and changes in human capital (e.g., a total quality transformation). Therefore, a much more comprehensive framework of measuring cognitive and behavioral learning, such as those discussed in chapter 9, are necessary to track progress and benefit from learning.

PURSUING META-LEARNING: GE's SUCCESS STORY

Since 1981, GE has undergone a radical transformation (Sherman, 1989). Jack Welch began this transformation by cutting GE's forty-three Strategic Business Units (SBUs) to fourteen by 1988, each with commanding shares of their markets. By 1989, ten of GE's SBUs were ranked first in their industry; two were ranked second, and two were in markets that were too fragmented to rank. During the twelve years from 1981 to 1993, Welch sold over two hundred of GE's SBUs worth $10 billion while acquiring and consolidating over three hundred businesses worth $20 billion into thirteen SBUs. Welch sold low-profit units such as small appliances, TVs, and houseware, and went into such high-profit areas as broadcasting, high-tech manufacturing, investment banking, insurance, and medical systems. He closed seventy-eight production facilities and invested $25 billion in automating GE's remaining 200 U.S. facilities and 130 facilities abroad in twenty-four countries, making them world-class manufacturing facilities. Welch shed 150,000 employees, delayered the chain of command from nine to five layers of management, decentralized power, widened the span of control, built a new executive team, revamped the corporate culture, restructured the operating division, and replaced all independent business leaders.

These radical changes over a relatively short period of time changed GE's strategies and structures dramatically. Looking back, in 1988, Welch recounted: "Now, how we went at this can be described from two totally different perspectives. One perspective would use words like downsizing, reducing, cutting. We think that view misses the point. We see our task as a totally different one aimed at liberating, facilitating, unleashing the human energy and initiative of our people" (GE, *Annual Report*, 1988). Eleven years later, in 1992, GE's sales rose from about $28 billion in 1981 to over $62 billion; profits rose from about $3 billion to almost $5 billion; and GE's stock appreciated 300 percent, with stockholder equity reaching about $74 billion. GE became the fifth largest industrial corporation in America, the third largest in profits, and the second largest in stockholder equity (*Fortune*, April 9, 1993: 185). The stage was set for mobilizing acceptance for, and institutionalizing the change.

In the speech quoted above, Welch planted the seeds for the new vision: "At the beginning of the decade, we saw two challenges ahead of us. One external and one internal. Externally, we faced a world economy that would be characterized by slower growth with stronger global competitors going after a smaller pie. In the context of that environment we had one clear-cut major competitor: Japan, Inc. . . . powerful . . . innovative . . . and moving aggressively into many of our markets." Realizing that GE would have to reinvent itself if it was to meet this global challenge and become a world-class competitive organization, Welch provided his vision of GE's renewal: "Internally, our challenge was even bigger. We had to find a way to combine the power, resources and reach of a big company with the hunger, the agility, the spirit and the fire of a small one." And so the journey toward the second revolution in GE's contemporary history had begun. The vision for the eighties was to change the system; the one for the nineties was to change people. The tool for this change was called Work-Out.

WORK-OUT

Initially, Work-Out started out with four main objectives (see figure 8.1):

1. Build trust
2. Empower employees
3. Eliminate unnecessary work
4. Create a new paradigm—a boundaryless organization (Tichy & Sherman, 1993)

Work-Out began in fall 1988 as a series of local gatherings patterned after New England town meetings. In groups ranging in size from thirty to one hundred, employees of a particular business would typically spend three days at an off-site conference to discuss all sorts of common practices with promises of no retribution and immediate feedback and action by management. The typical format for a Work-Out process is shown in figure 8.2. Work-Out sessions involve six phases:

1. *Group start up*

   - Mission, goals, and objectives
   - Operating principles (how individuals will work within the team, make decisions, resolve conflicts, give everyone an opportunity to express opinions, agree on solutions)

Figure 8.1. Work-Out

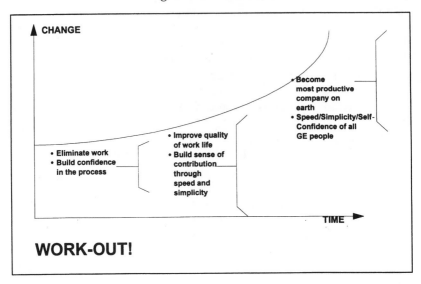

Source: An interview with Jack Welch, *Monogram*, 1990.

2. *Data collection (information dump)*

   • Perception sharing
   • Brainstorming (what's working and what's not)
   • Input from colleagues back home
   • "RAMMP analysis"—reduction or elimination of unneces-
     sary reports, approvals, meetings, measures and policies.

3. *Data sorting and analysis*

   • What is critical to fix?
   • Storyboarding to group or cluster data
   • Further clarification of data from team members
   • Visionary/outcome thinking (what the group would rather
     see instead)

4. *Problem selection and analysis*

   • Problem definition and analysis
   • Problem prioritization
   • Tools like fishbone diagrams and force-field analysis

Figure 8.2. The Work-Out Process

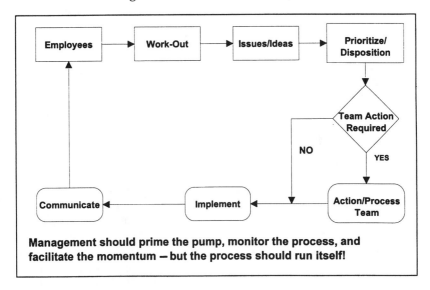

Management should prime the pump, monitor the process, and facilitate the momentum — but the process should run itself!

Source: GE publications.

5. *Solution selection*

- What will solve the problem
- How the group knows it will work
- Solution impact matrix
- Projected cost/impact analysis
- Contingency diagram

6. *Recommendation formulation*

- Action plan
- Potential obstacles
- Implementation

To ensure the free flow of ideas and candid sharing of concerns, managers were not allowed to participate in the meetings. Meetings were run by outside facilitators. Bosses would come in during the final day of the meetings to discuss proposals made by employees and make on-the-spot decisions. Those proposals needing further consideration had to be acted upon within a month. The process invariably exposed GE managers whose words were not consistent with their behaviors and it redefined the relationship between superiors and subordinates.

COMMUNICATE OBJECTIVE
PERFORMANCE STANDARDS

Still, Work-Out has not been a miracle cure and some bugs remain. Mark Potts, a writer with the *Washington Post*, reported that some GE employees, mindful of the more than 100,000 jobs eliminated by Welch in the 1980s, worry that the process would be used to have them unwittingly identify additional jobs that could be cut, something that Welch has adamantly denied. Employees in GE's various businesses know their fate: If the division does not meet the objective of being first or second in market share in its respective industry it is going to be sold! Apparently this is what Work-Out is really about: Supervisors of local work areas are more informed about the change than are front-line employees. Supervisors communicate the change directly to their employees, putting pressure on them to outperform their previously achieved targets. First-line supervisors, not remote managers, communicate performance directly in face-to-face communication. Then plans and programs are modified based on suggestions that come from the people who do the work.

There have also been problems getting some GE managers to go along with the Work-Out sessions. It often takes a change in management style and behavior to get a new value to be accepted and an executive to listen to, much less act quickly and effectively on the tough suggestions, particularly those that touch on management turf issues such as approval systems, meetings, and planning that come out of Work-Out sessions. On another issue, GE's management thinks that Work-Out helps labor relations by increasing dialogues between workers and management. "I am sold on it, and I am probably one of the bigger radicals," says the president of local 761 of the Electronic, Electrical Salaried Machine and Furniture Workers Union, which represents 11,000 workers at one of GE's largest plants, the appliance-making complex in Louisville. "It's empowering people . . . it brings people together. It gives people the feeling that they've got a part of the business . . . You can go into a room and feel you have as much power as the guy sitting beside you" (Tichy & Sherman, 1993).

THE BOUNDARYLESS ORGANIZATION AND
LEADERSHIP ROLES

> We would not knowingly hire anyone in our company that wasn't boundaryless, that wasn't open to an idea from anywhere, that wasn't excited about a learning environment.
>
> —Jack Welch, CEO, General Electric

Learning organizations must develop key competencies and mindsets that embrace change as a norm. Organizations that develop cultures which support change and risk taking, as well as experimentation across functional units and boundaries, increase their chances to evolve and adapt to environmental changes. Erasing organizational boundaries and creating a network of boundaryless organizations becomes a reality for many organizations through strategic alliances with competitors, partnerships with suppliers, and outsourcing to vendors and distributors. Within an organization, having no boundaries suggests the removal of barriers among levels and functions. It also presents management with a new challenge; maintaining creative tension among widely different but complementary skills and points of view. This challenge involves four important facets of intraorganizational boundary management:

1. Managers must pay more attention to facilitation, coaching, and leading. They must avert their attention from institutional relationships to interpersonal communications and resolution of conflicts. In a boundaryless organization, managerial authority is geared toward containment of the conflicts and anxieties that disrupt productive work. (Hirschorn and Gilmore, 1992)
2. Since work constellations involving people from diverse units defy boundaries and call for team interdependence, functional roles and responsibilities must be redefined and relationships realigned.
3. The political arena must be preserved to ensure that the various interests within the organization are advanced without undermining the effectiveness and coherence of the organization as a whole.
4. Blurred organizational boundaries create paradoxes that must be managed by encouraging unified diversity and by allowing team norms to thrive within organizational core values and culture.

This trend toward a boundaryless organization has become a tool of survival for many large-scale organizations trying to adapt quickly to merging world markets. Once they streamline their domestic operations, large corporations are now looking for efficiencies abroad. During the spring of 1994, IBM announced that it would reshuffle its worldwide sales, manufacturing, and engineering operations to be in a better position to take advantage of global markets, and also to break down internal barriers. Ford benchmarked Volkswagen and Toyota, as well as GE and Xerox, and in a decision to make more efficient use of its engineering and product development resources, merged its European and North American auto operations (Armstrong, 1994). The risks of becoming stateless are greater since standardization tends to take over customization. Local markets can contain misjudgments and errors. Global markets do not tolerate mistakes. Yet the opportunities for savings are great, since pooling resources and eliminating turf wars could save money. Some companies do both: McDonald's and Pepsico have globalized product development and customized through product differentiation. To be successful, however, external adaptation through globalization must also be aligned internally. Redrawing organizational charts must be followed by redrawing organizational culture. Equally important is the need to facilitate cooperation and communication across the borders. The challenge for the global CEO is to lead the process. As ABB's Barnevik says: "He (*sic*) has to be convinced, and he has to be convincing" (Armstrong, 1994, p. 25).

In the boundaryless organization employees and managers are supermen and superwomen who are versatile, multitalented, and cross-trained to perform diverse roles effectively. Being able to respond simultaneously to a range of different requirements also requires self-confidence and strong mental capacity. These individuals are critical of the success of the boundaryless organization. Free of preconceived notions of turf, hierarchical power, and functional expertise, these individuals are responsible for breakthrough innovations affecting the ability of top managers to reposition their organization strategically within its global market. Human resources, in this view, are the most important assets of the company, and so it follows that employees must be active participants in all facets of work. Information is not a tool for the accumulation of power, but rather a resource that must be shared to ensure continuous learning and breakthrough. "In the new culture, the role of the leader is to express a vision, get buy-in, and implement it. That calls for open, caring relations with every employee, and face-to-face communication. People who can't convincingly articulate a vision won't be successful. But those who can will become even more open—because success breeds self-confidence" (GE, *Annual Report*, 1989).

COMMUNICATING THE VISION

At the same time that Work-Out has been revolutionizing GE, Jack Welch has shared his vision of GE which includes the values of integrated diversity, boundarylessness, global leadership, and the "business engine" in which the business fits into the corporate whole. With Work-Out in place and the vision trickling down the lines, GE has been transformed into a powerful learning organization. During an annual meeting with stockholders, Welch described the new culture as one in which "the walls that separate us from each other on the inside, and from other key constituencies on the outside" were broken down (GE, *Annual Report*, 1989). The boundaryless company has no artificial boundaries between functions, levels, and locations. It reaches out to key suppliers and makes them part of a single value chain aimed at satisfying customers. Welch envisioned the replacement of command structures with cross-functional teams, the transformation of transactional managers into sensitive leaders, the transitioning of GE into a vertically loaded structure with few layers, and the sharing of knowledge and information across people and units.

The call for caring and supportive leadership must be met by organizations undergoing reengineering or restructuring, or for those becoming virtual organizations. Surviving managers and employees are looking ahead to renew the bond between themselves and the organization. Yet the nonmaterial rewards that come in large measure from collegiality and commonality of interest are diminishing (Patterson, 1994). As more and more companies outsource their noncore operations, and as they make dramatic personnel cuts, a widespread erosion of morale becomes evident. Patterson (1994, p. 86) reported that close to 25 percent of those employed are temporary, part-time, or contract employees. Outsourcing allows companies to avoid paying fringe benefits to contingent workers, saving about 40 percent in labor costs. A contingent workforce is also flexible: when business sags, the "temps" go first. Surviving employees and managers, in the meantime, are required to gain new skills to keep up with improved technology and processes. In a nonhierarchical structure, such as the boundaryless organization, they are expected to work smarter and make responsible decisions. Since the organization is much leaner, they are also expected to work harder to fill in for those who have left. Such pressures lead to alienation, lack of confidence, and mistrust in management. The inevitable outcomes are hypertension, high psychological stress, psychosomatic illnesses, and emotional distress. But this is exactly where leadership must move in with passion and empathy, coaching and counseling. In a work environment that is perceived as hostile, nonfriendly, and uncooperative, leaders must reestablish the bond between employees and the boundaryless organization. As Patterson (1994, p. 87) has warned:

> The danger I see is that the intangible but indispensable values I discovered at work will be lost: the sense of community, the shared goals, the spirited exchange of ideas, the pride of achievement. They are not, I admit, the concepts managers generally use to measure employee performance. But without them, I think, permanent gains, efficiency and quality will be difficult or impossible to achieve.

At GE, Jack Welch envisioned the replacement of command structures with sensitive leaders and the sharing of knowledge and information: "We cannot afford management styles that suppress and intimidate" (GE, 1990 *Annual Report*), Welch said, adding that the ultimate test for GE's success lies in mutual trust and respect that must be sustained. Yet, not everything worked well in realizing that vision. Functional walls and bureaucratic rules still prevailed, creating buffers between enthusiastic Welch followers and frustrated managers. When GE employees tried to test the ideas of a boundaryless organization, they very quickly found themselves up against a wall of bureaucrats and middle managers fighting off illusionists. *The Albany Times Union* (April 15, 1995) published the story of Robert Lemire, a "transformed" GE engineer in Schenectady, New York, who found that Welch's vision actually has boundaries (this story was published originally by William Carley a *Wall Street Journal* reporter). Lemire, a true believer and a follower of Welch, got so caught up in Welch's inspirational motivation and charisma, that he decided to take action. His first move was to suggest the establishment of a Department of Creativity and Innovation, reporting directly to Welch. The department would set up life-size photos of Welch at GE plants around the country, captioned "Tell it to Jack," and give employees an 800 number for calling in ideas. Workers would get a substantial slice of any savings or income generated by worthy proposals.

When his supervisors did not support him, Lemire worked his way up the chain of command until he reached the general manager of GE's power plant systems in Schenectady, Tamir Hamid, but was turned down by the lack of enthusiasm there too. Hamid, in a letter to Lemire, wrote that "during the past months this suggestion has been reviewed by no less than four managers at three different organization layers, as well as with [the] patent counsel, and each has come to the same conclusion . . . It does not warrant further discussion." Hamid then added that, given the feedback Lemire had received, he should re-examine the merits of his proposal and "move on to other challenges facing our business." But this is not the end of the story: Welch kept hammering out his values about a boundaryless organization. During the April 1994 Annual meeting, Welch again expounded on GE's "boundaryless" behavior. "It opens us up to ideas from anywhere," Welch told shareowners. "It ignores hierarchy and functional boundaries and cares only about the value of an idea, rather than the title of its source." Lemire, who came to this meeting, stood up and nominated himself for the board of directors, suggesting that Welch was like "the naked emperor" who needs an honest lieutenant to tell him when he is naked. The results were disappointing, but not for Lemire.

Lemire, who reportedly was also the recipient of innovation awards at GE, decided to take a different approach to find out whether the company walks the talk. One morning (at 1:00 A.M.) he sent out a survey on creativity over GE's e-mail system asking employees for their opinions about whether management is really interested in innovation. Lemire received mixed results from employees along with a big blow to his effort. His e-mail was cut off and two weeks later he was fired for abusing the e-mail system. Lemire was left quite bitter about his encounter with GE. "This was a test of whether GE really is open to new ideas . . . It seems the company is boundaryless on the way down but full of boundaries on the way up." GE officials see it differently. Hamid in his letter to Lemire wrote that he was "disappointed that [Lemire has] not recognized the progress made within the company in tearing down walls, eliminating bureaucracy and providing a setting that encourages employee participation." It should also be noted that GE's power division has a program in place that awards $4,000 after taxes to the "Innovator of the Year."

This story has an important message—communication from top executives does not trickle down the same way they envision it. Their mental map of where the company should be in the future is too soft and unrealistic for line workers. It is merely a dream, fantasy, or theory of the business—a construct space that is too vague and meaningless. To senior executives, this "vision" is important in gaining the agreement of diverse stakeholders and in widening the support base for the organization. Although the boundaryless idea is an extremely important concept for legitimizing the mission of and direction for the organization, it is still a symbolic metaphor that was conceived intellectually, but has been difficult to achieve. The boundaryless idea was strategically ambiguous in its goal to promote adaptation and change and to increase cohesion by highlighting pieces of Jack Welch's ideological puzzle of general ideas that help obscure disagreements over specific details. Lemire, although sincere and persistent with his idea to test the practicality of the boundaryless GE, was too naive in expecting such a glorified idea to happen. But he is not to blame: this mental abstract that exists in Welch's mind was communicated as a value to GE employees. Why communicate the (amorphous) value of boundaryless structure when you can achieve the same effect through communication about the vitality of cross-functional synergies and joint performance?

BEST PRACTICES

While Welch's vision and the Work-Out process transformed GE into a giant learning organization, a second phase called 'Best Practices' got underway. Best Practices was an effort to extend the learning process to the generic benchmarking of world-class organizations. In 1989, and after a senior team of business development staff scanned the world's most successful organizations, a list of six points was developed as the "secrets of success":

1. All manage processes rather than people. They focus on customer/supplier relationships rather than on results.
2. All use process mapping and benchmarking to identify opportunities for improvement.
3. All emphasize continuous improvement.
4. All rely on the customer as the source/instigator for performance improvement.
5. All stimulate productivity by introducing innovative products designed for efficient manufacturing.
6. All treat their suppliers as partners.

Welch reportedly became an instant convert. He quickly adopted the logic of Best Practices as "legitimized plagiarism" and assigned the task of spreading Best Practices and process mapping throughout GE to Work-Out teams. By 1990, the learning loop had been expanded to involve cross-functional teams. Self-sufficiency became a key goal: GE trained its own people as facilitators to replace the outsiders. When the Quick Response program at GE's Louisville-based appliance business was successful in reducing cycle time by more than 75 percent, reducing inventory by $200 million, and increasing ROI by 8.5 percent, it quickly became a target for internal benchmarking at GE. Louisville became a regular stop for executives from all over the company. Moreover, to create a corps of Quick Response experts, every GE business sent a few managers for a full year of "action learning" in Louisville. The result was the build up of a core competency that could spread the new technology throughout GE. Action learning was being reinforced by the powerful vision of trust, boundarylessness, and the sharing of knowledge and information.

ACCELERATING LEARNING: KAIZEN

The third stage of Work-Out began in 1992 with the Change of Acceleration program (CAP). This stage centered on transforming all GE leaders into change agents. The idea was to institutionalize learning by disseminating all of GE's accumulated knowledge and wisdom about the change process and the management of change to top managers. The expectation was that managers would become coaches and facilitators who would act as driving forces and initiators of learning and change. Work-Out represents Welch's personal commitment to the Japanese idea of Kaizen or continuous improvement. Kaizen, the Japanese term for continuous improvement, is a prominent approach in the battle to boost America's manufacturing process.

The following is a list of what is required to make Kaizen pay off (Treece, 1993, p. 136):

- *Worker cooperation*: a no-layoff pledge is necessary to assure workers that their suggestions for productivity improvements will not cost them their jobs.
- *Management commitment*: top management must back the Kaizen team with the resources and authority to make the sweeping changes necessary in search for radical efficiency gains.
- *Measurable goals and results*: besides validating the teams' successes, measuring enforces a reality check.
- *Diverse teams*: Kaizen teams should be drawn from disparate backgrounds and not just manufacturing to elicit a variety of ideas.
- *Bias for action*: the teams should favor immediate action on many fronts, opting for small improvements over costly, technological big fixes.

- *Follow-up*: not everything can be accomplished in one week, so follow-up work is needed to implement medium-term suggestions.

Kaizen takes Work-Out one notch further into the action and the doing or to the implementation of improvement ideas. GE's interpretation of Kaizen is:

K—Candor (*sic*): Participate in an improvement team and share your ideas.

A—Attitudes: Be result oriented. Go for quantum leaps rather than incremental ones. Make a difference.

I—Ideas, immediate actions: Be creative. Think outside the box. Look for implementation. Never kill an idea. For every *NO* bring two ideas.

Z—Zero sacred laws.

E—Energy that effects effort and motivation. Expertise geared toward process mapping. Empowerment to decide to implement.

N—No boundaries. Every idea is legitimate. The focus is on "doing."

GE's Work-Out demonstrates that learning is a journey that constantly challenges existing management philosophies and ways of doing things. Learning has become an important part of GE's culture, one which puts great emphasis on the values of self-organizing and self-designing, and which is supported by training and education. On April 25, 1990, in his presentation at the annual GE stockholders' meeting, Welch talked about the value of training and education:

> Education is a . . . great challenge we face in the '90s. If we ask our employees at every level of the workforce to win in a world seething with change we must provide them with tools to do so. We currently spend over $500 million a year on education and training—a figure that will grow to over a billion in the mid-nineties. Our educational infrastructure is among the best in the business—with our world-class management institute at Crotonville, New York and training centers and programs in place at our businesses . . . There is no more important investment this Company can make—because in the '90s, a decade that will roar with new technologies, geopolitical upheaval, cultural change, the difference between winning and losing will be how the men and women of our Company view change as it comes at them. If they see it as a threat—as an ill wind to be resisted by keeping your head down and digging your feet

in—we lose. But if they are provided the educational tools and are encouraged to use them—to the point where they see change as synonymous with opportunity—where they become receptive to it—even *demanding* of it—then every door we must pass through to win big all around the world will swing open to us—new markets—exotic technologies—novel ventures—dramatic productivity growth. (GE, *Annual Report*, 1990)

PROMOTING LEARNING THROUGH CULTURE, VALUES, AND IDEOLOGY

Jack Welch's transformational leadership created a rich system of values and beliefs that distinguishes GE from all others. It is a thick culture, but also one with the whole structure of the organization and management built around it. GE's managers and nonmanagers are socialized and in effect indoctrinated through the internalization of Work-Out goals. Work-Out, essentially a set of formalized programs intended to develop or reinforce a natural identification with the new ideology, has quickly become the force that integrates the organization. What holds GE together are not bureaucratic rules and regulations, planning and formal control, but rather the standardization of its norms and the sharing of values and beliefs among GE employees. Controls are conceptual not procedural. But this does not imply an absence of control. What takes the place of rules and bureaucratic control is the shared meaning of organizational goals. Control exists through capturing members' hearts and souls. Similar to Mintzberg's (1989) notion of the "missionary organization" GE's culture, too, had the following characteristics:

- A rich system of values and beliefs that differentiates it from other organizations.
- A culture rooted in a sense of mission associated with charismatic leadership, developed through traditions and sagas, and then reinforced through identifications.
- An ideology overlaid on the conventional organizational configuration, with centralized authority or sophisticated expertise, and a high level of commitment.
- A clear, focused, inspiring, distinctive mission.
- Coordination through the standardization of norms, reinforced by selection, socialization, and indoctrination of members.
- Small units, loosely organized and highly decentralized, but with powerful, normative controls.

- A mission to change or convert the world indirectly by attracting members and changing them.

Leadership in the missionary organization is charismatic and relies strongly on referent power; that is, the power to lead through the creation of natural identification and shared meaning. In the language of Mintzberg: "Leadership becomes not the imposition of direction so much as the protection and enhancement of the common ideology; the leader is expected to inspire others to pursue the mission, perhaps also to interpret the mission, but never to change the mission" (Mintzberg 1989, p. 229). GE, under Jack Welch's leadership, shares many of the characteristics of the missionary organization (see GE's value statement below). It is not uncommon in Work-Out sessions to hear participants mentioning Welch's name or talking about his views and ideology as if he were part of the session. Even though physically he is not there, spiritually he is constantly present.

GE VALUE STATEMENT: BUSINESS CHARACTERISTICS

Lean

- What: Reduce tasks and the people required to do them.
- Why: Critical to developing world-class cost leadership.

Agile

- What: Delayering.
- Why: Create fast decision making in a rapidly changing world through improved communication and increased individual response.

Creative

- What: Development of new ideas—innovation.
- Why: Increase customer satisfaction and operating margins through higher value products and services.

Ownership

- What: Self-confidence to trust others. Self-confidence to delegate to others the freedom to act while, at the same time, self-confidence to involve higher levels in issues critical to the business and the corporation.
- Why: Supports concept of more individual responsibility, capability to act quickly and independently. Should increase job

satisfaction and improve understanding of risks and rewards. While delegation is critical, there is a small percentage of high-impact issues that need or require involvement of higher levels within the business and within the corporation.

Reward

- What: Recognition and compensation commensurate with risk and performance that is highly differentiated by individual, with recognition of total team achievement.
- Why: Necessary to attract and motivate the type of individuals required to accomplish GE's objectives. A # 1 business should provide # 1 people with # 1 opportunity.

GE VALUE STATEMENT: INDIVIDUAL CHARACTERISTICS

Reality

- What: Describe the environment as it is and not as we want it to be.
- Why: Critical to developing a vision and a winning strategy and to gaining universal acceptance for their implementation.

Leadership

- What: Sustained passion for and commitment to a proactive shared vision and its implementation.
- Why: To rally teams toward achieving a common objective.

Candor/Openness

- What: Complete and frequent sharing of information with individuals (appraisals, etc.) and organization (everything).
- Why: Critical to employees knowing where they are, their efforts, and their business stand.

Simplicity

- What: Strive for brevity, clarity, the "elegant, simple solution." Less is better.
- Why: Less complexity improves everything, from reduced bureaucracy to better product design to lower costs.

Integrity

- What: Never bend or wink at the truth, and live within both the spirit and letter of the laws of every global business arena.

- Why: Critical to gaining acceptance in global arenas of our right to grow and prosper. Every constituency: shareowners who invest, customers who purchase, community that supports, and employees who depend, expect, and deserve our equivocal commitment to integrity in every facet of our behavior.

Individual Dignity

- What: Respect and leverage the talent and contribution of every individual in both good and bad times.
- Why: Teamwork depends on trust, mutual understanding, and the shared belief that the individual will be treated fairly in any environment.

Jack Welch's leadership style markedly fits into that of charismatic, transformational leadership. In describing his role in creating change Welch said:

> I haven't changed a thing! I try to adapt to the environment I am in. In the seventies, when I was helping grow new businesses . . . I was a wild-eyed growth guy. And then I got into the bureaucracy and I had to clean it out, so I was different in 1981. And now I am in another environment. But that's not being "born again" . . . the ideas were always the same. We have been talking about reality, agility, ownership, and candor since the beginning. We just got it simpler and more carefully articulated over time. Work-Out, eight years later, is a more meaningful way of communicating the idea of ownership—but it's the same idea . . . you don't get anywhere if you keep changing your ideas. The only way to change people's minds is with consistency. Once you get the ideas, you keep refining and improving them; the more simply your idea is defined, the better it is. You communicate, you communicate, and then you communicate some more. Consistency, simplicity, and repetition are what it's all about . . . We never changed; we just got better at it. And after a while it started to snowball. (Tichy & Charan, 1993, p. 31)

LEARNING FROM GE

Jack Welch's transformational leadership suggests three important objectives that effective leaders must pursue to turn their organizations into learning systems:

1. Create a new vision, reshape the organizational mission, and articulate values in support of that vision.
2. Mobilize commitment to the new vision and instigate ownership of the new values.
3. Institutionalize action learning as an organization-wide journey.

The revitalization at GE also suggests the following key elements that must preexist for effective organizational learning:

- *Vision*: integration, coordination, and control mechanisms must be in place to effectively link the organization from within and outside. The organization appears as a diverse system unified by a common purpose and shared mission.
- *Process learning*: through town meetings, cross-functional improvement teams, and adoption of best practices, the organization targets processes for streamlining or for reengineering. Process learning also allows for examination of "taboo" issues and identification of technical and behavioral problems that were not "allowed" to surface before.
- *Richness of information*: information flows within the system faster and in a nonbureaucratic way through communication bridges, direct contacts, and other electronic devices that connect all levels and locations.
- *Innovation*: debureaucratization and downsizing, a market-based form of organizing, and internal and external networking are the landscape for innovation and creativity. Creation of a leaner, more agile organization allows for fluidity and flexibility in coordination, direct contacts, and the free flow of ideas between individuals and work groups.
- *Risk taking*: people at all levels are encouraged to take risks and go beyond their comfort zone. They are encouraged to challenge the status quo, question the validity of current management practices, and propose alternative means of carrying out group charters and individual job performance. Leaders are expected to have a high tolerance for mistakes and ambiguity. They should develop a broad understanding of the tradeoffs between short-term costs and long-term payoffs. They must also use a diagnostic approach to problem solving and relinquish inappropriate styles of management caused by fear and intimidation.
- *Process feedback*: managers, professionals, and operators all need feedback about process outputs to prevent reoccurrence of

errors and eliminate rework and inefficiency. Employees must be empowered to tackle process difficulties and solve problems. They must also be held accountable for process flow and the impact of their work and improvement on the next process customer. Establishing a customer/supplier relationship within and outside the organization creates a great opportunity for fast learning and improvement along the entire value chain of the organization from vendor specifications upstream to end-user satisfaction downstream.

- *Shared ownership:* by reframing and redefining its vision and core values, and by mobilizing support and commitment to that vision, the learning organization is anchored in a continuous process of performance breakthrough and adaptation. Employees at all levels and in all units internalize the superordinate goals of the organization through socialization processes and training and education programs. To the extent that a new ideology is formed around the values of change and adaptation, the organization as a whole is transformed into a learning system geared toward continuous improvement.

Ownership is first and foremost a psychological element. People must feel and act in line with the new values. It is not indoctrination in the sense that the new movement is not geared to create mechanistic or robotlike responses to environmental stimuli. The learning organization is not a reflexive organization, but rather a responsive, proactive, and intelligent system with creativity and innovation as its flagship. Ownership can also be financial through gainsharing programs and stock options in which employees also become owners; that is, they have a stake in the survival and success of their organization. Thus, a sense of harmony among the parts and the whole is formed.

CONCLUSION: FACILITATING LEARNING AND CHANGE

Communication-based learning must be embodied in the thoughts and actions of organizational leaders performing the role of Facilitator. Knowledge management and transference require facilitation competencies and understanding of all facets of organizational behavior, processes, and outputs. In the role of Facilitator, organizational leaders must become strategic opportunists, globally aware, and capable of managing highly decentralized systems. In addition, they must be interpersonally competent, sensitive to issues of diversity and be community builders. How do leaders become proficient facilitators of knowledge and leaning? Jay Conger (1991) suggested patterning leadership training and action learning after the Center for Creative Leadership located in North Carolina. The Center uses art and visualization to expand leaders' interpretations of the complex dynamics they face. The goal is to encourage leaders to go beyond rational management and move into the exploration of other perspectives and options for situational analysis.

Conger's approach seems to be an extension of Quinn's (1988) suggestion that leaders should be encouraged to adopt a holistic approach through self-assessment and role modeling such as those discussed in chapter 9. The use of art and visualization is also consistent with Gareth Morgan's (1993) discussion of metaphorical analysis and applied imagination as cognitive tools that can help prospective leaders develop the conceptual skills and critical thinking needed to look at reality differently. By employing metaphors, leaders expand their views about the social construction of reality. They create a richer prism through which they can reshape interactional patterns and social processes. Applying metaphors diagnostically is also a learning tool— that is, a reflective process of reevaluating the meanings inherent in organizational sagas, rituals, and norms of behaviors. The paradoxical nature of organizations is such that contradictory themes and patterns of interaction are often simultaneously exhibited, requiring leaders to constantly use different metaphors for diagnosing decision situations effectively. Action turns into learning and learning becomes action when leaders initiate transformation processes that are also implemented. As Garvin (1993, p. 80) rightfully observed: Without accompanying changes in the way that work gets done, only the potential for improvement exists.

The renewal journey toward a learning organization requires not only changes in managers' thinking patterns, but also in their behaviors, actions, and performance. Their commitment is very important, and is a must. An article in *Industry Week* tells the story of a typical management saga in this context:

> Management group says, OK, we are going to be committed to quality. But we don't want to dictate what you are going to do. Each division is going to do its own thing. As long as you are doing something . . . So the senior group doesn't have any game plan or commitment. They also don't understand what the divisions are doing, and so they basically just get in the way most of the time because they manage the business the same way they always have . . . They tell others they have to change, but

back in their office they are still looking at the numbers. And when sales or production are off, they call their senior people and ask, "How come we are behind?" And when members of a quality improvement team come back from a meeting, their supervisor asks them why they aren't doing their job. This indicates that their real job has nothing to do with process improvement. The real job is getting the stuff out the door . . . Events like this are what make quality-improvement plans fall on their face . . . It's become something like the owner of a football team who shows up at the start of the season and gives the players a pep talk. He tells them to play hard, and at the end of the season to be sure to tell him how they did. (*Industry Week*, 10/90, p. 14)

Recently, Gemini Consulting completed a study involving the top business leaders of more than fifty companies in the United States, Europe, and Asia-Pacific. The top executives were asked their views about what factors contribute to successful facilitation of transformational learning. Their recommendations, published under the title "8 Essential Lessons For Change" (*Executive Edge*, vol. 26, no. 10, October 1995, pp. 1–3), are particularly relevant for leaders facilitating and managing the transfer of knowledge within organizations:

1. *All hands on deck*: Flatter hierarchies in which decision making is pushed down require the cooperation and involvement of all employees. Managers must learn to align their leadership style along the lines of coaching rather than commanding.
2. *Create great expectations*: Don't underestimate staff capabilities by padding goals or fudging estimates. Establish high standards and expect high returns. What you think is going to happen tends to happen. Today's competitive environment demands thinking out of the box. Accomplishments follow expectations: expect 80 percent improvement and you will get close to that.
3. *Turning vision into reality*: Including people in the vision and having open communication are critical for successful transformation. The vision must guide the goals of work units, managers, and employees. The goals must be clear and simple.
4. *Speed is of the essence*: Avoid complacency by moving forward with determination and confidence. Once the decision is made, move!
5. *Learning to change*: Top managers must structure the context for organizational change including raising the bar of tolerance for errors and encouraging risk taking. Change must be culti-

vated as an ongoing process with incremental gains that can be communicated widely and create a sense of "do-ability." Piloting or experimenting with the change to ensure early gains can be applied to other parts of the organization to accelerate successful implementation.

6. *Earning trust*: To become both responsive to the need to change and responsible for effective implementation, managers must instill trust in employees. Leaders' actions rather than their words are the barometer by which employees measure commitment.

7. *Communicate, communicate*: Create a culture of open communication and positive feedback. Support communication with good listening habits. Provide access to information, training, and resources.

8. *Inspiring leadership*: Managers must inspire staff and employees to stretch and take risks, build trust, and create a climate conducive to ongoing change.

Managers are faced with the challenge to learn to relinquish control by obliterating the old values and replacing them with new ones. Drucker (1988) rightfully pointed out that the task of management remains the same, that is to make people capable of joint performance by providing them with vision and direction, structure and ongoing training. But the very nature of this task changes when management helps to create highly knowledgeable employees. With a knowledgeable workforce, managers must also shed their traditional responsibilities and become coaches and facilitators of empowered teams. Concurrently, individual performers are expected to share the burden of defining their marginal contributions or their value adding to the organization. Effective leaders, in the role of Facilitator, must do more than that. They must be on the field and play the role of quarterback. They lead their employees by adopting multiple perspectives and shifting away from the perceptual error that their assumptions and views still have relevance to the environment in which they operate. They must be less emotional and sensitive to old paradigms and more open to new information which can ignite and energize the renewal process. They must be able to reason the change and physically display behaviors and actions that are in alignment with the change.

Learning follows needs—that is, when needs change the approach to learning must change. Under the new paradigm of redefining the total system and working in a boundaryless organization, an employee must move to center stage and become a proactive rather than a reactive partner in the learning contract. And the learning frame of reference must also move from the individual to the team (Burdett, 1993). In shifting the emphasis of learning to teams and engaging in experiential, work-based training activities, individuals develop the skills necessary for building cross-functional synergies. The focus, then, can be shifted toward reengineering work processes to create high value for customers and achieve innovative breakthroughs, rather than merely eliminating inefficiencies and reducing cost. Skill development and the transference of knowledge require organizational leaders to become effective facilitators and at the same time develop the sensitivity essential for self-improvement and developing others. Chapter 9 will address these issues within the context of competency education and development which define the domain of the manager enacting the Mentor role.

9

Learning to Learn: Competency Education for Management Development

We must learn to leverage the people resources in the organization as the fundamental strategy for success . . . The underlying assumption of the "competency movement" is that identifying the knowledge, skills, abilities, and behaviors required for successful job, team or total business performance is one of the most direct links to actualizing the shared mission of all organizations—to achieve and maintain competitive advantage necessary for survival in domestic and global markets.

—Vice President of Human Resources, MANOR Healthcare

With technology and working methods changing swiftly, companies increasingly are challenged to keep their managers and staff specialists abreast of current knowledge. Some organizations, in an attempt to cut costs and make education more relevant, have gone as far as granting their own degrees. Arthur D. Little, a management consultancy firm, offers a Master's degree in management. A survey of one hundred companies with well-developed education programs, conducted by Quality Dynamics, a New York based consultancy firm, found that one-third are considering such a move. Some companies have turned their educational programs from cost centers to profit centers by sourcing the programs to those who are willing to pay. Motorola, Xerox, Digital Equipment, and Disney offer seminars for hefty fees. IBM and Sun Microsystems use the Internet to market their courses. Often, making a profit becomes secondary to creating an image of a credible, trustworthy company with quality products and reliable service. Education is also a way to bind companies and their consumers. Dana Corporation, a car-parts company, trains its customers; Motorola its suppliers; Ford its dealers; Iams its dog-food distributors, and so on. *The Economist* (10/95) concluded that although it is not disputed that training and education help increase productivity, its main gain comes from boosting employee morale.

MODELS OF COOPERATION

Increasingly, companies have been establishing formal connections with colleges and universities who customize educational programs for them. In 1991, SUNY–Empire State College and New York Telephone established a partnership aimed at providing employees with opportunities to earn associate and baccalaureate degrees while not disrupting their work (Johnstone, 1994). Some corporate universities are trying to partner with higher education institutions to achieve the goal of a simultaneous melding of functional expertise (coming from the college) with innovation and market requirements (coming from companies). "The corporate universities are looking for flexible educational partners that might offer an onsite MBA or an onsite undergraduate degree. They do not want to just pay tuition reimbursement, they want to be a customer of education" (*AACSB*, p. 2). NYNEX, for example, outsourced much of its employee education to New England universities willing to partner a customized Associate's degree in telecommunication technology.

NYNEX, now part of Bell Atlantic has also partnered with FORUM/ESC to provide business management degrees to its level 1 and level 2 managers. What NYNEX has found with FORUM is a high degree of responsiveness and willingness to meet the needs of its middle managers for networking with managers from other companies, as well as cross-fertilization and the exchange of nonproprietary information. AT&T established a similar program for Associates degrees for its installers with the Center of Distance Learning of Empire State College. Motorola has formal relationships with the Kellogg School of Business, University of Michigan to develop curriculum in manufacturing. Dr. Duncan RyanMann, professor of economics at Empire State College and an expert in management education and adult learning, notes that labor market and corporate needs can be expressed through a variety of mechanisms. Differential wage rates across job categories and skill sets send a very powerful signal to individuals pursuing their education and training. Businesses or labor unions may contract directly with institutions of higher education for the provision of instruction in specific skill or knowledge areas. Private sector organizations may also play a role in the policy making process through which the goals and objectives of public higher education (or other education and training) are defined and supplemented.

Some companies have gone as far as supporting and even licensing local colleges to offer their curriculum. American Express, for example, has used its material to help Rio Salvador Community College in Phoenix, Arizona, develop an Associate's degree in customer service. Other companies use information technology to bring the classroom to the office. At Sprint's "University of Excellence," most classes take place via satellite and courses are provided by outside specialists. Hundreds of companies now offer management development courses to their own staff and managers in programs similar to the one run by McDonald's Hamburger University. New York University established a partnership with IBM Corporation to offer information systems courses over a global computer network to both IBM and non-IBM professionals worldwide. Why would colleges move to these models of cooperation?

An immediate answer would probably corroborate the need for symbiotic relationships between colleges and corporations. NYU sees corporate partnerships as a way to increase student enrollment and participation in its traditional as well as on-line programs. NYU also increases its outreach by using IBM's customer base to promote its programs and courses. The answer, however, involves a much deeper reasoning. In recent years, schools of business have been challenged to modify their structures, processes, and methods of teaching and learning to respond more effectively to the growing needs of adult learners in a new market segment—management development degree programs (Fortunato, Belasen, DiPadova & Hart, 1995; Shadle, Belasen & Benke, 1996).

RELEVANCE AND ACCOUNTABILITY

Criticism aimed particularly at traditional schools of business has called for the implementation of more innovative approaches to management education, increased access through greater feasibility, enhanced acceleration via the granting of credits for college-level learning, and, ultimately, increased program relevance. A call has gone out to make management education programs more responsive and accountable to market needs (Porter & McKibbin, 1988; Muller, Porter & Rehder, 1991).

Another stream of criticism has been aimed at pedagogies and the content of learning. It has challenged management education to shift its emphasis from management knowledge acquisition to management skills development and from an understanding-by-listening orientation to learning by doing (Whetten, Windes, May & Bookstaver, 1991; McEvoy & Cragun, 1987). More recently and consistent with the call to integrate cognitive and behavioral methods of learning into an integrated scheme of learning (Fleming, 1992; O'Connor, 1993), Whetten and Clark (1996) proposed an improved methodology for teaching skill development "in a way that systematically integrates the best features of a variety of traditional methods, and treats thinking and doing, and learning and applying as mutually enhancing learning processes" (p. 153). Their framework, basically an adaptation of Kolb's (1984) integration of action learning and reflection with practical and abstract thinking, resulted in the formulation of a dual learning cycle: assimilation through experience, understanding, and practice activities; and, post-course practice through reflection and application. Whetten and Clark argued that this integrated model, more so than existing management education methods, places students in the role of proactive learners, thus promoting long-term behavioral change through motivation for self-directed learning.

Criticism and assessment of management education programs have been useful in challenging institutional leaders to reexamine their programs. One source of criticism was the Task Force on High Performance Work and Workers (*Business-Higher Education Forum*, September, 1995). The goals of the task force were to recommend models of cooperation between business and higher education institutions and ultimately to provide higher education with parameters for future directions based on the viewpoints of the corporation. The observations corporate leaders of the task force were very specific:

- Higher education does not take the needs of the private sector seriously.
- In the face of global competition, higher education is behind the curve—unable to respond quickly and trapped in a discipline-bound view of knowledge.

- Corporate leaders are concerned less with a decline in the quality of higher education than with developing workers who can adapt and lead in business conditions characterized by dramatic change.
- Corporate leaders agree that graduates are deficient in a number of areas, including leadership and communications skills; quantification skills, interpersonal relations, and the ability to work in teams; understanding the needed to work with a diverse workforce at home and abroad; and the capacity to adapt to rapid change.
- Several leaders report a reduction in their emphasis on hiring graduates right out of college in favor of hiring more experienced workers.
- Some business leaders have significant reservations about the value of the MBA.

Although some schools have responded enthusiastically to these criticisms, most traditional schools have changed their methods and pedagogies only marginally, usually through an increase in the scheduling of evening classes or more "dramatically" through the introduction of weekend classes and the presentation of courses over the Internet. Brown University and the University of Pennsylvania, for example, have begun to offer graduate courses over the Internet (*USA Today*, 8/7/96). At Wharton School of Business, Dean Thomas Gerrity has taken steps to transform his program along the lines of the market model of reengineering by tearing down functional chimneys and relocation of staff specialists and students to interdisciplinary teams. He has also tried to remove the barriers which have separated his school from the university's other programs. Students now offer consultancy to other parts of the university. They are also sent on "global immersion" missions to become versed in international business management (*The Economist*, April 13, 1996). Harvard Business School, which has been criticized for its lack of innovative curriculum and turning out general managers that are good at selling themselves rather than effective leaders with strong interpersonal as well as computer-based analytical skills, has gone through a similar, although not as dramatic transformation. A "Foundations" course was added to its curriculum emphasizing analytical, interpersonal, and ethical skills. The school has also recruited more foreign-born teachers to add an international flavor to its curriculum. On the placement front, the school has also begun to pay more attention to business firms that employ its MBAs

(*The Economist*, Oct. 7, 1995, p. 69). Other schools have responded by increasing the number of evening classes and by establishing certificate programs.

However encouraging, these modifications seem more to be driven by the need to align organizational capabilities with strategies to become more competitive (input or institutionally oriented), than as a direct response to adult learners' professional and organizational needs (output or customer focused). It was not surprising, then, to find that although these schools changed some of their structures, their curriculum remained pretty much unchanged. Schools which develop distance learning to tackle the problem, such as Columbia and Pace University, focused their curricula on technology subjects. These schools, however, developed EMBA programs that are weekend based and typically take two years to complete. Despite their relative popularity (and high tuition costs), an experienced manager seeking formal education is still required to take the standard dose of functional and managerial introductory courses, regardless of his/her prior learning and practical knowledge. In addition to studying rigorously, adult learners maintain full workload obligations and family responsibilities. And according to *Crain's New York Business* (August 4, 1997, p. 14), executive MBA courses typically assume a certain level of knowledge and tend to be more practical than theoretical in nature.

Dr. Carolyn Jarmon, former Director of Graduate Studies, SUNY–Empire State College, explained why existing traditional models of higher education fail to respond to the needs of experienced managers. According to Dr. Jarmon, training initiatives in business today far outpace efforts of formal higher education. The learning opportunities provided for managers and administrators through their own organizations are based on the premise that these employees possess useful knowledge and that the goal of a particular training experience is to leverage and increase that existing knowledge. Higher education is not so enlightened. At both undergraduate and graduate levels, business students, regardless of prior experience or acquired knowledge, are required to study whatever the faculty member believes is useful for all to know—even if they already know it. Quality is defined by the supplier, higher education, who decides what is to be learned—that is, the same learning for everyone. Rightfully, Dr. Carolyn Jarmon concludes that the consumer, the student, buys a one-size-fits-all package. This is not a productive model.

Traditional schools have also responded to external pressures by creating more incentives for student enrollment, by easing up on admission requirements, by lowering academic standards, and by having a narrower focus. A new study sponsored by the National Association of Scholars (NAS) received national attention with its harsh critique: "By almost every measure, from curriculum requirements to time spent in class, 50 of America's top colleges have lowered their academic standards" (*Investor Daily*, March 1996, p. 1) . The NAS study reported dramatic changes in the way colleges and universities conduct their business—they now have less structure, looser content, and less rigor than in the 1960s. The patterns observed were alarming: fewer mandatory courses, fewer courses with prerequisites, more and narrower courses, less class time.

Although the reasons mentioned in the study for this downfall in academic standards are low-priority issues for teaching and hyperspecialization, management educators cannot clearly ignore market pressures and the institutional needs for adaptability and survival. The paradox is that the quest for flexibility and innovation has been met with the pathological adaptation of lowering standards rather than with increasing institutional responsibility and program effectiveness. William Simon, former Secretary of the Treasury, noted: "It is ironic that at the time when young Americans need a rigorous education to compete in the world marketplace, our colleges and universities are eliminating requirements and embracing the latest academic fads. It is also ironic that just when the rest of the world is embracing Western political and economic ideals, so many of our academic institutions are busy repudiating them" (*The Economist*, March 19, 1996).

Business schools are not changing their structures and processes fast enough, and when they do change, the rate and scope of change is only marginal. Increasingly, companies such as Digital Equipment and AT&T have formed their own universities to provide in-house quality training and education programs that are at college level. A recent report estimated that corporations with management education and/or training divisions referred to as corporate universities increased from four hundred to more than one thousand between 1988 and 1995 (*AACSB*, spring 1996). The major reason cited for this increase was rapid technological change and the need to keep managers abreast of knowledge and competencies. ACE and CLEPP are increasingly issuing college-level credits to employees participating in their corporate educational programs. Firms such as Arthur D. Little decided to take advantage of market opportunities by creating their own executive MBA educational programs and through joint ventures with local colleges. The problem is so acute, that in its special report *The Economist* (1990) came up with a prediction that business schools' major competitors in the near future will be in-house company schools.

A CUSTOMER-FOCUSED APPROACH TO
MANAGEMENT LEARNING AND EDUCATION:
A COMPETENCY-BASED MBA

Empire State College (ESC), part of the State University of New York, takes a different approach using a market-driven perspective. With a twenty-seven-year history of student-centered, undergraduate programs, SUNY–ESC designed a competency-based Master's degree in Business Administration, delivered by distance technology and augmented by strategically placed weekend residencies. Incubated and developed initially by Drs. Alan Belasen and Laurie DiPadova in the FORUM Management Degree Program at ESC, the philosophical basis of this degree is twofold: managers can demonstrate what they already know of the generally accepted MBA content and then learn what they do not know, building on the accumulated experience. Thus, there are two routes to credit for this degree: (a) the opportunity through a range of assessment techniques to demonstrate previously acquired, graduate-level knowledge, and (b) modular learning experiences delivered at a distance via information technology to acquire the needed MBA content.

Why would a college move to this model? According to Dr. Carolyn Jarmon, consultation with corporate partners and independent evaluations of MBA graduates in the workplace reported by others clearly indicated that managers with MBA degrees and their employers were dissatisfied with what students were learning, how they were learning, and how long it was taking them to learn it. In numerous research studies, MBA graduates were perceived as number-crunchers, rather than effective managers, and they spent significant amounts of personal and company time relearning what they already knew. When consulted, managers in traditional MBA programs indicated repeatedly that there is significant overlap between what they are assigned to learn and what they already know. Such a model is too resource intensive and frequently does not include the important concepts of effective managerial skills and leadership. SUNY–Empire State College, in keeping with its mission of meeting student and market needs, determined that moving to a competency model is productive for students, for employers, and for the college.

The program design and implementation team led by Drs. Alan Belasen, Michael Fortunato, and James Savitt expanded on the FORUM competency model (described below) to include functional components and assessment elements. Thus, the program design included both the quantitative or common MBA curriculum such as accounting and finance, management information systems, marketing management, operations management, managerial economics and managerial decision making, and the qualitative or behavioral studies needed for improving the effectiveness of managerial leadership, organizational communication, and the management of chance.

The MBA program utilizes a completely Web-based delivery system for all courses with the exception of the opening experience and the two capstone courses, "managerial reasoning" and "business strategy practicum" which combine residency and Web-based instruction. By July 1998 the curriculum of the competency-based MBA has evolved into 6 course blocks totaling 60 credits:

Scanning the business environment (the opening experience)	4 credits
The functional core	24 credits
Human systems and behavior	4 credits
The managerial roles	12 credits
Electives	12 credits
Business strategy practicum	4 credits

"Scanning the business environment" (the opening perspective) establishes the context for the study of management in today's changing workplace. The functional core consists of six 4-credit courses that represent the common body of knowledge that comprises most traditional MBA degrees. "Human systems and behavior" is a one-of-a-kind course that teaches students that managerial analysis can never take place effectively without a fundamental knowledge of people. The managerial roles block assesses, develops, and applies student competencies and skills. An important goal of the MBA is to enhance the overall level and balance of the students' managerial effectiveness profile. Thus, the managerial block includes the eight universal leadership roles covered by the Competing Values Framework as well as a capstone study, "managerial reasoning," that maps out the eight roles into an integrative scheme that places the roles within the context of rational problem solving, ethical choices, management learning, and the constraints on organizational effectiveness. The elective block is aimed at helping students specialize in a particular area (e.g., international business management, health care management) or achieve breadth of knowledge across a variety of subject areas (e.g., entrepreneurship, strategic management, organizational development.) "Business strategy practicum" (the culminating experience) integrates all the functional knowledge and managerial skills into an action learning framework in which teams of students apply what they have learned in the program, both functionally and managerially, to a real world situation of strategic importance. For example, a marketing analysis or a financial development plan could help improve an organization's competitive position.

Recognizing the need for high integration across the curriculum, a number of pedagogical strategies have been developed to facilitate the attainment of the goal: (a) a modular structure with integrative modules which provides opportunities for students to explicitly link their technical proficiency with the capability to accomplish appropriate managerial responses (for example, accounting and finance may interface with marketing [e.g., sales credit issues] and the managerial behaviors performed by managers playing the monitor role [e.g., cost control]; similarly, managerial economics may interface with the producer role [e.g., productivity issues] and operations management may cut across a number of courses and interface with the coordinator role); (b) the suffusion of three themes: managerial ethics, global perspective in decision making, and organizational effectiveness criteria; and, (c) the design of capstone courses in which student teams are engaged in residency presentations and computer supported collaboration to help client organizations meet a strategic challenge.

A key feature of this competency-based MBA program is the option granted to students to demonstrate functional knowledge of business or managerial competence for conversion into graduate level credits. Successful applicants to the program are expected to bring advanced-level knowledge from their experiences. It is expected that most students will normally earn 6–20 credits or up to a total of 28 credits for assessed knowledge and prior graduate study, while earning the rest of their credits from formal coursework. Very advanced students may complete their degree with as few as 32 credits of formal coursework. These assessments offer business professionals opportunities to validate their experience as graduate-level learning. Successful completion of these assessments leads to awarding of credit and serves as the basis for the design of the remainder of a student's program.

The inclusion of a limited number of weekend residencies provides the foundation for learning conflict-resolution and teamwork in a face-to-face setting. Since working well in this environment is also important for effective managers, the design of the program includes residency-based studies. Several representatives from different industries have indicated that managers must be able to function effectively in both types of working environments. Carolyn Jarmon expressed the view that the design of this well-thought-out competency-based MBA by Empire State College reflects the following values:

- A response to customer demand for a graduate program which prepares effective managers in both qualitative and quantitative content areas.
- Evidence of institutional accountability to taxpayers and society through its productive design.
- Recognition that working virtually is an organizational necessity for effective global business management.

This MBA degree combines a range of learning experiences using distance technology, while permitting the student to focus on particular areas of need via the option of assessing experiences to validate previous learning. Thus, the student's and concurrently the employer's time and resources are used productively. Society is enriched, as employees are prepared to work together in the same time and place, as well as at a distance in many time zones, and students are permitted to leverage their previous knowledge and experience as they acquire new understandings. The focus on how to manage, rather than teaching about management, offers students opportunities to practice and become proficient in applying requisite skills for effective daily management.

ADULT LEARNING AND MANAGEMENT EDUCATION

There are significant fundamental differences in the experience of operating in the academic world and the business world. Uncovering these differences is important for people who are trying to function in both arenas. Dr. Michael Fortunato, Director of the SUNY-FORUM Management Education devised a framework (table 9.1) to orient managers who are returning to school. The framework is presented below in terms of a comparison of the business and academic environments which might help adult learners to shape their pedagogy and instructional design.

Adult learners use a frame of reference and mental constructs that are based on their intuition and common sense regarding what works well and what fails. They were trained and developed requisite skills that conform to the need to become highly proficient and productive in fulfilling their tasks. They were taught to think critically, be decisive, initiate actions, and add tangible value to their work units and organizations. As table 9.1 indicates, while in the business world managers are expected to optimize results, in the academic world they are expected to satisfy process requirements. The academic world allows for unresolved arguments to coexist and for dialectical notions to surface and be

Table 9.1.
Back to School: Hints for Reducing Culture Shock

BUSINESS	COLLEGE
Focus is on getting the job done: the results are what count	Focus is on process: what matters is how you got there and whether or not you could repeat it
Work is expected to be relatively error free	Errors are essential—we learn more from our mistakes than from our successes
Learning is often by "apprenticeship": explicit directions are customary	Learning is by "self-discovery"; ambiguity is thought to be essential to the learning process
Solutions are formulaic: results can be described in a policy manual	Solutions are heuristic: creative inspiration is often needed to put knowledge to use
Gather just the facts necessary to makea good decision: redundancy is discouraged as "inefficient"	Research standards demand that "all" available evidence be considered: redundancy is encouraged as "comprehensive"
Solicit opinions of others "who have been there before"	Seek out other methods for approaching this or similar problems
Delegation is encouraged as "effective management"	Sensitivity to taking ownership of one's work and giving credit to whomever it is due
Tolerance for variety of processes/ work styles that lead to correct results	Tolerance for a variety of results that follow from correct processes: a tolerance for a variety of informed opinions
Risk acting on imagination without knowledge	Risk acting on knowledge without imagination

respected. For adult learners, these contradictions are a source of frustration and ambiguity—they represent equivocal issues that are not easily reconciled with their views of the world. Effective instructors must anticipate these reactions and be prepared to deal with these issues and help adult learners rebuild their confidence and trust in the system of management education. Notably, effective instructors must be familiar with contextual factors that uniquely affect adult learning, such as socioeconomic, psychological, perceptual, and cognitive factors.

The pedagogical challenge for the instructor of adult learners is to realize that the cognitive map of adult learners is different and unique: it is value-loaded and idiosyncratic. The challenge for instructors, who are expected to meet the educational and learning needs of their adult learners, is to shift away from the traditional, functional approach and move toward a more critical perspective that recognizes the richness of the world of adult learners. At minimum, instructors are expected to reconcile the two approaches by using a flexible and adaptive approach that is experientially based. The dilemma faced by instructors is in losing academic freedom and sovereignty in designing and delivering their curricula. They must give up or sacrifice some of their autonomy to create a learning environment that is flexible enough to accommodate the psychological, cognitive, and behavioral needs of adult learners.

PARTICULAR FRAME OF REFERENCE

Adult learners bring to the classroom an ample supply of experientially based knowledge and a practical prism through which they judge the utility of the process and content of learning. They measure theoretical constructs and conceptual models against their intuition and common sense that is both pragmatic and concrete. They use an inductive approach in explaining and relating to their surroundings and they expect instructors to have working assumptions and interpretations about the world that fits with their own. While instructors normally use a functionalist perspective for teaching and explaining organizational factors (e.g., factors in organizational communication may include information flow and networking, breakdowns, managerial responses to information overload/underload), most adult learners develop interpretations of organizational reality on the basis of shared meaning. They employ behavioral/intuitive criteria to judge the success of deliverables and the utility and relevance of material. Since they view the world from their own frame of reference, they also expect their instructors to reconfirm their assumptions about the world. Hence, adult learners expect their instructors to use a reflective approach rather than a deductive one to help them reconstruct images of their organizations and management practices.

How one frames professional problems and the range of solutions available is what differentiates the education of an expert from the education of the novice. Schon (1987) highlighted the need for reflection in learning and suggested the importance of the "right kind of telling" that takes place when students work closely with instructors. His explanation for reflection in learning begins with knowing in action, which is presumed knowledge. He follows this with reflection in action, which considers the possibility of surprise or an unexpected finding. Reflection about action is done through experimentation, which is particularly important for adult learners participating in structured educational programs. An experiential approach to learning also allows adult learners to reflect on the results of decisions and actions, a luxury not always evident in the business environment. Downplaying the importance of universal principles helps adult learners interpret events through the narrow prism of their experiences and understanding: it reinforces their preconceived ideas of what is working and what is not.

PSYCHOLOGICAL DIFFERENCES/NEEDS

Adult learners may have different goals and different motivation in going back to school. Some return to school in order to gain new skills or to get a promotion, while others enroll to meet a personal goal or because it is the requirement of continued employment. Whatever the reason, instructors should realize that adults differ from one another in their motivations and expectations. Some students need more direction and support than others and may place considerable claim against the time and attention of their instructors. These students are frequently also influenced by their own perceptions of their weaknesses and lack of inability to learn, thus requiring counseling and constant guidance. Learning activities that enhance self-confidence as well as personal competencies are valuable. Yet, instructors should recognize adult learners' personal limitations and use flexible instructional design to respond to the psychological needs of the students. Successful teachers of adult students with managerial experience seek to understand the prior experience, skills, and competencies of their students and to apply this understanding to the design of the learning activities. The study of management is enhanced by the experiences that managers bring along with them.

APTITUDE AND PERCEPTIONS

Adult learners generally have different needs and goals when going back to school than do young, full-time students. Adult learners may select and organize learning stimuli based on their perceptions of what is important and relevant to their work and what is not. Thus, they may respond differently to the context of learning (e.g., group activities versus independent learning), the type of communication used (e.g., verbal explanations versus visual aids), level of conceptualization (e.g., abstract versus concrete concepts), and problem-solving orientation (e.g., intuitive versus logical reasoning.) It is therefore important that instructors inform learners in advance about the format and mode of learning and how they are expected to demonstrate mastery of instructional objectives. Adults expect explicit instructions, reasonable deadlines, and realistic assignments because they are often juggling multiple expectations.

COGNITIVE FACTORS

The adult in a training or class session may have a great deal of prior knowledge in selected areas of the study ("positive depth,") but almost no knowledge in other key areas ("negative breadth.") This may require tailoring specific assignments to reflect the level of this knowledge, but also redirecting the adults toward the basic concepts or principles they need to know to be successful. Adult educators such as Freire (1992) and Cervero (1988) have long investigated the relationships between learning and the changing patterns of knowledge within a profession. Cervero advocates the need for a shift from a functionalist perspective to a critical view. Functionalism views professionals as a group who use knowledge to address problems that are important to society. The work of the manager is technical or specialized, so that more knowledge provides a basis for solving problems more effectively. When the functionalist approach is applied to education, deficiencies are corrected by expanding the knowledge base through training.

The functionalist (instructor) uses reasoning and logic to explain managerial and organizational dynamics. He or she supports the explanation with theoretical constructs and empirical models, using a deductive approach to generalize, infer, and draw conclusions. The result is often gross simplification of organizational and social reality. The interpretivist (adult learner) is less concerned with validity and reliability of measurement and about studies supporting general assertions about organizational behavior and/or managerial dynamics. Instead, the interpretivist is more likely to draw on his/her stories, organizational saga, rites, rituals, dynamics, and so on to draw conclusions about what is working. For example, the interpretivist is less concerned with the argument that feedback is crucial for establishing effective communication across levels and is more concerned with the reflections and uses of feedback in his/her organization and from his/her own frame of reference. Therefore, when working with adults, it is important to use a critical approach to clarify the sources of adult learning and, if necessary, change the actual knowledge. Instructors must have impact on how knowledge is shaped by working directly with adult learners.

THE SIGNIFICANCE OF WRITING SKILLS

Dr. Elaine Handley, a mentor who specializes in writing and literature and who coordinates the writing and research program at FO-RUM, Empire State College, has proposed to think of reading and writing as essential processes of sense making. According to Handley, reading and writing skills are critical tools of discovery, development, and extension of people's thinking patterns. These skills enable people to realize what they know and what they need to know to create meaning. The dialogue that takes place between readers' minds and the text they are reading or writing helps them interact creatively with the material as well as develop and clarify their own ideas. Critical reading requires active engagement with the text. The text becomes meaningful when we bring our own experience and questions to understanding the author's vision. Writing for both academia and business needs to be fostered as a humanistic tool for lifelong learning in diverse settings. As someone who has been working with middle managers returning to school, Handley calls attention to the enormous potential of developing writing skills to enhance managerial competence. In work that is bottom-line driven, the ability to access a thinking process and to become proficient at articulating clear ideas is a great advantage, especially for the manager selling ideas in a global marketplace.

Most of the writing that gets done in business is persuasive in nature, whether it is selling an idea, writing a memo, a report, addressed or unaddressed letters, or performance reviews. Persuasive writing calls for clarity, well-developed ideas, an appropriate tone, and logic. Elaine Handley concludes:

> These are learnable skills which should be the basis of any management training. As the writer and teacher Donald Murray says so aptly: "Writing can give you power, for we live in a complicated technical society, and those people who can collect information, order it into significant meaning and then communicate it to others will influence the course of events within the town or nation, school or university, company or corporation. Information is power." (Murray, 1984, p. 4)

Dr. Elaine Handley's experience teaching managers to write in college suggests that a relatively simple exposure to what has recently been learned about the process of writing can have significant value-added impact on the performance and productivity of managers. This may seem counterintuitive since business has to be concerned with the bottom-line results rather than a tedious, long-winded process. And yet, because managers are engaged in creative thinking that is typically required for effective decision making, their ability to yield those exponentially valuable ingredients of the human capacity to invent, communicate, and reinvent are immeasurable. As the poet Robert Frost said, "To learn to write is to learn to have ideas."

The writing process calls for writers to see writing as an effective means of stimulating thinking and bridging the gap between the transacting elements of communication (e.g., content) and the person's form of expression (e.g., language, words). Good writing begins with who the person is and what he or she knows, making connections and integrating learning through writing. This takes some retraining, especially for managers geared to efficiency and results. The process involves the new three Rs: *R*eflection, w*R*iting and *R*evision. In teaching adult learners, for example, we no longer advocate that learners think about what they want to say and then write it down, rather we encourage learners to do all their thinking on paper, from brainstorming to writing a draft and then revising.

By reflecting on readings, learners are encouraged to write freely and brainstorm what they know about a topic without being worried about the technicalities of writing. Learners think more freely and creatively and as a consequence come up with new ideas and thoughts that can be fashioned into a draft that will be revised. Adult learners bring rich work and life experience to the classroom and the job. It is rare for them not to have some knowledge of a topic, particularly in a work situation. Reflection through writing, then, is about revelation and human possibility. This sort of critical thinking helps people discover the depth and breadth of their thinking on a subject, as well as identify what aspects of a topic they need to know more about. And by revision, we do not mean just checking to make sure the writing is mechanically accurate, but rather the continuous process of reevaluating how our ideas are shaped and presented. Revision allows us to think in stages and to reprocess our thinking so that in the end we present our ideas with consistency, coherence, and unity. Dr. Handley explains that writing is about a writer trying to make ideas accessible and meaningful to his or her audience. Why process, and why think on paper? It is the way ideas are fully developed; through writing we are given access to both our consciousness and unconsciousness. Once people employ the writing process as a way to think, then it becomes an efficient and enriching way to explore and discover their knowledge and feelings about a topic.

Thinking spawns more thinking, which inevitably leads to imagination, risk taking, and innovative ideas. Our management students have told us that learning to use the writing process as a tool has boosted their self-confidence tremendously. Developing a strong, confident voice is no small matter, and neither is engaging in an authentic act of communication. It is relatively easy to start using the writing process, which requires minimal training. Using the writing process may lead to a better collaborative work environment since the writing process sensitizes individuals to value and consider many ideas and become more skilled at developing their own and others' ideas. Transforming managers into collaborative learners, problem solvers, and thinkers has many advantages for organizations. One such advantage is facilitating the transfer of knowledge and enhancing the quality of an organization's professional intellect.

The ability to understand the world from different perspectives allows an educated business manager to be more flexible, better able to compromise and negotiate, better able to cultivate useful working relationships, motivate workers, and understand diversity. Studying the arts and humanities forces people to think in new ways. It is not just about knowing more and gathering more information, but rather it is about coming to understandings which allow for a deeper appreciation of people and ideas, which in turn leads to development of the capacity to build community to develop human potential. This kind of "out of the box" thinking, whose currency is often imagination and intuition in the realm of the senses, is what adult learners often report to be most valuable outside of the management courses they take. The deeper appreciation they develop for the expression of the human spirit broadens their understanding of the world and gives them a perspective on their own life experience as well as the lives of others. Consequently they are better equipped to lead and motivate subordinates, think creatively, take risks, and pursue innovative thinking.

ENABLING MECHANISMS AND STRATEGIES

There are a number of ways by which instructors can create a high-energy learning environment that is both stimulating and appropriate for adult learners. It is highly recommended that instructors shift away from an "understanding by learning" edification to a "learning by doing" pedagogy by considering the following guidelines:

- Strike a balance between soft, value-loaded skills (e.g., mentoring, leadership, communication) and hard, analytically driven skills (e.g., decision science, math, statistics)
- Integrate students' on-the-job training into the instructional design by using an "executive development" style of short courses combining both work and study. Instructors should create opportunities for communication outside the class and via the electronic media (e.g., e-mail).
- Turn instruction into a more issue-based, focused approach utilizing students' work experiences and organizational (or social) images as living cases to examine the issues.
- Present knowledge and provide reasoning and analysis from a multiple perspective and integrative framework. Rely on cross-functional synergies by encouraging students to share their views from different perspectives (e.g., macro, micro, internal, external) and different levels of analysis (e.g., interpersonal, organizational).
- Teach using the case method by preparing data, arguments, and expectations in advance, in order to provide the adult learners with full ownership of the discussion. The activities involved in the case analysis must be driven by the students, and in particular by their images of what works and what does not work. Let them reason and explain the causes and effects of their diagnosis and action plan regarding the case. The instructor should also use questions in a rather provocative way to elicit different perspectives on the focal points under discussion. The tradeoff between depth and breadth of discussion will need to be managed. It is important to maintain mutual respect and a supportive climate by constructively managing intragroup dynamics and conflicts. An instructor might use humor to relieve tension or overcome barriers to group communication and turn the learning process into an enjoyable process.
- Use a competency-based approach to learning with built-in helping mechanisms to facilitate teaching and enhance learning. Center on application and the realization of skills essential for building cross-functional synergies, while also emphasizing

cognitive learning and the internalization of skills necessary for situational management. When used appropriately, the competency-based approach to learning can become a powerful teaching tool!

MANAGEMENT EDUCATION AND DISTANCE LEARNING: FORUM

Nontraditional (i.e., alternative education) schools have, usually since their inception, utilized more flexible structures and methods of teaching to accommodate adult learners' needs. FORUM Management Development Program of SUNY–Empire State College is a case in point. FORUM's philosophy is rooted in the assumption that everything that managers need to know is put in a learning context. Instead of acquiring knowledge through the prism of what they should know, participants are encouraged to use their wisdom and accumulated knowledge and skills and to look at things holigraphically—that is, how the whole fits together. The integrative capstone is implicit: managers create their own paradigms and conceptual frameworks within which learning takes place in an integrative way.

According to Dr. Duncan RyanMann, head of FORUM curriculum committee and an expert in preparing instructors and devising pedagogical strategies for teaching adult learners, the curriculum must simultaneously satisfy the educational goals of individual students, the academic expectations of the institution of higher education, and market-driven corporate needs for the development of skills that will enhance productivity and firm competitiveness. For the individual student, studies are needed that will challenge adult learners to move beyond their current understanding and functioning within an organization. Dr. RyanMann explains that this need can be met through a range of studies that broaden the individual's perception and understanding by engaging academic and professional disciplines that are outside of the adult learner's business functions. It can also occur by deepening the adult learner's knowledge and skill set within his or her chosen field.

In RyanMann's view, colleges and universities have their own set of expectations for skills and competencies and knowledge domains that all students are expected to demonstrate. These may include major or concentration requirements as well as a general education or a core curriculum. These sets of expectations have developed over time to reflect the academy's notion of what it means to be an educated person—

in the context of a particular discipline and in terms of any college diploma.

Building on participants' existing knowledge and work experience, FORUM seeks to facilitate learning that is most relevant to advance participants in their specialized areas while studying the other functions of the enterprise from their own perspectives. Hence, FORUM offers studies such as Accounting for Non-Accounting Managers and Finance for Non-Financial Managers so that nonspecialists can broaden their understanding in other disciplines without the burden of depth in specific areas normally required by traditional business programs. FORUM's added value is reflected in the breadth of studies provided through a flexible approach offering individualized programs through a combination of independent and residency-based learning studies.

FORUM participants are managers and team leaders who have worked their way up the ranks or who have excelled in leading their teams—often beyond the level normally associated with their noncollege backgrounds. The FORUM program allows these experienced managers to complete their degrees by earning substantial credit for their on-the-job learning, combined with guided independent studies and six weekend executive retreats (residencies) per year. The retreats are held in convenient locations around New York State. The substantial training and development program at the participants' companies and the learning acquired by individuals participating at either two-year schools or junior colleges may serve as the basis of advanced standing for the participants. In this way, the typical program participant earns an accelerated B.S. degree in a management discipline in about two years. FORUM also encourages its participants to choose and design their own area of concentration (major), for its philosophy of management development is deeply rooted in the value and importance of individualized programs tailored to individual needs (Fortunato et al., 1995; Belasen et al., 1996).

VALIDATION OF PRIOR LEARNING

Adult learners bring a wealth of knowledge with them from their prior learning experiences that can be converted into college credit. The college-level credit that has been gained comes from company training, work experiences, and personal/community experiences. For example, a student may enter our program with twenty-five years of experience managing a team of thirty individuals. He or she may be well versed in areas such as leadership, total quality management, management competencies, organizational development, human resource management, or labor relations, to name only a few. According to Robyn Silverman, a mentor with FORUM and an expert in evaluating prior learning, an important point to remember when considering converting this demonstrated learning into credit is that the knowledge gained must be college-level learning. This knowledge is often gathered through practice and application, and therefore, it is common for the credit granted to be nonliberal. Silverman explains that the credit-by-evaluation (CBE) process at Empire State College–FORUM Management Education Program begins at the degree-planning level. Students must undergo degree planning to determine which of the learning experiences fit into their chosen degree. Often a student has years of experience and training that, when translated into CBE, make up the bulk of his or her concentration. For example, consider the FORUM student who is developing a Business, Management, and Economics degree with a concentration in Technology Management. With company-based training courses in technology such as Programming and IBM/370; SUN Operating Systems; Oracle Design and Implementation; Database Concepts; Advanced Programming in PL1; and Main Frame Utilities and Process, this individual could receive twenty-three advanced-level technology credits toward his/her concentration.

It is through the credit-by-evaluation (CBE) interview that this information is communicated by the student and assessed by the evaluator. After the student has requested a CBE evaluation from the Assessment Center, an interview appointment is set up between evaluator and student. The evaluator, with a particular expertise in the needed field, assists the student in translating the knowledge into college-level credit. A student may request a specified number of credits in a certain subject at the lower or advanced level. After the interview is completed the evaluator may recommend any of the following: a change in the subject title (evaluator assesses college-level learning in a different, broader or more specific area); a change in the amount of credit (evaluator recommends more or less credit in a particular area); a change in the academic level (evaluator recommends lower-level credits for students who are familiar with facts, definitions, and concepts and upper-level credits for students who are familiar with relationships, knowledge of the discipline, and methodologies). Silverman concludes that the CBE interview gives students an opportunity to communicate the knowledge they have gained through their experiences in work and nonwork situations. Gaining credit for life experiences is a clear validation of the learning that has taken place over many years of hard work and training. Students communicate a great sense of accomplishment when they see that their prior learning is evaluated, converted to credits, and translated into advanced standing to use toward their degree.

OUTCOME ASSESSMENT

Nontraditional schools with a long-term commitment to adding value to their stakeholders have launched outcome assessment programs aimed at receiving feedback about their program effectiveness. These assessment programs have become part of a long-term strategy to further anticipate industry needs, preparation for the future, and institutional legitimacy as a program geared toward relevance, innovation, quality, and credibility. At the operational level, outcome assessment has provided important information about gaps in curriculum and areas for improvement. One such effort, described in Boyatzis and colleagues' *Innovation in Professional Education* (1995), involved curriculum innovation at Weatherhead's MBA program. More recently, SUNY–FORUM has undertaken a similar initiative, but with a much broader focus and more rigorous methodology (Shadle, Belasen & Benke, 1996).

FORUM's outcome assessment has pinpointed the need to aim the curriculum more toward the specific needs of businesses in the context of what is required and anticipated by the companies to meet the changing demands of the marketplace. FORUM students clearly echo the above sentiment by demanding a more vigorous business management program tailored not only to their current professional needs, but also to prepare them to deal more effectively with future changes. They appreciate the opportunity for professional growth, but also want it to become integrated into the whole scheme of corporate change. Moreover, they want to become skilled at dealing and adapting to this change. Curriculum development around the ideas of change and innovation, organizational transformation and leadership roles, competency-based management education, teamwork, time management, business communication, cultural diversity, critical thinking, decision making, and problem solving are the skills that seem to be most profitable for managers now and in the future. The outcome assessment also highlighted students' needs for greater knowledge in the area of social responsibility and citizenship. FORUM's research program also confirmed some of the observations made by corporate leaders—middle managers are concerned about their professional development, but also want it to be within the overall context of their institution and the society at large. Management education programs have an enormous responsibility to meet these needs by involving employers more directly in the process of developing and renewing the curriculum thereby aligning the mission and objectives of the management education programs more effectively with the leadership development and succession planning programs of corporations.

COMPETENCY-BASED MANAGEMENT EDUCATION

Competency-based education is aimed at assuring that participants can take best management practices and transfer them into their everyday experiences. FORUM's competency model is geared toward action learning and rooted in skill assessment, development, and application, similar to the way in which transformational learning involves a shift from the "unconscious ignorance" to the "conscious competence" (Tobin, 1996). Through the process of self-discovery, managers identify what they need to know, locate relevant information, and apply that information to improve work situations. FORUM's competency-based management program is modeled after the Competing Values Framework to leadership, is individually focused, value-added, and outcome oriented.

INDIVIDUALLY FOCUSED

A competency-based program is individually based in that the students' values, knowledge, abilities, and needs are incorporated into the pedagogy of management development through an experiential approach to learning. This experiential approach involves cognitive as well as applied learning. Using diagnostic instruments, students are able to identify their special managerial and professional needs. They then pursue competencies in areas where they are relatively weak or in areas where they have a special interest. A student is encouraged to construct a personal model of self-directed learning matched to his/her particular needs. These needs can be immediate, emergent, or anticipated, and are triggered by the demands of the position or task environment, organizational or technological changes, as well as career and professional opportunities. Since the student is at the center of learning, he or she becomes involved in determining learning priorities and in establishing the boundaries for the learning process. For example, if the student wants to improve her conflict management skills (objective) so she can become more proficient in facilitating group processes (need) in the near future (anticipated), she will initiate action learning in that direction which may include interpersonal communication and resolution strategies (boundary). Much of the learning draws on personal experiences and real work situations and integrates these within a theoretical framework of concepts and approaches. Students are encouraged to use their office desk as a laboratory where they are engaged in applying concepts to practice.

VALUE-ADDED

A competency approach to management education assumes that knowledge is acquired and skills are developed through action learning. As such, the emphasis is on adding value to the students' capacity to act through anticipating changes in their task environments and adapting to these changes through the development of new behavioral skills. Adult learners (e.g., managers) are able to reflect on the outcomes of this adaptation through insights and cause/effect analysis, and leverage the new learning to create high value for themselves, their organizations, and their customers. The value that is added through action learning is then reflected practically through the realization of important abilities and skills that are essential for effective management, and cognitively through internalization of methodologies and knowledge necessary for reasoning and evaluation of the work environment. Thus, a competency approach provides students with a unique opportunity to apply their knowledge and to conceptualize new frames of reference, replicate managerial experiences in individualized, structured learning environments, and to utilize real-life events in learning situations.

A competency-based approach to management integrates the vision that effective managers must have attributes of transformational and transactional managers. These managers are self-defining with strong internalized values and ideals about the future role and direction of their organizations. In performing their roles, these managers are expected to have the skills and abilities to do the following:

- Anticipate industry discontinuities and short product life-cycle shifts.
- Initiate a vision of frame-breaking change that shakes up the preexisting patterns of communication, values, and beliefs

within the organization while at the same time coping with internal organizational stress.

- Align employees with the direction of change through communication processes, skills training, and cultural transformation.
- Motivate and inspire employees to move toward the new vision even if the mission needs to be revised and updated or if the transformation is a long-term process.
- Institutionalize action learning to continually question traditional assumptions and realign employees' attitudes and behaviors around the vision.
- Empower process champions and cross-functional teams to implement the change.
- Develop employees effectively as critical resources for the accomplishment of the transformation.
- Adjust leadership style based on personal insight into strengths and weaknesses.
- Manage paradoxes, deal with contradictions, and cope with tension and discomfort, particularly during periods of restructuring and agenda setting, which leads to greater employee involvement.
- Transcend the culture by shifting the rules governing the organization and positively influencing the norms guiding collective actions.
- Create the conditions for optimal communication competence so that employees are able to redefine the parameters and assumptions of the existing systems and processes, roles and relationships.

These skills cannot be taught through traditional methods of transferring knowledge through low-tech teaching. What effective managers need is art and visualization to expand their interpretations of the complex dynamics they face.

OUTCOME ORIENTED

The focus of the competency-based approach is on the needs, expectations, and objectives of students. It is an approach with a built-in bias toward an outside-in perspective. The structure of the program, its strategy, goals and processes as well as rewards for faculty are driven directly by the values of the "end users"—for example, those who are affected by the learning process. A competency approach creates a commitment structure in which the educational system becomes more responsive to the needs of individuals adapting to the changing needs of their work environment. It runs counter to the traditional, control structure approach in which predetermined disciplines and functions both constrain and define the boundary of learning. As such, a competency-based approach is anchored in meeting and/or exceeding students' needs, values, and expectations.

COMPETING VALUES FRAMEWORK AS A COMPETENCY MODEL

At SUNY–FORUM the Competing Values Framework has been used to construct the competency-based management program. The framework divides what managers do along the lines of roles and competencies. These roles are: director, coordinator, monitor, mentor, facilitator, innovator, broker, and producer. Together these roles represent the range of behaviors and activities which optimize managerial effectiveness. Each role depicted by the CVF has three competencies. Since there are eight roles, the framework currently contains twenty-four competencies.

The framework was discussed at length in chapter 1. Briefly, the domain requiring continual adaptation, innovation, and resource acquisition creates pressures to activate the roles of innovator and broker. The relationships between these two roles and the need to employ flexible managerial behavior is described by the open systems model. The pressures toward standardization and bureaucratization can be described within the context of the internal processes model, which also houses the monitor and coordinator roles. Investments made to improve the quality of work life, achieve greater participation, teamwork, and synergy place a high premium on the HR model and its two roles, the facilitator and mentor. Finally, the need to respond to bottom-line pressures gives rise to the producer and director roles, both of which fall within the boundaries of the rational goal model. To increase the likelihood of responding effectively to these pressures and optimize the behaviors associated with these eight managerial leadership roles, managers can assess their skills in each area, identify the gaps between their current abilities and future needs, and develop action plans and evaluation processes to help improve their existing skills. The program that can help accomplish this goal is called competency-based management education.

COMPETENCY-BASED MANAGEMENT PROGRAM: MODEL BUILDING

Identifying and addressing learning values and needs is essential for a successful competency-based management education program. FORUM's competency program includes components of assessment, analysis, practice, and application. What follows is a short discussion of each of these components.

Assessment of Current Level of Skill Competence and Knowledge

Assessment often includes a judgment that is both intuitive and analytical as to how frequently the skills appear in the student's managerial behavior and whether he or she is consistent in performing specific managerial roles. Some assessments also provide students with images of ideal managerial skill competence against which they can measure their own competence. Other approaches rely on the students' inputs in constructing images of actual and desired competence level. The desired images, of course, become targets to shoot for: the expected outcomes of learning and development. In either case, the goal is to identify a behavioral skill gap which then serves as the baseline for personal development and self-improvement. At FORUM we use a model (depicted in figure 9.1) that combines elements of both approaches and, therefore, allows students to "customize" the form and pace of their self-improvement.

Conceptual Learning of Principles of Management

Learning in this context includes conceptual frameworks, models of behavior, and concepts that have wide applicability across situations. This learning spans over topics with theoretical underpinnings and practical applications with the operating assumption being that a learning curve is both cumulative and developmental. The theory provides the student with a comparative basis against which common managerial practices are measured and intelligent conclusions can be drawn. This learning helps enrich and expand the knowledge of the student rather than rewrite it. Learning can take any pedagogical form—readings, group discussions, role modeling, creative writing, critical thinking, and so on. Since the student is in "control" of the learning process, he or she is also responsible for maintaining enough creative tension to keep the momentum of learning alive. Self-directed learning becomes a powerful medium for improvement when the learner is self-motivated and when the drive is generated internally.

Figure 9.1. FORUM's Competency-Based Program

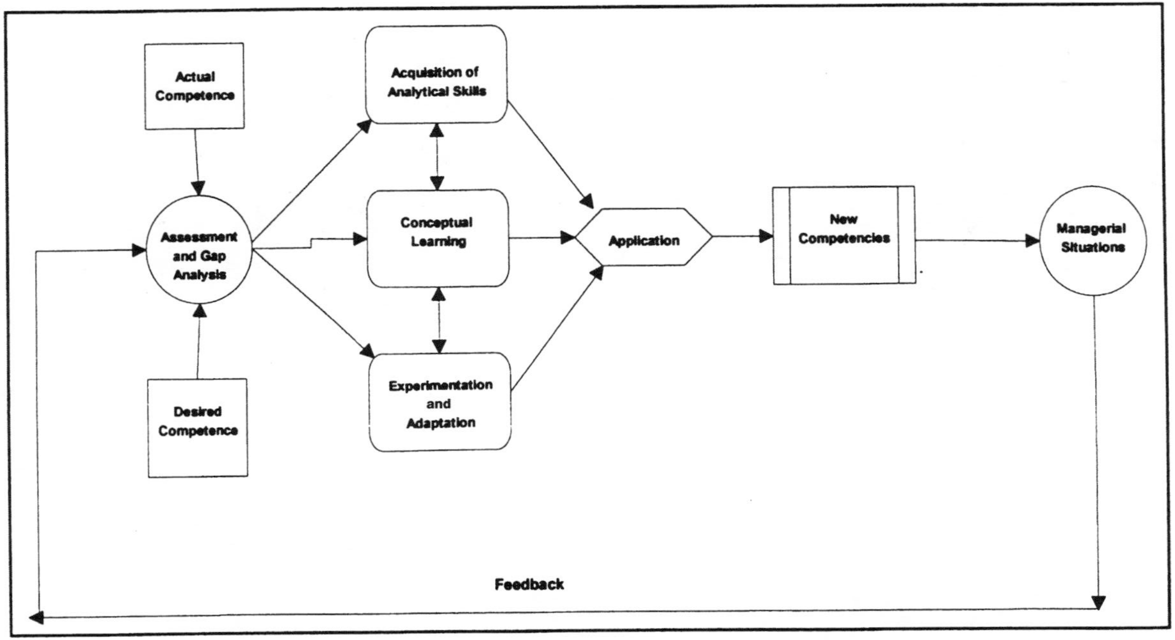

Acquisition of Analytical Skills to Bridge the Gap between Intellectual Assimilation and Behavioral Application

Gaining analytical skills can help students move from cognitive learning to the actual application of new behavioral skills. A competency-based approach to management is geared toward identifying the skills essential for analyzing situations. Students are put into structured learning environments and given opportunities to practice their skills. They receive systematic feedback that is both reinforcing and evaluative. They then reflect back on their analysis and experiment with contingencies. As they strengthen existing skills or develop new ones, knowledge is gained and expanded.

Experimentation with and Adaptation of the Behavioral Principles to Individual Needs

Once new behavioral skills and competencies are developed and refined, students become the center stage for experimenting and adopting new modes of behavior which reflect their learning. For example, if the outcome of goal setting using the SMART principles (mentioned in Chapter 1) proves successful, and the student practices and experiments with the new competency in a number of variations, then the student is expected to expand his or her cognitive map to include this competency on a consistent basis.

Skill Application to Sustain Learning over Time

Once the new behavioral skills have been adapted and a pattern of competent behavior is exercised across situations, the learning is complete. At this point the student is expected to reflect back on his/her experience and check the behavioral skills against the expectations of others, as well as changes in the environment. This process is important for it provides the student with valuable feedback to adjust the behavioral skills, add new elements to the competence that has been previously developed, or redefine its boundaries and scope. This process inevitably leads to a new assessment of needs whereby current skills are reassessed and weighted against the changing conditions of the managerial environment. Thus the process of learning is recycled.

THE STRUCTURE OF FORUM'S COMPETENCY-BASED PROGRAM

FORUM's competency-based program draws on the Competing Values Framework of leadership discussed above. The program, essentially a competency-based management concentration, consists of three sequential key components: Preassessment, 8 × 3 core competencies, and postassessment. Credit by evaluation (CBE) can be generated at the core component. The preassessment, core competencies, and postassessment together constitute the essence of the concentration for a total of twenty-three credits. The rest of the credits typically come from "complementary" studies such as quantitative (e.g., math, statistics), sociobehavioral (e.g., organizational behavior), and performance (e.g., operations management). The preassessment and/or core competencies can also be taken as stand-alone studies to satisfy the requirements for a degree. However, students are generally advised to complete the entire sequence to conclude their concentration in competency-based management.

PREASSESSMENT

The underlying assumption of this component is that via the process of self-assessment, students will be able to identify managerial values and attitudes, determine their capabilities and needs to guide themselves through a process of self-directed learning, which ultimately should lead to self-improvement. The purpose of this component, therefore, is to learn a method for self-assessing students' management-related knowledge and abilities, diagnose strengths and weaknesses, and formulate plans for skill development. Students coming into the concentration use assessment instruments and engage in some guided activities. The assessments include input from self and associates that results in a composite profile highlighting the students' managerial strengths and weaknesses within the Competing Values Framework of leadership.

8 × 3 COMPETENCIES BY ROLE

Eight learning contracts (independent, guided) paralleling the eight leadership roles comprise the core of the competency management concentration. Each role has three interrelated competencies and, taken together, all twenty-four (8 × 3) define the core content of the concentration (see figure 9.2). The objectives of these learning contracts (LCs) are:

- To appreciate both the values and the weaknesses associated with the particular role
- To acquire and use the competencies associated with the particular role

Figure 9.2. The Sequence of the Competency-Based
Management Concentration

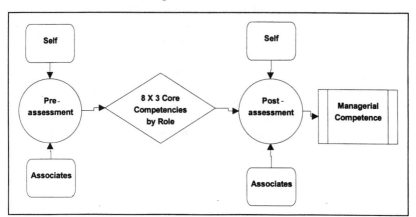

- To integrate dynamically the competencies associated with the particular role in managerial situations

Each learning contract is a series of short assignments involving elements of the competency approach: learning, analysis, practice, and application as discussed above. The assessment instruments help identify areas of weakness and strength in students' abilities and skills. Students can suggest CBEs in the areas where they feel particularly strong and take learning contracts to remedy deficiencies or further develop their skills.

POSTASSESSMENT

This is the capstone component of the competency-based management concentration. Essentially, students who participate in the concentration are expected to replicate the same procedure suggested in the preassessment, except that here the intention is to verify whether the gap between the initial profile and the desired one has been narrowed, or whether the desired goal or target-profile has been attained. Students also engage in learning and applying a series of strategies aimed at helping them sustain the results of their self-improvement effort and achieve higher levels of competence.

SUMMARY: LEARNING AND COMPETENCE IN MANAGEMENT EDUCATION

The methodology of SUNY–FORUM's competency-based management program integrates cognitive and behavioral methods of learning into an integrated framework of learning, thus responding effectively to market and academic challenges. Competency-based management education helps to reconcile both realities "in a way that systematically integrates the best features of a variety of traditional methods, and treats thinking and doing, and learning and applying as mutually enhancing learning processes" (Whetten and Clark, 1996, p. 153). An important outcome of participating in a program such as the one described above is a competency-based management degree at the baccalaureate level. This program provides students with a unique opportunity to engage in a continuous learning process. Continuous learning is like a race without a finish line—students create a baseline (the actual skill-competence) and a benchmark line (the desired skill-competence profile), in effect constructing a mental map of where they wish to be in the future. The benchmark is the lighthouse that guides and directs their actions and self-improvement efforts. Once achieved, the benchmark becomes a basis for a higher-level goal to be challenged.

Learning and competence are dialectically related and both are important elements of effective managerial leadership: Learning is a dimension of competence and competence is embedded in learning. Learning leads to competence and competence facilitates and even triggers new learning. As global change increases in speed and complexity, managers must be prepared to face the challenge of developing new competencies and increasing their capacity to learn. A management education program with a mission compatible with these goals is both responsive and accountable.

I have always emphasized competency-based management education as constituting the essential link between academe and market. I continue to argue that competency-based management education responds constructively to market criticisms of academic institutions as being too broad, abstract, impractical, nontransferable, and as being "unable to respond quickly and trapped in a discipline-bound view of knowledge" (to cite a view expressed by corporate leaders). Competency-based management education is rooted in action learning and skill development and includes an assessment of the competencies needed by managers to become effective and help align organizational capabilities with organizational strategies. Competency-based manage-

ment education represents a value-adding and outcome-oriented pedagogy that is sensitive to the needs of organizations and managers to
"learn by doing" rather than "understand by listening."

Competency-based management education also responds to challenges coming from the academe that markets and organizations are
only concerned with a "bottom-line" approach to management education, based on a focused, application-oriented methodology that is at
best inductive and therefore noninclusive and noncomparable. Markets
rely more on nontheoretically based assumptions, are geared toward an
idiosyncratic view of the world, are empirically driven, and are interested in skills development more so than acquisition of knowledge.
Since competency-based management education is a theoretically
founded framework that has been tested and validated across situations (e.g., organizational life cycle, organizational culture, organizational hierarchy, managerial leadership), it is as valid and reliable a
theoretical construct as are other organization and leadership theories
used and taught by academic institutions. FORUM's competency-based
management program helps its students/managers become more proficient in performing their managerial roles, while adding value to their
organizations. The value of competency-based management education
is in making management education programs more relevant and accountable and in challenging managers to continuously pursue self-
development through life-long learning.

CONCLUSIONS: DEVELOPING MANAGERIAL COMPETENCIES AND THE MENTOR ROLE

The key to successful mentoring is developing and maintaining
effective relationships between managers and their employees or team
members. Studies showed that the cycle of developmental relationships
between pairs of mentors and mentees moves through the phases of initiation, cultivation, separation, and redefinition. Each phase is characterized by particular affective experiences, developmental functions,
and interaction patterns that are shaped by both individual needs and
organizational circumstances. A mentoring relationship has the potential to enhance the career and professional development of employees
or team members. Through career functions, including sponsorship,
coaching, protection, exposure and visibility, and challenging work assignments, team members can learn the ropes of organizational life.
Through psychosocial functions including role modeling, acceptance
and confirmation, counseling, and friendship, team members can de-

velop a sense of competence, confidence, and effectiveness in the leadership roles (Kram, 1983).

In the role of mentor, managers know the importance of self-development and developing the managerial competencies of future organizational leaders. As discussed in chapters 4 and 7, developing the leadership capabilities of members of horizontal organizations and particularly those participating in self-managed teams is an important responsibility of managers performing the mentor role. Developing the human capital of the organization and particularly the competencies associated with managerial leadership is an important part of organizational strategic staffing. Strategic staffing or closing the gap between current competencies and anticipated needs is a human resource management goal that can support and enhance organizational capabilities and ultimately improve organizational effectiveness. Redesigning core competencies, leadership, and succession around strategic objectives, while upgrading managerial skills to create the "right fit" talent for management positions can help support corporate vision.

Earlier we discussed how competitive markets and industry discontinuity are the driving forces behind the adaptive responses of organizations. Two important requirements were stressed:

- Organizations are expected to do more with fewer resources.
- Leaders are expected to rethink radically how to move people and successfully revitalize and navigate organizations in their domain of operations.

These requirements call for leaders who are both transformational and instrumental, to whom we refer as high-performance leaders. These leaders are self-defining with strong internalized values and ideals about the future role and direction of their organizations. High-performance leaders recognize people as resources rather than costs. They have trust and confidence in employees, and therefore, are first to empower and delegate authority. The most important role of the leader, in this context, is to recognize the importance of the mentor role by instilling trust, communicating values, and creating a learning environment where everyone participates and contributes. An important responsibility of high-performance leaders enacting the mentor role is to develop a cadre of competent managers with an inner purpose and direction and with congruent values, who potentially can become future organizational leaders. Chapter 10 expands on these ideas by describing the characteristics, capabilities, and skills of high-performance leaders initiating and leading the learning organization.

Conclusion

10

High-Performance Leadership: Initiating Transformational Learning

Our challenge is to drive for a culture that enables all employees to fully contribute to the success of our company. We must help transform today's managers into tomorrow's leaders.

—George M. C. Fisher, Eastman Kodak

High-performance leadership is the moving force that helps organizations create a vision of success, embrace a new ideology, and carry out a reshaped mission. High-performance leadership involves frame-breaking and shaking up the equilibrium. High-performance leaders believe in constant renewal, thrive on chaos and discontinuity, worship inconsistency, and produce movement. This leader combines an authoritative personality with referent power to produce a committed followership. High-performance leaders are navigators with anticipatory skills who lead their organization through threatening territories without losing direction. This leader is what Drucker has labeled a "monomaniac with mission."

A high-performance leader has conceptual skills and enough creative tension to fold and unfold, frame and reframe, to understand contradictory demands and deal with them effectively. A high-performance leader is both charismatic and instrumental at the same time. Charismatic leadership involves:

- Having a long range perspective, envisioning and generating excitement in followers
- Energizing people through role modeling
- Influencing people's attitudes and enabling them to challenge goals innovatively
- Inspiring trust

An instrumental leader channels organizational energy and member aspirations in the right direction through:

- Focusing on systems, initiating structures, and defining roles and responsibilities
- Determining performance standards and monitoring and evaluating results
- Having a short-term perspective, motivating and rewarding employees
- Administering programs and controlling people

High-performance leaders have the cognitive capacity to perceive the world as a constantly evolving complex/dynamic system. To interact effectively with this world, high-performance leaders employ multiple perspectives or frames. In responding to the readings of their environments, these leaders often combine a highly structured and analytical frame of reference with intuitive, more flexible patterns of thinking. These leaders thrive on randomness, ambiguity, and contradiction, and they transform paradoxes and problems into opportunities for generating innovative responses. High-performance leaders maintain relatively longer periods of peak performance and are better equipped for coping with stress than are average leaders. They use imagination to develop new insights, pose new challenges, and improve their organization capacity for learning, dialogue, and change. High-performance leaders possess a "built-in" creative tension that allows them to employ more than one frame of reference to make sense of the world. They are engaged in Janusian thinking, transcending or reframing perceptual tensions that help them achieve important breakthroughs. Janusian thinking was found to be the common thought pattern behind all breakthroughs and significant contributions made to society by such highly creative individuals as Mozart, Picasso, and Einstein. Their innovations occurred when opposites were brought together (Quinn, 1988).

Creative tension and dissatisfaction with the status quo ignite action learning and energize the process of intellectual arousal toward peak performance. Creative tension is the force that helps leaders constantly search for and identify new "comfort zones" and new patterns of possibility. Burdett (1993) lists ten principles that high-performance leaders employ to create the context for action learning and for the regeneration of creative tension. High performance leaders:

1. Benchmark with both the best in the industry and the best, period
2. Move from seniority to meritocracy
3. Improve the quality and openness of performance feedback by including peers and subordinates in the process
4. Remove senior managers who present poor role modeling
5. Encourage risk
6. Take nondecision-making levels out of hierarchy
7. Reward success
8. Destroy concepts of turf
9. Strive for synergies
10. Focus on outputs

High-performance leaders generate energy from within; when it erupts, it captures the minds and hearts of employees. It is positive energy transformed into a centripetal force that pulls people together by creating a shared meaning and commitment to core values. As Jack Welch has described: "No [CEO] can come to work and sit, no one can go off and think of just policy, no one can do any of these things. You've got to be live action all day. And you've got to be able to energize others. You cannot be this thoughtful, in-the-corner-office guru . . . you cannot be a moderate, balanced, thoughtful, careful articulator of policy. You've got to be on the lunatic fringe" (*The Washington Post*, March 23, 1997, H1). This "out-of-balance" leadership is what helps transform learning into action. The inner motivation that inspires people to believe in the new direction and support that belief. This is the essence of referent power exercised through exemplary leadership and the assimilation of organizational values by employees. The leader forms an ideology that preserves a type of order within the organization and that guides people's thoughts and belief systems, giving the illusion that organizational members are united by superordinate goals. This illusion, however, is positively associated with conformity and support for the vision of top leadership. The new rules of behaviors, patterned after high-performance leaders, are intended to be emulated and adopted by followers. Hence, high-performance leaders achieve control that is socially construed. Active consent, rather than passive acceptance, occurs through self-regulated behavior that is concertively and socially controlled. Organizational members identify themselves and their values with that of high-performance leaders, thus giving legitimacy to the leader's goals and actions. Once the leader broadens the support for his/her ideology, a new culture evolves that serves to operationalize that ideology. These leaders enact the culture to which they later adapt. The leader's ideology and the organizational ideology are inseparable. It is difficult to understand the significance and consequences of artifacts and paradigms of behavior or to anticipate them without knowing the beliefs and core values that influence them.

A strong culture can provide alternate forms of structure and control without the need to resort to formal, bureaucratic mechanisms of control (Kotter & Heskett, 1992). High-performance leaders do not need to exercise their formal sources of power. The social structure of the organization and its core values symbolize their power. This power goes almost unnoticed. Members are infused with normative behaviors and regularities that serve to legitimize actions. Influential members with high value congruence are also perceived as powerful. These people are routinely associated with socializing, indoctrinating, sanctioning, and/or rewarding people who demonstrate conformity or deviation. Often, however, they achieve greater compliance by the simple method of role modeling, hence reinforcing desired behaviors and strengthening value congruence. Role modeling is what makes the ultimate leader an exemplary leader.

EXEMPLARY LEADERSHIP

Percy Barnevik, former CEO of Asea Brown Boveri (ABB), a global holding company, is an excellent example of a high-performance leader who used a unique approach in applying many of the above principles. In an interview, Barnevik revealed the secrets of his company's success story:

> ABB is a company with no geographic center, no national ax to grind. We are a federation of national companies with a global coordination center. Are we a Swiss company? Our headquarters is in Zurich, but only 100 professionals work at headquarters and we will not increase that number. Are we a Swedish company? I am the CEO, and I was born and educated in Sweden. But our headquarters is not in Sweden, and only two of the

eight members of our board of directors are Swedes. Perhaps we are an American company. We report our financial results in U.S. dollars, and English is ABB's official language. We conduct all high-level meetings in English. My point is that ABB is none of those things—and all of those things. We are not homeless. We are a company with many homes. (Taylor, 1991, p. 92)

ABB is a large-scale transnational company but with the attitude of a small business due to its five thousand (!) profit-center teams. These centers operate with a great deal of autonomy balanced with accountability. This way, managers or engineers can make decisions without the approval of headquarters while the top managers move around the different areas to spread their expertise. "I now have an army of 25,000 in profit-center teams," says Barnevik. "If you can really build a small-business atmosphere, you don't have to push or entice managers every day. It becomes a self-motivated force" (Schares, 1993, p. 204). Committed to this value, in all sixty acquisitions worth $3.6 billion made between 1987 and 1990, Barnevik slashed administrative staff by up to 90 percent. Such radical restructuring did not come without protests from unions and governments. "The important thing is to judge how much you can rock the boat without sinking it" (Schares, 1993, p. 205), he says. Seven years after becoming CEO of Sweden's Asea, Barnevik merged his company with Switzerland's Brown Boveri, creating Europe's largest electrical engineering company. One year later, he initiated the massive process of consolidation and rationalization in the merged company. The Zurich headquarters staff was slashed by 95 percent—from four thousand to two hundred people! Peripheral businesses were dropped, five thousand profit centers were created, and seven layers of management were reduced to four. Finally, he restructured the entire organization creating thirteen hundred companies, some of which had as few as ten employees. "When it comes to shaking up a big company," he said, "you can practically never do too much at one time" (Schares, 1993, p. 205).

Large organizational size becomes a liability by making adaptation a slow process and change too difficult to implement. Therefore, by divesting or decentralizing their operations, large organizations can create new, smaller units that are capable of adapting to rapid marketplace changes. These self-contained units, which operate as profit centers, are better equipped to deal with shorter product life cycles than are large, hierarchical organizations. This structure allows top management to establish control systems to oversee unit performance. Business units are responsible for creating strategic alliances with other organizations, as well as interdependencies with sister units. Headquarters acts as a holding company responsible mainly for pooling resources and coordination across the units. As a federation of thirteen hundred national companies with a global coordination center, ABB's companies have the leverage to create joint ventures and network with other regional, national, or international companies to achieve a quick response time to market changes and demands.

This global federation of national companies has become the new model of competitive enterprise: a holding company which combines global scale and world-class technology with deep roots in local markets. It is what Barnevik has called a "multidomestic organization" that in certain aspects is superglobal, as he explained:

> The vast majority of our businesses . . . fall somewhere between the superlocal and the superglobal. These are the businesses in which building a multidomestic organization offers powerful advantages. You want to be able to optimize a business globally—to specialize in the production of components, to drive economies of scale as far as you can, to rotate managers and technologies around the world to share expertise and solve problems. But you also want to have deep local roots everywhere you operate—building products in the countries where you sell them, recruiting the best local talent from the universities, working with the local government to increase exports. If you build such an organization, you create a business advantage that's damn difficult to copy. (Taylor, 1991, p. 92)

Barnevik has articulated three principles for encouraging personal initiatives in all of the companies:

- Managers must make decisions fast and be right.
- They must make decisions fast and occasionally be wrong.
- They cannot make decisions slowly.

The results of the restructuring and the new management philosophy were astonishing: By 1989, sales rose 54 percent and profits jumped 53 percent! During the same year, Barnevik further penetrated the American market. He acquired both Combustion Engineering, a manufacturer of power-generation and process automation equipment, for $0.6 billion and Westinghouse Electronics' electrical transmission and distribution business in a transaction involving twenty-five factories with revenues of $1 billion, thus making ABB the world's top electrical engineering company. ABB acquired turbine manufacturer Zamech during 1991 and began restructuring, sending technology, finances, and skills eastward.

One year later, Barnevik launched a Swedish pilot program to cut the time to perform all company tasks from administrative to R&D by 50 percent. During 1992, he had launched his global competitiveness drive by cutting cycle time by up to 50 percent. Since 1988 and by the end of 1992, productivity as measured by sales per employee rose by about 40 percent and profitability as measured by return on capital, although short of his goal of 25 percent, stood at 18 percent. Finally in 1993 he carved up ABB's global business into a triad: Europe, America, and Asia. He shrank the size of the board from twelve to eight and actively scanned the Asian markets for new business opportunities. In August 1993, due to market slowdown and a 17 percent plunge in profits, he took a $500 million write-off charge to close fifteen plants around the world. Additionally, he made plans to trim about 1000 employees per month from ABB's 218,000 personnel.

LEARNING AND BENCHMARKING

One of Barnevik's most potent weapons for creating converts was through action learning. He typically got one factory running at peak efficiency and then brought in skeptical managers from less profitable units across the world to evaluate it. "You have to exploit your success stories to break resistance," he argued frequently, "We human beings are driven by habit, history . . . to break direction you have to shake people up, not by threatening them, not by offering a bonus, but by illustrating in a similar situation what can be accomplished" (Schares, 1993, p. 208). Barnevik is also a strong fan of communication. Walking the talk is what management is about. Open communication encourages employees to break the mold and innovate. Everyone is involved in communication and so information about performance is disseminated across levels and between profit centers. Giving workers access to performance figures helps energize a competitive spirit within the organization. And Barnevik even takes it the extra mile through internal benchmarking. Monthly performance rankings at ABB's fifty transformer plants, for example, put managers on the spot if they are not near the top of the list. "The absolute overriding successful thing is cases, cases, cases" he asserts, "we don't wonder how a competitor does it. The competitor is inside ABB. We can go and look at his books" (Schares, 1993, p. 211).

In 1990, Barnevik set goals of $1.5 billion in Eastern European sales by 1995, investing $1 billion in Asia, where he expects to generate one-third of ABB's sales by the year 2000, a 25 percent return on capital and a 10 percent profit margin by 1995, thus making ABB a dominant company selling power equipment to the world. His vision of ABB has included more decentralization down to the factory floor in Sweden, breaking up work patterns, and promoting continuous learning and teamwork without formal supervision. He wanted to delegate more and more autonomy to each small work group, widen responsibility and rotate jobs to foster versatility. Barnevik viewed problems and challenges as catalysts for improvement. "You can get enormous change when you are forced to redesign your processes all the time . . . You constantly have new targets, new targets, new targets" (Schares, 1993, p. 211). In his vision, the revolution never stops.

The sluggish results of 1993, however, turned ABB's attention to benchmarking its most powerful and successful yet fiercest competitor in the electromechanical field, GE. The purpose of the benchmarking was to see why GE's economic performance is superior to its competitors' and what ABB can learn from GE. The benchmarking effort centered on GE's transformation at two levels: (a) strategically in its portfolio and businesses, and (b) culturally in creating a company committed to change and innovation. The targets for benchmarking were GE Power Systems, ABB's main competitor in the gas and steam turbine markets, and GE Capital Services, the financial arm of GE. Power Systems showed GE's depth and Capital Services indicated GE's width. In fact, GE Power Systems is in direct competition with ABB's power division. GE reported signing its largest contract for 1995, a $1.3 billion deal to supply power generation equipment to two power plants in Saudi Arabia (*Albany Times Union*, June 6, 1995, A-9). This win parallels GE's billion-dollar plus deal to supply equipment to Tokyo Electric Power in 1993. Both deals represent important steps in GE's effort to become a global player in the power generation market and a strategic threat to ABB. Benchmarking this division represented a challenge and an opportunity for ABB to learn what makes GE's Power Systems so successful. GE's Industrial and Power Systems overlap ABB in the key areas of steam turbines, gas turbines, nuclear reactors, and environmental control. In fact, GE developed products in the turbine business for both gas and steam, which increasingly topped its best competitor's market share: 1.7 for steam and 1.6 for gas for the two years between 1990 and 1992.

ABB decided to benchmark GE for several important reasons:

- Sales to value-added ratio per employee was $224,000, not far behind Mitsubishi Electric ($261,000), with ABB at $70,000 closing the list of the seven best companies in the global market.

- In 1992, GE's operating profits were higher than those of all of its competitors combined! Its profits amounted to $7.7 billion, while that of its six competitors (ABB, Hitachi, Siemens, Mitsubishi, Toshiba, and GEC Alsthow) was $6.84 billion.
- GE led its major competitors in terms of return on sales of about 13 percent in 1992, with its best competitor settling for about 7 percent and the worst competitor at a flat 2 percent margin.
- During 1984–1992, not only had GE outgrown its competitors by achieving growth revenues of 10 percent, it was also the only one which had reduced its workforce by 2 percent. Comparatively, ABB achieved a 7 percent growth in revenues and a 4 percent growth in its number of employees.
- By mid 1993, GE's market value (capitalization) reached over $79 billion, while ABB's was $10.7 billion. Moreover, market value per employee clearly showed that GE is the best: $269,000 versus ABB's $43,000 for the end of 1992.
- With its overlapping market, power systems, and industrial businesses (transportation systems, motors, electrical distribution and control, and lighting), totaling $13.3 billion, GE clearly outperformed ABB by showing 11 percent increase in its total earning for 1992. Moreover, GE's revenues from international businesses showed a steady increase to 10 percent overall in 1992.

What does all of this mean for ABB?

A benchmark team analysis for ABB proposed two critical issues to boost the company's competitiveness in the global market:

- ABB can do more in terms of profits, new business opportunities, and culture.
- ABB must focus on processes and people instead of functions and politics in serving external customers, managing and propelling businesses, fostering change, and further globalizing the company.

But the conclusion of the benchmark team analysis suggested the kind of competition ABB faces in the marketplace: Competing with GE means aiming for a rapidly moving target! Satisfied with the drive toward quality and higher productivity, Barnevik turned his attention during 1994 to speed and reduction of cycle times as the prime strategic goal for the company. Famous for its T-50 (that is time minus 50 percent) program, Barnevik set out to decrease lead times and further improve customer service. His goal was to decrease cycle times 90 percent for field work, 60 percent for manufacturing, and 30 percent for engineering. Due to robotics, ABB has been able to increase manufacturing speeds by 25 percent while improving path accuracy by six times. Additionally, computer simulations have reduced engineering times and improved accuracy. According to Barnevik, ABB spent about $700 million on information systems and at any given time ABB computer networks are being used to track fifteen thousand projects involving as many as fifty thousand companies (*Forbes*, 12/5/1994, p. 65).

During 1996, Barnevik kept stressing expansion into emerging markets, especially the former Soviet Union, India, China, and Southeast Asia, as well as Eastern Europe. Here, again, Barnevik's strategy was to train native engineers and managers to run local operations. With the matrix management structure still in place to promote internal integration, these managers reported simultaneously to a country manager and to a business area manager. By June 1996, ABB reported a 22 percent increase in net income to $556 million, despite a slowdown in Western Europe and the United States. About one year later, however, the *New York Times* (10/22/1997, C2) reported that the company will cut ten thousand jobs in Western Europe and the United States and will shift its attention to Asia. The restructuring will cost ABB an estimated $850 million and will reduce its global workforce to about 115,000 people. The announcement about the massive cut came under the leadership of Barnevik's successor Goran Lindahl a year after Barnevik stepped down as the chairman and chief executive of ABB.

A MATRIX STRUCTURE THAT WORKS!

ABB's competitive advantage does not just come from restructuring and maintaining highly decentralized structures. ABB's strength also comes from its technological edge, particularly in the areas of tilting trains and high-speed rail networks. Second, the business diversity at ABB has allowed it to nationalize and specialize across international borders, and thus have a competitive leverage versus other competitors. Third, ABB's unique structure allows it to become a superlocal company and take advantage of opportunities as they arise in local markets. But it also provides ABB with a sociocultural, economic, and geographic familiarity with different countries, thus rendering adaptation smoother and faster. Sourcing components locally helps global firms reduce costs, gives them a better understanding of local markets and regulations, and can improve their chances of winning contracts.

ABB is aiming to increase the share of local content in its power-generation equipment from 25 percent to 50 percent. Its competitor, Siemens, recently struck a series of deals with a Chinese state-owned firm to manufacture large coal-fired power stations. In recent bids for IPPs in Thailand, Japan's Marubeni, Belgium's Tractebel, and America's Bechtel all have became involved in joint ventures with Thai companies (*The Economist*, October 28, 1995, p. 79).

Barnevik created a matrix organization that has successfully resolved three internal contradictions: ABB is global and local, big and small, and radically decentralized with centralized reporting and control. "The matrix is the framework through which we organize our activities. It allows us to optimize our businesses globally and maximize performance in every country in which we operate" (Taylor, 1991, p. 96). ABB's matrix has two dimensions: along one dimension the company is a distributed global network with top executives making decisions and forming strategies regardless of national boundaries. A collection of national companies, each serving its home market as effectively as possible, is organized along a second dimension. ABB's global matrix holds the two dimensions together. Barnevik leads ABB, together with twelve members of the executive committee, who share multiple responsibilities for eight businesses. Leaders of the fifty business areas (BA) located worldwide report to them. The BA leaders form and champion global strategies, hold factories around the world to cost and quality standards, allocate export markets to each factory, and share expertise by rotating people across national borders. Parallel to the BA structure is a country structure with presidents, balance sheets, income statements, and career ladders. The BA structure meets the national structure at the level of ABB's member companies. There are thirteen hundred member companies spread around the world. Each member company has a local president who reports to both the national president and to the BA leader, who is usually located outside the country. In this grid ABB's multidomestic structure becomes a reality.

The matrix structure allows ABB to integrate the flow of resources globally and bring together supplies, manufacturing, and marketing. It also allows ABB to maintain an optimal balance between globalization-strategy through standardization, and multidomestic-strategy through differentiation and customization. "The BA leader is a business strategist and global optimizer. He decides which factories are going to make what products, what export markets each factory will serve, how the factories should pool their expertise and research funds for the benefit of the business worldwide' (Taylor, 1991, p. 97). The presidents of the local companies must be excellent profit center managers and must be able to balance the requirements that come from the global boss (i.e., the BA manager) with those coming from the country boss.

ABB's unique structure permits top management to take full advantage of a centralized control philosophy within coordinated decentralized profit centers, thus enjoying a world of both integration and flexibility. Once a decision is made, it is communicated down to the BA level, country level, and local company level for quick implementation. The members of the executive committee meet every three weeks to discuss global strategy and performance. "These same managers individually monitor business segments, countries, and staff functions. So when we make a decision—snap, it's covered. The members of the executive committee communicate to their subordinates, the BA managers and the country managers, and the implementation process is under way" (Taylor, 1991, p. 100). The matrix structure allows ABB to respond quickly through the application of technical expertise by its diverse business areas and the operating companies located worldwide. The company has evolved through acquisitions, mergers, geographical dispersion, and national diversity to become a transnational organization. The matrix, with its centralized control, permits ABB to achieve global coordination. The decentralized profit centers, at the local level, provide flexibility and adaptability to local markets. The matrix, then, creates a huge strategic advantage for ABB. The matrix design incorporates both unity and diversity; it promotes action learning both globally and locally. ABB is an information technology (IT) organization that is constantly learning and adapting through worldwide cooperation among self-sufficient units.

Another transnational company employing the matrix design is Unilever, which sells food products and detergents. The matrix structure at Unilever consists of a committee of an executive triad collectively in charge of five strategic groups. Reporting to them are the operating national companies. Through selective recruitment, management education systems, and a network of attachments (where a manager can be placed temporarily in either a head-office department or a subsidiary), Unilever has instituted a continuously evolving action learning program. In addition, Unilever maintains informal transnational networks with managers from across the company's functions, business units, and local operations. These networks are engaged in information sharing, problem solving, and even strategy formulation. One of Unilever's vice presidents evaluated the company's structure:

> The very nature of our products requires proximity to local markets; economies of scale in certain functions justify a number of head-office de-

partments; and the need to benefit from everybody's creativity and experience makes a sophisticated means of transferring information across our organization highly desirable. All of these factors led to our present structure; a matrix of individual managers around the world who nonetheless share a common vision and understanding of corporate strategy." (Maljers, 1992, p. 46)

The matrix is the utmost mechanism of coordination through mutual adjustment and direct communication. A matrix structure fosters creativity and innovation and promotes efficiency and fast response. Floris Maljers, the cochairman and CEO of Unilever, uses the analogy of the quadrille dance to illustrate the essence of the matrix design: "This is an old-fashion dance, in which four people change places regularly. This is also how a good matrix should work, with sometimes the regional partner, sometimes the product partner, sometimes the functional partner, and sometimes the labor-relations partner taking the lead. Flexibility rather than hierarchy should always be a transnational motto" (1992, p. 51).

BUILDING CORPORATE LOYALTY: MERGING CULTURES

Creating a seamless organization is a long and evolving process that should be managed carefully, especially when the acquiring firm seeks to impose its own culture without regard to the core values of the acquired firm. Organizational cultures that are separated by contradictory values and realities challenge leaders to foster loyalty and facilitate the assimilation process to reduce cultural clash and resistance. The acquisition of a firm often implies new organizational practices, new rules, new goals, and the need for a new identity. Senior managers must renew employees' commitment to the organizational goals and establish the trust and identity essential for rebuilding corporate loyalty. Paying more attention to the history and norms of behaviors underlying the culture of the merged company, showing respect for employees' feelings, and working toward rebuilding trust and regaining employees' commitment will transcend into more loyal customers and investors for the corporation. For Reichheld (1996), for example, the fundamental goal of a business is not profit but value creation. Companies create value by understanding that they can only retain loyal customers with a base of loyal employees.

Nahavandi and Malekzadeh (1995) devised an interesting typology that can help managers understand the dynamics involved in the integration of cultures, particularly those involving global mergers. The typology is based on two dimensions with incompatible values: First, "multiculturalism" describes the degree to which an organization values cultural diversity and is willing to tolerate and encourage it. In contrast, a company favoring "uniculturalism" will tend to impose its own culture and organizational practices. Second is the type of diversification strategy used by the company in its acquisitions, whether it acquires companies with related or unrelated business lines (see figure 10.1).

While integration implies that both firms keep their own identity, assimilation is only structural. A full assimilation occurs when the acquiring firm culturally absorbs the acquired firm. A separation occurs when both firms keep their organizational and cultural systems; the acquired firm is autonomous. Deculturation implies that no cultural identity emerges. For example, while GE's strategy is generally to acquire unrelated companies with high profit potential and to transpose its own culture on the acquired company (deculturation), ABB acquires its direct competitors (related firms) and encourages them to keep their identity. Thus, ABB's mode of acculturation relates more to integration. Preferably, the mode of acculturation must be the result of a mutual agreement between the acquired and acquiring firms. This also helps reduce unnecessary tension, conflict, and resistance that can slow down the integration process. Resistance is greater when the employees of the acquired company perceive the need for change as threatening. While they may accept the acquiring firm's right to introduce new structural arrangements, procedures, policies, and so forth, they may resist the goals and norms of the dominating organization. Managing organiza-

Figure 10.1. Acculturation in Mergers and Acquisitions

Culture: Degree of Multiculturalism

		Multicultural	Unicultural
Diversification strategy: Degree of relatedness of firms	Related	**INTEGRATION**	**ASSIMILATION**
	Unrelated	**SEPARATION**	**DECULTURATION**

Source: A. Nahavandi and A. Malekzadeh (1995). "Acculturation in mergers and acquisitions." In T. Jackson (ed.), *Cross-cultural management*, p. 333. Oxford: Butterworth-Heinemann.

tional transitions, therefore, requires sensitivity to the need to rebuild loyalty and recreate organizational shared purpose through the management of shared reality. GE Plastics use of a "share to gain" approach to help assimilate a rival it had acquired through a community service project that pulled employees together is a wonderful story in building corporate loyalty.

When GE decided to acquire Borg-Warner Chemicals and merge the company with its GE Plastics division, the challenge was quite heavy. Borg-Warner had a much more paternalistic culture with an emphasis on technical and manufacturing core capability. GE Plastics relied more on younger people and had a much more aggressive marketing group. The challenge was how to integrate the two discordant work cultures and how to cultivate trust and loyalty among former Borg-Warner Chemicals employees who elected to join and assimilate with GE Plastics. Instead of using such traditional techniques as teambuilding, management hypothesized, and later proved, that GE Plastics could build team spirit more effectively by putting its employees to work helping the San Diego community. The workforce was divided into thirty pre–selected teams, each containing members ranging from entry-level marketing employees to senior management and including a deliberate mix of former Borg-Warner and veteran GE Plastics workers (Bollier, 1996). While before the activity many Borg-Warner employees referred to GE Plastics as "the competition," the San Diego event, called "share to gain," led many of them to change their perceptions about GE. To illustrate the enthusiastic change of heart Bollier (1996, p. 22) stated, "These employees returned from San Diego and told their families [in West Virginia] to pack up, they were going to Pittsfield [Massachusetts]." Remarkably, the renovations cost GE Plastics no more than one of their traditional teambuilding activities.

GLOBAL MANAGERS: MINDSETS AND COMPETENCIES

Rhinesmith (1992) identified six important mindsets, which form the foundation for global management competencies:

- *Managing competition*: Global managers look for the context rather than the elements. They constantly look for the larger constellation by scanning their environments for market and technological opportunities. Having a global perspective expands the scope of leaders' technical, business, and industry knowledge. It provides leaders with breadth and vision.

- *Managing paradoxes*: Global managers view the world as a contradictory system requiring the constant act of balancing incompatible forces. A global manager recognizes the tradeoffs that exist among diverse constituencies and deals with adversity creatively. A global manager does not impose solutions: priorities are established in an act of reconciliation and through the simultaneous appreciation of contradictory ideas in a way that energizes rather than paralyzes. Dealing with paradoxes requires the ability to conceptualize and have a holistic view of the world through "action inquiry" (Torbert, 1987), "creative tension" (Quinn, 1988), or "systems view" (Senge, 1990). A systems view requires an intuitive, right-brain ability to understand different levels of business vision, mission and strategy, and organizational consequences. But maintaining a global mindset and ability also requires left-brain capacity and analytical skills to break down the complexity of issues and problems into manageable solutions.
- *Managerial adaptability*: Global managers center on organizational processes rather than structures and politics. They emphasize leadership, communication, and decision making rather than control as a means to increase adaptability. Global managers are flexible and adaptive, resilient, and creative. They achieve successful results by working with decision-making and problem-solving processes, rather than policies and procedures.
- *Managing diversity and teamwork*: Teamwork, interdependence, and team play are fundamental filters for a global mind. Team members with diverse backgrounds and cultures require leaders to be sensitive and flexible in meeting their needs. These needs must be balanced against the goals of the organization. Learning to be cross-culturally sensitive requires an awareness of individual differences and showing trust and confidence in the abilities of others. It takes personal ego and attitudes to be well integrated and emotionally stable. But global leaders also have a predisposition to accept new challenges and question their presumptions, values, and beliefs about themselves and about the world.
- *Managing uncertainty*: Global leaders with global mindsets are comfortable with change and have a high tolerance for ambiguity. They realize the unpredictability of their global surroundings because of its complexity, dynamism, and diversity. Global leaders are intuitive thinkers who use their experience to make

judgments about changes in the environment. Often they make decisions without complete information, and instead use their perceptions and interpretations of the world to make sense of complex, uncertain situations. "Effective global managers often display a good mix of self-confidence and humility. They are experienced enough to be confident in their judgment, but they are also experienced enough to know that there is seldom only one right answer to any issue of importance" (Rhinesmith, 1992, p. 66).

- *Managing learning*: Global leaders envision change and new directions by rethinking boundaries, finding new meaning, and changing and adapting their behaviors. They constantly seek new ways to improve themselves and others. They are interested in developing competencies to deal with changes and surprises rather than avoid them. Global leaders are effective learners, for they learn how to prepare themselves for surprises proactively as opposed to being trained in ways to deal with them retrospectively. Global managers are continuous learners who use reflection and communication skills to deal with new challenges and adjust to the world around them.

Communication is a key success factor in transnational organizations such as ABB and Unilever involving diverse people communicating in different languages. ABB global managers are open minded, fast moving, imaginative, and incisive. "They sort through the debris of cultural excuses and find opportunities to innovate" (Taylor, 1991, p. 94). Global managers have a high tolerance for ambiguity and diversity. They must handle the frustrations of language and semantic barriers and minimize communication problems. Global managers must have a broad perspective on their task environment, and therefore, must be able to work in or with mixed nationality teams. Global managers must be highly intuitive with both people and solutions. They must make decisions fast, take risks, and act with speed. "I tell my people that if we make 100 decisions and 70 turn out to be right, that's good enough. I'd rather be roughly right and fast than exactly right and slow" (Taylor, 1991, p. 101).

In a highly competitive market with constant pressures to respond just-in-time (JIT), there is no substitute for speed. "Why emphasize speed at the expense of precision? Because the costs of delay exceed the costs of mistakes" (Taylor, 1991, p. 104). In a turbulent global environment, organizations must develop the capacity to respond rapidly to changes in their environment by dramatically revamping their organizational vision and mission, altering business lines, reorganizing labor, readjusting technologies, and reshaping strategic alliances. A new kind of leadership is required to lead the organization through the age of change and discontinuity. A high-performance leader like Percy Barnevik must have the inner capabilities to reframe his organization through critical decision making and significant goal setting. This form of leadership is not evolutionary but rather revolutionary. Leadership must employ a high-speed management style to achieve performance breakthrough.

HIGH-SPEED MANAGEMENT

Originated by Cushman and King (1994), high-speed management (HSM) is a quick, quality response to customers' needs that beats out competitors. It is a fast-cycle approach to product development, product delivery, and customer service and management. Once a strategy is formulated, a synergistic team consisting of experts in design and engineering, production and marketing, constantly monitors the progress of product development and makes necessary adjustments. For example, when Unilever was confronted with a rapidly growing ice-cream market in Europe, they needed to respond quickly to intense demands for ice-cream snacks. A multifunctional team was put together to develop strategies and suggest a new product line.

> A group has been charged with the strategic planning and monitoring of what we call ice-cream snacks. In this rapidly growing market, which requires equally rapid innovation, Unilever sells a number of extremely successful products, like Magnum, Europe's most popular chocolate ice-cream bar. The strategy team is chaired by a marketing director . . . and has five additional members . . . from other operating companies . . . This team cooperates closely with the relevant strategic group at the head office but also has the authority to implement strategy on its own. (Maljers, 1992, p. 50)

High-speed management draws on management control and adaptation theories as well as on the value-chain theory (see figure 10.2), which focuses on customer-supplier relationships with sequential or reciprocal interdependencies within the value chain.

These relationships span organizational processes from upstream systems involving suppliers and vendors to internal systems involving performers and downstream systems involving external customers. Earlier we discussed the importance of horizontal congruence and the

Figure 10.2. Organizational Value Chain

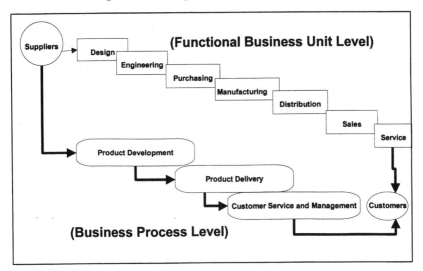

need to eliminate nonvalue-added tasks through quality improvement, reengineering, and benchmarking. Value-chain theory also centers on the need for a continuous quality evaluation of the major functions within the organization and their interfaces to achieve higher levels of performance that meet or exceed customer requirements. At the functional level, the evaluation may include design, engineering, purchasing, manufacturing, distribution and sales, and customer service. Externally, it involves evaluation of whether suppliers meet quality specifications, JIT delivery, and whether external customers are fully satisfied. At the business process level, evaluation is applied to the linkages between the functional units that make up product development, product delivery, service, and management processes.

High-speed management (HSM), then, is applied as an overall strategy aimed at achieving realignment of the organization vertically and horizontally, both inside the organization and outside its boundaries. Consistent with the earlier discussion on action learning, and following Cushman and King (1994), HSM seeks to improve an organization's communication capabilities in three major areas:

1. Scanning the environment for threats and opportunities to minimize the effects of undesired outcomes and to maximize

the benefits of readaptation. Strategic planning, stakeholder analysis, SWOT analysis, and intelligence gathering are communication mechanisms used to monitor, enact, and achieve a better fit with the environment.

2. Adjusting the value chain of the organization and reintegrating or realigning organizational processes to boost both the efficiency and effectiveness of resource utilization and product development and delivery. Adjustments involve incremental changes in structures and processes, deployment of cross-functional, quality-improvement teams, creation of self-managed profit centers, and establishment of linking programs with other organizations.

3. Anticipating trends and patterns of possibilities in the future and restructuring the organization through continuous process improvement (CPI) to take advantage of opportunities as they arise. The improvement strategies recommended by HSM theory are benchmarking and reengineering, while the communication processes used are information technology, EDI, and networking.

Cushman and King (1994) suggest the application of HSM in volatile environments that require innovative strategies coupled with information and communication capabilities. These capabilities must provide for a rapid coalignment of the elements within the value chain of the organization in response to environmental change and discontinuity. Thus, HSM relies heavily on high-speed communications. The communication processes involved are integration, coordination, and control, all of which are linking mechanisms used by high-speed managers. These managers must have communication and information skills that make it possible for organizations to scan the external environment, secure appropriate realignment across the value chain and continuously improve their performance. The aim is to maintain a sustainable competitive advantage through constant matching functions and processes across the value chain of the organization with subenvironments that are linked with the organization and that include suppliers, customers, and competitors (Oblog, Cushman & Kozminski, 1994).

High-speed managers must recreate their organizational culture and redesign their organizational structure to maintain high flexibility and achieve optimal integration. They must also establish effective mechanisms for linking the various parts of organizational processes to achieve optimal coordination. Centralized information technology, LAN & WAN systems, and electronic mail can be used along with teleconferencing and other forms of telecommunication networking. High-speed managers use control to evaluate process capabilities and use process outputs to make quick adjustments for optimal delivery of high-quality products.

ABB, described earlier, is a HSM organization with all of the characteristics mentioned above. ABB uses a matrix design to integrate the organization as a whole. The business area executives act as global co-ordinators, while the country presidents audit factory performance and results to check whether predetermined targets have been met. Percy Barnevik is a high-performance leader who constantly searches for ways to enhance the effectiveness of processes in his company. He acts to institutionalize high-speed management in his company as a strategy and culture. High-performance leaders enacting HSM require unique skills and capabilities that can help them revitalize and lead their organizations successfully in volatile environments.

COMPETENCIES AND CAPABILITIES

Earlier we discussed how competitive markets and industry discontinuity are the driving forces behind such adaptive responses of organizations as restructuring, downsizing, and outsourcing. Two important requirements were stressed:

- Organizations are expected to do more with fewer resources.
- Leaders are expected to rethink radically how to move people and successfully revitalize and navigate organizations in their domain of operations.

These requirements call for leaders who are both transformational and instrumental, refer to as "high-performance leaders." These leaders are self-defining with strong internalized values and ideals about the future role and direction of their organizations. High-performance leaders are willing, at times, to sacrifice their prestige and reputations when making such difficult decisions that affect organizational members as cutbacks and layoffs. They demonstrate a strong sense of inner purpose and direction that is viewed by others as the great strength of their leadership. High-performance leaders are capable of looking beyond short-term needs and self-interests. They are the first to recognize people as resources rather than as costs. They have trust and confidence in their followers, and therefore, they are the first to empower and delegate authority.

Such transformational, self-defining leaders are able to energize followers to take actions that support higher purposes rather than their own self-interest, and they are able to create an environment in which people are encouraged to address problems and opportunities with creativity and personal commitment . . . They can consider the long-term goals and interests of the organization, as well as of the individual, rather than being shackled by immediate or short-range goals . . . [they] delegate autonomy . . . to others and develop them in ways that can enhance learning and build a high-performance team and work environment. (Kuhnert, 1994, pp. 18–19)

High-performance leaders recognize the value of creating interdependence through empowerment rather than creating dependence through hierarchical authority. Empowered organizations mitigate the dependence on leaders through the initiation of self-managed teams and through empowering others and sharing the mission of the organization. The role of the leader is to instill trust, to initiate communication and coordination, and to create a learning environment where everyone participates and contributes. An important responsibility of high-performance leaders is to develop a cadre of competent managers with an inner purpose and direction and with congruent values, who potentially can become future transformational leaders.

DEVELOPING FUTURE LEADERS

We take people with great results and ask them to move on to other companies because they don't have our values.

—Jack Welch, CEO, General Electric

After Jack Welch realized the goal of transforming GE into the most competitive organization in the world through closing plants, consolidation, downsizing, and dismissing workers by the thousands, he turned his attention inward. Welch emphasized the set of values essential to take his company rapidly forward through the 1990s and beyond. The thrust of his new set of values was trust and respect between workers and managers, and developing managers as leaders. "In the first half of the 1980s we restructured the company and changed its physical makeup—that was the easy part. In the last several years, our challenge has been to change ourselves—an infinitely more difficult task that, frankly, not all of us in leadership positions are capable of" (*New York Times*, March 4, 1992, D-1).

In line with this view, Welch set out to identify and develop a cadre of "Type I" leaders (see figure 10.3), who deliver on commitment, financial or otherwise, and share the values of the company. These leaders' future "is an easy call," claims Welch, "onward and upward" (GE's 1990, *Annual Report*). The other three types are lower quality leaders: a "Type II" leader is one who does not meet commitment nor does he or she share GE's values. Type II leaders are obviously limited in terms of upward mobility at GE. A "Type III" leader misses commitment, but has a high value-congruence with the company's culture. This Type III leader, according to Welch, usually gets a second chance, possibly in a different environment. The most incongruent type is the "Type IV" leader, who delivers on commitments by meeting goals and numbers, but who does not believe in the new management philosophy.

> This is the individual who typically forces performance out of people rather than inspires it; the autocrat, the big shot, the tyrant. Too often, all of us have looked the other way—tolerated these "type 4" because "they always deliver"—at least in the short term . . . In an environment where we must have every good idea from every man and woman in

Figure 10.3. Leadership: Commitment and Values

VALUE CONGRUENCE	COMMITMENT	
	Low	High
LOW	Type II not a pleasant call but easy	Type IV walk the talk
HIGH	Type III gets a second chance, preferably in a different environment	Type I onward and upward

Source: GE publications.

the organization, we cannot afford management styles that suppress and intimidate . . . Whether we can convince and help those managers to change—recognizing how difficult that can be—or part company with them if they cannot, will be the ultimate test of our commitment to the transformation of this company and will determine the future of the mutual trust and respect we are building. (GE, 1990, *Annual Report*)

The desirable Type I leader is measured along the dimensions of placing a high priority on customers, resisting bureaucracy, cutting across boundaries, thinking globally, and demonstrating "enormous energy and the ability to energize and invigorate others" (GE, 1990, *Annual Report*). Jack Welch himself assumed such values by developing each of his division CEOs as future transformational leaders. These transformational leaders must set the right momentum for undertaking changes and ensuring that the changes are embedded in their divisions. They must master the arts of simplicity, excitement, inspiration, and challenge by offering employees a vision of success and a strategy for implementing the vision. They must master both the task dimension of work (commitment) and sociopsychological dimension (values) of moving and managing people. These leaders, congruent with Welch's philosophy, must focus their efforts on helping self-managed teams and cross-functional teams sustain their breakthrough innovations. They must support lasting impact of adopted best-practices and they must ensure consistency of integration, coordination, and control across the value chain of their businesses. Perhaps, the six principles formulated by Welch capture the essence of future leadership:

1. Control your own destiny or someone else will.
2. Face reality as it is, not as it was or as you wish it were.
3. Be candid with everyone.
4. Don't manage, lead.
5. Change before you have to.
6. If you don't have a competitive advantage, don't compete.

In fact, developing senior managers at GE as future transformational leaders has led to the labeling of GE as the "CEO Boot Camp" (Reese, 1991). In pursuit of high-quality leaders, many companies are willing to pay for GE experience and have lured top executives away from GE. Here is a sample list: Harry Stonecipher, VP of a GE aircraft unit became CEO of Sundstrand; Norman Blake, GE's credit VP became CEO of USF & G; Michael Emmi, GE World Sales VP became Systems & Computer Tech's CEO; Stanley Hoch GE's treasurer became General

Public Utilities' CEO; Richard Miller, GE Consumer Electronics president became Wang Labs CEO; Stanley Gault, GE Senior VP, Industrial Products, became Rubbermaid's CEO. The list goes on and on. Perhaps the best example is Lawrence Bossidy, the former number two at GE, who in July 1991 became Allied Signal's CEO. Bossidy's vision for his new company markedly resembled that of GE. "[Our goal is] to identify people who have passion, who are willing to make a commitment, take ownership, and make it a premier company" (Weber & Driscoll, 1991, p. 28). Jack Welch himself is often engaged in teaching and developing leadership. Says Steve Kerr, VP for corporate leadership development at the Crotonville facility: "Jack teaches that a good leader must have situational flexibility, that you cannot be locked into a way of behaving or source of information—but also that you cannot operate in the absence of a moral compass. For instance, across businesses, GE has widely different work practices, but a nonflexible set of values" (*Industry Week*, 11/18/96, p. 17).

An important aspect of developing highly committed managers with shared values at GE involves the systematic assessment of the performance and style of GE's top managers. Since 1989, GE has been rating its top two hundred managers along the lines of the desired Type I leadership and has relied on these ratings in decisions about compensation and rewards. The top core business managers' leadership capabilities are assessed directly by the respective CEOs and Jack Welch through what has been known as "Session C." Typically, Welch meets one day per year per business to analyze the managers' profiles. The examination is based on hard data such as accomplishment analysis or regular periodic reviews. Here is an account of Richard Stonesifer, president and CEO of GE Appliances, published in *Industry Week* (11/18/96, p. 17): "Jack made it a practice to approve every general manager's slate in the company [about five hundred positions]. Every slate has sometimes two, sometimes four people on it, and he certainly has his own view on each. Sometimes he'll take people off the slate, sometimes add. Then the hiring manager would be able to select someone from that slate Jack has worked with him on and approved. He personally reads thousands of EMS forms [a combination performance appraisal and career path document] and makes comments on the higher level folks like 'I don't like the way that's worded—that's not Joe as I see him' or 'Be sure you add this—be sure he or she knows this is a knockout blow if they don't get it fixed.'"

At the operating core, with his Six Sigma, the quality-control program pioneered at Motorola, Welch's goal is to reduce the number of product defects in goods or services to 3.4 per million.. Welch believes that anything less than Six Sigma quality can cost a company from 10 percent to 15 percent of its revenue. This translates to about $12 billion a year for GE. Thus, managers must be trained and receive Green Belts, Black Belts, and Master Black Belts, which represent a progressive training in statistical process control. And the message is clear: Managers unwilling to participate in the training that leads to a Belt lose their chances to be promoted (*The Washington Post*, March 23, 1997, H1).

THE SIGNIFICANCE OF DIAGONAL COMMUNICATION

High-performance leaders are role models and the point of reference not only for those who report directly to them, but also for people with whom they have an indirect (or diagonal) relationship. High-performance leaders have a responsibility to develop people at all levels and all locations within the organization. These leaders are expected to use vertical, horizontal, and diagonal directions of communication. This communication occurs not only through the intermediation of mass media but often also through direct, interactive, and spontaneous contacts with individuals working in different units or hierarchical levels. Percy Barnevik, for example, set a goal for himself to meet and communicate directly with people across all business areas of his transnational company. He made it clear that top leaders in his company must be involved in diagonal communication with all levels and locations. The matrix design used by ABB facilitates such lateral communication and Barnevik's role modeling has reinforced it throughout the organization.

Closely related to indirect leadership is the "cascading" modeling of leadership behaviors at successively lower levels of management (Yammarino, 1994). Those who are influenced directly and informally by the high-performance leader will also exhibit similar behaviors and adopt the values of the leader. In turn, behaviors of those below them in the hierarchy will be a manifestation of the behaviors and values of the high-performance leader. The point is that the qualities of high-performance leadership transcend levels and locations. Cascading is also a tested, useful approach for action learning and transformation of the total system. Xerox's training program is based on a cascading approach from the CEO level all the way down to the performer level. The most direct contacts between high-performance leaders and followers at all levels occur through communication bridges, the use of e-mail with direct access to and from the leader, or through applications of communication bypasses. ABB's internal networks, for example, are based on communication bridges and direct contacts between business area managers all over the world. Bypass supports an organic structure (such as the matrix) in which a level of management is skipped in the communication relationships between leaders and followers. Bypass is a common practice in organizations in Norway where the CEO communicates directly with people at the bottom levels, who in turn pass the information along to their peers. Bypass is an effective mechanism that helps circumvent the rigidity of the bureaucracy, or connects geographically dispersed units. Bypass may help develop a better bond between leaders and followers for it provides greater opportunities for followers to interact more directly and informally with their leaders (Yammarino, 1994).

MANAGERIAL LEADERSHIP: VALUES AND SKILLS

> Ironically, perhaps, the transformational leader is expected to meet organizational needs for change and adaptation while denying his or her subordinates' fundamental need for stability in their work environment. This is just one of the many contradictory obligations of leadership.
>
> —Dr. Michael Fortunato, Director, Management
> Education, FORUM, Empire State College

To compete successfully in today's volatile business world, managers must have transformational leadership capabilities. They must be visionary, innovative, flexible, and persistent leaders who must manage change through building and coaching teams and removing possible barriers to team performance. Transactional or instrumental leaders adopt an exchange perspective toward leading people, whereby recognizing the extrinsic values of employees and administering rewards and sanctions to enhance the motivation and effort of employees. Transformational leaders, however, use conceptual power to inspire and guide employees by shaping their attitudes, creating followership, and influencing followers' views of the organization's mission and future. In this perspective, leadership is a rhetorical process, whereby the transformational leader articulates a vision about future organizational goals that is both utopian and realistic (Barge, 1994, p. 176). The vision becomes a roadmap that directs and synergizes the efforts of managers, staff specialists, and workers toward achieving organizational superordinate goals.

Conceptual and empirical studies of the shift in management style that focused on the relationships between employee extra effort, employee satisfaction, and organizational effectiveness found these variables to be more highly correlated with transformational styles of leaders than with transactional styles (Bass, 1985; Deal & Kennedy, 1982; Peters & Austin, 1985). These early predictions led to studies supporting the view that transformational roles would become relatively more important in dynamic environments (Bass & Avolio, 1994; Mintzberg, 1989; Tichy & Ulrich, 1984). Quinn and Kimberly (1984) argued that these roles are also vital to managers during transitions. Later studies showed a correlation between transformational role playing and satisfaction with performance appraisals (Waldman, Bass & Einstein, 1987), group performance (Avolio, Waldman & Einstein, 1988), empowering employees (Barge, 1994), and the sophistication of the managers' cognitive maps (Quinn, Spreitzer & Hart, 1992; Quinn & Hart, 1993; Zorn, 1991). The principal conceptual finding of this literature is that more successful managers and more successful organizations do indeed transform in predictable patterns, which tend to follow external pressures.

Byrd (1987) suggested five essential skills for effective transformational leaders: anticipation, visioning, value congruence, empowerment, and self-understanding skills.

Anticipating skills involve the ability to project into the future, understand the consequences of present actions, scan the environment for trends and opportunities, take risks, and proactively engage the organization in adaptation processes. Leaders must demonstrate competencies in exploiting company strengths and networking and building coalitions. Other competencies for leaders involve intuitive decision making, scanning, and building trust.

Visioning skills involve creating a mental and verbal roadmap of a preferred future organizational environment in which internal and external stakeholders can participate. Vision provides organizational stakeholders with a sense of direction. The vision spells out what contributions the organization is going to make to society, how the organization will fit into the future marketplace, and how organizational resources will be allocated among major functions and processes. Ultimately, a vision serves as an organizing paradigm for helping organizational stakeholders understand where the organization is headed, what their role and expected contributions will be, and why certain behaviors and actions are important to achieve the desired state of affairs.

Leaders with visioning skills must be proactive and forward thinking. Leaders should be futurists with dreams, but also with realistic goals and ideas that can inspire and motivate others. Visioning involves getting people to become true believers in the dreams and goals of the organization through high acceptance and high commitment. People become committed to organizational goals partly because the vision helps them infuse meaning into their task environment. At the emotional level, a vision connects with the attitudes, beliefs, and values of employees and inspires them to perform with high commitment and energy. The acceptance of the vision also depends on the rhetorical skills of the leader for creating a sense of identity, unity, and purpose within the organization. Generating commitment to the vision is highly dependent on the reliability and credibility of the leader. To the extent that leaders are perceived as legitimate and credible emotional and informational sources for their employees, they are able to either structure situations using various sources of power or structure followers' attitudes using influence strategies. Trust, confidence, and credibility are important enhancements for open communication and motivation. Communicating the vision through both the oral (e.g., public speeches, informal discussions) and written (e.g., in-house publications) media are essential for pulling people together and synergizing their activities.

Visionary leadership is aimed at supporting two broad communication processes: *object mediation*, which is the ability to make sense of information within the environment and *action mediation*, aimed at removing obstacles for better adaptation and alignment with the external environment (Barge, 1994). Object mediation and action mediation involve the management of meaning. Viewing organizations as systems of shared meanings (Pfeffer, 1981) leads to the conclusion that visionary-inspirational leaders engage in communicating the meaning of goals, values, and ideologies to organizational members to create a sense of common purpose, mobilize support, and gain commitment to the vision. As Pondy (1978, pp. 94–95) proposed:

> The effectiveness of a leader lies in his ability to make activity meaningful for those in his role set—not to change behavior but to give others a sense of understanding what they are doing and especially to articulate it so they can communicate about the meaning of their behavior . . . If in addition the leader can put it into words then the meaning of what the group is doing becomes a social fact . . . This dual capacity . . . to make sense of things and to put them into language meaningful to large numbers of people gives the person who has it enormous leverage.

Leaders must demonstrate competencies in connecting their organizations with the larger environment, creating a vision of success, and sharing that vision with others.

Value-congruence skills allow the leader to articulate values that, when internalized by organizational members, become a source of motivation and energy. The leader must communicate the values by role modeling and through vicarious learning to achieve member identification with these values. Transformational leaders also communicate values through rhetorical devices such as analogies, metaphors, sagas, and stories. The rhetoric taps into members' emotions and elicits the response necessary for value congruence and for realizing the vision (Conger, 1989). Leaders must demonstrate their competency in understanding employees' values, establishing clear standards for making choices, creating value congruence with the corporate mission, and translating the values into daily behavior.

Empowering skills involve the delegation of authority and distribution of power. Empowerment also involves providing members with opportunities for developing into future leaders. Essential skills associated with empowerment are coaching, facilitating, counseling, and leading. Empowerment also facilitates teamwork and collaboration among employees. Important interpersonal communication skills for teamwork are listening, high tolerance for ambiguity, and giving constructive feedback. Leaders must demonstrate competencies in sharing power, creating conditions for involvement, consensus and shared decision making, unlocking motivation in others, and initiating human development.

Self-understanding skills relate to self-assessment and the realization of one's own strengths and weaknesses. Recognizing personal limitations is important—it should lead to greater interdependence rather than to an obsession with power to cover up a lack of skills and qualifications. Leaders must demonstrate competencies in giving and receiving feedback, continuous learning, and developing and motivating themselves.

THE POWER OF INNER CAPABILITIES

Bass and Avolio (1994) suggested a developmental model of leadership that can help individuals in leadership capacities assess their styles and competencies to determine how effective they are in fulfilling leadership responsibilities and the type of self-improvement strategy they can initiate. Their taxonomy involves five predominant styles: laissez-faire, passive management by exceptions, active management by exceptions, constructive transactional, and transformational leadership.

1. The "laissez-faire" leader is a nontransactional leader who abdicates responsibilities, avoids decision making, is indecisive, uninvolved, disorganized, and an isolationist. This passive orientation is undesirable, unacceptable, and pathological.

2. A manager with an orientation characterized as "passive management by exception" has a wider range of acceptance but with ineffective monitoring capabilities. Although not as passive as the laissez-faire, this manager is still quite reactive in responding to external stimuli. This leader waits for problems to occur, reacts to mistakes, and reluctantly gets involved in solving the problems. He or she is a status-quo keeper who would change only if necessary. The passive management by exception manager is a believer in the axiom of "if it ain't broke, don't fix it."

3. The more active style of management by exception involves a leader who selectively pays attention to deviations and emergencies and is more concerned about making sure that "things are under control." Hence, behaviors and actions involve setting standards, monitoring and taking steps to correct mistakes and solve problems. This is a retrospective (rather than prospective) attitude, which focuses attention on irregularities and nonroutine problems that require intervention via direct supervision.

4. The transactional leader is one who exchanges rewards for performance and who sets goals and clarifies the path to achieve these goals. This model of leadership is constructive in a sense that the manager negotiates and agrees with employees about their responsibilities, the measurement of their performance, and the inducements they receive. This style, unlike the previous ones, sets the parameters for the work flow and the results of the work, and gives recognition to employees when they meet predetermined targets.

5. Transformational leaders have inner capabilities that distinguish them from all other leaders. These capabilities include individual consideration, intellectual stimulation, inspirational motivation, and idealized influence.

- *Individualized consideration or human focus* refers to the capability of leaders to adopt a coaching, mentoring, and counseling style. The human-focused leader is concerned with the well-being of employees and uses a developmental approach that recognizes the psychosociological needs of individuals and groups. The leader acknowledges the value of cultural diversity and individual differences by applying a variety of learning tools and incentive mechanisms to develop and motivate different people. The leader is expected to maximize the use of different communication media, interact, and delegate tasks. An important objective fulfilled by a human-focused leader is the creation of a positive climate conducive to both action learning and instilling self-confidence in followers.

- *Intellectual stimulation* is an inner capability that triggers people to think creatively and innovatively. By stimulating employees intellectually, the transformational leader can help them think in a nonvertical fashion, broaden the scope of their diagnostic skills, and think critically. Intellectual stimulation also functions as a catalyst by influencing people to develop self-examination skills through questioning their own assumptions and through reframing problems. It is an ability that helps others challenge the status quo, use reasoning as well as emotion, generate simpler solutions, and look at problems in new ways.

- *Inspiration* involves passionate communication of the idealistic map of the future organization and depiction of the path that leads to the visionary organization. Inspired employees, excited about the vision, participate and become involved in attaining organizational objectives. Transformational leaders are truly empowered by their constituents, who supply them with the energy and support they need to navigate the organization through fluctuating environments. The leader, in turn, releases that energy to unlock constituents' motivation in pursuit of optimal performance. The inspirational leader clarifies future states, treats threats as opportunities, and elevates expectations. This leader sets higher standards for employees while projecting a high tolerance for ambiguity and mistakes. The inspirational leader is a great communicator who uses symbols and images to focus employees' efforts and who manages meaning skillfully.

- *Idealized influence or charisma* generates referent power that, when activated, becomes a centripetal force that energizes people and brings them together. The charismatic leader relates the work and mission of the group to values, ideals, and aspirations commonly shared by an organizational culture. The charismatic leader highlights desired outcomes and clarifies the path for attaining these outcomes. This leader helps members achieve emotional arousal through excitement, enthusiasm, involvement, and commitment to group objectives. The charismatic leader advances the vision and engages in the transmission and management of organizational purpose and direction (Smith and Peterson, 1988). Charisma is the ability to prompt someone to internalize the values of the leader and so become a firm believer in the vision articulated by that leader. A vision connects people at an emotional level: employees idealize the leader and often develop a strong emotional bond with that leader. The leader is admired, respected, trusted, and emulated. The idealized influencer is determined, confident in the vision, emphasizes accomplishments, and exhibits persistence in pursuing objectives. The inner power of this leader creates energy that pulls people together. This leader is emotionally attractive to his/her followers.

TRANSFORMING ABILITIES AND COMPETENCIES

Transformational leadership goes beyond rational management and the use of formal authority to achieve compliance. Transformational leadership involves influencing a shift in followers' mindsets and core values. Transformational leaders must be great communicators, be able to resist stress, have a negative need for security, a perpetual drive for achievement, and a positive need for challenges. In addition, they must demonstrate high standards of ethical and moral conduct, have a high tolerance for uncertainty and ambiguity, take risks, and initiate innovative breakthroughs. These leaders fulfill the interpersonal, information processing, and decision-making roles of effective managers by initiating and carrying out the organizational mission, while manifesting the appropriate concern for their constituents. Transformational leaders use their discretionary power to carry out a vision that moves people synergistically to meet organizational goals. They trust people and show them respect. They value followers' contributions and support and develop them to be successful and make temporary sacrifices for long-term gains. Transformational leaders sculpt the organization to reestablish a tight fit with the external environment. They think and act strategically and they select from a wide range of means to carry out the transformation including training, quality improvement, benchmarking, reengineering, outsourcing, networking, and rightsizing. But most importantly, transformational leaders have a positive image of their ultimate ideal organization as manifested in their dreams.

Steve Jobs, founder and former CEO of Apple Computer, had a vision: to create a high-tech innovative organization without the burden of a bureaucratic structure. During the 1984 Super Bowl football game, Apple aired a one-time commercial to introduce its new Macintosh computer. Patterned after George Orwell's novel, *1984*, the commercial went like this: An auditorium is filled with people mindlessly watching as Big Brother talks on an oversized movie screen. A female athlete runs into the auditorium and throws a hammer into the screen, shattering it and causing the people to react. The commercial represented IBM as Big Brother. When the screen was shattered, people could emerge as individuals. Similarly, in a subsequent address given to the Boston Computer Society, Jobs again used the 1984 theme, projecting an oversized image of himself on a back wall as he spoke (Conger, 1989). In both instances, the message was aimed at persuading others to break away from the conformity and tradition associated with bureaucracies. Apple, designed to counter this tradition, has sought to breed innovativeness. Its employees are encouraged to emphasize innovation, change, and creativity when approaching any situation, decision, or action (Barge, 1994, p. 183).

High-performance leaders must have transforming skills and abilities to do the following:

Anticipate industry discontinuities and short product lifecycle shifts.

Initiate a vision of frame-breaking change that shakes up the preexisting patterns of communication, values, and beliefs within the organization, while at the same time coping with internal organizational stress.

Align people with the direction of change through communication processes, skills training, and cultural transformation.

Motivate and inspire people to move toward the new vision even if the mission needs to be revised and updated, or if the transformation is a long-term process.

Institutionalize action learning to continually question traditional assumptions and realign employees' attitudes and behaviors around the vision.

Empower process champions and cross-functional teams to implement the change.

Develop employees effectively as critical resources for the accomplishment of the transformation.

Adjust leadership style based on personal insight into their strengths and weaknesses.

Manage paradoxes, deal with contradictions, and cope with tension and discomfort, particularly during periods of restructuring and agenda setting, which in turn leads to greater employee involvement.

Transcend the culture by shifting the rules governing the organization and positively influencing the norms guiding collective actions.

Create conditions necessary for optimal communication competence so
that members are able to enable members to redefine the parameters and assumptions of the existing systems and processes,
roles and relationships.

EXEMPLARY HIGH-PERFORMANCE LEADERSHIP

Jack Welch's well-orchestrated transformation of GE into a highly
competitive global company is testimonial to his ability to develop, articulate, and effectively communicate a vision of what the company
should be. Welch's anticipatory skills were evident throughout the
transformation of GE in the 1980s. During the early 1990s, he projected
a tremendous opportunity for GE in the Asian countries for GE's steam
turbines as a predominant technology. GE forecasts that such machines
will be selected over gas turbines because of the vast coal reserves in
China and India and insufficient supplies of natural gas. GE expects
that more than 460 billion watts of power generation will be ordered by
the end of the century (*Albany Times Union*, Feb. 6, 1994). GE's Power
Systems represents only one expansion area. Almost every one of GE's
SBUs has a stake in an Asian country or in Mexico with plans to increase investments and expand. For example, Medical Systems has a
joint venture in China to develop low-cost imaging equipment; GE
Capital has a $2.5 billion stake in an Indonesian plant; Plastic is build-
ing a compounding facility in India; and the list goes on and on. "The
way Welch sees it GE's aggressive push into India, China, and Mexico
are no longer a matter of choice: They could well determine the future
of the $57 billion titan, America's third-most-profitable company"
(Smart, Engardino & Smith, 1993, p. 64).
　　Inspired by his own anticipation, Welch has set out the strategy
for shifting the focus of GE from the Western world to Asia and Latin
America. His forecasts are that those markets could provide more than
$20 billion in annual revenues, doubling the current level and account-
ing for more than 25 percent of GE's total sales. Welch is aware of the
risks associated with huge investments, but he emphasizes the tremendous potential for growth if this strategy is realized. "If the strategy is
wrong, it's a billion dollars, a couple of billion dollars. If it's right, it's
the future of the next century for this company." The potential of this
expansion stands in sharp contrast to the modest growth forecasted for
the United States and European markets. Welch concluded that these
new markets are just right for the optimal mix of GE's capital and technology. A perfect match! "We are a company with great infrastructure

strengths and, therefore, a company that ought to go where the growth is. It's clear to anyone that the growth will be in the Pacific Rim, India, and Mexico" (Smart, Engardino & Smith, 1993, p. 66).

With this anticipation came a vision of GE as a fully transnational company. GE has never really been a global company in an organizational structure sense. Rather GE has been a U.S. company operating internationally with most of its activities concentrated in the industrialized world, particularly Europe and Japan. With the strategy of expansion into new world markets in place, GE has begun to transform itself into a global company. Since 1987, revenues from outside the United States have risen at an annual rate of 30 percent and now account for 40 percent of the company's total sales. The day when GE will make more money outside its U.S. "domestic" market is coming soon. "Being national doesn't pay" suggested GE's Vice Chairman Fresco (p. 66).

To this end, Welch is taking GE through its third major revolution in less than fifteen years—GE is shifting its center of gravity to Asia and Mexico. Along with this global expansion, GE has begun transforming its management ranks by moving Welch confidants to front-line positions in the field in an adaptive move with the purpose of creating a cadre of "global brains" to manage operations in distinctly Third World cultures. To institutionalize the change and achieve value congruence of its employees across the globe, GE has begun exporting its training programs, particularly those focusing on lean management, quick response, speeding up product cycles, and high productivity. To sharpen their interpersonal skills and adjust their leadership styles to accommodate multinational and multicultural diversity, Welch sent teams of executives on a mission to study the specific cultures in countries in which GE has a stake. He has also indicated that newly hired managerial-level employees should be given courses in global issues at GE's Crotonville training center. GE will be transformed into what Welch has titled a multipolar and multicultural company. The third revolution of the renewal cycle of GE during the last fifteen years has started to gain momentum.

THE MAKING OF THE HYPERCOMPETITIVE COMPANY

> The only way to be more competitive was to engage every mind in the organization. You couldn't have anybody on the sidelines.
>
> —Jack Welch, CEO, General Electric

By early fall 1996, the fruits of Welch's third revolution began to emerge with GE's stock up 86 percent since early 1995 and GE achieving the most remarkable market performance by becoming the most valuable company on the globe with a total market capitalization of $157 billion. By the end of 1996, GE's market capitalization had risen to $170 billion. With earnings topping the $7.4 billion for the year, GE was also expected to become the most profitable company in the United States. Although GE is one of America's most competitive companies, its revenues grew an average of around 5 percent a year between 1990 and 1994. Looking at these four years as transition time, Welch pointed to GE's 17 percent hike in revenues and 11 percent increase in earnings during 1995 as the new growth goals for the coming years—in the upward range of 10 percent. *Business Week* (October 28, 1996, p. 155) reported that Jack Welch has become the gold standard against which other CEOs are measured.

For Jack Welch, sustaining these results has meant continuing to push his agenda for overseas expansion, manufacturing efficiencies, and product quality. During 1995, for example, GE's revenues from its global operations soared 34 percent and GE's quality effort was projected to lead to a cut of $7 billion to $10 billion from its operating costs by the end of this century. But with product life cycles shortened and technology that is easy to emulate, Welch is concerned that without moving more aggressively into services it will become increasingly difficult to retain a competitive edge in the global market and achieve double digit returns on capital. Hence, the strategic emphasis of GE during 1995–1996 pointed to his new vision, pushing GE into services by leveraging its core industrial capabilities and by relying more on outsourcing. While 60 percent of GE's profits now comes from services, more than three times greater than the 1980s, Jack Welch is envisioning a higher ratio—somewhere in the neighborhood of 80 percent. To that end, GE has increasingly positioned itself as a consultant showing other businesses how to cut costs and operate more efficiently in running power plants, servicing engine shops for airline, hospital chains, railroads and locomotive, and corporate computer networks. A few examples follow.

GE Aircraft Engines signed a $2.3 billion, ten-year contract with British Airways in the spring of 1996 to service 85 percent of the carrier's engines and another deal worth $1 billion to service USAIR's GE engines. GE is also involved in transforming British Airways into a more responsive company with a JIT inventory system for parts and the establishment of self-directed work teams. GE Power Systems entered a joint-venture agreement with the Milan-based power company Societa Norddelettrica to offer utility maintenance and operation services throughout Europe. GE Transportation also signed a deal worth over half a billion dollars to sell and service 150 new locomotives for Burlington Northern Santa Fe Corporation. GE Transportation also formed a joint venture with Harris Corp. to design and sell global positioning systems similar to those used in air-traffic control. In addition, GE Medical Systems, in pursuit of this vision via acquisitions of medical service shops, acquired National Medical Diagnostics, a leading independent servicer of imaging equipment in early 1996. Yet that's just the beginning. GE Medical spent $80 million building a state-of-the-art training center complete with a TV studio to develop educational programming to help its customers better run their businesses (*Business Week*, October 28, 1996, p. 158). GE Capital Services, which accounts for about a third of GE's operating profits developed a $5 billion global computer outsourcing business to help run computer networks for client corporations, competing head on with IBM and EDS. Meanwhile GE's rivals responded either by dismissing GE's shift toward becoming more of a service company or by rushing to develop strategic alliances of their own. But they also needed to wrestle with Welch's hypercompetitiveness and learn the hard way. In a 1995 deal that GE executives hoped will prove valuable, GE and Andersen Consulting, a software-services leader, joined forces to beat major competitors for a ten-year, $350 million contract to manage LTV Corporation's mainframe-based computer needs (*Business Week*, October 28, 1996, p. 159).

Jack Welch continues to challenge and motivate his executives to think and act strategically and shift toward a more entrepreneurial mindset. The third revolution, which began with the realization of Welch's vision to transform GE and establish it as a dominant, most valuable global player, is in an advanced stage of transitioning toward becoming a hypercompetitive company.

LEARNING AND TRANSFORMATION

The success stories of GE and ABB clearly demonstrate that learning and cultural transformations have a reciprocal relationship and both must be supported by strong, charismatic, high-performance leadership. Over time, maintaining a flexible balance between culture and learning is essential. Thick culture is quickly transformed into dogmatism and rigidity, which may block renewal. Alternatively, a loose culture with no core values does not allow for a repository of learning. These two predicaments fail to provide a context conducive to learning, are limited in scope, restrictive in action, and consequently are both dysfunctional. One way to institutionalize learning as a positive force is by lengthening the organizational span of attention (Burdett, 1993). This span of attention should cross several territories along the renewal cycle. The first renewal concerns internalizing the value of change, revising internal processes, and readjusting structures to move the organization to higher levels of performance. Quality improvement initiatives in this context include:

1. Customer focused process design
2. Cross-functional improvement teams
3. Partnership with key vendors
4. Empowered leadership
5. Employee involvement
6. Knowledge-based rewards
7. Technical system design built along the lines of a prevention approach
8. Shorter cycle time through streamlining and elimination of rework
9. Data-based feedback and communication
10. Formulation of a vision of success

The second renewal involves organizational frame-breaking through redesigning the whole system and restructuring and realigning organizational structures and processes with the environment. This renewal moves the organization toward an advanced stage of external adaptation and internal consistency through the use of:

1. Process reengineering
2. Benchmarking
3. Internal networking
4. Horizontal management
5. Outsourcing
6. Transformational leadership
7. Self-managed work teams

The third renewal involves the entire value chain of the organization and is centered on the institutionalization of change as a core value reflected in the behaviors and activities of organizational members and as a competitive strategy linking the organization externally. The key elements included in this renewal are:

1. Action learning and revitalization
2. High-speed management and communication

3. Cross-training
4. Virtual organization
5. Boundaryless system
6. Strategic alliances
7. Globalization
8. Matrix organization
9. Information technology

THE REVOLUTION OF GE: DOING IT JACK'S WAY!

The potential outcomes/benefits of transitioning the organization toward an organic system characterized by teamwork, commitment, and flexibility should offset or at best outweigh the costs of transformation. While GE of the 1980s was different from GE of the 1970s, GE of the 1990s has unique characteristics that were absent in the previous organization. The company is smaller in size, but richer in financial and technological resources, and is worth more in terms of market capitalization than ever before. GE under Jack Welch has undergone three "revolutions" that reflect important points on the renewal cycle. During the mid-1980s, the company pursued two important goals through structural adjustments, consolidation, acquisitions, and selling off unproductive assets. GE's strategic business units (SBUs) had to be number one or two in their industry or they would not remain GE businesses. GE would remain lean, agile, and able to respond quickly to changes in its environment. After achieving these goals faster than expected, in 1988 Welch shifted his focus to adaptation processes that further advanced GE into the most competitive company in the world and the most valuable corporation in America. Two important goals were identified:

- An organization-wide drive to identify and eliminate unproductive work and unnecessary bureaucracy.
- Transformation of employees' attitudes toward creativity, self-confidence, and ownership.

In 1993, following the creation of a highly responsive giant through Work-Out and internal and external benchmarking, the company began its third transformation, by moving from a predominantly American-based company to a global-transnational organization through massive investments in Mexico, China, and India. The goals identified in this context were:

1. Aggressive penetration of foreign countries with opportunities for GE to capitalize on its technological and financial resources, which are GE's primary distinctive competencies.
2. Creation of strategic alliances with other national companies.
3. Globalization of GE's structure.
4. Networking through information technology to achieve coordination.

The lesson from GE's revolution for successful rethinking and reframing structures, processes, and leadership roles is simple yet powerful:

- Create a vision that is credibly communicated and lived
- Set very tough objectives from the top
- Initiate rapid decision making with limited analysis
- Instigate rapid implementation by empowered employees
- Sponsor a continuous push for improvement and change
- Strive for short feedback and learning cycles
- Push delegation and ownership back to where it belongs

The above list is what makes GE an outstanding performer and what differentiates GE from all the rest of its competitors, including ABB. And, ABB knows this very well, for it is the list prepared by its analysts in an attempt to brainstorm new ways to benchmark GE!!

THE IMPORTANCE OF PARADOXICAL SKILLS

Heifetz and Laurie (1997) suggested that effective leaders are more responsive and adaptive when asking the right questions rather than providing the solutions. Providing leadership and not just authoritative expertise is extremely difficult due to patterned leadership behaviors and a self-fulfilling prophecy that prevent excellence from happening. "This tendency is quite natural because many executives reach their positions of authority by virtue of their competence in taking responsibility and solving problems. But the locus of responsibility for problem solving when a company faces an adaptive challenge must shift to its people. Solutions to adaptive challenges reside not in the executive suite but in the collective intelligence of employees at all levels, who need to use one another as resources, often across boundaries, and learn their way to those solutions . . . [The problem is that] many employees are ambivalent about the efforts and sacrifices required of them.

They often look to the senior executive to take problems off their shoulders" (Heifetz & Laurie, 1997, p. 124). However, the roots of this problem are much deeper and require spiritual and visionary leadership that is also frame-breaking and discontinuous. All too often organizational leaders tend to be selected or promoted from within. As a result, only certain types of leadership styles and communication patterns that may conform to the decision makers may be chosen.

Witherspoon (1997) suggested that such styles may generate little change and, therefore, little effects on organizational outcomes. These organizational leaders tend to protect the status quo by providing satisfactory solutions that are understandable and acceptable but that are not frame-breaking solutions. When these leaders function at a lower organizational level, the impact of their influence and actions is relatively small and usually is contained locally. However, when these leaders are the top executives who direct and lead giant organizations, they also need to be charismatic and have independent thinking. When Percy Barnevik stepped down after eight years as president and CEO of Asea Brown Boveri, he turned the job over to his longtime sidekick Goran Lindahl, who was responsible for the Middle East and North Africa operations. In passing the baton to Lindahl, Barnevik said: "If you want to keep momentum and continuity, it is best to get an internal candidate." And Lindahl's response was no different: "I see no reason to change strategy just because we are changing the CEO" (*Business Week*, October 28, 1996, p. 66). To the external observer, this answer may hinge on a drift in favor of incrementalism and continuity. The more serious objective for Lindahl, however, has been to identify the adaptive challenges and frame key questions and issues that brought Barnevik his fame as the human perpetual-motion machine.

Leading horizontal organizations is a challenge that transcends rational management and that requires paradoxical capabilities and behavioral complexity and competencies that distinguish great organizational leaders from others. The challenges that face high-performance leaders are to continue to lead in the midst of discontinuity, to develop biases toward action and adaptive change, and to embrace learning and "relentless consistency," as Jack Welch has labeled it, to inspire people to achieve peak performance. Effective executives must simultaneously embody the status quo and question it (Jonas, Fry & Srivastva, 1990). While top executives who are high-performance leaders are challenged by organizational members and stakeholders to stabilize the system, they are also expected to challenge the existing structural arrangements and patterned behaviors and to ask frame-breaking questions. Citing Itami's (1987) concept of "dynamic fit," Hart and Quinn (1993) suggested that the paradoxical nature of executive leadership and high performance leaders is manifested in the leaders' ability to create and destroy at the same time. "Senior management must send consistent messages and align strategy with structure but must never allow the organization to settle into complacency. As soon as 'balance' is achieved, it must be destroyed. The organization must be challenged to acquire new competencies so that it might be positioned for the future" (p. 555).

EXECUTIVE LEADERSHIP: A MODEL OF THE COMPETING ROLES

Hart and Quinn (1993) tested the hypothesis concerning the relationship between roles executives play and firm performance, using data gathered from a large sample of top managers. They identified four competing roles that executives play with each matching different domains of organizational operation with competing demands: The Vision Setter is geared toward the future and responds to the need for change and innovation; the Motivator focuses on the organization and challenges people to increase their commitment; the Analyzer is attentive to the operating system and is oriented toward efficiency; and the Task Master responds to the market and emphasizes performance. These roles correspond to the Competing Values Framework's quadrants and are depicted in figure 10.4.

High-performance leaders have multiple frames of reference which require cognitive complexity but also behavioral complexity or the ability to perform a variety of roles in the domains facing them (Hooijberg & Quinn, 1992). Managers who demonstrate competence in playing the roles associated with the Competing Values Framework also have been found to be perceived as more effective by their associates as compared with managers who have less paradoxical capabilities or behavioral complexity (Quinn, Spreitzer & Hart, 1992). These findings and empirical observations have led Hart and Quinn (1993) to hypothesize that "The simultaneous use of the Vision Setter, Motivator, Analyzer, and Task Master roles by executives [are] associated with high performance on all three performance dimensions—financial, business, and stakeholder" (p. 556). The main characteristics of these roles are described below.

Top Managers as Dynamic Vision Setters

Top managers are concerned with strategic decisions that affect the equilibrium and effectiveness of the organization. Effective execu-

Figure 10.4. Competing Values Framework: Roles Executives Play

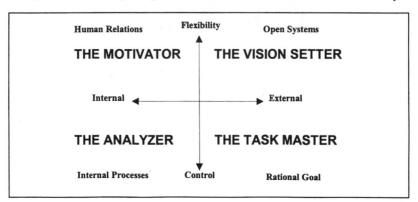

Adapted from: S. L. Hart & R. E. Quinn (1993). "Roles executives play: CEOs, behavioral complexity, and firm performance." *Human Relations*, 46: 115–42. Plenum Publishing Corp.

tives have the ability to articulate an emotionally meaningful vision of change or a mission that is clear, consistent, and compelling and to mobilize support for that vision using their charisma. These executives are exemplary leaders who influence the core values of the organization, shape its structural arrangements, and institutionalize the new vision through personal example. Top managers are engaged in maintaining the effective flow of communication both internally (through informal networks of communication) and externally (through environmental scanning) to sense emerging trends and shape the direction of the organization. Effective top managers have great interpersonal skills and a good deal of knowledge about the inside workings of their industry.

Top Managers as Motivators

As Motivators, executives influence the construction of organizational shared reality—a core set of concepts and priorities which infuse and energize organizational members. Through innovative structures, programs, and processes, the top manager must challenge people to assume new responsibilities, gain new competencies, and achieve higher levels of performance. The Motivator role essentially is involved in the management of meaning through symbols, metaphors, sagas, and rituals that help to create a commitment toward the overarching goals and the cross-functional synergies needed to attain these goals.

Top Managers as Analyzers

As Analyzers, much of top managers' span of attention involves overseeing internal operating efficiencies through decision and rule making that shape internal processes. Effective top managers ask difficult questions which force business and functional managers to think in new ways. Thus, an important skill of the Analyzer is to assure that organizational capabilities and core competencies are in place to help achieve the vision set by the top managers.

Top Managers as Task Masters

The top manager is concerned about the bottom line and meeting stakeholders' needs. The Task Master typically emphasizes external goals, effective performance, and optimal results. The main concern of the task-oriented organizational leader is to improve productivity and profitability.

Hart and Quinn (1993) found that the top managers in their sample rated the Task Master role as the most common role they play, followed by the Analyzer, Vision Setter, and Motivator. However, when these roles have been correlated with measurements of firm performance (i.e., market share, sales growth, and new product development), the Task Master role was found to contribute the least. The results specifically underscore the significance of the Vision Setter and Motivator roles to firm performance. These researchers also found that the unbalanced playing of the Task Master and Analyzer roles appears to hamper performance. This finding is also interesting in light of the study by Belasen, Benke, DiPadova, and Fortunato (1996), in which middle managers indicated that both the transactional and transformational roles are important, but playing the transformational roles more often was needed to achieve better business performance and organizational effectiveness.

Hart and Quinn (1993, p. 569) also found that "The highest levels of performance were achieved by CEOs with high levels of behavioral complexity—leaders who were able to play, at a high level, all four roles. That is, they saw themselves as focusing on broad visions for the future while also providing critical evaluation of present plans. They also saw themselves tending to relational issues while simultaneously emphasizing the accomplishment of tasks." These researchers also observed that those executives who have been playing the four roles simultaneously did so regardless of organizational size or the nature of the competitive environment. This may seem to point to a very interesting implication: that a high degree of behavioral complexity is a universal capability of high-performance leaders! They went on to propose that "the capacity to balance competing demands and play all four roles at a high level suggests lengthy experience, hard work, and the development of knowledge and relationships over a long period of time" (Hart & Quinn, 1993, p. 569). Finally, no strong correlation was found between playing the roles and financial performance indicators (i.e., ROA, ROS, and ROA) of firms whose managers participated in the study by Hart and Quinn. Rather environmental context (e.g., degree of change) and organizational factors (e.g., accounting practices) were assumed to have greater influence on short-term earnings. Although this finding is consistent with common expectations about the lag effect between leadership and profit, it also underscores the significance of the role of top managers as future-oriented Vision Setters. Jack Welch captured the essence of the job of those who lead their organizations to greatness, the job of the CEO:

> Today's CEO in 1997 knows it's the beginning of a career, that the battles are just beginning. No one can come to work and sit, no one can go off and think of just policy, no one can do any of these things. You've got to be live action all day. And you've got to be able to energize others. You cannot be this thoughtful, in-the-corner-office guru . . . you cannot be a moderate, balanced, thoughtful, careful articulator of policy. You've got to be on the lunatic fringe. (Swoboda, 1997)

The road toward initiating, transforming, institutionalizing, and leading horizontal organizations is paved with hurdles and is full of surprises. High-performance leadership involves breaking existing hierarchical structures and functional walls to obtain great results in a somewhat reminiscent old adage—in order to build you must tear down. Like the "piñata"—you must sacrifice the old structure to get to the good things. The list outlined below contains the characteristics and conditions for high-performance leadership:

- High-performance leaders are both instrumental and transformational.
- Transformational leadership is anchored in action learning.
- Action learning requires flexibility and adaptation.
- Adaptation requires the creation of a fluid organization with horizontal management, multifunctional teams, and self-management.
- Renewal and continuous improvement are important for the success of team-based organizations.

- Quality improvement and process reengineering are vital for achievement of performance breakthrough and transitioning the organization toward a world-class organization.
- World-class organizations use internal and external networking to continuously realign themselves with the external environment.
- Realignment is an ever-evolving process which can be (a) supported by a high-speed management system, (b) sustained by action learning, and (c) inspired by high-performance leaders.
- High-performance leadership is the moving force that helps organizations create a vision of success, embrace new technologies, structures, and processes, and carry out a reformulated mission with excellence and compassion.

The menu is impressive. The ideas are innovative and stimulating. The challenge is not how to interpret the social context of organizing; that can be reduced to a simple task due to the enormous amount of knowledge and information that has been amassed over the years about how social systems work. The primary challenge facing high-performance leaders seems to be how to change the social construction of reality and how to create and sustain a new meaning that individually is inspiring and collectively is acceptable. Transforming learning into action is an exciting and inspiring challenge. Intentions alone will not do it. As Welch has said: "Without leaders who walk the talk, all of our plans, promises, and dreams for the future are just talk!" But can they meet the challenge?

References

Adams, J. D. (1984). Achieving and maintaining personal peak performance. In J. D. Adams (ed.), *Transforming work* (pp. 191–207). Alexandria, Va.: Miles River Press.

Adler, P. & Adler, P. A. (1987). Role conflict and identity salience: College athletics and the academic role. *Social Science Journal*, 24, 443–55.

Aggarwal, S. (1993). A quick guide to Total Quality Management. *Business Horizon*, May/June, 36.

Allender, H. D. (1993). Self-directed work teams: How far is too far? *Industrial Management*, 35(5), 13–15.

Alter, C. & Hage, J. (1993). *Organizations working together.* Newbury Park, Calif.: Sage.

Armstrong L. (1994). Borderless management. *Business Week*, May 23, 24–26.

Ashforth, B. E. & Mael, F. (1989). Social identity theory and the organization. *Academy of Management Review*, 14, no. 1, 20–39.

Atkins, S. (1995). *The name of your game* (9th printing, 2d ed.). Beverly Hills, Calif.: Ellis & Stewart.

Avolio, B. J., Waldman, D. A. & Einstein, W. O. (1988). Transformational leadership in management game simulation. *Group and Organization Studies*, 13(1), 59–80.

Back to the laboratory, *The Economist*, October 7, 1995, p. 69.

Badiru, A. B. (1993). *Quantitative methods for project planning, scheduling and control.* Westport, Conn.: Quorum Books.

431

Baker, W. E. (1994). *Networking smart.* New York: McGraw-Hill.

Barge, K. J. (1994). *Leadership: Communication skills for organizations and groups.* New York: St. Martin's Press.

Barker, J. R. (1993). Tightening the iron cage: Concertive control in self-managing teams. *Administrative Science Quarterly,* 38, 408–37.

Barnes, S. & Greller, L. M. (1994). Computer-mediated communication in the organization. *Communication Education,* vol. 43, April, pp. 129–33.

Barry, D. (1991). Managing the bossless team: Lessons in distributed leadership. *Organizational Dynamics,* 20(1), 31–47.

Bass, B. M. (1985). *Leadership and performance beyond expectations.* New York: Free Press.

Bass, B. M. & Avolio, B. J. (1994). Introduction. In Bass, B. M., & Avolio, B. J. (eds.), *Improving organizational effectiveness through transformational leadership* (1–9). Thousand Oaks, Calif.: Sage.

Bassett, G. (1993). *The evolution and future of high-performance management systems.* Westport: Quorum Books.

Beam, H. H. (1997). Transformational learning: Renewing your company through knowledge and skills (book review), *The Academy of Management Executive,* vol. 10(3), pp. 73–75.

Beckhard, R. & Harris, R. T. (1977). *Organizational transition: Managing complex change.* Reading, Mass: Addison-Wesley.

Beer, M., Eisenstat, R. A. & Spector, B. (1990). Why change programs don't produce change. *Harvard Business Review,* November–December, 158–66.

Believe in yourself, believe in the merchandise. (1997). *Forbes,* 160(5), September 8, 118+.

Belasen, A. T. (1997). An application of the competing values framework to self-managed teams. In Rahim, A. M., Golembieski, R. T. & Pate, L. E. (eds.), *Current topics in management,* vol. 2, (79–111). Greenwich, Conn.: JAI Press.

———. (1996). The transformation of the middle line. *FORUM Chronicle,* Empire State College, Saratoga Springs.

Belasen, A. T. (1994, April). *Leadership roles and communication patterns in self-managed teams.* Paper presented at the annual convention of the Eastern Communication Association, Washington, D.C.

Belasen, A. T., Benke, M. & DiNitto, A. (1996). Integrating experiential learning and competencies into management education—Challenges and methods in teaching adults. In DiPadova, L. N. (ed.) *Instructional guide to accompany becoming a master manager: A competency framework.* (2d ed.), 59–71. New York: John Wiley & Sons.

Belasen, A. T., Benke, M., DiPadova, L. N. & Fortunato, V. M. (1996). Downsizing and the hypereffective manager: The shifting importance of managerial roles during organizational transformation. *Human Resource Management Journal,* 35(1), 87–117.

Bennis, W. (1989). *On becoming a leader.* Reading, Mass.: Addison-Wesley.

Bennis, W. & Nanus, B. (1985). *Leaders: The strategies for taking charge.* New York: Harper & Row.

Benson, T. E. (1993). TQM—A child takes a first few faltering steps. *Industry Week*, April, 16–18.

Berry, T. H. (1991). *Managing the total quality transformation.* New York: McGraw Hill.

Blake, R. R. & McCanse, A. (1990). *Leadership dilemmas—Grid solutions.* Houston: Gulf Publishing.

Bluestone, B. & Bluestone, I. (1993). *Negotiating the future.* New York: Basic Books.

———. (1992). Workers and managers of the world unite. *Technology Review*, 95(8), 30–40.

Bollier, D. (1996). Building corporate loyalty. *Management Review*, vol. 85(10), October, pp. 17–22.

Bolman, L. G. & Deal, T. E. (1995). *Leading with soul: An uncommon journey of spirit.* San Francisco: Jossey-Bass.

Bounds, G. M., Dobbins, G. H. & Fowler, O. S. (1995). *Management: A total quality perspective.* Cincinnati, Ohio: Southwestern.

Boyatzis, R. E. (1982). *The competent manager: A model for effective performance.* John Wiley & Sons.

Boyatzis, R. E., Cowen, S. S., Kolb, D. A. & Associates (1995). *Innovation in professional education.* San Francisco: Jossey-Bass.

Bracken, D. W. (1994). Straight talk about multirater feedback. *Training and Development*, September, 44–51.

Bradford, D. L. & Cohen, A. R. (1984). *Managing for excellence: The guide to developing high performance in contemporary organizations.* New York: John Wiley and Sons.

Brewer, M. B. (1993). Social identity, distinctiveness, and in-group homogeneity. *Social Cognition,* 11, no. 1, 150–64.

Brigham, S. E. (1993). TQM lessons we can learn from industry. *Change*, May/June, 42–48.

Brown, M. G., Hitchcock, D. E. & Willard, M. L. (1994). *Why TQM fails and what to do about it.* Burr Ridge, Ill.: Irwin Professional Publishing.

Brown, R. W. (1986). *Social psychology,* 2d ed. New York: Free Press.

Bruton, G. D., Keels J. K. & Shook, C. L. (1996). Downsizing the firm: Answering the strategic questions. *Academy of Management Executive*, 10(2), May: 38–45.

Bryan, E. (1990). The world turned upside down? IBM in the 1990s. *Business Horizon*, November/December, 39–47.

Buchholz, S. & Roth, T. (1987). *Creating the high-performance team.* New York: John Wiley & Sons.

Buhler, P. (1995). Managing in the 90s. *Supervision*, 56, 24–26.

Burdett, J. O. (1993). Managing in the age of discontinuity. *Management Decision*, 31(1), 10–17.

Burrows, P., Hamm, S. & Judge, P. (1997) Is this Apple's Grand Plan? *Business Week*, August 25, 44.

Byrd, R. (1987). Corporate leadership skills: A new synthesis. *Organizational Business*, 34–43.

Byrne, J. A. (1994). The pain of downsizing. *Business Week*, May 9, 60–63.

———. (1993a). Belt-tightening the smart way. *Business Week/Enterprise*, December, 34–38.

———. (1993b). The virtual corporation. *Business Week*. February 8, 1993, 98–103.

Cadwell, Bruce & Gambon, Jill. (1996). Virtual office gets real. *Information Week*, January 22, n563, p. 32.

Cameron, K. S., Freeman, S. J. & Mishra, A. K. (1991). Best practices in white-collar downsizing: Managing contradictions. *Academy of Management Executive*, 5(3).

Carlvert G., Mobley, S. & Marshall L. (1994). *Training & Development*, June, 48(6), 38–43.

Carpenter, T. (1996). Corporate anorexia: A dangerous epidemic. *The Magazine of the American Scene*. 125 (2614), July, 36–38.

Cascio, W. F. (1993). Downsizing: What do we know? What have we learned?" *Academy of Management Executive*, 7(1), 95–104.

Case, J. (1993). A company of business people. *INC.*, April, 79–93.

Caudron, S. (1996). Teaching downsizing survivors how to thrive. *Personnel Journal*. 75(1–6) January, 38–48.

Cervero, R. M. (1988). *Effective continuing education for professionals*. San Francisco: Jossey-Bass.

Chang, R. Y. (1994). Improve processes, reengineer them, or both? *Training & Development*, February, 54–58.

Charan, R. (1991). How networks reshape organizations for results. *Harvard Business Review*, September–October, 104–15.

Chung, R. K. (1993). Benchmarking performance. *Business Credit*, May, 19–21.

Clark, J. & Koonce, R. (1995). Engaging organizational survivors. *Training & Development*, 49, pp. 24–30.

Clark, T. P, Varadarajan R. & Pride, W. (1994). Environmental management: The construct and research propositions. *Journal of Business Research*, 29, 23–29.

Cofsky B. (1993). Digital's self-managed accounting teams. *Management Accounting*, April, 39–42.

Cohen, M. D., March, J. G. & Olsen, J. P. (1972). A Garbage can model of organizational choice. *Administrative Science Quarterly*, 17, March, 1–25.

Cohen, W. M. & Levinthal, D. A. (1990). Absorptive capacity: A new perspective on learning and innovation. *Administrative Science Quarterly*, 35, 128–52.

Cole, R. E. (1993). Introduction. *California Management Review*, Spring, 7–11.

Communication, 28, Fall, 348–65.

Conger, J. A. (1996). Inspiring others: The language of leadership. *Academy of Management Executive*, 5(1), 31–44.

———. (1991). The brave new world of leadership training. *Organizational Dynamics*, 46–58.

———. (1989). *The charismatic leader: Behind the mystique of exceptional leadership*. San Francisco: Jossey Bass.

Covey, S. R. (1989). *The seven habits of highly effective people: Powerful lessons in personal change*. New York: Simon & Schuster.

Covin, J. T. (1993). Managing workforce reduction. *Organization Development Journal*, 11(1), 67–76.

Crouch, J. M. (1992). *An ounce of application is worth a ton of abstraction.* Greensboro, N.C.: LEADS Corporation and Piedmont Pub. Partners.

Cummings, T. G. (1978). Self-regulating work groups: A socio-technical synthesis. *Academy of Management Review*, 3, 625–634.

Cushman, D. & King, S. (1994). *High-Speed Management: Organizational Communication in the 1990s.* Albany: State University of New York Press.

Daft, R. L. (1989). *Organization theory and design.* New York: West Publishing.

Daft, R. L. & Lengel, R. H. (1984). Information richness: A new approach to managerial behavior and organization design. In Barry Staw & Larry L. Cummings (eds.), *Research in organizational behavior*, vol. 6, Greenwich, Conn.: JAI Press.

Daft, R. L., Lengel, R. H. & Klebe Trevino, L. (1987). Message equivocality, media selection, and manager performance: Implications for information systems, *MIS Quarterly*, 11, pp. 355–66.

Daniels, T. D. & Spiker, B. K. (1994). *Perspectives on organizational communication.* Madison, Wisc.: Brown & Benchmark.

D'Andrea-O'Brien, C. & Buono, A. F. (1996, Summer). Building effective learning teams: Lessons from the field. *SAM Advanced Management Journal*, 4–9.

Dansereau, F., Graen, G. & Haga, W. J. (1975). A vertical dyad linkage approach to leadership within formal organizations: A longitudinal investigation of the role-making process. *Organizational Behavior and Human Performance*, 15, 46–78.

Daughtrey, A. S. & Ricks, R. B. (1989). *Contemporary supervision.* New York: McGraw-Hill.

Davidson, F. J. (1994). *The new project management.* San Francisco: Jossey-Bass.

Dayal, I. & Thomas, J. M. (1968). Operation KPE: Developing a new organization. *Journal of applied behavioral science*, 4, 473–506.

Deal, T. E. & Kennedy, A. A. (1982). *Corporate cultures: The rites and rituals of corporate life.* Reading, Mass.: Addison-Wesley.

Del Polito, G. A. (1993). *The Advertising Mail Marketing Bulletin*, 31, March/April.

Delavigne, K. D. & Robertson, J. D. (1994). *Deming's profound change.* Englewood Cliffs, N.J.: Prentice-Hall.

Dellecave, T., Jr. (1995) Charged with change. *Information Week*, September 18, n545, 100–103.

Deming, W. E. (1982). *Out of the crisis.* Cambridge, Mass.: Cambridge University Press.

Denison, D. R. (1984). Bringing corporate culture to the bottom line. *Organizational Dynamics*, 13(2), 5–22.

Denton, K. D. (1991). *Horizontal management.* New York: Lexington Books.

DePree, M. (1990). *Leadership is an art.* New York: Currency-Doubleday.

DiPadova, L. N. (1996). *Instructional guide to accompany becoming a master manager: A competency framework* (2d ed.). New York: John Wiley & Sons.

———. (1995). *Managerial leadership and organizational hierarchy: An exploration of the similarities and differences in managerial roles at hierarchical levels.*

Unpublished doctoral dissertation, Rockefeller College, University at Albany.

DiPadova, L. N. & Faerman, S. R. (1993). Using the Competing Values Framework to facilitate managerial understanding across levels of organizational hierarchy. *Human Resource Management,* 32(1), 143–74.

Dobbs, J. H. (1993). The empowerment environment. *Training and Development,* February, 55–57.

Dopson, S. & Stewart, R. (1990). What is happening to middle management? *British Journal of Management,* 1, 3–16.

Doran, G. (1981). There's a S.M.A.R.T way to write management's goals and objectives. *Management Review* (November).

Dorfman, J. R. (1991). Stocks of companies announcing layoffs fire up investors, but prices often wilt. *Wall Street Journal,* December 10, C1, C2.

Drucker, P. F. (1993). *Managing for the future.* New York: Truman Talley Books.

———. (1990). The emerging theory of manufacturing. *Harvard Business Review,* May–June, 94–102.

———. (1988a). The coming of the new organization. *Harvard Business Review,* January–February.

———. (1988b). Management and the world's work. *Harvard Business Review,* September–October, 65–76.

Dué, R. (1994). The productivity paradox revisited. *Information Systems Management,* Winter, 11(1), 74–76.

Dumaine, B. (1993, February 22). The new nonmanager managers. *Fortune,* 80–84.

Dumaine, B. (1990, May 7). Who needs a boss? *Fortune,* 52–60.

Dyer, W. G. (1995). *Team building.* Reading, Mass.: Addison-Wesley.

Engel, B. (1995). Self-managed teams. Working paper, Department of Communication, State University of New York, Albany.

Etzioni, A. (1961). *A comparative analysis of complex organizations.* New York: Free Press.

Faerman, S. R., Quinn, R. E. & Thompson, M. P. (1987). Bridging management theory and practice: New York State's Public Service Training Program. *Public Administration Review,* 47 (3), 310–19.

Farnham, A. (1991, October 7). Who beats stress best—And how. *Fortune,* 71–86, (February) 55–57.

Filley, A. C., House, R. J. & Kerr, S. (1976). *Managerial process and organizational behavior* (2d ed.). Glenview, Ill.: Scott, Foresman.

Fisher, K. (1993). *Leading self-directed work teams.* New York: McGraw-Hill.

Fitzgerald, P. (1996) Benchmarking pays off. *Chemical Marketing Reporter,* April 8, 249(15), SR16+.

Fleming, R. K. (1992). An integrated behavioral approach to transfer of interpersonal leadership skills. *Journal of Management Education,* 16, 341–53.

Floyd, S. W. & Wooldridge, B. (1996). *The strategic middle manager: How to create and sustain competitive advantage.* San Francisco: Jossey-Bass.

Fortunato, M. V., Belasen, A. T., DiPadova, L. N. & Hart, D. W. (1995). Relevance, accountability, and competencies in management education. *American International College—Journal of Business,* Spring (7), 36–63.

Frazee, V. (1996). When downsizing brings your employees down. *Personnel Journal*, 75(3), 126–27.

Freire, P. (1992). *Education for critical consciousness*. NY: Continuum.

Fuchsberg, G. (1992). Total quality is termed only partial success. *Wall Street Journal*, October 1, B-1.

Fulop, L. (1991). Middle managers: Victims or vanguards of the entrepreneurial movement? *Journal of Management Studies*, 28, 25–44.

Galbraith, J. R. (1993). The business unit of the future. In J. R. Galbraith, E. F. Lawler III and Associates (eds.), *Organizing for the future: The new logic for managing complex organizations* (pp. 43–64). San Francisco: Jossey-Bass.

Galbraith, J. R. & Lawler, E. E. (1993). *Organizing for the future*. San Francisco: Jossey-Bass.

Garfield, C. S. (1986). *Peak performers*. New York: Avon Books.

Garvin, D. A. (1993). Building a learning organization. *Harvard Business Review*, July–August, 78–91.

Geber, B. (1994). Guerrilla teams: Friend or foe? *Training*, 31(6), 36–39.

———. (1988). Not just another printing shop. *Training*, May, 65–69.

Geisler, E. (1994). How strategic is your IT? *Industrial Management*, 36(1), 31–32.

Gendron, G. & Burlingham, B. (1986). Printer Harry Quadracci, *Inc*. December, 24–38.

Gertz, D. L. & Baptista, J. P. (1995). *Grow to be great: Breaking the downsizing cycle*. New York: Free Press.

Goldhaber, G. M. (1993). *Organizational Communication* (6th ed.). Dubuque, Iowa: Brown & Benchmark.

Goll, E O. & Cordovano M. F. (1993). Construction time again. *CIO*, October 15, 32–36.

Grain's New York Business (1997) vol. 13, no. 31 (August 4–10).

Grant, R. M., Shani, R. & Krishnan, R. (1994). TQM's challenge to management theory and practice. *Sloan Management Review*, Winter, 25–34.

Gray, B. (1991). *Collaborating: Finding common ground for multiparty problems*. San Francisco: Jossey-Bass.

Greising, D. (1994). Return on quality. *Business Week*, August 8, 54–59.

Grimsley, K. D. (1996) For workers "surplused" by IBM, lives forever changed. *Washington Post*, March 31, A1.

Guzzo, R. A., Jette, R. D. & Katzell, A. (1985). The effects of psychologically based intervention programs on worker productivity: A meta-analysis. *Personnel Psychology*, 38(2), 275–92.

Hackman, J. (1990). *Groups that work*. San Francisco: Jossey-Bass.

Hackman, J. R. & Oldham, G. (1975). Development of the job diagnostic survey. *Journal of Applied Psychology*, 60, 159–70.

Hall, G., Rosenthal J. & Wade J. (1993). How to make reengineering really work. *Harvard Business Review*, November–December, 119–30.

Halpp, L. (1993). *Journal for Quality and Participation*, December, 64–70.

Hamel, G. (1991). Competition for competence and inter-partner learning within international strategic alliances. *Strategic Management Journal*, 12, 83–103.

Hammer, M. (1990). Reengineering work: Don't automate, obliterate. *Harvard Business Review*, July–August, 104–112.

Hammer, M. & Champy, J. (1992). What is reengineering. *Informationweek* May 5, 10–24.

———. (1993). *Reengineering the corporation.* New York: Harper Collins.

Harcourt J., Richerson V. & Wattier, M. J. (1991). A national study of manager's assessment of organizational communication quality. *Journal of Business.*

Harrington, J. H. (1987). *The improvement process.* New York: McGraw-Hill.

Harrington-Mackin, D. (1994). *The team-building tool kit: Tips, tactics and rules for effective workplace teams.* New York: AMACOM.

Harrison, R. (1972). Role negotiation: A tough-minded approach to team development. In W. W. Burke & H. A. Hornstein (eds.), *The social technology of organization development* (pp. 84–96). La Jolla, Calif.: University Associates,.

Hart, S. L. & Quinn, R. E. (1993). Roles executives play: CEOs, behavioral complexity, and firm performance. *Human Relations,* 46: 543–74.

Hecksher, C. (1996). *White-collar blues: Management loyalties in an age of corporate restructuring.* New York: Basic Books.

Heifetz, R. A. & Laurie, D. L. (1997). The work of leadership. *Harvard Business Review.* January–February, vol. 75(1), pp. 124–34.

Heimovics, R. D. & Herman, R. D. (1989). The salient management skills: A conceptual framework for a curriculum for managers in nonprofit organizations. *American Review of Public Administration,* 119, 295–312.

Heller, R. (1995). *The leadership imperative.* New York: Penguin Books.

Hersey, P. & Blanchard, K. H. (1993). *Management of organizational behavior: Utilizing human resources.* Englewood Cliffs, N.J.: Prentice-Hall.

Higher education and work readiness: The view from the corporation, Task force on high-performance work and workers: The academic connection. *Business Higher Education Forum,* September 1995, pp. 1–17.

Hildebrand, C. (1994). A resourcing maybe. *CIO,* 7 (8), 34–37.

Hill, R. C. & Freedman, S. M. (1992). Managing the quality process: Lessons from a Baldridge award winner: A conversation with Wallace, J. W., CEO of the Wallace Co. *Academy of Management Executive,* 6(1), 76–88.

Hirschorn, L. & Gilmore, T. (1992). The new boundaries of the "boundaryless" company. *Harvard Business Review,* May/June, 104–15.

Hitchcock, D. & Willard, M. (1995). *Why teams can fail and what to do about it.* Chicago: Irwin Professional.

Hogg, M. A. & Turner, J .C. (1985). Interpersonal attraction, social identification and psychological group function. *European Journal of Social Psychology,* 15, 51–66.

Hooijberg, R. & Quinn, R. E. (1992). Behavioral complexity and the development of effective managers. In R. L. Phillips & J. G. Hunt (eds.), *Strategic leadership: A multiorganizational-level perspective* (pp. 161–76). Westport, Conn.: Quorum Books.

Hotch, R. (1993). Managing from a distance and the well-equipped telecommuter. *Nation's Business,* 8(2), 24–26.

House, R. J. (1971). A path goal theory of leadership effectiveness. *Administrative Science Quarterly,* September, 321–39.

Hsu, J. & Lockwood, T. (1993). Collaborative computing. *BYTE*. March, 113–20.

Huber, G. P. (1991). Organizational learning: The contributing processes and literature. *Organization Science*, 2, 88–115.

Huey, J. (1994). The new post-heroic leadership. *Fortune*. February 21, 42–50.

Ibarra, H., (1992) Structural alignment, individual strategies, and managerial action. In Nohria, N. & Eccles, R. (eds.), *Networks and organizations*. Cambridge, Mass.: Harvard Business School Press.

Imai, M. (1985). *Kaizen*. New York: Random House.

Isgar, T., Ranney, J. & Grinnell, S. (1994). *Training and Development*, April, 45–47.

Itami, H. (1987). *Mobilizing invisible assets*. Cambridge, Mass.: Harvard University Press.

Jacob, R. (1993). TQM more than a dying fad? *Fortune*, Oct. 18.

Jessup, H. R. (1990). New roles in team leadership. *Training and Development Journal*, November, 79–83.

Johnson, L. W. & Frohman, A. L. (1989). Identifying and closing the gap in the middle of organizations. *The Academy of Management Executive*, 2, 107–14.

Johnstone, D. B. (1994). College at work—Partnerships and the rebuilding of American Competence. *Journal of Higher Education*, 65(2), March/April, 166–82.

Jonas, H., Fry, R. & Srivastva, S. (1990). The office of the CEO: Understanding the executive experience. *Academy of Management Executive*, 4, 36–48.

Jones, S. (1995). Computer-mediated communication and community: Introduction. *Computer-Mediated Communication Magazine*, vol. 2(3), p. 38, March 1.

Kanter, R. M. (1989). The new managerial work. *Harvard Business Review*, 67(6), 85–92.

———. (1986). The reshaping of middle management. *Management Review*, January.

———. (1983). *The change masters: Innovation and entrepreneurship in the American corporation*. New York: Simon & Schuster.

———. (1979). Power failure in management circuit. *Harvard Business Review*, 57, 65–75.

———. (1977). Some effects of proportions on group life: Skewed sex ratios and responses to token women. *American Journal of Sociology*, 82, 965–90.

Katzenbach, J. R. (1995). *Real change leaders: How you can create growth and high performance at your company*. New York: Times Business Random-House.

Katzenbach, R. & Smith, D. K. (1993). *The wisdom of teams: Creating the high-performance organization*. Boston: Harvard Business School Press.

Kaufman, H. (1985). *The Limits of Organizational Change*. University, Alabama: The University of Alabama Press.

Kehrer, D. M. (1989). The miracle of theory Q. *Business Month*, September.

Kendrick, J. (1992). Benchmarking survey builds case for looking to others for TQM models. *Quality*, March.

Kerr, S. & Jermier, J. M. (1978). Substitutes for leadership: Their meaning and measurement. *Organizational Behavior and Human Performance*, 22, 375–403.

Kerzner, H. (1989). *Project management: A systems approach to planning, scheduling, and controlling* (3d ed.). New York: Van Nostrand Reinhold.

Kimberly, R. J. & Quinn, E. R. (1984). *Managing Organizational Transitions.* Homewood, Ill.: Irwin.

King, D. (1988). Team excellence. *Management Solutions,* 10, 25–28.

Kirschen J, (1989). Rewriting the rule book: A success story at Quad. *Printing Impressions,* June, 24–28.

Kolb, D. A. (1984). *Experiential Learning.* Englewood Cliffs, N.J.: Prentice-Hall.

Kotler, P. & Armstrong, G. (1994). *Principles of marketing* (6th ed.). Englewood Cliffs, N.J.: Prentice Hall.

Kotter, J. P. (1990). *A Force for Change.* New York: Free Press.

———. (1982). *The general managers.* New York: Free Press.

Kotter, J. P. & Heskett, J. L. (1992). *Corporate culture and performance.* NY: Simon & Schuster.

Kram, K. E. (1983). Phases of the mentor relationship. *Academy of Management Journal,* 26(4), 608–25.

Kram, K. E. & Isabella, L. A. (1985). Mentoring alternatives: The role of peer relationships in career development. *Academy of Management Journal,* 28, 110–32.

Kuhnert, K. W. (1994). Transforming Leadership: Developing people through delegation. In Bass, B. M. & Avolio, B. J. (eds.), *Improving organizational effectiveness through transformational leadership* (10–25). Thousand Oaks, Calif.: Sage.

Kunda, G. (1992). *Reengineering culture.* Philadelphia: Temple University Press.

Larkin, T. J. & Larkin, S. (1994). *Communicating Change.* New York: McGraw-Hill.

Latham, G. P. & Wexley, K. N. (1994). *Increasing productivity through performance appraisal* (2d ed.). Reading, Mass.: Addison-Wesley.

Lawler, E. E., III. (1992). *The ultimate advantage: Creating the high-involvement organization.* San Francisco: Jossey-Bass.

———. (1988). Substitutes for hierarchy, *Organizational Dynamics,* Summer.

Lawler, E. E., III & Mohrman, S. A. (1987). Quality circles: After the honeymoon. *Organizational Dynamics,* Spring, 42–54.

Lawler, E. E., III, Mohram, S. A. & Ledford, G. E. (1992). *Employee involvement and total quality management.* San Francisco: Jossey Bass.

Lawrence, P. R. & Lorsch, J. W. (1967). *Organization and environment: Managing differentiation and integration.* Homewood, Ill.: Richard D. Irwin.

Ledford, G. E. & Mohrman, S. E. (1993). Self-design for high involvement: A large scale organizational change. *Human Relations,* 46(1), 143–73.

Letter-Perfect Operations at USPS. (1997). *Geo Info Systems,* June, 7(6), 17.

Leuchter, M. (1995) Slimmed down Fleet tries to keep momentum in NY. *Crain's New York Business,* February 20, 4.

Levinson, M. (1993). Playing with fire. *Newsweek,* June 21, 46–48.

Levitt, B. & March, J. G. (1988). Organizational learning. *Annual Review of Sociology,* 14, 319–40.

Liebowitz, S. L. & DeMeuse, K. P. (1982). The application of team building. *Human Relations*, 35, 1–18.

Lipnack, J. & Stamps, J. (1993). *TeamNet factor*. Vermont: Oliver Wright Publications.

Locke, E. A. & Latham, G. P. (1984) *Goal setting: A motivational technique that works*. Englewood Cliffs, N.J.: Prentice Hall.

London, M. (1996). Redeployment and continuous learning in the twenty-first century: Hard lessons and positive examples from the downsizing era. *Academy of Management Executive*, 10(4) 67–78.

Long, C. & Vickers-Koch, M. (1994). Creating a vision statement that is shared and works. *Journal for Quality and Participation*, June, 17(3), 74–77.

Lutz, R. (1994). Implementing technological change with cross-functional teams. *Research Technology Management*, April, 14–18.

Mael, F. A. & Ashforth, B. E. (1995). Loyal from day one: Biodata, organizational identification, and turnover among newcomers. *Personnel Psychology*, 48, 309–33.

Mael, F. A. & Tetrick, L. E. (1992). Identifying organizational identification. *Educational and Psychological Measurement*, 52, 813–23.

Magjuka, R. J. (1993). The ten dimensions of employee involvement. *Training and Development*, April, 61–67.

Magnet, M. (1994). The new golden rule of business. *Fortune*, February 21, 60–64.

Maisel, L. S. (1996). Proactive and powerful: The new CEO. *Financial Executive*, 6, 13–17.

Maljers, F. A. (1992). Inside Unilever: The evolving transnational company. *Harvard Business Review*, September–October, 46–51.

Management: Fishing for ideas. (1997) *Financial Times* (London Ed.), July 9, 8.

Manz, C. C. (1992). Self-leading work teams: Moving beyond self-management myths. *Human Relations*, 45(11), 1119–40.

Manz, C. C. & Sims, H. P. (1987). Leading workers to lead themselves: The external leadership of self-managing work teams. *Administrative Science Quarterly*, 32, 106–28.

Manz, C. C., Keating, D. E. & Donnellion, A. (1990). Preparing for an organizational change to employee self-management: The managerial transition. *Organizational Dynamics*, August, 15–26.

McCarroll, T. (1992). How IBM was left behind. *Time*, December 28, 26–28.

McDermott, L. C. (1993). Jump-starting managers on quality. *Training and Development*, September, 37–40.

McEvoy, G. M. & Cragun, J. R. (1987). Management skill-building in an organization behavior course. *Organizational Behavior Teaching Review*, 11(4), 60–73.

McKee, B. (1992). Turn your workers into a team. *Nation's Business*, July, 80, 126–27.

McWhinney, W. (1992). *Paths of change*. Newbury Park, Calif.: Sage.

Meadows, I. S. G. (1980). Organic structure and innovation in small work groups. *Human Relations*, 33, 369–82.

Micklethwait, J. & Wooldridge, A. (1996). *The witch doctors: Making sense of the management gurus.* New York: Random House.

Miles, R. & Snow, C. C. (1978). *Organizational strategy, structure, and process.* New York: McGraw-Hill.

Miller, D. & Friesen, P. M. (1982). Structural change and performance: Quantum versus piecemeal-incremental approaches. *Academy of Management Journal* (25), pp. 867–92.

Miller, K. & Monge, P. (1986). Participation, satisfaction, and productivity: A meta-analysis review. *Academy of Management Journal*, 29, 727–53.

Miller, W. H. (1997). Runyon delivers a turnaround. *Industry Week*, February 3, 246(3), p. 44.

Mink, O. G., Owen, K. Q. & Mink, B. P. (1993). *Developing high performance people.* Reading, Mass.: Addison-Wesley.

Mintzberg, H. (1989). *Mintzberg on management: Inside our strange world of organizations.* New York: Free Press.

———. (1983). *Structure in Fives.* Englewood Cliffs, N.J.: Prentice Hall.

Mitchell, R. (1994). Managing by values. *Business Week*, August 1, 46–51.

Mitchell, R. & Weber, J. (1994). And the next juicy plum may be . . . McKesson? *Business Week*, Feb. 28, 36.

Moats Kennedy, M. (1996). Why managers get fired. *Across the Board.* March: 53–54.

Morgan, G. (1993). *Imaginization: The art of creative management.* Newbury Park, Calif.: Sage.

———. (1988). *Riding the waves of change—Developing managerial competencies for a turbulent world.* San Francisco: Jossey-Bass.

———. (1986). *Images of organizations.* Newbury Park, Calif.: Sage.

Morris, D. M. (1996). Everybody's doing it. *Business Credit*, July/August, pp. 51–52.

Morris, D. & Brandon, J. (1993). *Reengineering your business.* New York: McGraw-Hill.

Muller, H., Porter, J. & Rehder, R. (1991). Reinventing the MBA the European way. *Business Horizon*, vol. 34(3), May/June.

Murray, D. (1984). *Write to learn.* New York: Holt, Rinehart & Winston.

Myers, T. E. (1993). Downsizing blues: How to keep up morale. *Management Review*, 82 (April), 28–31.

Nadler, D. A., Gerstein, M. S., Shaw R. B. & Associates. (1992). *Organizational architecture—Designs for changing organizations.* San Francisco: Jossey-Bass.

Nahavandi, A. & Aranda, E. (1994). Restructuring teams for the reengineering organization. *Academy of Management Executive*, 8(4), 56–68.

Nahavandi, A. & Malekzadeh, A. (1995). Acculturation in mergers and acquisitions. In T. Jackson (ed.), *Cross-cultural management*, pp. 326–41. Oxford: Butterworth Heinemann.

Naisbit, J. & Aburdene, P. (1985). *Re-inventing the corporation.* New York: Warner Books.

Nelton, S. (1993). A flexible style of management. *Nation's Business*, 81. 12, 24–31.

Noer, D. M. (1995). *Learning from the past: The survivor syndrome across time*. San Francisco: Jossey-Bass.

No more easy money. (1996). *Traffic World* September 9, 247(10), 22.

Nonaka, I. (1988). Creating order out of chaos. *California Management Review*, 30, 57–73.

Obloj, K., Cushman D. & Kozminski, A. (1994). *Continuous improvement: Theories and practices*. Albany: State University of New York Press.

O'Connell, S. E. (1988). Human communication in the high tech office. In Goldhaber, G. M. & Barnett, G. A. (eds.), *Handbook of Organizational Communication* (473–82). Norwood, N.J.: Ablex.

O'Connor, E. S. (1993). People skills as a discipline, pedagogy, and set of standard practices. *Journal of Management Education*, 17, 218–27.

O'Dell, C. A. & McAdams, J. (1987). *People, performance, and pay*. Houston, Tex.: American Productivity Center.

Orsburn, J. D., Moran, L., Musselwhite, E. & Zenger, J. H. (1990). *Self-directed work teams: The new American challenge*. Homewood, Ill.: Irwin.

Ostroff, F. & Smith, D. (1992). The horizontal organization. *The McKinsey Quarterly*, 1, 148–68.

Ouchi, W. G. (1981). *Theory Z: How American business can meet the Japanese challenge*. Reading Mass.: Addison-Wesley.

———. (1980). Markets, bureaucracies, and clans. *Administrative Science Quarterly*, 25, 129–41.

———. (1979). A conceptual framework for the design of organizational control mechanisms. *Management Science*, 25, 833–48.

Parker, G. M. (1994a). *Cross-functional teams: Working with allies, enemies, and other strangers*. San Francisco: Jossey-Bass.

———. (1994b). Cross-functional collaboration, *Training & Development*, October, 49–53.

———. (1990). *Team players and teamwork*. San Francisco: Jossey-Bass.

Parsons, T. (1960). *Structure and process in modern organizations*. New York: Free Press.

Partnering drives success at Honda. (1995). *Electronic Buyers News*, May 22, n956, 8+.

Partnership or nothing philosophy. (1995). *Management Consultant International*, February, n66, 5.

Patrick, M. B. (1994). Outsourcing has many potential benefits for PR firms. *Public Relations Quarterly*, 39, pp. 37–39

Patterson, J. (1994). Welcome to the company that isn't there. *Business Week*, October 17, 86–87.

Pelz, D. C. (1952). Influence: A key to effective leadership in the first-line supervisor. *Personnel*, 29, November, 209–17.

Pentland, B. T. & Reuter, H. H. (1994). Organizational routines as grammars of actions. *Administrative Science Quarterly*, 39, 484–510.

Perrow, C. (1986). *Complex organizations*, New York: Random House.

Peters, T. J. & Austin, N. (1985). *A passion for excellence: The leadership difference*. New York: Random House.

Peters, T. J. & Waterman, R. J. (1982). *In search of excellence.* New York: McGraw-Hill.

Pfeffer, J. (1981). Management as symbolic action: The creation and maintenance of organizational paradigms. In Cummings, L. L. & Staw, B. M. (eds.), *Research in Organizational Behavior,* 3(1–52). Greenwich, Conn.: JAI.

———. (1978). The micropolitics of organizations. In Meyer, M. W., et al., *Environments and Organizations* (29–50). San Francisco: Jossey-Bass.

Piore, M. J. & Sabel, C. F. (1984). *The second industrial divide: Possibilities for prosperity.* New York: Basic Books.

Pondy, L. R. (1978). Leadership is a language game. In McCall, M. W., Jr. & Lombardo, M. M. (eds.), *Leadership: Where else can we go?* (88–99). Durham, N.C.: Duke University Press.

Porter, L. W. & McKibbin, L. E. (1988). *Management education and Development: Drift or thrust into the twenty-first Century?* New York: McGraw-Hill.

Prahalad, C. K. & Hamel, G. (1990). The core competence of the corporation. *Harvard Business Review,* May–June (3), 81– 91.

Preble, J., Rav, P. & Reichel, A.. (1988). The environmental scanning practices of U.S. multinationals in the late 1990s. *Management Information Review,* 28(4), 4–14.

Quinlan, T. (1996). Vendor strategy Apple contemplates leadership void. *InfoWorld,* vol. 18(3), January 15.

Quinn, R. E. (1988). *Beyond rational management.* San Francisco: Jossey-Bass.

———. (1984). Applying the competing values approach to leadership: Toward an integrative framework. In Hunt, J. G., Hosking, D., Schriesheim, C. & Stewart, R. (eds.), *Leaders and managers: International perspectives on managerial behavior and leadership.* Elmsford, New York: Pergamon Press.

Quinn, R. E. & Cameron, K. S. (1988). Paradox and transformation: A framework for viewing organization and management. In Quinn, R. E. & Cameron, K. S. (eds.), *Paradox and transformation* (289–308). Cambridge, Mass.: Ballinger.

———. (1983). Organizational life cycles and the criteria of effectiveness. *Management Science,* 29, 33–51.

Quinn, R. E., Faerman, S. R., Thompson, M. P. & McGrath, M. R. (1996). *Becoming a master manager: A competency framework.* New York: John Wiley and Sons.

Quinn, R. E. & Hart, S. L. (1993). Roles executives play: CEOs, behavioral complexity, and firm performance. *Human Relations,* 5, 543–74.

Quinn, R. E. & Kimberly, J. R. (1984). Paradox, planning, and perseverance: Guidelines for managerial practice. In Kimberly, J. R. & Quinn, R. E. (eds.), *Managing organizational transitions* (295–313). Homewood, Ill.: Richard Irwin.

Quinn, R. E., Spreitzer, G. M. & Hart S. L. (1992). Integrating the extremes: Crucial Skills for managerial effectiveness. In Srivastva, S., Fry, R. E. &

Associates, *Executive and organizational continuity—Managing the paradoxes of stability and change* (222–52). San Francisco: Jossey-Bass.

Quinn, R. E. & Rohrbaugh, J. (1983). A spatial model of effectiveness criteria: Towards a competing values approach to organizational analysis. *Management Science*, 29(3), 363–77.

Ray, D. & Bronstein, H. (1995). *Teaming up: Making the transition to a self-directed, team-based organization.* New York: McGraw-Hill.

Redding, J. C. & Catalanello, R. F. (1994). *Strategic Readiness: The making of the learning organization.* San Francisco: Jossey-Bass.

Reengineering the MBA. *The Economist*, April 13, 1996, p. 65.

Reese, J. (1991). General Electric as CEO boot camp. *Fortune*, April 8, p. 12.

Reichheld, F. F. (1996). *The loyalty effect: The hidden force behind force, profits, and lasting value.* Boston: Harvard Business School Press.

Remick, J. (1991). Using communication to manage following a major reorganization. *Supervisory Management*, 35, July, 3.

Rhinesmith, S. H. (1992). Global mindsets for global managers. *Training and Development*, October, 63–68.

Rice, R. E. & Love, G. (1987). Electronic emotion: Socioemotional content in computer-mediated communication network. *Communication Research*, vol. 14, pp. 85–108.

Robbins, S. P. (1990). *Organization theory: Structure, design, and applications.* Englewood Cliffs, N.J.: Prentice Hall.

Robey, D. & Sales, C. (1994). *Designing Organizations*, Burr Ridge, Ill.: Irwin.

Robinson, B. & Drucker, M. (1991). Innovative approaches to downsizing: The experience in Maine. *Employee Relations Today*, Spring, 79–87.

Rogers, P. S. & Hildebrandt, H. W. (1993). Competing values instruments for analyzing written and spoken management messages. *Human Resource Management Journal*, 32(1), 121–42.

Rubach, L. (1995). Downsizing: How quality is affected as companies shrink. *Quality Progress*, 28(4), April, 23–28.

Rummler, G. & Brache, A. P. (1990). *Improving performance: How to manage the white space on the organization chart.* San Francisco: Jossey-Bass.

Sayles, L. R. (1993). Doing things right: A new imperative for middle managers. *Organizational Dynamics*, Spring, 5–14.

Schares, G. E. (1993). Percy Barnevik's global crusade. *Business Week/Enterprise*, December, 204–11.

Schmidt, W. H. & Finnigan, J. P. (1994). *TQManager.* San Francisco: Jossey-Bass.

———. (1992). *The race without a finish line.* San Francisco: Jossey-Bass.

Schmit, J. (1997). Apple trims 4,100 jobs, tighten focus. *USA Today*, March 17.

Schon, D. A. (1987). *Educating the reflective practitioner: Toward a new design for teaching and learning in the professions.* San Francisco: Jossey-Bass.

Sendelbach, N. B. (1993). The Competing Values Framework for management training and development: A tool for understanding complex issues and tasks. *Human Resource Management*, 32(1), 75–99.

Senge, P. (1990). *The fifth discipline: The art and practice of the learning organization.* New York: Doubleday.

Shadle, C., Belasen, A. T. & Benke, M. (1996). Part one of an outcomes study: Implications for management education. In *Visions and Revisions,* 16th Annual Alliance/Ace Conference, An Association for Alternative Degree Programs for Adults and the American Council on Education, October, pp. 202–12.

Sherman, D. (1989). The mind of Jack Welch. *Fortune,* March 27, 39–50.

Sherman, S. (1995). Wanted: Company change agents. *Fortune,* December 11, 197–98.

Sims, H. P. & Lorenzi, P. (1992). *The new leadership paradigm.* Newbury Park, Calif.: Sage.

Smart, T. & Dobrzynski, J. H. (1993). Jack Welch on the art of thinking small. *Business Week/Enterprise,* December, 212–16.

Smart, T., Engardino, P. & Smith, G. (1993). GE's brave new world. *Business Week,* November, 8, 64–70.

Smith, P. B. & Peterson, M. F. (1988). *Leadership, organizations and culture: An event management model.* London: SAGE.

Smith, R. & Lipin, S. (1996) Odd Numbers: Are companies using restructuring costs to fudge the figures? *Wall Street Journal,* January 30, A1.

Snow, C. C., Miles, R. E. & Coleman, H. J. (1992). Managing twenty-first-century network organizations. *Organizational Dynamics,* Winter, 5–20.

Solomon, C. M. (1991). Behind the wheel at Saturn. *Personnel Journal,* 70(6), 72–74.

Sorohan, G. E. (1994). When the ties that bind break. *Training & Development,* February, 28–33.

Spreitzer, G. M. & Quinn, R. E. (1996). Empowering middle managers to be transformational leaders. *Journal of Applied Behavioral Science,* vol. 32(3), 237–61.

Stanley, B. (1995). Outsource this, you turkeys! *Fortune,* December 11, 132 (12), 43–44.

Stroh, P. & Miller, W. W. (1994). Learning to thrive on paradox. *Training & Development,* September, 28–39.

Stundza, T. (1993). Intel uses suppliers to cut order-to-delivery cycle time. *Purchasing,* 115, November 25, 16–23.

Sundstrom, E., DeMeuse, K. P. & Futrell, D. (1990). Work teams: Applications and effectiveness. *American Psychologist,* 42, 120–33.

Swoboda, F. (1997) Talking management with chairman Welch. *Washington Post,* March 23, H1.

Tajfel, H. (1982). Instrumentality, identity and social comparisons. In H. Tajfel (ed.), *Social identity and intergroup relations* (pp. 483–507). Cambridge, England: Cambridge University Press.

———. (1978). The achievement of group differentiation. In H. Tajfel (ed.), *Differentiation between social groups: Studies in the social psychology of intergroup relations* (pp. 77–98). London: Academic Press.

Tang, T. L. & Fuller, R. M. (1995). Corporate downsizing: What managers can do to lessen the negative effects of layoffs. *SAM Advanced Management Journal,* 60(4), 12–15.

Tannenbaum, S. I., Beard, R. L. & Salas, E. (1992). Team building and its influence on team effectiveness: Conceptual and empirical developments. In K. Kelley (ed.), *Issues, theory, and research in industrial/organizational psychology* (pp. 117–53). Amsterdam: North-Holland.

Taylor, W. (1991). The logic of global business: An interview with ABB's Percy Barnevik. *Harvard Business Review*, March/April, pp. 91–106.

Telecommuting. (1997). *Business Week*, October 7.

Telecommuting will define much of the twenty-first-century workforce. (1997). *Direct Marketing Magazine*, 60, n3, July, p. 64.

Thompson, J. D. (1967). *Organizations in action*. New York: McGraw-Hill.

Tichy, N. M. (1983). *Managing strategic change: Technical, political, and cultural dynamics*. New York: John Wiley & Sons.

Tichy, N. & Charan, R. (1989). Speed, simplicity, and self confidence: An interview with Jack Welch. *Harvard Business Review*, 112–20.

Tichy, N. M. & Sherman, S. (1993). Walking the talk at GE. *Training and Development*, June, 26–35.

Tichy, N. M. & Ulrich, D. (1984). Revitalizing organizations: The leadership role. In Kimberly, J. R. & Quinn, R. E., *Managing organizational transitions* (240–64). Homewood, Ill.: Richard Iwin.

Tjosvold, D. (1993) *Learning to manage conflict: Getting people to work together.* New York: Lexington Books.

Tobin, D. R. (1996). *Transformational learning: Renewing your company through knowledge and skills.* New York: John Wiley & Sons.

Tompkins, P. K. & Cheney G. (1985). Communication and unobtrusive control in contemporary organizations. In McPhee, R. D. & Tompkins, P. K. (eds.), *Organizational communication: Traditional themes and new directions* (179–210). Newbury Park, Calif.: Sage.

Torbert, W. (1987). *Managing the corporate dream: Restructuring for long-term success.* Illinois: Homewood.

Trapp, R. (1996). Downsizing or "corporate anorexia"? *World Press View*, April, 34–35.

Treece, J. B. (1993). Improving the soul of an old machine. *Business Week*, October 25, 134–36.

Trist, E. L. (1981). The evolution of sociotechnical systems. Occasional paper no. 2. Toronto: Quality of Working Life Center.

Trist, E. & Murray, H. (1993). *The social engagement of social science.* Philadelphia: University of Pennsylvania Press.

Tudor, T. R., Trumble, R. R. & Diaz, J. J. (1996, Autumn). Work teams: Why do they fail? *SAM Advanced Management Journal*, 31–39.

Turner, I. (1994). Strategy and organization. *Manager Update*, 6, 1–9.

Turner, J. C. (1981) The experimental social psychology of intergroup behavior. In J. C. Turner & H. Giles (eds.), *Intergroup Behavior* (pp. 66–101). Chicago: University of Chicago Press.

Umanath, N. S. & Campbell, T. L. (1994). Differential diffusion of information systems technology in multinational enterprises: A research model. *Information Resources Management Journal*, 7(1), 6–18.

United States General Accounting Office, Washington, D.C. 20548. (1991). National Security and International Affairs Division, 91, 190 Management Practices, 2–42.

Van Cauwenbergh, A. & Cool, K. (1982). Strategic management in a new framework. *Strategic Management Journal*, 3, 245–64.

Venkatraman, N. (1994). IT-enabled business transformation: From automation to business scope redefinition. *Sloan Management Review*, Winter, 35(2) 73–87.

Vroom, V. H. (1973). A new look at managerial decision making. *Organizational Dynamics*, Spring, 66–80.

Vroom, V. H. & Jago, A. G. (1988). *The new leadership*. Englewood Cliffs, N.J.: Prentice-Hall.

Wal-Mart ups the pace. (1996). *Information Week*, December 9, n609, 37+.

Walther, J. B. (1996). Computer-mediated communication: Impersonal, interpersonal, and hyperpersonal. *Communication Research*, vol. 23(1), February, 3–43.

Walton, M. (1986). *The Deming management method*. New York: Putman.

Walton, R. (1985). From control to commitment in the workplace. *Harvard Business Review*, 63(2), 76–84.

Weber, J. & Driscoll, L. (1991). Jack Welch's jackhammer nails corner office. *Business Week*, July 15, 28.

Weedman, J. (1992). Informal and formal channels in boundary spanning communication. *Journal of the American Society for Information Science*, 43(3), 257–67.

Weick, K. E. (1985). Cosmos vs. chaos: Sense and nonsense in electronic contexts. *Organizational Dynamics*, 14, 51–65.

———. (1976). Educational organizations as loosely coupled systems. *Administrative Science Quarterly*, 21(1), 1–19.

Wellins, R. S. (1992). Building a self-directed work team. *Training & Development*, 46(12), 24–28.

Wellins, R. S., Byham, W. C. & Wilson, J. M. (1991). *Empowered teams*. San Francisco: Jossey Bass.

West III, P. G. & Meyer, D. G. (1997). Communicated knowledge as a learning foundation. *The International Journal of Organizational Analysis*, vol. 5(1), 25–58.

Westley, F. (1990). Middle managers and strategy: Microdynamics of inclusion. *Strategic Management Journal*, 11, 337–52.

Whetten, D. A. & Cameron, K. S. (1995). *Developing management skills*. New York: Harper Collins.

Whetten, D. A. & Clark, S. C. (1996). An integrated model for teaching management skills. *Journal of Management Education*, 20, 152–81.

Whetten, D. A., Windes, D. L., May, D. R. & Bookstaver, D. (1991). Bringing management education into the mainstream. In Bigelow, J. D. (ed.), *Managerial skills: Explorations in practical knowledge* (pp. 23–40). Newbury Park, Calif.: Sage.

Wigglesworth, D. C. (1996). A guide to motivating the survivors. *HRMagazine,* February, 98–99.

Witherspoon, P. D. (1997). *Communicating leadership: An organizational perspective.* Boston: Allyn & Bacon.

Yammarino, F. J. (1994). In Bass, B. M. & Avolio, B. J. (eds.), *Improving organizational effectiveness through transformational leadership* (26–47). Thousand Oaks, Calif.: Sage.

Yukl, G. (1989). Managerial leadership: A review of theory and research. *Journal of Management,* 15(2), 251–89.

Ziegler, B. (1997a). Gerstner's IBM Revival: Impressive. *Wall Street Journal,* March 25, B1.

———. (1997b). Gerstner, meeting analysts, paints an optimistic IBM. *Wall Street Journal,* May 8, B4.

Zorn, T. E. (1991). Construct system development, transformational leadership and leadership messages. *Southern Communication Journal,* 56(3), 178–93.

Index

451